The Washington Post

GARDEN BOOK

ADRIAN HIGGINS

Illustrations by
Susan Davis

Published by
Washington Post Books
1150 15th Street, N.W.
Washington, D.C. 20071

First Edition

The text of this book is composed in Times Roman,
with display types in Geometric, Century Gothic,
Galliard and Flemish Script.

Manufactured by Chroma Graphics, Largo, Md.,
in association with Alan Abrams

ISBN: [0-9625971-5-5]

Publisher and Editor: Noel Epstein
Graphic Designer: Robert Barkin
Composition: Kathy Myrick
Manuscript Reviewers: Trish Gorman,
Michael Farquhar and Carolyn Ruff
Distribution Director: André Denault

This used to be among my prayers
— a piece of land not so very large,
which would contain a garden, and near
the house a spring of ever-flowing water,
and beyond these a bit of wood.

— HORACE

Acknowledgments

Many editorial debts have been accumulated in the course of writing this book. Numerous friends and acquaintances in the worlds of gardening and landscape design generously gave me the benefit of their expertise. Colleagues at *The Washington Post* lent invaluable support and counsel. And, as always, I owe more than I can say to my wife, Trish, and our children, Mary and Patrick. I get the glorious feeling of having done the book, they get the computer back.

In the world of horticulture, I owe special thanks to H. Marc Cathey, president-emeritus of the American Horticultural Society, and to Holly Shimizu, managing director of Richmond's Lewis Ginter Botanical Garden. They not only shared their knowledge, but they have unhesitatingly provided counsel and encouragement over many years. Similarly, I have learned a great deal from Phil Normandy about woody plants, from Gordon Riggle about daylilies, from Jack Shaffer about rare and unusual plants and from Don Humphrey about rock gardens and vegetables.

I also have had the good fortune to receive expert advice on many other subjects, from shade gardens and aquatic plants to bulbs, ornamental grasses, pest management and others. My deep appreciation for this assistance goes to Scott Aker, Marc Aveni, Lynn Batdorf, Katherine Bull, Barbara Bullock, Edwin Burkhardt, Henry Eastwood, Florence Everts, Joan Feely, Andrew Gerachis, Joseph Gorman, Wanda and Charles Hanners, Robert Howell, Don Hyatt, Kevin N. Morris, Charles Moutoux, Hiu Newcomb, Wolfgang Oehme, Mary Painter, Ellen Polishuk, Margaret Pooler, John E. Roe, Peter J. Schenk Jr., Judy Springer, Jon Traunfeld, Donald Voss, Nicholas Weber and Michael Zajic.

At *The Washington Post*, this book would not have come to pass without the support of Managing Editor Robert Kaiser, without years of encouragement and creativity from *Home* section Editor Linda Hales, and without the endorsement and enthusiasm of *Home* Deputy Editor Belle Elving. Indeed, I am grateful to all of my colleagues at *Home*, especially fellow scribes Charlie Fenyvesi and Adrienne Cook, whose gardening columns have long graced *Washington Post* pages.

Not least, I owe much to those who worked directly on the book. Noel Epstein conceived the book and asked me to do it. He then went at my prose with the precision and eye (and alacrity) of a master gardener pruning a rose that tended to ramble. Thank you, friend. Graphic designer Bob Barkin gave the work its wonderful form. Illustrator Susan Davis, a fellow gardening spirit whose art has touched and enriched so many lives, bestowed her special beauty upon the book. And Kathy Myrick meticulously turned manuscript into finished pages.

Finally, I would like to devote this book to the memory of my father, Patrick Higgins. He was not a gardener, but he had sound advice for those who were: "Now, don't go tiring yourself out."

Contents

ACKNOWLEDGMENTS **5**

INTRODUCTION: THE YEAR-ROUND GARDEN **9**

SECTION I: GETTING STARTED

Chapter 1: Designing Your Garden **15**

Chapter 2: Garden Tools **21**

Chapter 3: Preparing Your Land **27**

Chapter 4: The Lawn **39**

Chapter 5: Getting Help **49**

SECTION II: PILLARS OF THE GARDEN

Chapter 6: Azaleas and Rhododendrons **57**

Chapter 7: Boxwood **63**

Chapter 8: Other Popular Shrubs **67**

Lilacs • Viburnums • Hydrangeas • Crape Myrtles • Mountain Laurel
Japanese Pieris • Cotoneasters • Pyracantha

Chapter 9: Dogwood **77**

Chapter 10: Japanese Maples **81**

Chapter 11: Magnolias, Cherries and Crab Apples **87**

Chapter 12: Hollies and Yews **93**

Chapter 13: Conifers **97**

Chapter 14: Bests and Worsts **103**

SECTION III: THE PLANT PALETTE

Chapter 15: Perennials **117**

Chapter 16: Annuals **129**

Chapter 17: Bulbs **133**

Chapter 18: Ornamental Grasses **151**

Chapter 19: Ground Covers **153**

Chapter 20: Roses **159**

Chapter 21: Dahlias and Mums **167**

SECTION IV: SPECIAL GARDENS

Chapter 22: Shade Gardens **175**

Chapter 23: Hillside and Rock Gardens **183**

Chapter 24: Water Gardens **187**

Chapter 25: Natural Gardens **193**

SECTION V. THE EDIBLE GARDEN

Chapter 26: Vegetables **203**

Chapter 27: Herbs **217**

Chapter 28: Fruits and Nuts **225**

APPENDIX **231**

Plant Hardiness Zones • Average Freeze Dates
Common Pests & Diseases • Specialty Plant Sources
Extension Agencies • Public Gardens • Plant Societies

INDEX **247**

Introduction

THE YEAR-ROUND GARDEN

ONCE, AFTER I wrote an article about the problems of deer eating plants, an animal lover called to complain that all gardeners were vain, that they had no right to grow those flowers for their own glory and then carp when a hungry Bambi showed up. She was right in one sense: More than a few gardeners are vain. They take great pride in their little Edens, and some are not above showing them off. She was mistaken, however, in believing it wrong to deter deer. How many people want deer in their homes?

The caller did not seem to understand that gardens are integral parts of our homes, essentially outdoor rooms. They are dining rooms where we take our meals on patios and living rooms where we entertain guests and sometimes hold our weddings. They are playrooms for our children and bedrooms where we doze on hammocks. They are outside dens where we read books beneath trees and extensions of kitchens where we grow and gather vegetables and herbs. They are open-air studios where we design and nurture works of living art, punctuated with paths and ponds, gates and gazebos, benches and borders, and in the process nourish our souls.

This guide for Greater Washington and the Mid-Atlantic region is designed to help you develop and delight in the garden of your choice, whether you have an urban backyard, a suburban landscape, a rural spread or an apartment balcony. But it especially encourages you to think about creating a year-round garden, to look for the ornament of leaves, bark and berries as well as of flowers, to imagine blooms tucked amid a larger canvas of trees, shrubs, ground covers, herbs and ferns. In the process, you will discover many enchanting plants that appeal through three or four seasons, not just two weeks in spring.

Unfortunately, there is a lingering notion that gardening centers on flowers, arranged in individual beds. This idea first took hold in the 19th century, when gardeners also used dynamite to prepare planting holes. We no longer employ high explosives, but, alas, we still lean too much on separate groupings of annuals like marigolds and ageratum, wax begonias and red salvias.

Gardens that rely less on fleeting flower displays and more on a year-round tapestry of plant forms and foliage are not only more rewarding aesthetically. They also have practical advantages, such as minimizing requirements for maintenance, for chemicals and for check-writing. A large fothergilla, for example, is not as showy as a rhododendron that is briefly in flower, but its leaves will look clean and untroubled in high summer, it won't need chemical support, and its fall coloration will be breathtaking. By all means use forsythias, rhododendrons, azaleas or lilacs, but don't depend on them too heavily, especially not if you are sacrificing plants that provide longer-lasting joy.

Mindful of our busy lives and of the expense of gardening, the guide notes other ways as well to create low-maintenance paradises while holding down costs. This is just one reason, for example, why the book favors wonderful perennials that flower for long periods and, without much work by the gardener, are reborn year after year.

You also will find here other ways of avoiding chemicals. In books and on radio, gardeners too often are encouraged to make free use of herbicides and pesticides. This is an anachronism, not only because many gardeners today feel uncomfortable about damaging the environment but because there are less toxic alternatives, including horticultural oils, insecticidal soaps and beneficial parasites that devour bad bugs (it's a jungle out there). In addition, you can and should choose plants with a natural resistance to pests and diseases, or varieties and hybrids that have had those traits bred into them. This can make all the difference in escaping needless labor, bills and disappointments as well in reducing garden toxins.

Granted, certain plants — modern roses, for example, or a collection of lilies or dahlias — cannot be grown without chemical sprays. You should keep this in mind when choosing them. But if you have to employ chemicals for much of your garden to exist, something is wrong

This guide is intended for every level of gardener, from beginners to old hands, from those starting with bare landscapes to others wishing to embellish or mend existing gardens. It examines plant choices, cultivation techniques and much else that is specific to plant hardiness Zones 6b and 7a. The area embraces all of Greater Washington, which is bisected by Zone 7a to the south and east and the colder Zone 6b to the north and west, but extends all the way from Richmond, Va., to Wilmington, Del., and beyond.[1]

Although the guide is filled with recommendations, it seeks to avoid pedantic instruction. Some garden writers seem compelled to bark orders, insisting that if it is past noon on November 3 it is too late to plant daffodils. This is nonsense. Nor should you view our plant hardiness zones rigidly. Because climates within a zone can vary greatly, zone maps are imperfect tools for deciding what to grow. Gardens inside the Capital Beltway, with their low elevation and shelter against winter's northwest winds, for example, will do better with a fig or a camellia than those around Reston, Va.

All of us in the Mid-Atlantic region, however, are fortunate in having a large repertoire of plants that thrive here — from northern plants such as sugar maples and lilacs to southern plants such as crape myrtles and osmanthus — and a long growing season. The summers can be hot and steamy, and this sometimes makes plant and gardener a little edgy. On balance, though, it is a wonderful place for creating your own series of outdoor rooms.

If you are lucky, and millions are, the chore of tending the yard will then turn into the joy of nurturing a garden and of allowing the garden to nurture you back. You will embark on a long journey, uncertain of precisely where you might end up, but you can rest assured that it will be fun and enriching along the way. Think of this book as your travel guide.

[1]See Appendix for a map of the region's plant hardiness zones.

Section 1

GETTING STARTED

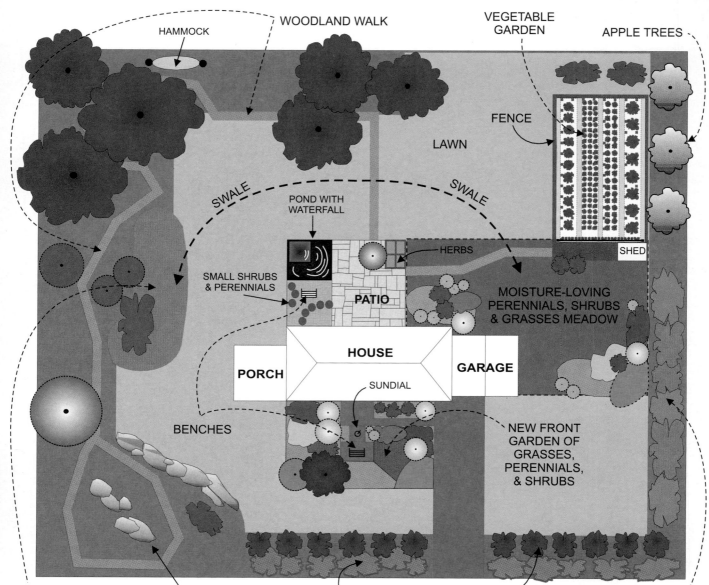

HAMMOCK

WOODLAND WALK

VEGETABLE GARDEN

APPLE TREES

FENCE

LAWN

SWALE

SWALE

POND WITH WATERFALL

HERBS

SHED

SMALL SHRUBS & PERENNIALS

MOISTURE-LOVING PERENNIALS, SHRUBS & GRASSES MEADOW

PATIO

HOUSE

PORCH

GARAGE

SUNDIAL

BENCHES

NEW FRONT GARDEN OF GRASSES, PERENNIALS, & SHRUBS

FERNS & OTHER MOISTURE-LOVING SHADE PLANTS

ROCK GARDEN

LANDSCAPE ROSES, GROUND COVER

HABITAT HEDGEROW

Master Plan

PHASE 1:
Rear patio, pool & swale

PHASE 2:
Front garden, lawn rejuvenation and landscape roses

PHASE 3:
Woodland trail & rock garden

PHASE 4:
Vegetables & fruit trees

PHASE 5:
Habitat garden & wet meadow

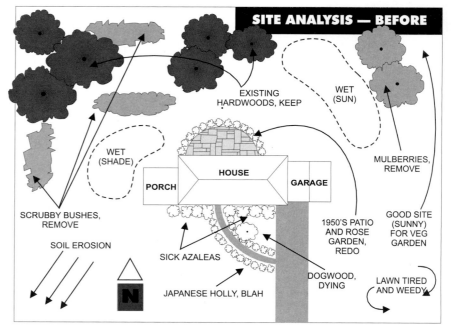

SITE ANALYSIS — BEFORE

EXISTING HARDWOODS, KEEP

WET (SUN)

WET (SHADE)

HOUSE

PORCH

GARAGE

MULBERRIES, REMOVE

SCRUBBY BUSHES, REMOVE

GOOD SITE (SUNNY) FOR VEG GARDEN

SOIL EROSION

N

SICK AZALEAS

JAPANESE HOLLY, BLAH

1950'S PATIO AND ROSE GARDEN, REDO

DOGWOOD, DYING

LAWN TIRED AND WEEDY

Chapter 1

DESIGNING YOUR GARDEN

WHETHER YOU ARE moving into a newly built home or an existing one, or have long wanted to enhance or transform your own grounds, you can turn your yard into a beautiful garden, raise the value of your property and, above all, enrich your life. Other people do it all the time. The key is to do it wisely, in ways that will be satisfying for years, and without wasting money.

A noted designer once advised house shoppers to take along a landscape architect. This is wishful thinking for most of us. But if you are considering buying a property, you would do well to scrutinize the grounds carefully. It can prevent serious mistakes.

Look at the condition of the landscape, both vegetation and physical architecture. Do you see evidence of poor drainage? Does the land slope away from the house? Some drainage problems are easy to fix, while others may take a second trust. Examine the condition of concrete or asphalt driveways, garden paths or steps, walls or fences. These can be expensive to replace, especially if you have to use a contractor. Look at the plants. Old, sick trees may need to be removed, along with brittle, soft-wooded shade trees that endanger the house. The site might be overrun with brambles and weeds that not only need removing but that mask deteriorating masonry or failed drain tiles.

Most problems like these can be fixed, if at something of a price. You should understand, though, that some problems are virtually unsolvable: adequate drainage in a flood plain, thin soils on rocky ground or the presence of a septic field.

Don't allow every flaw, however, to cloud your judgment. Use your imagination. A hillside might be an area of weeds and erosion now, but in the future it can make for a dramatic change of level in a landscape that is far more interesting than a purely flat site.

SKETCHING A MASTER PLAN

WHILE YOU CANNOT create or transform a garden in a weekend or two, you can get to work right away on developing a master plan, one of the creative joys of the enterprise. The plan itself may take a year or more to complete. You will need this time to learn about your site: the nature and condition of the soil, wet areas and dry ones, changing patterns of sun and shade, special features of the terrain.

You can easily develop your ideas on paper, using a bird's eye view of the property. The plan doesn't have to be a work of art. Go to an art supply store and buy some oversized sheets of graph paper with one-inch grids, subdivided into ten squares. Each tiny square becomes one foot in the garden, each grid 10 feet. Buy a plastic template of circles, so you can draw in the spaces occupied by plants, and some tracing paper. Use your property's deed plat to set the boundary lines (you may have to compensate for a difference in scale), or take actual measurements and transfer them to your plan. Locate and draw in paths, driveways and any other permanent structures. Also add large shrubs and trees.

Use tracing paper overlays to examine different aspects of the site. Record areas of sun and shade, dampness and dryness, views out and views into the site that need screening. Show the service areas, places where you have to put trash cans, the car, the woodpile, the storage shed, the air conditioner, the compost pile.

Show paths, existing or desired, that will allow access between garden areas and connect entrances to the property. You might need a path between the driveway and the front entrance, which would give you an excuse to build a delightful front garden of specimen shrubs, bulbs and perennials. The front yard doesn't have to be a lawn. In the garden, the shortest distance between two points is often the dullest. Make turns and landings in formal paths and curves in natural ones. Break up the journey with a bench or a special plant and, if possible, screen a special garden area so that you come upon it unexpectedly.

On another overlay, show slopes. This will reveal drainage patterns and areas that are difficult to mow but that might make wonderful places for attractive ground covers and shrubs or for natural-looking rock gardens anchored by boulders.

If you have a hillside or a side lot or a wooded corner that is seemingly impossible to integrate with the rest of the property, put in a path or trail that loops in and out of the space, so you don't have to backtrack. This will allow for a succession of plantings, surprises and moods and link the space with the rest of the property. On a hill, let the path wind from side to side, rising lazily to the top before it snakes back down. The result will be a journey that is easier on the feet as well as longer, giving you a chance to install and admire many more plants in the years ahead.

SUN OR SHADE?

Shade changes by the hour and by the season. This must be considered in identifying areas of sun and shade. Generally, full sun is a term gardeners use to mean at least six hours of direct afternoon sunlight, while shade comes in varying degrees: partial, dappled, high and full. Remember that a shady area in April, when you do a lot of planting, might be flooded with sunshine in July and August. Let the sun do its dance before deciding where to throw your bouquets. Get a compass and find north. The afternoon sun will come from the southwest in winter, the west in spring and the northwest in summer. The northwest sun is the deciding factor in sorting your garden into sunny and shady areas.

Sunny areas are precious, particularly in heavily wooded neighborhoods. It is here alone where you can place the main lawn, the vegetable garden and the showiest flowers. If you have just a little pocket of full sun, you will have to make hard choices. Many wonderful plants, though, thrive in shade, so remember that shaded areas can be turned into striking parts of your garden (see Chapter 22 on shade gardens, including definitions of different degrees of shade).

Once you've taken stock of the site, note what you need or want: a place to read in solitude, a ramp for an infirm family member to reach a shady patio, swings for the children, a place for parties or summer meals.

PATIOS AND DECKS

The single most useful element in the garden is the patio. Some people use decks in the same way, to put them more into the landscape than a screened porch but not so far that they can't hear the doorbell. People with delightful gardens tend to spend much of their time on the patio between April and October. You might consider an overhead arbor, which will create the cocooning sensation of a ceiling and support shade-giving vines and fragrant plants for summer use. Candidates include wisteria, kiwi vine, silver fleece vine, grapevine and the climbing rose New Dawn.

The object is to take what you are after and match it to the site conditions. For example, you may have the perfect spot for a patio, except that it needs a screen from the neighbor's house on the right where the land remains wet. Select the tree to match the site and the requirement, in this case perhaps a stand of bald cypress or, in smaller confines, of Heritage birch.

If decks are well made and well designed, they add considerably to a garden. They are particularly suited to naturalistic gardens where the property is set in or near woodland. The problem with many decks is that they are nothing more than a balcony off the second floor. If there is any connection to the landscape, it is by a narrow flight of stairs, usually leading to nowhere. Instead of becoming a link to the landscape, these decks separate us from the garden, physically, psychologically and emotionally.

It is better to build a multi-layered deck that brings you down, gently, to the garden, or one with broad stairs and landings. You can incorporate planters and seats into a deck, making it a garden unto itself. And nothing imparts as much magic in the garden as a deck that embraces the thick trunk of an existing shade tree. It returns us to childhood and to notions of tree houses. Look for books of deck plans and ideas at bookshops and hardware stores. A deck must meet local building codes and engineering standards so that it is safe for users (see the Chapter 5 section on contractors).

FENCES

Local ordinances and covenants dictate the placement and height of fences. Typically, a rear fence might be six or seven feet, while a front fence might have to be no higher than three feet and semi-open. A picket fence is easy to install and does wonders in providing an attractive frame for the front yard without shutting out the world. Fences aren't just for perimeters. They are terrific for establishing distinctive spaces within the property. This also gives the illusion of making the property seem larger. Consider picket or rail fences with gates to surround and define vegetable gardens, herb gardens, patios and transitional points in the garden. Chain link fences are durable and cheaper, but they are simply unattractive.

DESIGNING WITH PLANTS

In planning your plants, realize that shrubs, trees and even grasses and perennials can and should be used as building blocks, not just as ornaments. Tall conifers or shade trees can be more effective as screens and backdrops than fences or walls, because they grow much bigger. Any specimen tree or shrub with bright flowers, bark, berries or leaves will be better presented against the dark green of a large evergreen, such as an American holly or a Siberian spruce. On slopes, small trees and large shrubs of layered, horizontal habit slow the eye and hold interest. Candidates include several dogwood species, the doublefile viburnum, the Washington hawthorn and witch hazels.

One of the most common mistakes — made in gardens ranging from large, grassy suburban lots to small, rectangular townhouse and city yards — is to push all shrubbery and other plants to the outside, in two-foot-wide or three-foot-wide beds. Rather than create the sense of the most space, such boundary planting accentuates the property's limits. If your yard is narrow enough, consider replacing the lawn entirely with planting beds and a four-foot-wide path.

BEDS AND BORDERS

A bed is a freestanding planting area, while a border is one that has some sort of backdrop — a wall, a hedge, a house or simply a screen of trees. Beds tend to be viewed from all sides, so taller plants should be placed in the center. A border is linear by nature, to be viewed from one side, so layer the taller plants at the back and step down the scale of the plants as they move to the front.

Generous borders are a wonderful way to grow many plants in beautiful arrangements of color and texture, with a succession of flowers and other year-round ornaments. If you have some existing trees and large shrubs on the property, imagine a border or two that can be configured to incorporate them.

In the glossy magazines each spring you will see breathtaking, English-style borders replete with roses, delphiniums, larkspur, baby's breath, poppies, lavender, phlox and on and on. Don't try to stuff a border full of flowers. You are setting yourself up for a garden of high maintenance, high expense, chemical dependence and early demise. Compose a plant border using trees, shrubs, perennials, grasses and bulbs chosen for their har-

CLIPPED HEDGES AND TOPIARIES

CLIPPED HEDGES and topiaries can be effective design elements, but they require high levels of maintenance. You should understand what is involved when considering them.

Clipped hedges are created by shearing the foliage (not by pruning the branches). The leaves then form a dense wall, an elegant, living piece of architecture. Plants used for clipped hedges are set more closely than if they were left unclipped, usually three to four feet apart. It generally takes three to five years for a tall hedge to reach its desired height. Young plants are lightly clipped on all sides, and half the new growth is cut back each summer. This is done to ensure that the bottom of the hedge is bushy. For the same reason, the hedge should be shaped so that the top is narrower than the bottom.

Later, when the hedge has reached the desired size and is to be sheared, don't "eyeball" it. Make a form from bamboo stakes and string. Electric shears are the best tool for beginners.

Once the basic form is established, the hedge will need clipping once and sometimes twice a year, depending on the amount of summer rain. With large hedges, this is a major job requiring several hours and a good stepladder. Don't clip a hedge later than early September or the new growth won't harden off in time for the November frosts.

In our climate, shearing often stresses a shrub or tree and invites diseases. By selecting plants that have a naturally tidy and compact habit, it is possible to have a clean-looking hedge that doesn't have to be clipped. Candidates include edging boxwood, Japanese and Chinese hollies, osmanthus, red-tipped photinia, certain upright junipers, Hicks yew, arborvitae, especially the variety Green Giant, European hornbeam, variety Fastigiata (deciduous) and hemlocks.

If you still want a clipped hedge, consider the following plants:

TALL: American holly; Chinese holly (either species or cultivar Burfordii); Southern magnolia; tree or American boxwood; hemlock, Leyland cypress and European beech (deciduous but effective, twiggy winter screen).

MEDIUM: Hicks yew, Russian olive, juniper, glossy abelia (semi-evergreen), osmanthus and pyracantha.

LOW: Barberry, edging box, lavender, Japanese holly and low-growing yew varieties.

Some people have an urge to turn broadleaf evergreens and conifers into geometric shapes, usually dotted around the foundation of the house or along the front path. This comes down to one's aesthetic sense. The natural beauty of plants is destroyed by this practice, and you will lose floral display if you cut at the wrong time of year. Perhaps that would not be such a bad thing. If you inherit a yard where this has been done, allow the plants to grow out and do some selective pruning to help them attain a natural and more open shape. Forsythia, yew, holly and many other plants can be cut back hard and will regenerate.

TOPIARIES. Topiaries are plants that have been shaped into an object or a purely geometric form. In one style of topiary, the plant is clipped into shape like a hedge and certain stems are allowed to grow to fashion in time into ears, hats, handles and the like. The second type of topiary consists of a hidden metal mesh or armature on which evergreens or vines are trained. A garden of topiary can be a place of great whimsy and fun. It will also requires a lot of work to keep the shapes trimmed and the plants healthy.

diness, resistance to diseases and pests, low maintenance and multi-seasonal ornament. You will have a garden of enduring beauty that will repay the initial investment for many years.

A bed or border should be composed of different types of plants. Select large shrubs, broadleaf evergreens and mid-sized trees as anchoring plants, positioned toward the back of the border (allow room for growth on all sides). These big-boned plants might be quite different in character: an arborvitae, which is large yet unassuming and constant, or a cherry, which bursts into glorious bloom in April and then recedes. Connect them with large, spreading shrubs that might be massed to span 15 or 20 feet in a large border, plants such as redtwig dogwood; viburnums; Japanese aucuba; forsythias or rugosa roses. Use smaller, showier shrubs to form accents and a reduced scale toward the front of the border; candidates might include azaleas, nandina, mahonia, pieris, hydrangeas and mountain laurel.

Create blocks of color and texture with masses of perennials and grasses, and fill in gaps with ground covers and bulbs. At a strategic point — the start or end of the border or where it curves or passes a patio or pool — plant a specimen shrub or tree such as a Japanese maple, stewartia, crape myrtle, paperbark maple, witch hazel or sourwood. Remember, these are the stars of the show specimens, so plant just one (see Chapter 14 for the best — and worst — trees and shrubs for our region).

You should resist the urge to put in one of everything. The result will look like a jumble. Instead, reduce the variety of plants and increase the quantity of chosen varieties.

Place stepping-stones into borders and beds so that you can prune and remove dead flowers without trampling on the soil, which will compact the earth and impede root systems. The bed or border should be dressed once a year with a three-inch layer of mulch or compost, to keep weeds at bay, retain moisture, build the soil and fill in gaps. Perennials should be cut back in the fall. Ornamental grasses should be cut back in late winter. Mulch or compost is best laid in the fall. In the spring, you risk injuring emerging bulbs and perennials.

PLANNING FOR PLANT SPACING

Perhaps the most common error in creating a garden is not allowing for the correct spacing of plants. With annuals and perennials, mistakes are easily if laboriously remedied: You dig up the plants later and set them farther apart. With large shrubs and trees, it usually is too late to do anything once the plant is established and the problem noticed.

It is difficult to imagine that a shrub that is at first two feet tall and 18 inches across will, in a decade, be the size of a pickup truck. It is our instinct to want instant gardens, and so we plant shrubs three feet apart instead of six feet or 10 feet. The years soon creep along and we become victims of our impatience.

The problem is that gardens are a moving target. Do we plant them for how they will look in five years, or 10 years, or 15 years, or 30 years? We are told that Washington is a transient city, but most people I know have been in the same gardens for at least a decade and usually for much longer.

Plant labels give pretty accurate indications of the size of plants at or approaching maturity. These tend to reflect the true size after about seven years, when most trees and shrubs slow their growth rate. If the label says oakleaf hydrangeas will grow six feet high and five feet across, believe it, and plan to plant them out from under the canopy of low-branched trees and no closer than four or five feet apart.

With shade trees and conifers, it's not the height you have to worry about but the width. A white oak actually will squeeze into a tight space so long as its roots are not disturbed, but certain trees demand elbowroom. These include American hollies, beeches, Leyland cypresses, Eastern white pines, maples, Southern magnolias, Bradford pears, spruces and cedars. Choose these species only if you have the room. You may decide that the whole scale of the garden must come down. In that case you should choose patio trees in place of shade trees, broadleaf evergreens instead of huge conifers, medium-sized shrubs instead of large ones, maidenhair ferns instead of ostrich ferns and so on.

If you plan your woody plants correctly, you will end up initially with large expanses of dark mulch between barely discernable twigs. The gaps can be filled in with ground covers, perennials and grasses, which reach maturity after two or three seasons and generally are planted two feet apart. Or plan on using annuals, which fill out in one season. Or do nothing but keep weeds at bay and wait for your woody plants to grow up (and out). If your neighbors and friends are underwhelmed at first, they will come to admire your prescience.

You can accelerate the growth of a plant by setting it in deeply worked and enriched soil and making sure that it is watered, especially during dry spells. The plant will form a large, healthy root system, and then the top growth will take off. You can cheat and gorge your plant on fertilizers; this will make it long-stemmed and leafy initially, but excessive fertilization also will invite insects and diseases.

EFFECTIVE SCREENS

Most gardens need a strategically placed screen or two to provide privacy or block out an undesirable view. Yards in urban and older suburban neighborhoods tend to be smaller and the gardens more closely packed, but they are blessed with mature shade trees and evergreens. In new suburban gardens, home builders and property owners have an understandable craving to put in fast-growing trees. Popular species include silver maple, Leyland cypress, spruces, white pine and Bradford pear. Within a few years, these trees can outgrow their allotted space and come to dominate and oppress the garden. Don't choose them unless you have the room, usually a half-acre lot at the least. Some trees are tall but narrow, making them better suited to the smaller yard. If you allow yourself deciduous screens as well as evergreens, your choices will be much greater. The screening effect will not be as great in winter, but you may not need a screen in winter.

Good screening trees for tight spaces include ginkgo, Japanese cryptomeria, American holly, hemlock, dawn redwood, Japanese snowbell, pin oak, upright Japanese maple, fastigiate hornbeam, crape myrtle, Foster's No. 2 holly and Serbian spruce. Bamboo is effective but should be grown only in planters. In the ground, it will spread and become a weed, and putting it in submerged containers, as some advise, is risky. In colder winters, its top growth will be killed. Cut it back in late winter. Then new shoots will emerge.

If you are surrounded by high-rise buildings or houses that look down on your property, you can place patio trees at strategic points to block sight lines and/or use the overhead arbor with dense vines.

Sometimes it is impossible to hide adjoining structures. In these cases, design a garden that is inward looking, so the eye will be loath to move beyond the entertainment. Build in just one or possibly two distractions, perhaps a piece of statuary at the far end of the garden framed by cherry trees or a little lily pond. Don't place anything directly beneath the offending structure, such as a storage shed or a showy plant; that will just draw the eye to it. Corners form natural focal points, because that's where fence lines come together. Plantings, paths, bed edging and fences all should be used to lead the eye to the desired spot.

SWIMMING POOLS

Before deciding on a swimming pool, speak to friends who have them and ask if the initial expense, the continual maintenance requirements and the loss of the area to other uses were worth it. From a design standpoint, pools work well if they are integrated successfully into the rest of the landscape, often an expensive proposition that relies on extensive masonry decking to tie the pool to terraces near the house. If a pool is constructed as an afterthought, it will show. If and when it comes time to sell your property, the pool actually may reduce the number of interested buyers.

Chapter 2

YOUR GARDEN TOOLS

$\mathcal{G}$ ARDENING TODAY is a multibillion-dollar industry, with many makers of gadgets and gizmos seeking a share of the take. You will need proper equipment for all of your garden work, and my advice is to spend your money on high-quality, basic manual tools that, with a little care, will last for decades. If your property is large, you may need power equipment. These machines save labor and can be fun to use, but they are noisy and smoky, so be considerate of your neighbors. With both manual and powered equipment, you generally get what you pay for.

Look for digging tools whose heads are forged from one piece of heavy-gauge steel, rising to a single socket that envelops the handle shaft. Sockets that cover only part of the shaft are much weaker.

ESSENTIAL TOOLS

ROUND-POINT SHOVEL

This is essential for most earthwork: digging planting holes, slicing through small roots, mixing soil and amendments, skimming turf and prying out buried stones. Spades may be great for turning well-worked loam, but they are practically useless on the unimproved clay soils most of us must work with in this region. Don't get a shovel that is too big, no matter how strong you think you are. An oversized shovel will soon become tiring when a lot of material needs to be moved. The longer the handle, however, the more leverage you will have, so try to find a shovel with a smaller blade and the longest shaft you can comfortably manage.

GARDEN FORK

This, too, is indispensable for our heavy clay soils and for subsoil that is particularly unyielding or laced with stones. The fork is also useful in working areas close to precious garden plants, where a shovel would risk more root damage. And this is the tool for turning a compost pile. It is foolish to buy a cheap garden fork; the tines will soon bend, rendering the tool useless.

BASIC HOE

A good basic hoe is worth its weight in gold. You will use it for weeding and for fine grading between plants, where a rake will not fit. It is also a lot less tiring than a rake for smoothing soil and mulch. In the vegetable garden, use the corner of the hoe blade to form a row for sowing.

RAKES

You will still need a garden rake for smoothing flower and vegetable beds in some cases and for leveling new lawns. If you are tall, make sure that the handle is long enough to use without straining your back. Leaf rakes are essential for a lawn: Select a broad one that can collect many leaves in one stroke.

HAND TOOLS

You will need a trowel and a cultivator, for planting in tight spots, transplanting seedlings and working soil in containers. The cultivator, which looks like a three-pronged claw, is used for loosening and breaking up soil before you employ the trowel. A trowel of thin, pressed metal, connected to the handle with an inferior tang and ferrule, will bend in clay soil and become useless.

WHEELBARROW

A wheelbarrow is many things: a wagon for carrying seedlings, a dump truck for delivering peat, a dolly for large plants, a mixing basin for soil amendments, a hod for bricks. Large, contractor-grade barrows allow you to ferry more materials at one time, but they can become overloaded. Avoid barrows with narrow wheels: They damage lawns and planting beds. Broad pneumatic tires are best. Fancy, spoke-wheeled carts can be useful, but they are bulky and less maneuverable, and you can't subject them to the same abuse as a wheelbarrow.

HAND PRUNERS

These are essential for light pruning, cutting flowers, deadheading spent blossoms and removing the dead top growth of perennials and grasses. Avoid anvil-action blades, which crush stems. Get the best quality you can afford: Light ones are hard on the hands. A telescoping pole pruner and lopper is useful for reaching high branches, but it has drawbacks. It is difficult to cut branches precisely and cleanly with it, and you have to worry about falling branches and overhead power lines.

ESSENTIAL CLOTHING

Winter or summer, you will need thick leather or suede gloves for digging, pruning thorny plants, sawing wood and moving stones or firewood. Wear heavy work boots for digging. In summer, wear white cotton clothing and a white, wide-brimmed hat.

OPTIONAL EQUIPMENT

In time, you should get a few other tools:

MATTOCK

This is like a pick, but with a flattened blade. It is good for working the worst hardpan, breaking up the subsoil to mix with amendments. You will need it to remove stubborn stones. The other end of the head has a vertical blade used like a hatchet for cutting through roots. However, if your garden is afflicted with many subsurface roots, a well-balanced and sharp ax is a better tool for the job.

BOW SAW

A sharp bow saw is as effective and almost as fast as a chain saw on most small to mid-sized pruning jobs. It's also a great deal quieter and less expensive.

PUMP SPRAYER

A 1.5-gallon pump sprayer delivers pesticides, when they are needed, in a more measured and accurate way than hose-end sprayers. The pump sprayer is more maneuverable, though heavier when full, and it can be used for spraying more environmentally friendly products, including horticultural oils, glyphosate and insecticidal soaps. Ideally, you should have two sprayers, one solely for herbicides. Then any residue will not be sprayed accidentally on ornamental flowers.

LAWN AND YARD CARE

GASOLINE-POWERED MOWERS

The walk-behind, gasoline-powered mower is still the most popular type in America, though modern technology has given gardeners attractive alternatives to a machine that is disdained in certain quarters for being noisy and polluting. (What people fail to recognize is that during the worst smog days of summer, no one cuts the grass anyway — the lawn usually is brown and dormant then.)

If your lawn is relatively flat and your lot under half an acre, a push mower is sufficient. For hillier ground and larger lawns, you may want a self-propelled model. These generally need larger engines, four or five horsepower, to do the job.

Mulching mowers are popular today. They are designed to cut grass blades finely so that they are returned to the lawn as beneficial mulch. Conventional mowers will do the same job, if not as efficiently. To return grass clippings as mulch, you must mow often, as much as every five days in the spring. Even if you use a mulching mower, there may be times when you want a bag on the machine, to gather leaves in the fall, for example.

ELECTRIC AND MANUAL MOWERS

On smaller lawns, you have a choice of electric or push-reel mowers. Electric mowers have cords, which can be a nuisance if they batter small plants and get tangled in the bushes. Advanced battery technology has led to efficient cordless mowers with rechargeable power packs. They can still run out of power before the job is finished if the grass is too long or wet or there's too much of it, but they are much better today than just a few years ago and can only improve further in the future.

Push-reel mowers hark back to the dawn of mower technology in the 19th century. They are still effective, and a machine in good condition does not need unusual strength to operate. They are terrific for small town gardens, with one caveat: The highest setting usually is 2 1/2 inches. The optimum height for turf-type tall fescues is three inches. You risk stressing the turf if you use one, but the environmental friendliness and ease of storage may be worth the chance. You can compensate by ensuring that the lawn is maintained properly (see Chapter 4).

TRACTORS

At the other end of the scale from push-reel mowers is the lawn tractor. A top-of-the-line model costs thousands of dollars, but it can be justified if you have a large property. In addition, more powerful models take attachments for all manner of yard chores, from snow plowing to lawn dethatching. Generally, brands sold at mass-merchandise stores are less expensive — and of a lesser quality — than those sold through dealerships.

Manufacturers make different types of machines, based on market sectors and consumer preferences. The bottom-of-the-line ride-on mower with a rear-mounted engine is still available but is now considered passé, replaced with more powerful and desirable tractor types. These are divided into two categories: regular lawn tractors, designed primarily for lawn cutting, and garden tractors, with larger mowing decks and the power to take a range of attachments. More recently, manufacturers have introduced commercial-style mowers that maneuver on the spot, minimizing or eliminating the need to edge the lawn with a push mower in areas tractors cannot reach.

SPREADERS

Spreaders are used to apply, evenly and at the correct rate, seed, fertilizer, lime and pesticides. Drop spreaders are simple to use but are bulkier and slower. Broadcast spreaders use a spinning plate to scatter contents. They are more efficient but require some skill to achieve uniform coverage. For small lawns of less than 3,000 feet, use a hand-held broadcast spreader, which is easily stored. Fertilizers are highly corrosive, and metal spreaders tend to rust. Plastic ones last longer but still should be washed thoroughly after use.

EDGERS

There are many types of manual and mechanical edgers for tidying turfgrass where it meets edges that lawn mowers cannot cut: along fence lines, around woodpiles, next to plant beds and the like. The English border edger is the best tool for creating a crisp earthen edge between lawn and plant bed. It has a handle and shaft like a spade, but the head is a flat, half-moon-shaped blade that makes beautiful vertical slices. A border edge should be laid out with a line of string, pegged with tent stakes or nails to create an evenly wide bed with a straight edge. Don't try to eyeball it.

Hand shears have blades that resemble a large scissors and are worked by using one hand to squeeze two handles set one above the other. To minimize the strain on the hand and wrist, buy a high-quality brand and keep the blade sharpened and the action oiled. Hedging shears take both hands to operate and are less fatiguing. Long-handled shears let you to edge while standing up. They are easier on the back but a little unwieldy.

For a crisp vertical edge to the lawn where it meets paths and sidewalks, you will need a rotating edger. You can buy manual ones with a star-like blade attached to a rubber roller, on the end of a long pole. In my experience, they require a lot of strength and leave a ragged edge. Electric or gasoline rotating edgers are far more effective but are costly for the amount of work they get (they are used perhaps half a dozen times a season).

STRING TRIMMERS

If you are skilled at using a string trimmer, you can turn it so that the nylon cutting string forms a vertical blade, and you can edge lawns in that way. Take precautions against flying debris. Otherwise, the trimmer is used like the shears to cut back overgrown grass in areas mowers cannot get to. You must take extreme care not to lacerate stems or trunks of cherished plants. A string trimmer in the wrong hands will do more plant damage than a plague of locusts. Be careful, too, not to trim your ankles and shins. I wear high rubber Wellington boots for the occasion. Cheap, two-stroke, gasoline-powered trimmers are noisy, smoky and difficult to keep running. An electric trimmer is kinder to your neighbors.

BLOWERS

Similarly, gasoline-powered blowers are extraordinarily anti-social. If you have large areas of lawn that need raking in the fall and you don't enjoy long periods of solitude or quiet, use an electric blower. If you have a lot of steps or corners where leaves keep piling up, an electric blower actually is a useful tool. You should be aware, though, that the blast of air picks up tiny specks of dried leaves and soil and can be as destructive as a sandblaster on annuals, perennials and ground covers, not to mention lawn furniture and windowpanes.

CHIPPERS/SHREDDERS

These devices use a powerful grinder to turn whole leaves into leaf mold ready for composting or into mulch for beds. They also chip twigs and small branches into mulch. Small electric ones are especially limited in the amount of leaves they can take at one time and the size of the branches they accept. However, larger gasoline models are remarkably expensive. They are potentially dangerous machines; some have better safety features than others, but they are not for unsupervised teenagers. A chipper/shredder might be of long-term value to someone with a large, wooded lot. You don't have to have one to make compost.

ROTOTILLERS

Like most specialty tools, the rototiller will sit idle for months on end and then is indispensable for a moment. A vegetable garden is tilled under twice, maybe three times a season. You will need a plot of at least 750 square feet to make a tiller worth the expense.

The tiller is useful, too, in the ornamental garden, but only for major projects, not small bed preparation. It has two applications, one for re-seeding a large lawn, the other for creating a large new plant bed. A tiller will cultivate soil only to a depth of seven inches, ample for a lawn but not for a bed or border that is to last 50 years. You will have to use the tiller to "double-dig" the bed by tilling an area, raking aside the loose earth, tilling it again, and then returning the original topsoil to the area, along with soil amendments, for a final tilling.

Tillers fall into two types. The cheaper, inferior style has front tines that propel the machine in addition to cultivating the soil. A machine in good order will do the job adequately. However, if the spring holding the notched depth guide has weakened, the guide will not stay on the higher settings. The tines will grab too deeply into the soil and take the user on a wild and back-straining ride. The better design uses tines in the rear and a set of forward, tractor-type pneumatic tires that propel the machine. Some brands, on the largest models, allow you to remove the tines and install snow blowers, sweepers, shredders and other heavy-duty attachments. They function as mini-tractors and cost several thousand dollars. Even a mid-sized, rear-tine tiller will cost close to four figures.

You can rent tillers, but most rental centers have only the front-tined tiller. You also will have the challenge of delivering it. It takes two strong people to lift these machines safely.

A good machine can do the work of a crew, but rototilling at its best also requires a fair amount of physical strength. The knack of using a tiller is to allow the machine to do the work. If you end up fighting it, you will lose. Six-, seven- and eight-horsepower tillers are powerful beasts. There are gardeners with expensive tilling machines looking for work. You can hire them by the job or the hour. Look for ads in the newspaper or signs at community gardens.

GARDEN HOSES
Again, you get what you pay for. The heavier the gauge of hose, the longer it will last. Look for a solid rubber or four- or five-ply vinyl hose with brass couplings. Hoses will last much longer if kept wound, out of the sun and unpressurized (i.e., dry). If your hose is pressurized and it then freezes, you might as well throw it out.

NOZZLES
Spray wands that mimic the gentle action of a watering can are useful for patio plantings and hanging baskets. Otherwise, avoid pistol-grip nozzles and instead use an adjustable, straight brass nozzle that is twisted to control the force of water. Wide open, it provides a far-reaching jet of water, but twisted near-shut it gives a fine mist that will not damage tender plants or wash away soil.

Chapter 3

PREPARING YOUR LAND

*Y*OU MAY WANT TO TAKE shortcuts, going straight to planting a rose garden here or a flower border there, but this would be a mistake. It wouldn't fix an underlying problem, wouldn't be part of a considered design for the entire site, and probably would fail horticulturally. Proceed in an orderly way and your patience and forethought will be rewarded.

The first tasks, which might take an entire growing season, are to learn about your soil and to clear and clean up the property. In the process, you will come to understand more about the land's characteristics, both good and bad. Among common revelations: areas of soil erosion, poor drainage, failed lawns or grassy banks that are too steep to mow safely. The cleanup itself can include everything from taking down an ailing crab apple tree, pruning shrubs, removing bamboo or weeds and reseeding the lawn to wholesale clearing of the lot.

A word of warning about cutting down trees: The U.S. Occupational Safety and Health Administration regards tree work as among the most hazardous occupations. A mature tree can weigh thousands of pounds and often must be taken down piecemeal by experts. Don't attempt to fell trees or remove limbs unless you are experienced and have the correct equipment, clothing and assistance. On no account should you do this work with children or neighbors in the vicinity.

Even if tree felling is beyond you, you can do certain things yourself. Valuable old shade trees and conifers get smothered in vines, which must be removed. Common offenders include poison ivy, English ivy, wisteria, Hall's honeysuckle, trumpet vine and porcelainberry. Look out for the poison ivy. It is identified by its leaves — they are alternate and have three leaflets — and, on older vines, by a hairy covering to the stem. Cut the stem about two feet above the ground and paint glyphosate on the cut surfaces. Repeat every two weeks for six weeks. Once the vine has shriveled and dried, it can be pulled out. Wear protective clothing around poison ivy — and remember that the toxic oils persist on gloves, so keep them away from skin and eyes.

Several vines, including English ivy, are not easily killed by herbicides. You will have to cut them and rip them out by hand. If English ivy is also forming a ground cover at the base of trees, don't pull it up until you have decided on a new planting plan for that part of the garden. As a ground cover, it will keep weeds at bay and check soil erosion until you replant the area. However, do stop it from climbing up the tree again. Be sure to water and fertilize newly rescued trees.

CLUSTERS OF THREE GLOSSY LEAVES ARE THE QUICKEST WAY TO RECOGNIZE THE POISON IVY VINE

On oaks and other hardwoods, choking vines may cause lower branches to die. A tree with a number of dead branches, however, can rejuvenate after being freed of vines. Assuming the tree isn't patently dead (no bark is flaking off to reveal bone-white cambium or there are no swarms of woodpeckers), give it a year or two to see if it comes back.

Vines are but one killer of neglected trees. Gypsy moths, fungal diseases, lightning strikes, drought and pollution all take their toll. On all but large rural properties, where dead trees are used by woodpeckers and other fauna, such trees should be removed. Some may be alive but beyond salvation. Weak trees invite insects and diseases and break up in storms.

Some trees might be flourishing, but you may need to have them removed to get the garden you want. This is especially true of weed trees such as tree-of-heaven, mulberry and the related paper mulberry (*broussonetia*), mimosa, silver maple, Siberian elm and loblolly pine.

Some people heartily dislike black locust, catalpa, Norway maple and paulownia trees. Beauty is in the eye of the beholder. But if a tree is too large for your site, weak-wooded and messy, bullies out other plants or casts a gloomy shade over everything, you may wish to get rid of it. Black walnut trees exude a poison in their roots that prevents many (but not all) other plants from taking hold; perennials are the best bets under black walnuts, particularly hostas, daylilies, sweet woodruff, bloodroot, Solomon's-seal, ajuga, Siberian iris and sedums. Don't be in a hurry to take the walnut down. In maturity it is one of our prettiest native trees, even if the fruit is indescribably messy.

Because some plants may regenerate from their roots, and because tree roots take years to rot away, it is best to dig out or employ someone to grind out stumps or root systems of trees and shrubs you want removed. Sometimes a tree root is too expensive to take out. If this is the case, use it as a support for climbing roses, climbing hydrangea, clematis, tomato vines, pole beans, morning glories or other pleasing vines. Some people, however, leave a stump five or six feet high and turn it into a primitive sculpture. This is not to be encouraged.

THE NATURE OF YOUR SOIL

BEFORE DECIDING whether you do indeed want that rose garden, you not only have to consider your overall design but whether your soil is slightly acidic, which is what roses require. Indeed, you have to make sure that all of the plants you desire have the soil they need.

Most soil in our region is heavy clay, sticky when wet, like concrete when dry. If the land is low-lying, or there is subsurface shale or hardpan, the clay soil does not drain and becomes waterlogged and devoid of air. In periods of drought, this suffocating gum turns to rock. It is no place for a plant. In areas close to the Chesapeake Bay and the Atlantic Ocean, this clay yields to sand. Sandy soil has plenty of air, but it cannot hold water or nutrients. It is also no place for most plants.

The third fundamental component of soil is silt — particles that are smaller than sand but bigger than clay. Silt tends to be charcoal gray in color, sand a light or washed-out brown and clay a range of colors from blue-gray to orange to red. A dark soil usually is a sign of fertility, but not always. Test the consistency of your soil. If it balls up when squeezed, like Play-Doh, it has too much clay. Ideally, a ball of it should slowly fall apart in your palm in large particles.

The optimum soil is a blend of clay, silt and sand. This is loam. Technically, it has no more than 27 percent clay, 28 to 50 percent silt and less than 52 percent sand, but a heavy loam typically has a higher content of clay.

You can change the consistency of your soil with humus, decayed organic matter that further lightens the earth and makes it more productive. Humus might have some nutritional benefit, but it is added primarily to improve the soil's structure. Loam enriched with humus is the best combination. It is like a sponge that is wrung: It holds moisture but also contains the oxygen that roots must have to live. In addition, it is loose, allowing tiny feeder roots to grow freely in their search for food and water, and it permits taproots to tunnel deeply.

Vehicles, machinery and human feet compact the soil, squeezing the air and nutrient-holding qualities out of it. This is why vegetable gardeners contrive slow, lingering deaths for those who trample in their beds.

If you have heavy clay soil, you can improve small areas instantly with bales of peat moss, bags of topsoil and humus from the hardware store. At some point, bulk delivery of topsoil is more cost effective, but you have to be extremely careful that you are getting sound material, not clay-heavy soil that has been fluffed up by machine and darkened with mulch. You may also add gypsum or calcium sulfate. Another option in a small area is to create a raised bed over poor soil, making it thick enough to allow roots to develop and to account for the soil settling.

If you chisel out a hole in hard clay, fill it with premium soil and stuff in a shrub, all you are doing is creating a pot plant with no drainage hole. The roots will drown and rot. Some people earnestly add a bag of sand to a planting hole. This does no good: It takes great quantities of sand to alter the composition of clay soil. It is better to lighten clay with a mixture of topsoil and humus. Don't be afraid to incorporate mulch into the soil.

SWEET OR SOUR?

The pH level, a measure of hydrogen ions in the soil, tells you whether your soil is acidic or alkaline. If the pH is not within a narrow range needed by a specific plant, the plant will not be able to take up required nutrients and minerals and trace elements. It will then become stunted and even change color. A pH of 7.0 is neutral; anything below 5.0 is very acidic, or sour, and anything above 8.0 is highly alkaline, or sweet.

Using iron sulfate or aluminum sulfate generally lowers the pH of alkaline soils. This is rarely needed in our region unless you have beds close to newly built concrete paths, pools or mortared walls, which leach lime, or you are planting certain plants, such as lavender, beets and onions, which prefer slightly sweet soils. Lawns, however, will need a program of liming (see Chapter 4). Some garden beds may need to be limed, too, because soils tend to get increasingly acidic over the years as a result of acid rain, leaf decomposition and the use of mulches and chemical fertilizers.

Most plants prefer a pH range of 6.0 to 7.0, which is what you typically might find in our region. But you won't know if your soil is right until you have it tested. This is easy and cheap to do through your county extension agency. The helpful people there will tell you how to take soil samples, which you then send off in a box. After a few weeks, you will receive an analysis of your soil's composition, pH, nutrient deficiencies and precise quantities of lime and fertilizers needed. It works for lawns, ornamental beds, vegetable plots and orchards.

Building soils on a large scale takes several years and is best begun by starting and replenishing a compost pile. A continual top dressing of compost (and other materials such as mulch, leaf mold and grass clippings) on garden beds will work wonders.

COMPOST

A compost pile is not only the recipient of yard waste that otherwise would go into municipal landfills, but it is the cheapest and most convenient source of soil enrichment. You may get a special feeling the first time you start a compost pile and return a week later to find it cooking. It is alchemy, and you are the wizard.

For some people, compost piles have a bad name. This is because, done incorrectly, they give off a foul odor and attract vermin. But building compost piles correctly is easy. Unlike 10 or 20 years ago, you now can turn to a force of composting experts in local government recycling offices and county extension agencies, all ready to provide help.

Compost piles generally go bad when there is too much of one type of material, particularly lawn clippings, and when the pile is allowed to mat and get soaking wet. Conversely, a pile that is well balanced, turned occasionally and kept moist but not wet will break down quickly.

Certain animal manures, of course, do smell badly when fresh — the dung of horses, cattle and poultry, for example — but they soon break down, adding important nutrients and structure to the finished compost. (Dog

SOIL AMENDMENTS

THERE ARE TIMES when even the enlightened gardener with a big compost operation needs additional soil amendments brought in, usually to establish a new plant border, backfill a newly retained terrace or build up a lawn.

Here are some tips:

TOPSOIL. There is no regulated control of the sale of topsoil, and it is easy to end up with an inferior product and disastrous results, especially when buying in bulk. Before purchasing, go to look at the product. Almost all topsoil has been shredded in huge machines, which bestows flattering qualities: The soil will look dark and loose. After the first rainfall, however, it may well turn to impenetrable clay. If you see tiny strands of mulch, the seller may have incorporated the mulch to give the soil a darker, richer appearance. Pick up a handful of the soil and give it the Play-Doh test to see if it has too much clay content. Sometimes, you can find a major property development under construction where the topsoil has been scraped off and piled up. If there is surplus, the builder might be willing to let you have some. Avoid offers of free fill dirt unless you are a potter.

HUMUS. It is hard to find sources of humus in bulk, but they are around. Some of the major mulch-supply companies sell humus products. Montgomery County, Md., has an extensive bulk humus operation that includes the sale of ComPRO, a composted sewage sludge that is particularly good as a top dressing for lawns (but not for ornamental beds, because it is blended with lime and has a high pH). It is also possible to buy well-rotted animal manures from the National Zoo in Northwest Washington, but you must provide the pickup truck yourself. If you have such a vehicle, you also can get horse manure from local stables, but it will need to be composted for several months before using in the garden.

Many municipalities sell leaf mold, sometimes called leaf mulch, which is useful as a mulch or blended with humus, but it is not a growing medium in itself. Often, it is also not screened for trash.

Some mulch companies sell their own compost, but if you go that route make sure that your batch is from the center of the pile. Otherwise, you can get a product loaded with noxious weed seeds. Ask mulch companies if they would be willing to blend acceptable topsoil with a compost or sewage sludge product before delivery.

For quantities of amendments, figure working in two inches of material, which would require 166 cubic feet, or 6 cubic yards — two full-sized pickup truckloads — per 1,000 square feet of lawn (e.g., 50 feet x 20 feet).

and cat waste should never be used, nor should kitchen scraps consisting of meats, fish, lard, vegetable oils or dairy products.) Horse manure is readily available at stables, often given away to those who want it. It will be partially composted there, and its mixture with bedding straw — litter — makes it an even more valuable ingredient.

You don't have to use manure, though, for a compost pile to work. Yard waste and other kitchen scraps — fruits and vegetable peelings, coffee grounds, egg shells and pumpkin shells are recommended — can provide an adequate waste stream. You should be careful, however, not to add weeds or plants that are diseased, and twigs and stems should be included only if they have been chipped finely first. You also do not need additives to speed the bacterial action; just shovel in a bit of garden soil or finished compost

Compost needs a pile that is large enough to achieve a critical mass but not so big that turning it becomes difficult or impossible. The optimum size is one cubic yard. Imagine a box that is 3 feet long on each side. The pile can be freestanding — a freestanding pile will drain well if it is properly turned and not matted — but it will be more efficient and look tidier if put in a bin.

Some people make bins from wooden pallets, scrap lumber or cinder blocks. Snow fencing and chicken wire are other options. The Rolls Royce of composting systems is a three-bin unit, framed in pressure-treated lumber, sided with one-inch wiremesh called hardware cloth, and with slide-in wooden fronts to hide the piles from view. The unit is a production line of sorts. The first bin is for a starter pile, the second for semi-composted matter, the third for the finished product. If you want the end product to look like soil, you will have to pass it through a screen to remove twigs and matter that has not been fully composted. This excess can be returned to the pile.

There is a thriving industry in plastic compost bins, some furnished as barrels that you roll about to turn the compost. These might be useful if you have a rodent problem, but they are expensive and not necessary for a successful pile.

There are two basic types of compost pile. The first is a fast pile, in which the organic material forms humus in less than a month from frenetic microbiotic action. This takes the active involvement of the gardener. The pile must be at least a cubic yard in volume, comprised of equal parts of nitrogen and carbon ingredients, finely chopped and watered lightly and turned every three or four days. If a pile becomes too hot, don't hose it down. Rather, just turn it thoroughly two or three days in a row.

The second and easier method is the slow pile, which needs far less attention and which breaks down over several months. You should still keep the pile moist, turn it occasionally and be sure there is a mix of material.

You have to turn compost because the microbes that break down the pile need the oxygen. If a pile becomes matted and devoid of oxygen, different microbes go to work, the bad ones that create a stink. Turning compost is best done with a good garden fork, but this is too strenuous for many people. You can buy agitators — metal rods with handles — to poke in and get air to the middle of the pile. Another method is to build the pile on several perforated drain pipes, placing one vertically like a chimney. This will aerate the pile, making turning unnecessary.

The microbes that feed on organic matter need a mix of materials high in carbon and nitrogen. High-nitrogen materials, called "greens" by composters, include grass clippings, kitchen scraps and livestock manures. High-carbon materials, called "browns," include leaves, straw, shredded newspaper and sawdust.

The problem is that there is a surfeit of grass clippings in the spring, when browns are scarce, and a glut of leaves in the fall, when greens are falling off. Of the two, the surplus grass is the more likely to cause a compost pile to fail. You can stockpile leaves in the fall for use the following spring (oak leaves are preferred; they won't mat like maples leaves) or work plenty of shredded newspaper into grass clippings in the spring.

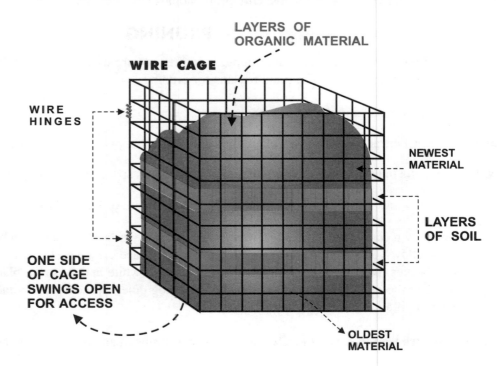

WIRE CAGE

LAYERS OF ORGANIC MATERIAL

WIRE HINGES

NEWEST MATERIAL

LAYERS OF SOIL

ONE SIDE OF CAGE SWINGS OPEN FOR ACCESS

OLDEST MATERIAL

Finished compost has some nutrient quality, but it is not used as a fertilizer. Rather, it is a fabulous soil conditioner for both clay and sandy soils. Used over the years as a top dressing or incorporated into the soil, it makes your plants healthier and happier and less dependent on chemical sprays and excessive irrigation.

DRAINAGE

SOMETIMES DRAINAGE PROBLEMS can be fixed simply by tilling soil, adding amendments, eliminating low spots and raking the land so that the water sheets away from buildings. But in our region, more seriously waterlogged soil and damp basements are facts of life. Often, correcting drainage around the house worsens soil conditions for the gardener, but the house must come first. However, correcting a house drainage problem also may fix the problems of wet, flooded soil that severely limits the range of plants that can be used.

The remedies should be progressive. First, check to see that gutters and downspouts are working correctly. Next, install downspout extenders to take storm water away from the foundation. Use solid, four-inch, flexible plastic pipe, sold in 10-foot sections at the hardware store. (It can be cut with a hacksaw and, once positioned, hidden by mulch). If you still have water seeping into the house, use a tamper and heavy clay excavated from another part of the yard and create a slight slope around the entire house extending out about 10 feet or so. Compact the soil with the tamper. A common problem is water seeping into cavities that have formed over the years below the concrete stoop. Make sure all holes are filled and tamped. Another source of water and woe is an old subsurface drain that has failed through silt buildup, root growth or compaction. If you have such a drain, it will need to be dug up and replaced.

If problems persist, hire a private house inspector for an examination. Inspectors usually are trained engineers and don't have an interest in recommending expensive in-basement drains and pumps. Often, a flagstone or brick terrace around the house will solve the problem, draining away surface water before it gets to the foundation wall.

If you have to install a drain, a number of legal and technical issues need to be considered. You must be careful not to direct your storm water on to a neighbor's property; this is not only anti-social but usually unlawful. In some instances, jurisdictions require connections to municipal sewer systems. Before you dig, you also must know the location and depth of underground gas, electricity, water, sewerage, cable TV and telephone lines, drains, storage tanks and septic fields. Hire professionals to design and install any elaborate systems.

PRUNING

MANY PEOPLE are confused about pruning. If you're not sure whether you should prune, don't cut. You can do far more harm than good. The main reasons for pruning:

■ To remove diseased and damaged branches

■ To restore an attractive shape to a plant that has become twiggy and overgrown.

■ To reduce the bulk of a tree or shrub that has outgrown its space and let in more light.

■ To promote more vigorous growth, a bushier habit and more or larger flowers.

Some overgrown conifers and broadleaf evergreens, notably yew and junipers, can be thinned or cut back hard. Others will allow you to remove lower branches. Sizable space can be reclaimed by doing this, sensitively, to American hollies, Norway and Colorado spruces, Eastern white and Austrian black pines and the Southern magnolia. But the branches of most conifers — including pines, spruces, arborvitae and false cypress — will not regenerate if all the needles are removed.

Neglected sites tend to have unlovely and overgrown shrubs, many of which can be transformed with artistic

DRAINAGE CHOICE I: A SWALE

THERE ARE TWO popular methods for draining waterlogged areas. The first is a surface drain called a swale. At its simplest, this is a shallow, grassy ditch that runs at the bottom of a slope, perpendicular to the hill. It collects rainwater and channels it to lower ground, where it might drain into the street gutter or a storm drain or an area of the property where it will do no harm. A typical swale might be four feet across and, at its midpoint, six inches deep. It is seeded like the rest of the lawn. Points to consider:

■ The contours of your land must be able to accommodate the swale, which has to lead to lower ground.

■ You will not be able to plant in the area of the swale.

■ Silt occasionally will build up, requiring the swale to be cleaned and reseeded.

Some gardeners make a feature of their swales, lining them with river stones, planting the sides (which are deceptively arid) and treating the feature as a dry river.

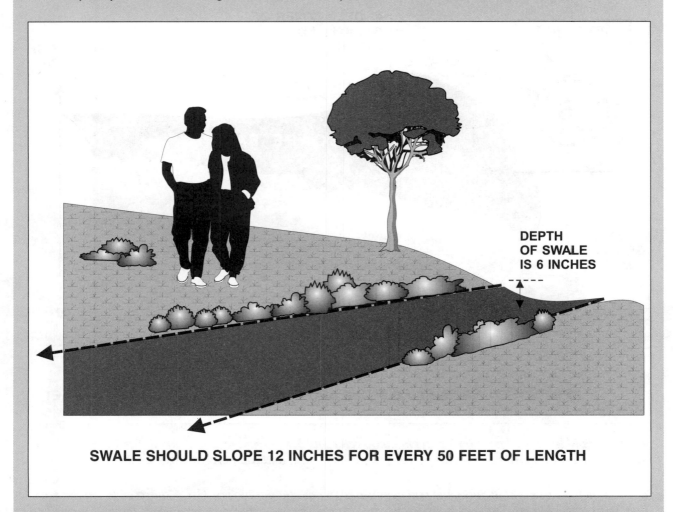

DEPTH OF SWALE IS 6 INCHES

SWALE SHOULD SLOPE 12 INCHES FOR EVERY 50 FEET OF LENGTH

The bottom of a swale should tilt at a constant minimum slope of 2 percent. Thus, if your swale is 50 feet long, it should be 12 inches lower at one end than the other. You can measure this by taking twine and pinning it with a nail at the high point of the swale. Thread a line level on to the twine, pull the string taut and raise it until the level is horizontal. The distance between the string and the bottom of the swale should increase six inches every 25 feet. The vertical measurement should be six inches at 25 feet, 12 inches at 50 feet, 18 inches at 75 feet and 24 inches at 100 feet. Obviously, this works only if the swale can be taken to lower ground.

DRAINAGE CHOICE 2: AN UNDERGROUND PIPE

AN UNDERGROUND PIPE is not as dependent on surface undulations and can be laid at the optimum tilt no matter what the ground above is like. However, it must still ultimately drain to a point lower than where it started.

If your land is flat, it is possible to empty a subsurface drainage pipe into a dry well, essentially a gravel-filled pit of modest proportions. Make sure it conforms to local codes.

Once you start shifting large volumes of water, it is best to get expert help in designing and building a system. For example, a large area of standing water will need a network of subsurface drainage and a proper place for it to go. Avoid draining water into a fishpond. It will carry pollutants from afar and also cause the pond to overflow during heavy rains.

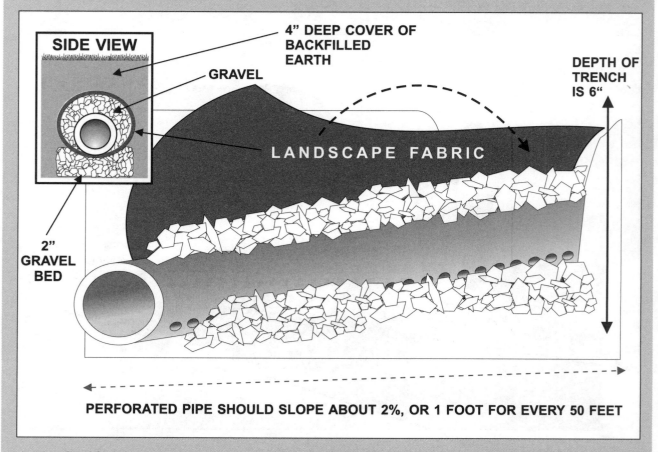

SIDE VIEW

4" DEEP COVER OF BACKFILLED EARTH

GRAVEL

DEPTH OF TRENCH IS 6"

LANDSCAPE FABRIC

2" GRAVEL BED

PERFORATED PIPE SHOULD SLOPE ABOUT 2%, OR 1 FOOT FOR EVERY 50 FEET

A pipe should tilt at no less than 1 percent, and preferably 1.5 percent or 2 percent. A 1 percent slope will drop 12 inches every 100 feet, a 1.5 percent slope 18 inches, and a 2 percent slope 24 inches.

Dig a trench that's eight inches wide and begins at a depth of eight inches. Use a sharp ax to cut the roots that invariably appear. Line the bottom and the sides with landscape or filter fabric, leaving enough to fold over to form a lid. This allows water in but filters out silt and keeps roots at bay.

Put in perforated, corrugated plastic pipe, four inches in diameter, centering the pipe in the trench. Fill the trench with gravel until it covers the pipe by two inches. Fold over the filter fabric to form a seal, pinning it with nails if necessary. Fill the top of the trench with a porous mix of sand and topsoil, and seed with grass or, if part of a flower bed, cover with mulch. Mark the pipe's location for future reference.

pruning. As with trees, remove shrubs only after all other options have been considered. Many shrubs — including forsythia, lilacs, crape myrtles, hollies and Japanese flowering quince — will regenerate in a pleasing way after being cut back hard.

You should not arbitrarily cut the branches of shrubs or trees or the central leader. Don't allow anyone to do this. It disfigures and weakens trees and causes shrubs to become hideously bushy as well as unhealthy. If the tip of a branch is broken, cut it back to just above the next pair of leaves or buds. If a branch is otherwise damaged, diseased or rubbing against another branch, remove the entire stem back to its union with a larger branch or the trunk.

Where a stem meets a branch, or a branch a trunk, the joint forms a collar that is often visible as a swelling. The cut must be made cleanly just outside this collar. Do not cut more than an inch away or the resulting stub will invite rot and disease. If the branch is more than two inches thick, it must be removed with three cuts to avoid having the falling limb rip bark off the plant. The old practice of dressing wounds with sealant is no longer recommended and may impede the plant's ability to heal itself.

Also, don't try to make a tree out of a plant that wants to be a large shrub. Lilacs, non-tree-form crape myrtles, shadbushes, blueberries, hydrangeas and other woody plants grow with multiple stems. They can be thinned, but don't go looking for a central trunk that isn't there.

While old and tired flowering shrubs can be rejuvenated through pruning, never remove more than a third of the plant at a time. Rather, plan to prune out a third of the oldest stems each spring over three years. If a shrub is not grafted (a grafted plant such as a rose or a cherry tree has a conspicuous bulge in its lower trunk) and produces suckers, it is desirable to let many but not all of the suckers grow. It will take several seasons for the plant to reach full flowering force again, but the wait will be worth it.

Whole branches can be removed at almost any time. Some trees bleed sap if pruned in March through May, but this is more unsightly than damaging. You should not cut stems, though, when temperatures are below freezing.

Plants that blossom on wood produced the previous season should be pruned as soon as they are finished blooming. These include virtually every spring-flowering woody plant, from winter jasmine to mophead hydrangeas. If you wait until late spring or summer before pruning them, you will lose flower buds set for the following year.

Plants that bloom in the summer and fall flower from wood produced the same season, so they can be pruned in the early spring. Examples include buddleia, rose-of-Sharon, smooth hydrangea, summer-flowering spirea and crape myrtle. (See table on next page for more information on what to prune.)

BAMBOO

BAMBOO IS A MEMBER of the grass family, spread by underground runners called rhizomes. The rhizomes make it exceedingly difficult to get rid of the plant once a colony is established. Unchecked for many years, a stand of bamboo will spread throughout a yard. Worse, it will spread into a neighbor's yard and may generate ill will. In winter, when it is covered in ice and snow, it flops over. This looks pretty but may block off a pathway. If the path belongs to your neighbor, ill will may turn to malice.

Contrary to conventional wisdom, you can get rid of bamboo if you are patient and persistent. Beginning in late summer, spray the foliage with glyphosate, being careful not to spray desirable plants. Glyphosate is a general herbicide that has low toxicity and soon breaks down in the environment. Roundup and Kleenup are two common brands. If you have more than just a small bed or two, it is far cheaper to buy glyphosate as concentrate, which you dilute with water and dispense in a hand-held pump sprayer.

KNOWING WHAT TO PRUNE

When you are deciding whether to prune during your first-year cleanup or in later years, you should know which plants gain from regular trimming — and which rarely need pruning.

Plants That Benefit From Annual Pruning

Redtwig and yellowtwig
   dogwood
Wisteria
Grapevines
Buddleias
Caryopteris
Ornamental Grasses
Bamboos

Japanese maples
Climbing roses
Modern roses
Apple trees
Pear trees
Raspberry canes
Pyracantha
Trumpet vine

Porcelainberry
Jackman hybrid clematis
Russian olive
Rose-of-Sharon
Smooth hydrangea
Willow
Winter jasmine

Plants That Benefit From Occasional Pruning

All small trees and shrubs that have grown too thick, with diminished flower and fruit ornament, should be periodically pruned, as should any with branches that have been killed by disease, cold or injury. Following are specific plants that gain from occasional pruning:

Eastern redbud
   (canker damage)
Abelia
Boxwood
Potentilla
Rugosa roses
Forsythia
Japanese flowering quince

Hollies
Hydrangeas
Leucothoe
Beauty berries
Aucuba
   (winter damage)
Camellia
   (winter damage)

Red-tip photinia
   (winter damage)
American yellowwood
   (tight crotches)
Clethra
Corylus
Deutzia
Winged euonymus

Plants That Rarely Need Pruning

Most conifers, especially pines
   (except Mugo pines) and
   cedars
Birches
Tree peonies
Azaleas
Rhododendrons

Mahonia
Sourwood
Fothergilla
Stewartia
Styrax
Viburnum

Witch Hazels
Cotinus
Enkianthus
Carolina silverbell
Crab apples
Deciduous magnolias

Wait two weeks and repeat the spraying. Repeat again in another two weeks. With a pair of loppers, remove stems as they shrivel and die, but don't remove them until then. The object is to get the stems to draw the herbicide into the roots. By November, all the top growth should be removed. The following spring, wait for new shoots to emerge, and let them grow tall. Once they leaf out, immediately cut them off at the ground again. Repeat this as a weekly or fortnightly chore until July. Allow the summer shoots to leaf out, then begin the glyphosate spray program again in August. After two or three seasons, you will kill the bamboo.

As the roots die, use an ax, a mattock, a sharp, pointed shovel and a good gardening fork to dig them up to make room for new plants. Be careful to gather the severed roots and throw them out. Do not put them on the compost pile, where they might re-shoot.

WEEDS

WEEDS ARE NOT a disease but a symptom, most often of the fact that a lawn that has not received proper care. It takes two to three years of diligent effort to beat back years of accumulated weeds. The key in almost all cases is to begin stopping the cycle of reproduction by preventing the weeds from flowering and setting seed. Your arsenal will consist of a sharp hoe, newspapers, mulch and glyphosate.

A tip: Weeds are far easier to pull or hoe when the ground is moist. If it has not rained a day or two before you weed, give the ground an advance soaking with the garden hose.

Here are the principal weeds that must be dealt with in inherited lawns and what to do:

CRABGRASS: Apply a pre-emergent herbicide before seeds germinate in mid-to-late March. Dig plants in the spring as they grow.

BROADLEAF WEEDS: Broadleaf weeds such as dandelions, oxalis and plantains should be dug or else killed with a broadleaf weed killer, which is effective only if the leaves have matured.

WILD ONION OR GARLIC: Repeated applications of a broadleaf weed killer or Roundup will beat back these weeds, but the best remedy is digging up the bulbs with a special weeding tool. The tool, which looks like a screwdriver with a notched tip, also is used to extract dandelions.

GROUND IVY: Like moss, ground ivy thrives in wet and shady sites with compacted soil. Its existence tells you that you probably need to improve drainage and loosen the soil.

BERMUDA GRASS: Bermuda grass is virtually impossible to eradicate. Repeated applications of Roundup will beat it back in late summer and early fall, but the stolons run deep, and some always seems to survive. Try digging up as much as possible. Bermuda grass moves into sunny thin spots in grass, so, ultimately, you can chase it off with thick turf cut high.

CHICKWEED: This winter annual is best tackled in early fall when its tiny seedlings break through the soil. By February it is covered in tiny white flowers and by late March with little seed capsules containing millions of the next year's plants. On bare ground, cover the seeds with a layer of mulch and pull any survivors.

In garden beds, pull out or hoe existing weeds. If there are too many, spray with glyphosate and repeat after two weeks. Don't expect the weeds to shrivel on the spot; they take several weeks to die. If possible, do this after mid-summer, when the weed killer is most effective. Spraying then also will give you a chance to see (and avoid) a range of plants — daffodils, lilies, peonies, poppies, hostas and other herbaceous stuff that may have been planted by previous owners — whose existence you may not have been aware of the previous winter. If the plants are in the wrong spot, most can be lifted and replanted with little effort.

Once weeds are croaking, lay sheets of newspapers and secure them with stones as you dump at least three inches of mulch on top. Many local governments deliver large amounts of leaf mulch or leaf mold for a modest sum. Alternatively, use shredded hardwood mulch. The mulching not only will give the yard a finished look until you implement your master plan, but both the newspapers and the mulch will decay and can be dug under to improve the soil. If you use plastic sheeting or landscape fabric, you would have to lift the material later. If and when weeds emerge in or through the mulch, pull them or spray with glyphosate.

For areas that are to be left open, plant either winter rye (November to January) or annual rye (early March to mid-May) until you can re-sow in late September with one of the permanent turfgrasses examined in the next chapter.

Chapter 4

THE LAWN

*A*T SOME POINT, efforts to keep a poor lawn going aren't worth it. The general rule is that a lawn with more than 50 percent weeds or bare spots should be redone. You should first figure out, though, why the old lawn declined. It could have been many things. Indeed, so many wrong steps are taken with lawns that they might be compared to minefields.

Some people use the wrong seed or too much fertilizer, or they apply the fertilizer at the wrong time of year. Others cut the grass too low, inviting weeds, or they fail to deal with insects or diseases. Still others don't fix drainage problems, let the ground become too compacted from heavy traffic, or try growing grass in full shade. Despite all of the potential pitfalls, however, a simple and methodical approach to lawn installation and care will give you a greensward to be proud of — and at minimal expense to you and the environment.

First, you need to decide what type of grass you want and whether you will use seed or sod.

SELECTING A GRASS

DIFFERENT CONDITIONS dictate different types of turfgrass. A beach house may do well with the southern warm-season type called zoysia. It greens up nicely in the summer but turns a straw brown with the first frost. While the neighbor's cool-season grass remains green (if wan) from November to March, the zoysia lawn looks dead. Great for Bethany, but not so great perhaps for Bethesda — and certainly not for anyone wanting a colorful year-round garden.

Another trait of zoysia is that once established, it starts to wander. It is not pleasant to see a cool-season turf invaded by zoysia — especially if the cool-season grass belongs to a neighbor.

Areas that are in partial shade and receive little foot traffic will do well with fine fescues; this also is a great variety for second homes that receive minimal landscape care or use. Gardeners who take great pride in having a pristine, fine-bladed and deep blue-green lawn will use Kentucky bluegrass — and then make the lawn one of their hobbies. But for most of us, who want a low-maintenance landscape that is aesthetically pleasing and kind to the environment, the grass of choice will be the turf-type tall fescue.

A. BUYING A PARTICULAR SEED

BEFORE DECIDING on your needs and preferences, you should keep one point in mind: *Don't buy grass seed on the basis of price.* Let others think that they are getting a bargain. The price difference between a superior variety, say Falcon II, and an inferior one, say Kentucky 31, might be $10 or $20 a 20-pound bag. Given the short-term cost in time and money of site preparation, equipment rental, hired help and soil amendments — and the long-term cost of keeping a bad variety going for years to come — trying to save a few dollars on seed is a fool's errand.

Kentucky 31 and other low-grade fescues tend to be coarse, clumpy and pale green, and they may come with many weed seeds. They might have their place on large rural properties where the owner needs to seed acres of outlying land or has flocks of hungry sheep, but they are best avoided in the suburban or city garden.

The extension services for this region put out lists of recommended grass seed varieties, chosen through extensive local trials. Almost all the rest of what you need to know about a seed is on the required label. If the label fails to name the variety or varieties of seed, don't buy the product. The label also must give the percentages of weed seed (which should be less than 0.5 percent) and undesirable grass seed (which should be zero). Some bags also have a fair amount of inert matter, in essence filler; the product should have as little as possible.

If a seed is advertised as high in endophytes, that's good. Endophytes are fungal organisms that improve resistance to diseases and pests. Your primary consideration, however, should be the quality of the variety and other ingredients. Everything else — from claims that a mix is right for this region to words like "landscaper" in the title to pictures of happy families barefoot on the lawn — is irrelevant. Here's a primer on grass seeds for our region:

- **ANNUAL RYE.** This is a temporary, one-season grass that is not for the permanent home lawn. In small percentages in a mix, it is useful as a nurse grass to keep weeds at bay and hold soil until permanent varieties get established. Annual rye also is useful to prevent soil erosion on bare dirt until it can be graded or seeded permanently in the early fall.

- **PERENNIAL RYE.** This, too, is not for the permanent home lawn in our region. It is useful as a nurse grass, but experts recommend against buying seed with more than 15 percent perennial rye in it. Otherwise, it will dominate the lawn and then do poorly in subsequent years.

- **KENTUCKY BLUEGRASS.** Once the ultimate in turfgrass, Kentucky bluegrass no longer enjoys the popularity it had. It is at its southernmost limit here, resents our summer heat and humidity and requires a high level of maintenance, including more frequent watering, feeding and dethatching, to endure. If you nonetheless select bluegrass, it should be a mixture of at least three different approved varieties in equal parts.

The following bluegrass varieties, recommended by the University of Maryland Cooperative Extension Service, are valid throughout the region:

Abbey	Georgetown	Livingston	Preakness
Aspen	Glade	Lofts 1757	Princeton 104
Baron	Gnome	Marquis	Ram I
Blacksburg	Julia	Merit	Rugby
Chateau	Kelly	Midnight	Shamrock
Cheri	Liberty	Monopoly	Suffolk
Classic Eclipse	Limousine	NU-STAR	Touchdown

For shade tolerance: Columbia, Eclipse, Georgetown, Glade, Midnight.

For low maintenance: Merit, Midnight, Monopoly, NU-STAR, Ram I and Washington.

In five-year trials by the National Turfgrass Evaluation Program in Beltsville, Md., the highest-scoring bluegrass varieties under a high-maintenance regime were Midnight, Limousine and Eva. For low maintenance, the best were Sophia and Ram I. Although some of these are not on the University of Maryland list, they are worth seeking out.

- **TURF-TYPE TALL FESCUE.** This is the preferred type for most lawns. It is not necessary to buy a blend, as with bluegrass. If you do buy a mixture, though, pick one with recommended varieties. Some varieties are dwarfs, which form thicker clumps and grow more slowly and thus don't need mowing as often. However, if they are injured they won't regenerate as quickly. The University of Maryland recommends these tall fescue varieties:

Amigo	Duke	Monarch	SR8300
Anthem	Eldorado	Montauk	Taurus
Apache	Finelawn 5GL	Olympic II	Titan
Arriba	Finelawn 88	Pixie	Tomahawk
Avanti	Guardian	Revel 3D	Trailblazer II
Aztec	Jaguar II	Revel Jr.	Tribute
Bonanza	Jaguar 3	Safari	Winchester
Chieftain	Lancer	Shenandoah	Wrangler
Cimmaron	Maverick II	Shortstop	
Crossfire	Mesa	SR8200	

Promising new varieties also are recommended. Note that many are improved versions of existing varieties:

Alamo	Crossfire II	Houndog V	Pyramid
Apache II	Debutante	Lexus	Silverado
Austin	Duster	MB-22	Southern Choice
Bonanza II	Falcoln II	Micro DD	Starlet
Chieftain II	Finelawn Petite	Minimustang	Titan 2
Coyote	Grande	Palisades	Vegas
Crewcut	Heritage	Phoenix	Virtue

In a three-year trial of tall fescues at Beltsville, Finelawn Petite, Genesis and Lancer excelled under a low-maintenance program. Other consistently high performers were Falcon II, Jaguar 3 and Houndog V.

The lists are updated periodically, and further improved varieties are likely. Any recommended variety, however, will do well in our region. The challenge is to find the seeds. Shop around and you'll spy at least one on the list.

■ **FINE FESCUES.** These fall into five categories: hard fescue, chewings fescue, creeping red fescue, slender creeping fescue and sheep fescue. Creeping red fescue, like Kentucky bluegrass, grows from rhizomes, or surface stems; this allows it to fill voids in a lawn in a way that most other grasses cannot. Both creeping red fescue and slender creeping fescue are not recommended for sunny sites. Sheep fescue is not considered attractive enough for home lawns. Hard fescues are useful for sunnier sites that get little attention.

The University of Maryland recommends the following fine fescue varieties:

Hard fescue: Attila, Aurora, Bardur, Biljart, Brigade, Discovery, Eureka, Silvana, SR 3000, SR 3100, Valda and Warwick.

Chewings fescue: Banner, Bridgeport, Epsom, Jamestown II, Longfellow, Proformer, Shadow, Southport, SR 5000, Tiffany and Waldorf.

Slender creeping fescue: Barcrown, Dawson, Marker, Napolie, Seabreeze and Smirna.

Creeping red fescue: Belvedere, Flyer, Herald, Jasper, Salem, Shademaster, Talus and Vista.

Sheep fescue: Bighorn, MX 86.

If you are paying others to seed your home, don't assume that they will use the correct grass. This applies as well to contractors who use hydroseed. Insist that they use a variety suited to your site and needs and one that is recommended by your state department of agriculture.

SOWING THE LAWN

THE OPTIMUM TIME to sow cool-season grass seed is from September 1 to October 15. This lets plants get established when they are least likely to be stressed by heat and drought or molested by weeds or insects. The seed takes up to two weeks to germinate. Kentucky bluegrass, which takes up to three weeks to germinate, should be sown earlier, between mid-August and September 30. Remember, these dates are for sowing, after your soil test and other site preparations are done. If your soil test indicates that both lime and fertilizer are needed, lay the lime a week or two before the fertilizer to establish the correct soil chemistry.

In late July to early August, you should spray the failed lawn with Roundup or its equivalent (do this carefully and on a still day, so the glyphosate won't kill desirable plants). Concentrate, as noted earlier, is a better value for your money and is generally used at a rate of six fluid ounces per gallon of water (follow the label instructions). This will treat 300 square feet. It takes at least two weeks for the old grass and weeds to die. Repeat the process in mid-August if necessary.

Around Labor Day weekend, cultivate the top two or three inches of the remnants of the lawn with either a garden fork or a rototiller. Rake out the dead vegetation, bag it and throw it away; it should not be used in the compost pile. Remove stones, sticks and other debris with a garden fork, and dig out as many Bermuda grass runners as your stamina and back allow. Grade the soil, making sure there is a slight slope away from buildings. Hose down the ground and look for low spots where water collects. Then wait a week, keeping people and pets off the bare earth.

The following weekend, fill the dips, and then spread soil amendments, fertilizers and, if needed, pulverized limestone in quantities specified by your soil analysis. Till in and rake the final grade. Don't worry if the soil sits high; it will settle after a few weeks.

Spread half the seed north to south, the remainder east to west. Coverage will be stated on the seed bag. Lightly rake the seed over the area, working backwards to rake out your footsteps. Cordon off the lawn for several weeks, until the young grass is established.

In small lawns, spreading a thin layer of sand on top is an excellent way of keeping seed moist and birds away. This is not practical on larger areas. Use weed-free straw (not hay), but spread it thinly, so that you see plenty of bare earth. The straw will keep the soil moist and discourage birds, but too much of it will impede seedlings and rip them out when you try to rake it up.

Seeded lawns need to be kept moist but not too wet, so hand watering with a good nozzle is preferred to a sprinkler. You will need to be much more vigilant about the seed drying out if it is sown in early September than in early October. Be prepared to mist the lawn morning and evening. Continue to water once the seed germinates. Don't worry if the grass looks thin. It will take two seasons to become fully established and thick.

Mow the seedlings when they grow to three inches. Don't wait too long. You must have a sharp blade on your mower. Do not apply fertilizers or weed killers until you begin a regimen of care the following season.

B. USING SOD

SOME PEOPLE PREFER sod, which has several advantages and some disadvantages over seed. The pluses include the fact that turf provides an instant lawn and can be laid during most months. It also is great for slopes where seed would wash out, and it keeps weeds at bay while its roots are established. The minuses are that sod is considerably more expensive and more laborious to install, and it still requires the same grading and soil amending as seed (you can't lay turf on orange clay subsoil and expect it to survive). The turf also may not be the type of grass you want.

If you are leaning toward turf, here are some things to keep in mind:

- **Know whether you are getting Kentucky bluegrass or turf-type tall fescue.** You may not want Kentucky bluegrass, with its attendant demands. However, sod made with tall fescues should have about 10 percent Kentucky bluegrass to bind the turf together.

- **Sod should be "state certified."** This guarantees that the turf has been grown with recommended varieties and with minimal pests or diseases in weed-free fields. "State approved" sod is a lesser designation, signifying turf that may have a broadleaf weed, a less pleasing color and slightly higher levels of insects and diseases. Read any landscape contract specifications carefully and know what you are getting. Since the burden of long-term lawn care falls on your shoulders (as well as on Mother Earth's), it is prudent to avoid turf that starts off disadvantaged.

- **The turf should be dense and well knitted.** You should be able to pick up a strip of sod at one end without having it tear under its own weight. Yet the thickness of the root and soil zone should be no more than three-quarters of an inch.

- **It is important to use freshly harvested turf.** It should be put down within 36 hours of harvest. If it is delivered and you cannot lay it for a day or two, unfurl the turf grass-side up, place it in an area of afternoon shade and the water it lightly.

LAYING TURF
You can't lay turf when the ground is frozen, and you shouldn't harvest or install turf in dry spells.

Sod should be laid with staggered joints, like bricks. You will need a sharp knife or a masonry trowel to cut sections to length at the lawn's perimeter. Make sure there's good contact with the subsoil. When you finish a section, hose it down and press it with a lawn roller. Have plenty of topsoil available to fill unanticipated depressions and spaces between joints where edges don't butt together well. Try to work on the soil side of the project; if you must step on the grass, use a plank to avoid compressing it.

Once the turf is laid, water it well and keep people and machines off it until you have to mow. It is essential to continue watering daily in the initial two-week to three-week rooting period.

If you are laying turf on a slope, you may need to secure sections with wooden pegs until the roots have grown. A tip: Don't seed or lay turf on a slope with an angle of more than 33 percent (meaning the ground rises three feet or more each 10 feet of distance). It will be too difficult and dangerous to mow. Instead, terrace the hill with retaining walls or use a ground cover that suits your site (see Chapter 19 on ground covers).

WHEN YOU BUY A NEW HOME

IN BUYING a new home, let the builder know that the quality of the yard is important. Builders typically budget for the bare minimum of yard materials and labor. Find out precisely what will be done as part of your deal.

Ask your builder to follow landscape contractor industry guidelines, which assure that the site will be properly prepared, that it is correctly amended and that an approved grass seed is used. This is a minimal approach. For example, the acceptable level of organic matter in the soil is just 1.5 percent. If you wish to negotiate a higher level, be prepared to pay a few hundred dollars more. In light of the long-term drain that a struggling yard will put on your resources and time, the initial sum may be worth it.

A reputable builder and his subcontractor should observe the Landscape Specification Guidelines of the Landscape Contractors Association of Maryland, the District of Columbia or Virginia.

The guidelines state that the landscape contractor will take a soil test and add, if needed, limestone, fertilizer and soil amendments. If the subsoil is exposed and of heavy clay, 50 pounds of gypsum per 1,000 square feet are supposed to be added, and the topsoil is supposed to be a loam or a silt loam. The subgrade should be cultivated to a depth of two to four inches. The topsoil then should be laid to bring the land to the correct final grade. The topsoil depth can be designated in the contract, but mixing the topsoil with the subsoil is especially important if three inches or less are added. Alternatively, the guidelines allow for an inch of compost, which should be incorporated into the top four to six inches of subsoil.

The contractor, too, is supposed to use state-recommended seed or "state certified" sod. If you want turf-type tall fescue (which you probably do), be sure to ask for it.

MAINTENANCE

AS ALL HOMEOWNERS know, maintaining healthy lawns requires careful attention. Here are the essentials to keep in mind:

MOWING
Set the lawn-mowing height to three inches (often the highest setting). Don't let the grass grow any higher than four inches before you cut it. This means that in wet springs, you may have to cut the grass every five days. (You can cut Kentucky bluegrass at 2.5 inches.) Replace the mower blade in late summer. Leave the collection bag off the mower and allow the clippings to fall to the ground.

If you are spending a lot of time pushing and pulling the mower into nooks and crannies, eliminate them by reshaping your garden beds. A lawn configured so that it can be trimmed in one go will take a lot less of your valuable time.

Push-reel mowers may not cut higher than 2.5 inches. Anything lower is not recommended for cool-season grasses in the Mid-Atlantic region. Check before you buy.

FERTILIZING
To maintain their vigor, grasses need the three primary nutrients in fertilizer — Nitrogen (N), Phosphate (P) and Potash (K) — as well as secondary nutrients and micronutrients. You should get a soil test every three or four years to determine if your lawn is deficient. Incorrect levels of nutrients can harm the lawn, are wasteful and pose a pollution risk. The soil test results will recommend which nutrients to apply and at which rates.

Lime is not a fertilizer but is necessary for fertilizer to work. Turfgrass prefers a slightly acidic soil to take up nutrients (a pH of 6.2 to 6.8 is considered ideal). In our region, soils tend to get more acidic with time. The powdered lime will raise the pH to the proper level. It can be applied at virtually any time, but common sense dictates that you do it slightly in advance of applying fertilizer in the fall.

Nitrogen makes lawns lush — but more is not better. On the contrary, too much fosters disease. Amounts slightly higher than those recommended on the bag can be used in high-traffic areas, but in shady areas you should reduce the level by a third to a half. On fine fescues in shade, reduce the amount even more (see table).

There are two basic types of nitrogen fertilizer, fast release and slow release. It is important to know which type you have for correct application amounts and schedules. Slow release allows more to be applied less frequently and also is preferred on sandy soils. This is how you calculate. The label will give the percentage of Water Insoluble Nitrogen (WIN), e.g., 8 percent. It will also give the amount of Total Nitrogen. That would be the first number in the analysis. Hence a fertilizer listed as 16-4-8 would have 16 percent total nitrogen. You then divide the WIN by the amount of Total Nitrogen and multiply the answer by 100 to give the percentage of Total Nitrogen that is water insoluble. Thus, 8 divided by 16 x 100 = 50 percent.

This is the schedule recommended by the University of Maryland Home & Garden Information Center:

OPTION 1 (less than 40 percent slow release)				
(Amounts are pounds per 1,000 square feet)				
	Sept.	Oct.	Nov.-Dec.	Mid-May-Early June
Tall Fescue	1	1	0	0-1*
Kentucky Bluegrass	1	1	0-1*	0-1*
Fine Fescue	0	1	0	0-1*

OPTION 2 (at least 40 percent slow release)			
	Sept.	Oct.	Mid-May-Early June
Tall Fescue	1.5-2	0-1.5*	0-1*
Kentucky Bluegrass	1.5-2	0-1.5*	0-1*
Fine Fescue	0	1	0-1*

*Apply only if lawn needs it — generally, if it's thin and weakly colored, growing on particularly poor soil or less than a year old.

WATERING
Watering is important to help a lawn get established, especially during its first spring and summer. Newly laid turf should be watered regularly until its root zone grows into the prepared subsoil.

Established lawns should be watered if they show signs of wilting, but the old practice of heavy watering in summer in an attempt to maintain a lush lawn is discouraged today as wasteful and unnecessary. When the lawn turns brown (a natural defense mechanism), stop mowing, keep off the grass and water deeply once a week. Even if the top growth looks dead, it will spring back in September. One method of checking the irrigation level is to push a screwdriver into the ground. If the lawn has had the inch of moisture a week that it needs, the screwdriver should go in four to five inches. Alternatively, place an old coffee can on the lawn until it contains an inch of water.

Watering is best done in the morning to minimize evaporation and to make sure the foliage is dry before nightfall, when fungal spores come out to play.

DETHATCHING
Thatch is the matted detritus that builds up at the base of the turfgrass crowns. Eventually it will form a barrier between the top growth and the root zone, impeding the watering, feeding and care of the individual grass plants. If the lawn has not been dethatched in more than five years, chances are high that a thick and harmful layer of thatch has grown. Raking the ground will reveal if large amounts of thatch have built up. Kentucky bluegrass and fine fescues tend to generate more thatch than tall fescues. Lawns that are excessively fertilized or have too little or too much lime also generate thatch quickly. Mulch mowers do not contribute appreciably to thatch problems.

The need for a full-blown dethatching can be delayed with proper care and a light dethatching each year with a dethatching rake. This has vertical blades that loosen the thatch with a minimum of damage to the grass. Rake up the debris, bag it and throw it out.

When the time comes for the heavy guns, the advice is this: Mechanical dethatching does damage, so do it in September or early October to let the grass regenerate at the optimum time of year, not in the spring when the grass would be stressed going into the summer. This also is a time to thicken the whole lawn, a process known as "overseeding," something a dethatched lawn will need.

Some outlets sell blades with a sprung prong at each end as a dethatching tool that you attach to the lawn mower. These are to be avoided; they scalp the grass terribly. It is better to rent a dethatching machine, which will have vertical blades that dangle loosely. Start off at the highest setting, lowering it only if necessary: The aim is to destroy as little healthy grass as possible.

You should have a work mate to rake and bag the debris as you work, to minimize rental time. Work the machine north and south, then east and west.

CORE AERATION

Core aeration is perhaps the single most effective way of tackling the hardpan clay left by new construction. It is also the best way to re-establish a dying lawn in areas where soil compaction and poor drainage have all but killed the turf. Finally, it is a great method of preparing the turf for overseeding. The avid lawn gardener will find an excuse to use the core aerator every fall. Otherwise, it is generally used to correct the deficiencies mentioned.

The core aerator is not to be confused with manual or powered aerators that simply stick metal spikes into the ground. The core aerator is a serious machine (self-powered or an attachment to a tractor) that uses sharp metal pipes to extract plugs of soil, perhaps a half-inch in diameter and four inches long. The plugs create something of a mess and should be broken up with a rake. The soil should be slightly moist to allow the aerator to penetrate the ground without compacting it.

The machine can be rented, but you'll need a pickup truck to transport it. Some lawn services will aerate your property for a fee, even if you are not a regular customer. If your lawn is too small for a powered machine, you can buy a manual aerator with a coring pipe on each end of a foot bar. It works in a city garden or on small patches. If the ground is dry, water it well the day before.

Aeration allows water and nutrients and gases to reach the root zone and removes physical barriers to the roots. Top-dress the lawn with humus after aeration, especially if you are overseeding in the early fall. You can aerate at other times of the year, but obviously not when the ground is frozen or waterlogged or when the lawn is in summer dormancy.

TOO MUCH SHADE

IF THE SITE is in full shade, maintaining a lawn will be extremely difficult, if not impossible. Consider replacing the grass with a shade-loving ground cover (see Chapter 19 on ground covers and Chapter 22 on shade gardens). If you have just partial shade, try the following:

■ Select a fine fescue variety recommended by the extension service.

■ Correct any drainage and soil compaction problems.

■ Check the soil pH. Often, moss is a sign of acidic soil that will need liming.

■ Consider removing lower branches of trees or shrubs (or whole trees if they are old and unattractive or pose a threat to the house) to bring more light into the area.

Once established, a lawn in partial shade will need fewer waterings and feedings than one in full sun, but you will have to be diligent about keeping leaves and other debris off the lawn.

PESTS AND DISEASES

PESTS AND DISEASES afflict all lawns, arriving when the grass is sick. If you keep the turf healthy by following the guidelines in this chapter, most problems can be prevented or contained.

Pest	Symptoms	Treatment
Japanese and June beetle grubs White, C-shaped grubs start small in September but grow to the size of a cashew nut in spring.	Lawn is thin and peels back when raked. The presence of moles and shrews often connotes large grub populations.	Bt or granular insecticide in late summer when grubs are young and near surface. Milky spore as long-term biological control. Re-seed with tall fescues.
Billbugs Small, legless grubs feeding on root crowns in the summer.	Brown patches two to six inches across. Blades of grass dying and easily pulled, and sawdust-like frass in heavy feeding areas.	Re-seed the following September with tall fescues high in endophytes.
Chinch bugs Tiny black insects with white wings, one-fifth of an inch long. Preceded by even smaller red nymphs with white bands. They feed on grass leaves and do most damage in July and August.	Localized yellow or brown areas.	Insecticide. Re-seed in September with tall fescues high in endophytes.
Sod webworm Caterpillar of a white moth, brown and active in June and July.	Brown patches. Look for white moths flying above turf and for caterpillars at the base of leaves.	Bt and endophytic tall fescues.

Diseases. Most diseases are fungal leaf spots encouraged by excessive nitrogen fertilizer (or, alternatively, lack of fertilizer), buildup of thatch and improper watering. Dollar spot results in dark-bordered leaf lesions and hourglass-shaped spots on neglected grass in late spring. Brown patch has elongated legions with brown margins and occurs in mid-summer. As a rule, bluegrass and fine fescues get more fungal diseases than tall fescues. Instead of resorting to highly toxic fungicides, correct summer watering practices, get a soil test and apply correct fertilizers in the early fall.

PATCHING AN EXISTING LAWN

MOST LAWNS NEED renovating about every five years. In addition to repeating previously noted steps — getting another soil test, carefully using glyphosate or a selective herbicide to kill broadleaf weeds and crabgrass without damaging desirable plants — you should mow the grass at the lowest setting and collect the clippings.

You cannot throw seed on an undisturbed lawn and expect it to germinate. After mowing, go through the lawn and identify bare and weedy areas that need reworking. Tackle these as a series of small patches, cut into rectangles. Slice off the vegetation with a shovel and then use a garden fork to work the top two or three inches of soil. Add two more inches of a topsoil-humus mix. Peat moss is useful, but it will lower the soil pH.

Even though you are only patching the worst areas, use the opportunity to overseed and thicken the whole lawn. You also must work the lawn to create good contact between soil and seed. The simplest way is to scratch the surface with a rake, add some amendments as a top dressing, rake the ground smooth and lay the seed. For large lawns where hand raking is onerous, consider first doing a dethatching, a core aeration or both. This also is a good time to fill dips with a blend of sand and topsoil or humus. Watering, fertilizing and mowing advice is the same as for new lawns

Use turf-type tall fescues, except in shady areas, where an approved variety of fine fescue can be applied. It is important to keep fallen leaves off germinating grass. If raking disturbs the seedlings, you may have to hand-pick the leaves.

A WORD ON LAWN SERVICES

MANY BUSY PEOPLE who can afford it hire lawn care companies. If you plan to be among them, you should make sure that you hire one of the reputable firms that have responded to growing concerns about excessive and needless applications of fertilizers and pesticides by changing those practices. You also should be wary of proposals to treat the lawn on a rigid, prescribed schedule if the firm has not first determined and explained the need for such treatment.

Consider companies that not only advertise integrated pest management techniques (a rather abused term) but that actually use them. The basic tenet here is using most toxic chemicals as a last resort, not first. An environmentally sensitive firm will take soil tests and have specialists monitor insect populations and diseases before arriving with tanker trucks. If a problem arises, it should be addressed first with the least intrusive method, perhaps something as simple as changing mower height or watering practices. If that is not enough, it might be fixed with insecticidal and herbicidal soaps and oils or with beneficial predatory insects.

Organic fertilizers, while slower acting and more expensive, are widely available and better for the long-term health of the lawn (and the environment) than more powerful synthetic fertilizers. Find a company whose agents listen as well as talk.

Chapter 5

GETTING HELP

*S*OME IMPROVEMENTS are easy for you to do, such as turning a moss-ridden patch of grass into a shrub bed, planting a screen of evergreens or laying stepping-stones through a garden bed. Other jobs, however, will be beyond your physical limits, your equipment, your expertise or simply your willingness to do them.

In many instances, site conditions will dictate the magnitude of a project and whether it is something for a do-it-yourselfer or a professional. A retaining wall of landscape timbers or dry laid stone that is 18 inches high (perfect for sitting on) is within the capacity of many do-it-yourselfers. Anything much higher, however, should be left to professionals. High retaining walls hold back enormous forces and must be engineered, drained and built correctly.

If you have more than one or two landscape projects in your sights, or need to address the whole yard, it is wise to turn to a professional designer before seeking out a contractor. You may have to spend, say, $5,000 or $10,000 to fix a drainage problem; a landscape architect might show you how to use the money to correct the problem while building a desirable garden feature as well.

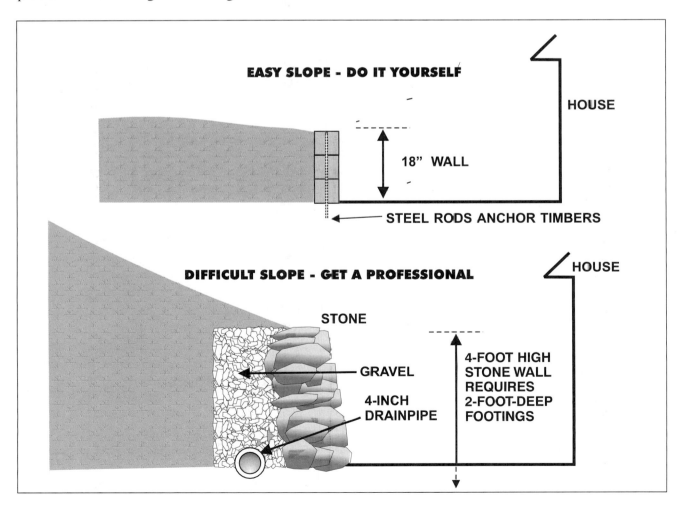

EASY SLOPE - DO IT YOURSELF

HOUSE

18" WALL

STEEL RODS ANCHOR TIMBERS

DIFFICULT SLOPE - GET A PROFESSIONAL

HOUSE

STONE

GRAVEL

4-INCH DRAINPIPE

4-FOOT HIGH STONE WALL REQUIRES 2-FOOT-DEEP FOOTINGS

If you can afford only one phase of an overall design at first, it is important that it be part of your long-term master plan, so that future improvements fit with your initial investment. This may sound grandiose, but a future phase might be something as modest as putting in a small lily pond or a collection of antique roses.

WHERE TO TURN

LANDSCAPE ARCHITECTS

Landscape architects are rigorously schooled and licensed by state boards. Some specialize in residential design, while others have large practices, with home gardens only a small part of their business. A frequent complaint is that landscape architects are lacking in horticultural knowledge, but this is a generalization. The design and construction-supervision services of landscape architects can run into thousands of dollars. If you can afford it, it usually is money well spent.

GARDEN DESIGNERS

Garden designers do not have the same level of education or regulatory control as landscape architects. This does not necessarily make them less gifted as designers or less competent at construction management. As a rule, their knowledge of plants and their needs is excellent. Garden designers often are good at inventive designs in smaller spaces. Satisfy yourself that a garden designer you are considering is capable and experienced. Look for designers who have graduated from the landscape design programs of universities.

DESIGN-AND-CONSTRUCTION FIRMS

These are landscape contractors, general contractors or contractor divisions of major retail nurseries. Often the design for your garden is listed as "free." The design and its execution may be entirely sound and satisfactory, but scrutinize the plan for the spacing and type of plants proposed, as well as for the quantity and quality of materials specified.

BUYER BEWARE

TURNING TO professional help costs money, often a lot of money, so you owe it to yourself to spend wisely. Have a clear idea of what you do — and don't — want before you go to a designer or contractor. If you are vague, you are apt to get features you don't like, and you will come to resent the cost of them. Allow a professional to bring form to your desires, but don't give a designer or contractor carte blanche.

Like it or not, turning to a professional is not the end of your involvement. Far from it. You have to stay engaged to ensure that the job is done correctly to specifications and to make decisions when unexpected problems or choices arise, as they inevitably will.

PLANTS

Contractors have been known to cram in far more plants than a garden should take. This creates an instant effect and makes for a more profitable job. Soon, however, the new garden is likely to become overcrowded, and you will be burdened with removing or constantly pruning plants. How do you know if a plan is plant heavy? Write down the name of the plant (use Latin names to avoid confusion) and look up its mature size. The cherry laurel Otto Luyken *(Prunus laurocerasus)*, for example, grows four to six feet wide; it should not be spaced at two feet. Bradford pears grow 15 to 20 feet wide; they should not be spaced four feet apart. The Eastern white pine *(Pinus strobus)* grows 20 to 30 feet wide; anything less than 15 feet apart is pushing it. Gardens are planted mainly for tomorrow, not today (see Chapter 1, plant spacing section).

MATERIALS

You cannot get an accurate comparison of contractor bids unless you and/or your designer specify the amount and grade of material, including precise dimensions. Virtually every building material for gardens comes in different grades. If you don't specify which grade, the contractor is likely to use the lowest grade available and base his bid on that. Sometimes the use of inferior materials is purely economic — cheap bricks might cost 25

cents apiece, expensive ones more than $1 — but often a lower-grade material translates into higher mainte-
nance costs and a shorter life span. A fence or deck made of low-grade, knotty pine, for example, will be inferior to one made of the highest grade of cedar or redwood.

Quarried stone comes in different grades (based on the type of stone, its size and its cut), as does flagstone
(based on thickness and cut). Large stepping-stones, often called landscape stones, are more expensive per ton
than small ones, but they may be essential for the scale of your project.

As a driveway material, gravel is cheaper than asphalt, but gravel must be kept contained, raked and weeded.
Asphalt is cheaper than concrete but must be at least two inches thick and on a compacted gravel base of six
inches. Concrete is cheaper than brick or pavers but must be on a well-drained, compacted base, be poured six
inches deep in welded wire fabric, and be designed with the correct number of expansion joints. Bricks or
other pavers are cheaper than cobbles or flagstone, but all should have a concrete base with curbing.

Before material is unloaded, check it to verify that it meets the specifications. Better yet, accompany your contractor to the stone yard, lumberyard and plant nursery to make sure the best materials are selected. Spend the
time to educate yourself. Understanding the type and quantity of specified materials provides the best basis for
accurate bid comparisons and minimizes misunderstandings and disappointments.

Your landscape architect or garden designer also will act as your general contractor or construction supervisor.
But even if your designer is hiring the contractor(s), you should be involved in the selection.

CONTRACTORS

The same rules for picking a contractor to build or enlarge a house apply outdoors. First, candidates must be
licensed in the state (and sometimes the community) where the work is to be done, and they must carry workers' compensation and liability insurance and produce proof of it.

One of the best ways of finding a suitable designer and contractor is through word of mouth — ask friends,
neighbors, relatives and co-workers for names. Try to get at least three bids, and be sure to request references
and check them out. Ask to see a portfolio of work, and arrange to visit completed projects, the more, the better. Each designer will have his or her own style. Look beyond style, though, to see that the design responds
to a garden's own unique site in some special way and isn't merely a copy of another garden.

A contractor has to juggle existing projects and look for new ones simultaneously, so it is unreasonable to
expect him to be at your site continuously. However, you should not be abandoned, either. Make sure the contract has a start date and a completion date.

Do not hire people who knock on your door looking for work or bother you on the telephone. Disregard prom-
ises of cut-rate prices, once-in-a-lifetime opportunities, sales drives, perilous site conditions that need fixing
immediately and other scams of fly-by-nights. Be especially careful of those offering to resurface your asphalt
driveway. A dandelion sprayed with black tar is still a dandelion.

Never give most or all of the money to anybody up front. If you deal with a reputable contractor, it is reasonable to pay a deposit once work has begun and to schedule payments as the job progresses. Save a large chunk
as a final payment, to be given once the project is finished to your satisfaction.

Don't go looking for a contractor between March 1 and Memorial Day. That is when everybody else is thinking about garden improvements. The contractor you want probably won't be available, and no one will be hungry for work. Also, it takes weeks and months to design a garden, prepare the construction drawings and put
the job out to bid. Plan your schedule so that you receive bids over the summer, with work to begin in the fall.
In mild years, it is possible to work well into December and even through the winter.

SAVING MONEY

DESIGN

If you are at a loss as to how to improve your garden, some landscape architects and garden designers will come out for a modest consultation fee and spend an hour or so walking the site, discussing your needs and wants and offering suggestions. For additional fees, they will provide some conceptual plans that might in themselves be sufficient for you to execute with the help of a mason, carpenter or laborer.

CONSTRUCTION

Certain projects are straightforward, stand-alone improvements — replacement of a cracked driveway, a new fence or renovated patio — that don't need to involve a large cast of characters. Again, ask neighbors and friends about workers they have used and go to see the results. If you are looking for a skilled mason for re-pointing or for a small wall, observe a crew working on a commercial project you admire and ask a member if he or she does work on the side.

You can arrange to pay for the design and construction drawings and take the project to your own contractor or, if you are brave, act as your own general contractor. This will save money, but it will saddle you with the burdens of hiring, supervising and scheduling subcontractors, getting building permits, calling Miss Utility and keeping building inspectors and neighbors happy. The savings might be offset by the cost of divorce lawyers.

PLANTING

As a rule, it is between one-half to two-thirds cheaper to buy your own plants and install them than to arrange for a nursery to do it, though the plants you install usually won't be guaranteed for as long. You will need to prepare the beds beforehand and have a stock of soil amendments and mulch on hand. You will also need some basic equipment — a wheelbarrow, garden fork, shovel, rake, and penknife — along with the services of a friend, neighborhood teenager or day laborer recommended by others.

If your garden plan calls for large numbers of perennials, grasses and ground covers, ask your garden center or mail-order nursery if they sell plugs. These are low-cost, tiny plant divisions that, with proper care, reach full size in a season or two.

Section 2

PILLARS OF
THE GARDEN

Chapter 6

AZALEAS AND RHODODENDRONS

*S*HRUBS AND TREES are the pillars of the garden, and the azalea is the ubiquitous flowering shrub of Washington-area neighborhoods, beloved for its bursts of bright colors in April or May. Similarly, the closely related rhododendron (both belong to the genus Rhododendron) is the first choice as a larger specimen shrub among many new gardeners, who rightly love its coarse-leafed texture and large, joyous trusses of flowers.

Azaleas long have had a special place in the hearts of Washington gardeners. The plant's rise and development coincided with the growth of Washington and its suburbs in the 20th century. Young homeowners in search of attractive foundation shrubbery needed look no further than the showy hybrids reaching plant nurseries from the 1930s to the 1960s. The rhododendron has similar needs to the azalea but is more difficult to grow. The key is to be highly selective in the variety you pick, even if that means passing up some of the most beautiful flowering rhododendrons in the nursery or plant catalog.

Here are some general suggestions for purchasing and growing both azaleas and rhododendrons:

1. Don't buy on impulse during flowering season. Know the plant you want and where it will go before you drive to the nursery. Better yet, don't get into the car until the hole is dug.

2. Select a variety for the ornament of its leaf as well as for its bloom. These plants will be in flower just two weeks a year. Think about their leaf texture the other 50 weeks, as part of a larger plant composition.

3. Use these plants sparingly, and look for others to substitute, unless you don't mind having one of our area's many look-alike azalea and rhododendron gardens.

4. Be choosy with the azaleas as well as the rhododendrons you grow. This not only will help make your garden special as well as disease-resistant in some cases, but it may well persuade retailers to start carrying valuable varieties that they often don't stock.

5. Keep the plants out of full sun and poor clay soil.

I. Azaleas

THE AZALEA PROPAGATES and interbreeds so easily that literally thousands of varieties are available, making it all the more important to acquire superior plants by name. If a generic pink azalea that you buy cheaply at a roadside stand does not die, you may discover one day that this no-name plant has grown to eight feet.

Despite the numerous azaleas that have been bred, relatively few make it to large retail nurseries and garden centers. Rather, these outlets tend to carry such common varieties as Hershey Red, Mother's Day, Delaware Valley White, Coral Bells, Hino Crimson and Pink Splendor, all of which are planted excessively. A number of outlets offer rare and unusual varieties (see Specialty Plant Sources in the Appendix).

Most azaleas are evergreen or semi-evergreen, but not all. Some of the best are deciduous. Growth habits of azaleas vary widely, and a common mistake is to plant some too close to foundations, windows and other plants, not realizing that they can grow to six or eight feet. Even low-growing varieties reaching just three feet in maturity generally will grow to four feet in diameter. Others might reach just two feet and are valuable as ground covers. Make sure that you know the mature size of the variety you are planting.

NOTABLE VARIETIES

- **KURUME HYBRIDS.** These were among the first showy Asian azaleas to make a splash in the West in the early 20th century. As a class, they tend to be smaller in habit and texture, growing to about three feet. They also tend to come in bright reds and magentas that can make them hard to place with other plants and against red brick walls. Common varieties include the overplanted Coral Bells (pink), the garish Hinodegiri (rose red) and the unrelenting Hino Crimson (red). More recent introductions are less garish and worth growing.

- **GABLE HYBRIDS.** These were developed by Joseph B. Gable in Stewartstown, Pa., making them reliably hardy in the Washington area. They tend to be low-growing. Worthy varieties include Herbert (purple), Rosebud (pink), Rose Greely (white) and Stewartsonian (red).

- **GLENN DALE HYBRIDS.** Developed by Benjamin Morrison, first director of the National Arboretum, in Glenn Dale, Md., these were selected for their flower form and color, plant habit and hardiness. Most varieties are medium-sized, but after many decades they grow tall and often too big for allotted spaces. Most are upright and arching; some are wide. Morrison emphasized large flowers, and his hybrids remain good choices for the Mid-Atlantic region. Look for Buccaneer (reddish-orange), Daybreak (white-blush), Delos (rose-pink), Gaiety (purplish pink) and Martha Hitchcock (white, edged purple).

- **SATSUKI HYBRIDS.** Compact plants with large flowers, these bloom very late, well into June. Of these, only Gumpo White and Gumpo Pink are commonly available, which is a shame, since this is a large and interesting group well suited to the small garden.

- **EXBURY HYBRIDS.** The most popular of the tall, deciduous azaleas, these have flowers of bright oranges, reds, yellows and blends of those hues, depending on variety. They and others that are in a group called Knap Hill azaleas are at their southernmost limit in Washington, preferring the cooler climate of the Northeast. If you grow them in Zone 7, make sure that they have optimum conditions and care. Don Hyatt, a grower in McLean, Va., recommends Cecile (pink), Marina (soft yellow), Chetco (stronger yellow) and Gibraltar (bright orange) for our region.

- **GIRARD HYBRIDS** (raised in Ohio and hardy), **ROBIN HILL HYBRIDS** (raised in New Jersey and hardy, typically three feet high and wide), and **VUYK HYBRIDS** (particularly Palestrina) are other worthy types.

The following lesser-known azaleas are harder to find but deserve to be used:

- **ROYAL AZALEA** *(Rhododendron schlippenbachii)*. This is an exceptional plant (see Chapter 14 on bests and worsts for details).

- **PINXTERBLOOM AZALEA** *(Rhododendron periclymenoides)*. This is a charming native plant, somewhat tall and spindly, growing to six feet, but beautiful in a native plant collection or a naturalistic garden. Its flowers, pink to violet, appear as fragrant clusters just as the plant begins to leaf out in early May. Connoisseurs consider the similar Roseshell Azalea *(Rhododendron prinophyllum)* a more handsome plant.

- **FLAME AZALEA** *(Rhododendron calendulaceum)*. Another deciduous, tall native, the flame azalea is like an exotic bird in bloom, flashing its brilliant flowers in June, and then receding from view the rest of the season. It is the showiest of the natives and a parent of the Exbury and Knap Hill strains, but it is a tougher plant.

Some varieties are yellow, others orange-red. Ideally, you should select your plant in bloom but wait until September to plant to avoid transplant shock in high summer.

Other unusual native azaleas worth trying are the **COAST AZALEA** *(R. atlanticum)*, a three- to six-foot-high suckering shrub with fragrant white and blush blooms in April; the **PINKSHELL AZALEA** *(R. vaseyi)*, seven feet high with rose-colored blooms, and the **SWAMP AZALEA** *(R. viscosum)*, a five-foot-tall shrub flowering in June. The swamp azalea is one of the few to take wet conditions.

CULTIVATION

AZALEAS WILL SURVIVE — barely — in poor soil, but they look their most vigorous and lush when raised in optimum conditions. This is easy to do, particularly if you are sparing with the number you plant. As with aging movie stars, lighting is everything. Azaleas need protection from the direct afternoon sun of high summer (plant for July, not April). An ideal spot would be in front of and on the east side of small shady trees or tall evergreens, on an east-facing hill or, best of all, beneath the high canopy of mature hardwoods. If you place azaleas in deep shade, they will grow leggy, and the flowering will diminish.

Azaleas have shallow, fibrous roots. This makes even big specimens easy to move. It also means the gardener must make sure the plant grows in soil that retains some moisture but is well drained. Azaleas prefer slightly acidic soil, which is easily achieved by planting them in a loam that has been amended with leaf mold or peat moss. The roots are then kept cool and moist in summer with a two-inch layer of mulch.

When planting, you must tease roots from their pot-like shape, set the plant at the same growing level as when it was in the container, and go easy on the peat moss. Too much, ironically, can cause the soil to repel water. Some growers lighten the soil a little with finely chopped pine bark.

Water the young azalea regularly, particularly when first planted and during its first summer. Once established, it won't need regular watering, but all azaleas should be watered slowly and deeply during a drought. Don't lay too thick a layer of mulch. You can prune a young plant, lightly, to give it a nice tiered effect, but as a rule healthy azaleas don't need pruning.

Azaleas should not be excessively fertilized and should not be fed later than Labor Day. Use correct amounts of either Hollytone or some other fertilizer formulated for acid plants or an acidifying organic nutrient called cottonseed meal.

If you cannot move a large, overgrown, evergreen azalea, chances are good that it will spring back, smaller, from a hard pruning. In early spring, cut stems to 12 to 18 inches above the ground. The plant will not flower that year and may take another two or three to regain its full flowering vigor.

Main Pests: Lacebugs, spider mites, whiteflies and deer. **Main Diseases:** Petal blight and chlorosis.†

USES IN GARDEN DESIGNS

THE USES OF AZALEAS depend on their size and the beauty of their overall habit, leaf form and color, not just on the flowers. Use tall, upright plants as back-of-the-border shrubs or as mid-sized screens. Compact, spreading azlaeas make great players in semi-shady gardens, used in small groups as accents. They are generally fine-textured.

If you plant too many azaleas, the plant volumes and textures will become monotonous. You should use them with other shrubs to bring out their beauty. Pick other foliage plants that enjoy partial shade — yews, hollies, pieris, aucuba, leucothoe, epimedium, sweet box, Solomon's-seal, ferns, hostas, liriope and Japanese maples, to name just some. Small azaleas work nicely as ground covers or massed on embankments.

AZALEA POT PLANTS

AZALEAS USED in potted plants indoors are grown for their showy blooms. Most are not hardy in our winters and should not be planted outside. After they flower, harden them off by exposing them to outdoor (above-freezing) daytime temperatures over two weeks, bringing them in at night. They can then be grown as patio plants, with partial shade, to be taken into a bright, cool room in the winter. They are likely to bloom indoors in late winter. Re-pot them as they grow larger.

Hardy azaleas can be grown the same way. In November, dig a hole in the ground to receive the pot for the winter, lifting it in late March. In summer, shield the plant from afternoon sun and be prepared to water it every two or three days.

A TIP: If your azaleas didn't bloom, it was because you pruned the plant after June the previous season, removing the following spring's flower buds. Or else deer did the job for you. They love azalea buds.

Exbury and other Knap Hill azaleas should be grown as specimens. They are strong in color and need to be used wisely. They will jar easily, but they also afford the opportunity to make a striking color combination, an orange or yellow, say, with a mass of blue flowers in the background provided by irises or Virginia bluebells. Ringing the house with azaleas is neither artistic nor good azalea culture: It guarantees that at least some will get too much sun.

II. *Rhododendrons*

WHILE AZALEAS ARE relatively easy to grow, rhododendrons are notoriously difficult. They are prone to stress and fatal diseases brought on by our hot and humid climate. Even when grown well, they often are not long-lived and never will attain the stature of rhododendron shrubs and trees you may have seen in the Pacific Northwest, Britain or Ireland, where they can grow to 20 feet. But you can grow large, healthy rhododendrons, raising simply spectacular plants, as long as you follow certain rules. If you have fallen in love with these plants and want to do well with them, join the American Rhododendron Society, Potomac Valley Chapter (see Appendix for Plant Societies list).

RECOMMENDED VARIETIES

RHODODENDRONS ARE plants from temperate climates and high elevations. They don't like the warm nighttime soil temperatures of lowland gardens in our area. You should therefore select rhododendrons developed by breeders on the East Coast, whose hybrids are proven in this region.

Look for Dexter Hybrids and Gable Hybrids as well as native species *R. maximum album* (white) and *purpureum* (pink-purple); and *R. catawbiense* and its hybrids *Album Grandiflorum* (white) and *Roseum Elegans* (pink-lavender). Certain Asian species and their varieties do well here, including the highly recommended metternich rhododendron *(R. metternichii), R. yakushimanum* and *R. makinoi.*

The following are recommended by Don Hyatt, a rhododendron hobbyist and breeder from McLean, Va.:

DEXTER HYBRIDS AND DERIVATIVES
GiGi (rose red)
Scintillation (lavender pink)
Wheatley (deep pink)
Janet Blair (white)

GABLE HYBRIDS
Disca (large white flowers)
Cadis (pale pink)
County of York (white)

RECENT EAST COAST HYBRIDS
Martha Phipps (pink/yellow)
Golden Star (yellow)
Donna Hardgrove (orange blend)

ASIAN SPECIES
Rhododendron fortunei (lavender to white)
R. metternichii (pink)
R. yakushimanum var. Yaku Angel (white, semi-dwarf)

CULTIVATION

CULTIVATION FOR rhododendrons is roughly the same as for azaleas, but the correct steps become even more critical because of the lower tolerance for abuse. You can't pull a rhododendron out of a pot and stick it in a hastily dug hole and expect it to survive. Again, plant in good loam that has been amended with pine bark, leaf mold or peat moss, and place the plant where it is protected from full afternoon sun. The east side of the house is ideal. Try to position the plant so the top growth is in sun while the roots remain shaded. Don't try to do this with a ground cover such as ivy or pachysandra — the rhododendron will resent the root competition.

Pot-grown rhododendrons typically have been gorged with fertilizers (and fungicides) before they reach the consumer. If left in pots for too long, rhododendrons become pot-bound; the roots assume an almost impenetrable mat, circling around on themselves. Try to examine roots before buying a plant to check for this.

Even if the plant is only moderately pot-bound, you must take a sharp knife and butterfly the roots at their base, score them along the side and attempt to tease them out with your hands. If you don't, the roots will form a barrier to watering and will dry out no matter how much you water them. You can avoid this problem by buying field-grown plants that have been balled and wrapped in burlap. They cost more but are more likely to do well.

Do not plant rhododendrons (or azaleas) too deeply or their surface roots will drown. When the blooms of rhododendrons fade, cut off the spent blossom, being careful not to damage the new lateral buds beneath the old flower. The object is to prevent the plant from expending energy in producing seeds. Rhododendrons wilt badly in freezing winter weather. To minimize this, water the plants well in mid-autumn before the ground freezes, and apply an anti-desiccant spray on the leaves.

Main Pests: Stem borer (the most serious) and lacebug. **Main Diseases:** Root rot and bytrosphaeria.[†]

USES IN GARDEN DESIGNS

RHODODENDRONS MAKE wonderful accents in mixed perennial shrub borders, as well as handsome screens and low, informal hedges. If you have high dappled shade from mature hardwoods, you will have a perfect spot for one of these beauties. Do not plant them in pairs (if one dies, you can never match the survivor), and do not plant them as specimens in key locations. A sick rhododendron draws attention to itself.

[†]See Appendix for common pest and disease ailments and remedies.

Chapter 7

BOXWOOD

EW PEOPLE are neutral about boxwood. Those in search of a sense of history and permanence crave the stuff. It's not just that its wood has been used for centuries by cabinetmakers (hence its name). It also was favored in the formal gardens of Colonial America, and the Colonial Revival movement of the early 20th century assured its continued popularity. There are those, moreover, who love boxwood's bittersweet scent, with some saying it reminds them of childhood gardens.

Others, however, detest both the plant and the scent. Some of them say that boxwood brings to mind people they don't like who grew it. This is not the plant's fault. They also dislike the fact that this passive plant remains unchanged throughout the year, that it is static and monotonous. Their opponents in the Great Boxwood Battle, however, view this trait as a distinct virtue, as giving a garden year-round structure.

Washington falls in the center of boxwood nirvana — it cannot be grown well much north of Pennsylvania, and it is not a plant for the Deep South. So if you are among the boxwood lovers, you would do well to take advantage of our location, though perhaps judiciously, for boxwood does not come without problems. It is prone to several maladies. These can be minimized with correct cultivation, but it is still a plant that you have to fuss over. If you are looking for low-care, broadleaf evergreens, you might want to consider such alternatives as Japanese holly, English ivy, barberry or lavender for formal garden edging, or osmanthus, various hollies or small upright conifers for screening

NOTABLE VARIETIES

- **ENGLISH BOXWOOD** *(Buxus sempervirens Suffruticosa).* This is in fact a variety of common box known more properly as edging box. It is the wonderfully tidy shrub that grows after many years to waist height or more in sensuous, billowing mounds. A dwarf form is even slower growing and preferred as a near-static edging plant for Colonial-style parterres and knot gardens.

- **AMERICAN BOX** *(Buxus sempervirens Arborescens).* Also misnamed (boxwood is not native to the United States), this is a tree-like variety. It is entirely different from edging box — more open, upright and massive, growing in time to 15 feet high and another 15 feet across.

- **KOREAN BOXWOOD** *(B. sinica var. insularis)* and **JAPANESE BOXWOOD** *(B. microphylla var. japonica).* These related species are not considered the most beautiful boxwoods, but they are hardy and tough. Japanese boxwood in particular takes on a bronze cast in the winter that is normal but looks sickly. (In other boxwoods it is a sign of stress.) While both grow to considerable size, *B. microphylla* varieties also include some of the smallest, slowest-growing plants in the garden. One, named either Kingsville Dwarf of Compacta, gets to about 12 inches after 30 years. Its leaves are tiny, and it is an effective plant in artful textural compositions. A variegated version named *B. sempervirens Elegantissima* has creamy yellow leaf margins. It grows high with age, to about seven feet.

- **HARLAND'S BOX** *(B. Harlandii).* This is a little-known Chinese species that is different and elegant, with long, glossy leaves. Growing about three feet high and six feet across, it makes a stunning low hedge, but it is marginally hardy in Washington and should be grown only in sheltered sites inside the Beltway. If you do plant it, make sure that you buy the hardier clone.

USES IN GARDEN DESIGNS

BOTH EDGING BOX and Harland's Box, left unclipped, make superb hedges. Edging box is the aristocrat of the bunch and desired for lining paths and defining formal beds. American, Japanese and Korean boxwoods all make useful evergreen screens and add passive structure to garden beds and borders. Be sure that you know their mature size before planting. The American box will grow after 40 years to a 15-foot tree. The Japanese box grows in a shorter period to about eight feet and the Korean box to six feet.

Select edging box for formal hedges along walks and decorative parterre and knot gardens, but be mindful of some practical problems. It is, for one, hard to give an entire bed the same light conditions. This will promote uneven growth and, possibly, some winter bronzing on one side but not the other. You also shouldn't space plants too closely, a common mistake. Set them four feet apart and be patient, and keep mowers and trimmers away from the shrubs. You might want to grow extra plants elsewhere (perhaps as patio container plants) so that they can be moved easily into the hedge to fill the gap of a plant that dies.

You should visit historic gardens where boxwood is grown well, which is fun as well as enlightening. Tudor Place in Georgetown has splendid hedges of edging box, including a knot garden of great beauty in spring. Many of Virginia's historic plantations, including Mount Vernon, are famed for their boxwood. Virginia Garden Week in April will take you to more boxwood gardens than you ever imagined existed. The finest gathering of boxwood gardens is at Colonial Williamsburg, and to see the remarkable diversity of form and habit, visit the boxwood collections at the National Arboretum or at the Virginia State Arboretum east of Winchester. Take along a tape measure and paper. Note how plants are arranged. In the parterre or knot garden, see how the bed is maintained between the boxwood and the interior space, whether planted with roses, ivy or herbs (see Appendix for Public Gardens information).

CULTIVATION

THE MOST IMPORTANT influences on the success of boxwood are where and how it is planted. It should be set in a well-drained site and in properly amended soil. If it is planted too low, its surface-growing roots tend to drown. If set too high, those roots dry out too much, stressing the plant.

Boxwoods also will not flourish in the shade. However, sun exposure needs to be regulated. The most common cause of stress, evidenced by winter leaf bronzing, is exposure to too much winter sun and wind. Protect it from afternoon sun in the winter. Do not plant in areas of a building facing south or west, except in the lee of another building or of evergreen vegetation. Remember that deciduous trees offering afternoon shade in May will be of little use in December, when their leaves will have dropped (and the sun will be more southerly).

If boxwoods are in the wrong site, they can be readily transplanted in a manner similar to Japanese maples (see box in Chapter 10). Wrap the foliage in burlap during transplanting to reduce the risk of stem damage. To curb water loss, large plants should be wrapped in plastic while they are on the back of a pickup truck.

Boxwood sulks when placed too close to other plants — it dislikes root competition — so give it its own space. Similarly, don't plant it right up to the edge of a walkway. Set it back 12 to 18 inches to allow for root development and future growth. You also shouldn't let winter salt wash into the root zone.

Boxwood prefers soil that is neutral or slightly alkaline. This makes it difficult to place with azaleas, which prefer acidic soil. If the two are in close proximity, top dress the boxwood with a cup of dolomitic limestone each spring. When planting boxwoods, avoid peat moss, which is acidic, as a soil amendment.

Boxwoods also detest drought. It is important to water them regularly during dry spells, especially in the summer, and in the fall before the ground freezes. But try not to water excessively, and remember that the soil must drain well. Overhead sprinkling is undesirable. It will set the foliage up for disease and encourage unwanted surface roots. Instead, soak the roots with a hose set to a slow trickle. If you have lots of boxwood, you may want to install a system of soaker hoses or drip irrigation.

Mulch lightly and avoid mulching against stems. When buying plants, look for specimens with a single trunk emerging from the root ball before branching. Those with multiple stems are less likely to do as well after several years.

Boxwood branches, which are brittle, often are snapped by winter storms. Large snowfalls (particularly of wet snow) and ice storms are the principal culprits. Shrubs planted beneath eaves often get battered by snow and ice falling from roofs. This can truly devastate old, mature plants.

In November, take twine and, starting at the base, wrap the bush in a spiral pattern, once up and once down, tying it at the base. Do not wrap too tightly, and it is essential to remove the twine at winter's end. Some people with old choice specimens go to greater lengths, building a wooden frame to place over the plant. Open-slatted snow fencing is then nailed to the top of the frame. Do not clad a frame in plywood. This will prevent air, moisture and light from getting to the plant.

If heavy snow is threatening your plant, you can sweep it off, using gentle upward strokes of the broom. Start from the bottom and work up. Sweeping from the top down or from side to side snaps branches. If your boxwood is encased in ice, leave it alone. Any brushing will damage the plant.

If a winter storm has broken a branch, remove it cleanly with a sharp saw once temperatures are above freezing. Do not try to close the gap by tethering branches together. The only thing you can do is wait for the boxwood to regenerate in the hole, which it will do, although it will never regain its original symmetry.

Main Pests: Leaf miners, psyllids and mites. **Main Diseases:** Macrophoma and volutella are particular to boxwood, as is boxwood decline, which especially afflicts edging box. These ailments usually attack stressed plants, so the best defense is keeping plants healthy. Phythophthora is another boxwood affliction.[†]

PRUNING AND SHEARING

THINNING BRANCHES is highly beneficial to edging box and to the dwarf forms of *B. microphylla*. This also is a way to collect holiday greens in November and December. Randomly remove whole stems at points all round the plant. A mature plant of edging box should yield about a trash bag full of stems. This will leave the plant with "holes" (that's what you want) that will soon be filled in. Do this yearly. After a season or two, the thinning — some call it "plucking" — will have encouraged foliage to grow not just in the plant's top two inches but down the stem to about six inches. The plant will be healthier, have more air circulation within it and be far less prone to disease.

Overgrown boxwoods can be cut back and will regenerate. Severe pruning is best done in two stages 12 months apart, when the plant is dormant in winter. Like hard-pruned yews and rhododendrons, the plants will look distressingly disfigured for two or three years. It is better to keep them shaped and pruned before they become overgrown.

Shearing, or giving the foliage a trim, involves slicing through leaves to present a flat plane. It is done on topiary and hedges and practiced with abandon in Europe. In our more difficult climate, however, shearing places heavy stress on the plant and is best avoided. Edging box has a naturally compact shape and does not need shearing. If you do shear a boxwood, promise yourself that you will look after it with proper feeding, watering and spraying. You still should thin it even if you shear. Shearing after August (or late applications of fertilizer) will encourage tender new growth in the fall that will be killed by frost.

[†]See Appendix for common pest and disease ailments and remedies.

Chapter 8

OTHER POPULAR SHRUBS

*S*HRUBS ARE one of the important pillars around which the garden is formed, but they should be far more than just building blocks. They should be beautiful and interesting in many seasons, resistant to disease and matched to their sites. These and other factors should be considered in choosing among the seven other popular Washington-area shrubs examined here.

I. Lilacs

THERE ARE FEW greater garden joys than the sweet fragrance of an old lilac bush heavy with blossoms. Spring is under way, and all's right with the world. The lilac is a splendidly old-fashioned plant, the type our grandmothers knew and grew, and for some of us the lilac flowers of early May unlock far-off memories of childhood.

Lilacs, however, do have their shortcomings. The first is that once the flowering is over, the shrub is rather dull. The second is that lilacs generally are big, easily growing in a few years to eight to 10 feet, with a six-foot spread. Owners of small gardens end up devoting much precious real estate to this one-season wonder. The common lilac has a place in large suburban or rural properties, especially grouped into broad natural hedges or living walls to mark off garden areas. In smaller gardens, diminutive lilacs should be used.

The third problem is that lilacs develop powdery mildew during our hot and alternately dry and humid summers. This turns their large leaves a sickly gray-white in late summer and through the fall, lowering the tone of the garden. You can minimize this problem by choosing varieties that are resistant to diseases and by siting them well.

NOTABLE VARIETIES

THE TYPE OF LILAC most grown is the common, or French, lilac *(Syringa vulgaris)*, with its hundreds of varieties differing little except in flower color, which ranges from light blue to deep purple and white. I prefer the richer colors, especially in the purples. The whites remind me too much of privet, and the paler colors and blues generally seem to get washed out in our bright light.

If you cannot resist having lilacs, here are the most notable varieties:

■ **CHINESE LILAC** *(Syringa x chinensis)*. This old hybrid has smaller leaves and flower panicles than the French lilac, making it finer in texture and a little (but not a great deal) smaller in size.

■ **PERSIAN LILAC** *(Syringa x persica)*. Although this is a more graceful and smaller shrub, reaching six feet, it needs room to spread. It produces masses of pale lilac flowers.

■ **CUTLEAF LILAC** *(S. laciniata)*. Similar to the Persian lilac, this one has interesting, deeply cut leaves, which is most unlike lilac plants, and the cutleaf does better in the heat of Zone 7a than other lilacs. The flowers are a pale lilac.

- **PRESTON HYBRIDS** *(S. x prestoniae)*. This version blooms two or three weeks later than common lilac and is valued for that alone, though its blooms are nowhere near as fragrant. There are many varieties to choose from, with handsome flowers ranging from white and light pink to magenta.

- **MEYER LILAC** *(S. meyeri)* The Meyer is a champ. Reaching just seven feet, it flowers early and is covered in masses of fragrant, violet-purple blooms. It also is tolerant of Zone 7 heat and resistant to powdery mildew. The most common variety is Palibin.

- **LITTLELEAF LILAC** *(S. microphylla)*. This is a broad, spreading shrub, 7 feet x 10 feet in maturity. Its smaller leaves give a finer texture, making the plant seem not as big as the common lilac. It flowers late, with fragrant, rose-colored blossoms, and is a worthy plant in larger gardens. For lilac fans, it's a great plant for extending the season.

- **JAPANESE TREE LILAC** *(S. reticulata)*. This is a different type of lilac altogether, not a thick shrub but a valuable ornamental tree, reaching 20 feet or more and with a spreading habit. It blossoms late (in rose season) and is spectacular in flower. The fragrance, such as it is, is bitter, like privet's. A hardy and trouble-free plant, the Japanese tree lilac brings up the rear in the grand parade of spring-flowering trees.

CULTIVATION

LILACS GROW HAPPILY in ordinary soil, but they resent a site that is too acidic. Mix wood ashes or limestone into the planting hole, or top-dress existing lilacs. Do not plant lilacs in poorly drained soil or in shade.

You must devote some time to your lilacs to make sure they bloom well each year. You should remove the spent flower panicles as soon as possible after they have finished blooming. Use a sturdy stepladder and good hand pruners. In spring, you also can apply a superphosphate fertilizer, worked into the soil at the edge of the dripline.

A pruning regimen is important with lilacs. Again, do this right after flowers fade. You can improve air circulation and minimize mildew by taking out some interior branches to let in air and light. Try to find an old thick stem to remove each year without disfiguring the plant. This will start a program of renewal pruning that will assure optimum flowering. You must also remove most, but not all, of the tiny suckering stems that appear each spring from the roots. Leave two or three and allow them to grow into mature stems.

If you have inherited a garden where lilacs have grown old and stopped blooming, remove all the old stems and allow several suckers to start growing in their place. It will take two or three seasons for the plants to regenerate and flower again, but the wait will be rewarded.

Some lilacs, particularly French hybrids of the common lilac, may be grafted on to privet or other root understock. Look for a swelling above the root ball where the two plants have been joined. Try to get a plant that is not grafted so that you can regenerate the lilac if necessary in years hence.

Main Pests: Borers and scale insects. **Main Disease:** Powdery mildew.[†]

USES IN GARDEN DESIGNS

LILACS RARELY are interesting enough year round to use as a specimen, even those trained into little lollipops. On larger lots, use them as driveway hedges, screens, windbreaks and to delineate garden areas. Smaller types make excellent anchoring shrubs for wide plant borders. Lilacs are extremely cold-hardy, making them good choices for exposed gardens at higher elevations.

II. *Viburnums*

VIBURNUMS HAVE at least two seasons of ornament. They are attractive in bloom in the spring, and many varieties have superb fruiting displays in the fall. The foliage is handsome, green and healthy looking throughout the summer. The viburnum is an asset to any garden, but like the lilac it demands a lot of space. Several smaller varieties are better suited to the city garden.

The late Donald Egolf, a gifted plant breeder at the National Arboretum, introduced some of the best viburnums available today. All were tested rigorously at the arboretum and do well in our region. (Egolf also produced superior varieties of crape myrtle and pyracantha, discussed later.) Generally, any plant developed by Egolf has good multi-season ornament, a superior form and resistance to diseases that typically afflict the plant. In other words, they are as close as you can get to a sure bet.

NOTABLE VARIETIES

■ **DOUBLEFILE VIBURNUM SHASTA** is considered the crowning achievement of Egolf's work with viburnums and is indeed one of the finest garden plants (see Chapter 14 on bests and worsts for more details).

■ **SIEBOLD VIBURNUM** *(Viburnum sieboldii)* is a large shrub or small tree valued for its glossy green foliage and handsome flowers. The leaf emits the most awful smell when bruised; perhaps this is why the shrub is not troubled by insect pests. Egolf bred a variety named Seneca, selected for its red berries and red berry stalks that (unlike those of other Siebold viburnums) are not quickly devoured by birds.

■ **LEATHERLEAF VIBURNUM** *(V. rhytidophyllum)* is a valuable, tall shrub useful for providing screens and backdrops, especially in the shade garden. The leaves are coarse, and you need to place it with care. The plant's one drawback is that the leaves will wilt to an unsightly degree in cold winters. A popular alternative is a leatherleaf hybrid named *Viburnum x pragense*, which is about two-thirds the size of the parent plant in leaf size and eventual height (10 feet). Egolf bred a hybrid named Alleghany that grows to 11 feet, with an equal spread.

■ **VIBURNUM CHIPPEWA AND HURON.** These two Egolf hybrids are splendid large landscape shrubs, developed for the South but hardy in Washington and to the north, with superior flower and fruit ornament as well as great fall leaf color. Chippewa has glossier leaves and grows to eight feet. Huron grows to nine feet.

In small gardens, side yards and corners of larger properties where a medium-sized shrub is required, the following are suitable (they grow wide, so you still must give them elbowroom):

■ **DOUBLEFILE VIBURNUM SHOSHONI.** This is a dwarf version of shasta, growing to four feet. Like shasta, it flowers in May and has a broad and tiered growth habit, but at two-thirds the scale.

■ **VIBURNUM ESKIMO.** This is a snowball-type developed by Egolf for its compact habit and dark, glossy, semi-evergreen leaves. It grows to four feet. A larger version named Chesapeake reaches six feet at maturity.

■ **VIBURNUM CATSKILL.** The Catskill is a compact variety of the linden viburnum *(Viburnum dilatatum)* that grows slowly to five feet. Another named Erie is slightly larger but still suited for residential use. Both have especially good fruit ornament.

■ **VIBURNUM X BURKWOODII CONOY.** This was the last of Egolf's introductions and, at five feet, also is suited to the smaller garden (though it has a place in any garden). It has small leaves, a fine texture and remains evergreen in the Washington area. The flower and fruiting displays are exceptional. A related selection named Mohawk grows larger, eventually to seven feet, and is valued for its compact growth and flowering ornament, which includes several weeks in spring of red buds that open to white petals with red blotches.

- **EUROPEAN CRANBERRY BUSH VIBURNUM COMPACTUM** (*V. opulus Compactum*). This grows to no more than six feet and is a good, dense, flowering (and fruiting) plant. Make sure to get this variety, not the species (that's still a good plant, but it grows about twice as large).

CULTIVATION

VIBURNUMS ARE EASY to grow, and they don't need coddling once established. They will do well in ordinary soil that has been lightened a bit with organic matter. They prefer the soil to be slightly acidic, and it must drain well. Viburnums will grow in full sun but prefer a little afternoon shade. In deep shade, viburnums grow leggy, and the flowering and fruiting diminish. To promote a good shape, the plant should be pruned lightly when it is young and again when it has become mature and twiggy. Soak the roots during dry spells and frequently during the plant's first season.

Main Pest: Aphids. **Main Disease:** Cited varieties generally are free of disease.[†]

III. *Hydrangeas*

HYDRANGEAS ARE old-fashioned plants that rightly are back in favor. A lot of gardeners like the showy mopheads, huge powder puffs of blues or pinks. They are great fun and wonderful for children, but the lacecap versions are altogether more elegant. Oakleaf hydrangea are an indispensable stalwart of wooded lots, while climbing hydrangea vines reward patient gardeners.

The mopheads and lacecaps, of which there are many varieties, fall under the species of bigleaf hydrangea (*Hydrangea macrophylla*). The only difference is in the size and the form of the flowers: The mopheads, sometimes called hortensias, consist entirely of showy but sterile flowers, while the lacecaps are daintier blooms, with a ring of sterile flowers surrounding a dome of the much tinier fertile flowers. Siting and care for the two, though, are the same (see cultivation).

These are medium-sized shrubs, reaching four to six feet in height and at least six feet across. Their leaves are large and coarse, making the plant seem bigger than it is. These hydrangeas bloom in July, and, like most of their kin, the flower heads dry on the stalk and can remain ornamental through the fall and winter.

For gardens on the cold side of Zone 7a, the *Hydrangea serrata* is a good substitute for the bigleaf hydrangea; its mopheads are smaller but more profuse.

NOTABLE VARIETIES

- **OAKLEAF HYDRANGEA** (*H. quercifolia*). This is deservedly a popular shrub. It is trouble-free, robust in leaf size and flower panicle, and well suited to the fringes of the woodland garden, where it flourishes. It also is a native plant. The showiest variety is Snowflake (see Chapter 14 on bests and worsts for more details).

- **SMOOTH HYDRANGEA** (*H. arborescens*). This is another native hydrangea but harder to love. It is handsome enough in an authentic native plant collection, but by any measure it gets twiggy and unkempt by late summer. It grows to five feet with white flowers. If you like this shrub, Annabelle is an improved variety worth seeking out.

- **CLIMBING HYDRANGEA** (*H. anomala subspecies petiolaris*). An aristocrat among vining plants, this grows not only up but across and out, making it a valuable vertical plant for covering walls. It is superb in almost every ornament: the leaves thick and glossy, the lacecap white blooms a delight of late spring, the bark, when revealed in autumn, a rich cinnamon and flaking. Like clematis, it quietly develops a good root system for its first two or three seasons and then grows rapidly.

■ **PEEGEE HYDRANGEA** *(Hydrangea paniculata Grandiflora).* A tall shrub or tree-type hydrangea, this plant suddenly bursts into bloom in late summer, its huge white panicles arching under their own weight. Many connoisseurs consider this a vulgar plant. The bark is a sickly tan and the leaves hold little interest. But I think that an artfully pruned specimen, with a leaning trunk and a posed imbalance to the plant, makes the PeeGee an enjoyable landscape addition. The flower heads dry to a rose and light brown color in the fall, and it is possible to pick up those colors in other autumnal plants such as winged euonymous, rugosa roses, viburnums and Japanese maples.

■ **ASPERA HYDRANGEA.** Though hard to find, this is a wonderful plant that grows tall, with its lacecap flowers well presented above leaves that are much narrower than those of the bigleaf hydrangea. A variety named Vilosa is particularly handsome.

CULTIVATION

THE OAKLEAF, smooth and aspera hydrangeas prefer some protection from full sun. Plant them on the east or north side of the house or on the fringes of a wooded area. The PeeGee is an unabashed sunbather. Bigleaf hydrangeas, particularly lacecaps, tend to do best with some shade in the afternoon. They can wilt terribly in drought conditions. The climbing hydrangea is content in sun or partial shade. All do well in heavy loam as long as it is well drained.

The smooth and PeeGee hydrangeas bloom on stems that grow in the current year. The smooth hydrangea benefits from being cut to the ground like a perennial each spring. Be careful with the others, which bloom on wood formed the previous year. In many gardens, the bigleaf hydrangea doesn't bloom after a severe winter, because the buds are killed by freezes. In mid-summer, after it flowers, prune out dead wood. Carefully remove faded flower heads, but leave intact the nearest leaf node, and make sure not to damage or prune any freshly emerging stems. In colder parts of Zone 6b, you may need to protect flower buds routinely in winter by circling the shrub with chicken wire and filling it with fallen oak leaves. Wrap the wire in burlap. In spring, dismantle the apparatus, removing the leaves by hand to avoid injury to flower buds.

Main Pests: Aphids and mites. **Main Diseases:** Leaf spot, powdery mildew and rust.[†]

USES IN GARDEN DESIGNS

USE THE SHRUB HYDRANGEAS as specimens, grouped as informal hedges or screens, or as part of a larger mixed border of shrubs and perennials. This includes the PeeGee hydrangea, which should no longer be used as a lone and forlorn lawn specimen. Treat the smooth hydrangea as a woodland perennial, chopping it back in March. The climbing hydrangea is superb growing up the walls of a house, a shed or breezeway, and it also makes a great embankment plant on a shady hillside. You must give it room, although it can be kept pruned to a desired dimension.

Bigleaf hydrangeas presented as pot plants can be set out in the garden, but you will have to harden them off by gradually acclimating them to the outdoors. If winter is looming (actually the first frosts of late October), wait until the next spring to do this. In the meantime, keep them indoors in a bright, cool environment.

IV. Crape Myrtles

THE VALUE OF crape myrtles to the garden cannot be overstated. They can be grown as medium-sized or large shrubs, exquisite ornamental trees and, with the impending introduction of another National Arboretum plant, as a compact, low-growing shrub. Crape myrtles bloom in July and August when few other trees and shrubs are in flower. New varieties, moreover, have stunning bark patterns and attractive fall leaf color, making them four-season plants. They are also hardier, making them reliably sound choices for Zone 7.

Again, we have Donald Egolf to thank for these beauties. There are so many Egolf selections and hybrids available today that it seems pointless planting the old crape myrtle, a multi-stemmed shrub known botanically as *Lagerstroemia indica*. Egolf's are prettier, hardier and much less prone to powdery mildew, which marks and damages leaves and flowers. Egolf did produce improved selections of the old species, but his choicest varieties are those resulting from crosses with a wild species of crape myrtle, *Lagerstroemia faurei,* discovered in Japan in the 1950s.

The variety Natchez, a beautiful all-round plant, has become the tree type of choice, but for the sake of variety, try others (see Chapter 14 on bests and worsts for more details). Miami is one of my favorites. Here are more than 20 from which to choose*:

MEDIUM TO TALL (7 to 9 feet)

VARIETY	FLOWER	TRUNK	FALL COLOR	HABIT
Acoma	white	silvery gray	red-purple	low/spreading
Caddo	bright pink	cinnamon	orange-red	spreading
Hopi	light pink	gray-brown	orange-red	low/spreading
Pecos	medium pink	dark brown	maroon	low/spreading
Tonto	dark fuchsia	beige	maroon	rounded
Zuni	lavender	brown-gray	dark red	low/upright

TALL (12 to 18 feet)

Apalachee	lavender	med. brown	orange-russet	upright/rounded
Comanche	coral pink	sandalwood	purple-red	upright/rounded
Lipan	lavender	beige	orange-russet	upright/rounded
Osage	pink	dark brown	red	trailing/rounded
Sioux	dark pink	gray-brown	red-purple	dense upright
Yuma	lavender	silvery gray	yellow-orange	upright/rounded

TREE TYPE (15 to 30 feet)

Biloxi	pale pink	dark brown	orange-red	vase-shaped
Choctaw	bright pink	cinnamon	bronze-maroon	rounded
Kiowa	white	cinnamon	orange	tree
Miami	coral pink	dark chestnut	red-orange	upright
Muskogee	lavender	gray-brown	red	broad/tall
Natchez	white	cinnamon	orange to red	broad/tall
Tuscarora	coral pink	light brown	red-orange	broad/vase
Tuskegee	pink-red	gray-tan	orange-red	spreading
Wichita	magenta	mahogany	russet	vase-shaped

*Source: U.S. National Arboretum

A series of compact, miniature crape myrtles is in the pipeline as others carry on Egolf's work. The first scheduled to be available to consumers is Chickasaw. It has pink-lavender flowers and grows to two feet. These miniatures will be useful for summer color in small and medium-sized beds, as container plants and, on larger sites, as ground covers.

CULTIVATION

The crape myrtle grows well in ordinary soil, but it will grow faster and reveal its bark patterns sooner if planted in enriched soil. It must have full sun to perform well. The new crape myrtles are hardier than the old. Indeed, they are reliably hardy in Zone 7 as a rule. In severe winters and exposed sites, however, they may suffer dieback in the coldest pockets of Zone 7a. This won't kill the plant — it will regenerate happily — but it may never attain the size needed for the bark to show its mature beauty. If you live in such a microclimate, plant one of the shrub types. Crape myrtles are among the last plants to leaf out, so don't assume until June that a branch is dead.

When watering in summer, avoid getting the foliage wet. Crape myrtles form a thick root system that makes it difficult to plant much beneath them, including spring bulbs. Do not plant in poorly drained areas.

Main Pest: Aphids. **Main Disease:** Powdery mildew.[†]

V. *Japanese Pieris*

JAPANESE PIERIS *(Pieris japonica)* is sometimes called andromeda, but nobody seems to know why. Anyway, it is an old favorite and deserves to remain one. A well-grown specimen is guaranteed to cheer gardeners who complain about having too much shade. The broadleaf evergreen has distinctive whorled leaves and an upright habit tempered by the blossoms, which are pendant clusters of tiny white bells. The plant is ornamental year round. The swelling flower buds provide interest through the winter, months before they burst open in early spring. While in flower, the new leaf emerges, in some varieties a light green, in others a copper bronze. In still other types, this new leaf growth is a glowing scarlet, so bright that it is mistaken at a distance for blossoms. Pieris is a slow-growing shrub, but after 10 years it can rise as high as eight feet.

Red-leafed varieties include Bert Chandler, a semi-dwarf pieris suited to the town garden, Red Mill, another smaller variety, and Mountain Fire. Other varieties are bred for the red tinge to their flower bells.

CULTIVATION AND USES

PIERIS SHOULD be grown in partial shade in organically enriched, evenly moist and acidic soil. It hates droughts and should be watered well in summer.

The pieris is a fabulous large specimen plant in the shade garden or, with smaller varieties, in the town garden. You could use it as a back-of-the-border plant, but try to surround it with neutral plants such as liriope, sweet box, Solomon's-seal or small, sober-colored azaleas so that you give it a chance to shine.

Main Pest: Lacebug. **Main Disease:** Phytophthora dieback.[†]

VI. *Mountain Laurel*

THE MOUNTAIN LAUREL *(Kalmia latifolia)* is one of the most attractive native shrubs in the garden repertoire. It blooms in late spring, providing a valuable bridge of color between seasons. Its flowers are among the most curious and beautiful in the plant world, developing as tiny ribbed globes that open into chalices of whites, pinks and roses. The *kalmia* is a broadleaf evergreen that grows slowly, compact in youth and becoming quite leggy in maturity. It is a choice plant for the native plant garden and a valued addition to any garden. There are several varieties, differing in leaf size and blossom color.

CULTIVATION AND USES

YOU MIGHT EXPECT a native plant to grow like a weed, but the mountain laurel demands exact conditions if it is to flourish. It shares the rhododendron's preference for a head in the sun and feet in the shade, and you will find the plant growing wild on the edge of woodland near streams and lakes. It requires acidic, evenly moist and well-drained soil. It should be mulched and watered during periods of drought. Prune out diseased or damaged branches, but do not prune this plant as a matter of course.

Mountain laurel should be massed on larger properties and used as specimens in smaller borders. It is a good companion to azaleas and rhododendrons.

Main Pests: Stem borers and lacebugs. **Main Disease:** Petal blight.[†]

VII. Cotoneasters

COTONEASTERS HAVE their drawbacks, aside from the name (pronounced co-TON-e-aster). Some people hate them because they collect leaves and litter, and on neglected embankments they soon will look trashy. But in the right setting and dutifully cared for, the cotoneaster is another of the more beautiful and interesting shrubs in the landscape.

Most varieties grown in our region are the creeping ones, valued for their lustrous, leathery leaves, arching stems and fall fruit display. The fruiting is the most obvious ornament, but the shrub's fine leaf texture makes it a terrific foil for other plants, especially taller-growing shrubs and perennials.

NOTABLE VARIETIES

■ **BEARBERRY COTONEASTER** *(Cotoneaster dammeri)*. Landscape companies value this shrub because it grows vigorously, covering large areas in a few years. It rises to 18 inches high but at least six feet across. It is semi-evergreen in the Washington area, depending on the severity of the winter. It is not the best cotoneaster for fruit display.

■ **CREEPING COTONEASTER** *(C. adpressus)*. As its name suggests, this variety hugs the ground, again growing to about 18 inches with a six-foot spread. It is a deciduous cotoneaster with fabulous fruit display and striking fall coloration.

■ **CRANBERRY COTONEASTER** *(C. apiculatus)*. One of the best fruiters, it produces plump red berries in late summer. It is a taller plant, rising to three feet, with a spread of four to six feet.

■ **ROCKSPRAY COTONEASTER** *(C. horizontalis)*. Similar to creeping cotoneaster, rockspray cotoneaster is a jewel, admired for the herringbone pattern of its tiny leaves and its fall leaf color. It forms a mounding, tiered shrub three feet high and five to six feet across.

■ **WILLOWLEAF COTONEASTER** *(C. salicifolius)*. The species grows as a large shrub. The variety normally sold is a prostrate version named Repens or Repandens. The willowleaf cotoneaster has larger, narrow leaves and a coarser effect. It, too, typically grows to 18 inches and six feet in width.

CULTIVATION AND USES

COTONEASTERS DO well in ordinary, well-drained soil. They flower and fruit best in full sun, though some protection from the afternoon sun will lessen problems with spider mites, which can cause serious trouble. You can cut back cotoneasters that have become too large, but be selective, and remove whole stems rather than heading them back to stubs. Also, on creeping types you should remove vertical stems that emerge, to maintain their mounding, prostrate habit.

Cotoneasters are attractive massed, but not on an institutional scale. They provide fabulous textural relief in the shrub and perennial border. They look best when they are allowed to cascade down a wall or alongside steps. Some dwarf varieties also are favored in the rock garden.

Main Pests: Aphids, leafhoppers, lacebugs and spider mites. **Main Disease:** Fireblight (which also afflicts pear and apple trees, so don't grow cotoneasters near them).[†]

VIII. *Pyracantha*

CLOSELY RELATED to the cotoneaster, the pyracantha, or firethorn, is another handsome broadleaf evergreen or semi-evergreen for the Washington area. In spring it is smothered in tiny white flowers, which later turn into generous clusters of orange, red and yellow berries that decorate the autumn and winter garden.

Neglected pyracanthas can become awfully straggly in habit and soon outgrow their bounds. You should either pick dwarf varieties or be prepared to prune annually. Pyracanthas also have extremely sharp thorns. This makes them useful as barrier plantings and as a place for birds to find shelter from cats, but it is not a plant to place close to an entryway or near where children play. Wear thick, high gloves when pruning.

NOTABLE VARIETIES

DONALD EGOLF enters the picture once more as the breeder of varieties suited to the home garden in the Mid-Atlantic region:

- **PYRACANTHA NAVAHO.** One of the best choices, this mounded shrub grows to six feet. Its orange-red fruit appears in November. It is resistant to both fireblight and scab, a disease that disfigures the fruit.

- **PYRACANTHA APACHE.** Suited to small gardens, this dwarf variety grows after many years to three to five feet. Its fruit is a glossy, bright red. It, too, is resistant to fireblight and scab.

- **PYRACANTHA MOHAVE.** This Egolf creation can grow tall and somewhat gangly if untended, but it is a favorite for training against a wall or clipping as a hedge.

- **PYRACANTHA TETON.** This is the least known and in some ways the most valuable Egolf plant. It has a naturally high but compact habit, growing in maturity to 12 feet or above and half that in spread. This makes it an ideal plant for an impenetrable screen or hedge that doesn't need clipping.

CULTIVATION

CULTIVATION IS basically the same as for cotoneaster: A little light shade will cut down on insect problems, and shelter from northwest winter winds will assure that more leaves are kept year round. The east side of a property is ideal. If you are growing a pyracantha as a hedge, prune it soon after it flowers. If you are training it against a wall, do not use wire or other ties that will cut into the bark of the stems. Attach the plant to a trellis or a network of wires with soft twine.

Main Pests: Aphids, lacebugs and scale. **Main Diseases:** Stem blight and scab.[†]

[†]See Appendix for common pest and disease ailments and remedies.

Chapter 9

DOGWOOD

ENTION DOGWOOD TO PEOPLE and the immediate image is of the flowering dogwood of April, its tiered form covered in a cloud of white blossoms. This is the most beloved of the dogwoods, but it is by no means the only one with a place in the garden. Unfortunately, this loveliest of native trees is afflicted by a new and deadly disease called dogwood anthracnose. You should consider alternatives, including another native species, the pagoda dogwood, or the Kousa dogwood from East Asia.

NOTABLE VARIETIES

■ **FLOWERING DOGWOOD** (*Cornus florida*). No other small tree has the appeal or look of the flowering dogwood, and even though it is overplanted, it is never trite. The tree is not carefree, so if you plant it, be prepared to look after it. The flowering dogwood is decorative year-round: its white flowers (actually bracts surrounding true flowers) in the spring, its tiered form in the summer, its berries and ruby foliage in the fall, and its pleasing outline and rugged bark in the winter. The tree is upright in habit when young, but after a few years it develops its distinctive spreading and layered shape. It will grow 15 feet to 25 feet in height, with a canopy spread of almost as much.

Several varieties are available, including a pink-flowering dogwood named Rubra, a variety with variegated foliage, a weeping form and even dwarf types.

■ **KOUSA DOGWOOD** (*Cornus kousa*). This is a handsome tree, quite different from the flowering dogwood. It blooms about three weeks later, and, after it has produced leaves, its blossoms — more pointed and star-like — are less showy. It is a larger, fuller tree, more upright than a flowering dogwood, but it develops a similar layered effect when mature. It grows to about 20 feet, with similar spread, but will take years to achieve that size. It is trouble-free and of interest all year. One of its greatest attributes is its bark: With age, it starts to flake, producing a mosaic of grays, browns and tans. The effect is stunning.

New hybrids have been introduced, crosses between flowering and Kousa dogwoods, in an attempt to overcome the disease problems afflicting the native species. The hybrids are indeed more disease resistant. Some have flowering dogwood blooms, others Kousa blossoms, but they flower in May after foliation and are not the same plant as flowering dogwood.

■ **PAGODA DOGWOOD** (*Cornus alternifolia*). Another alternative to the flowering dogwood, the pagoda dogwood is rightly being grown more these days. Also a native plant, its flowers — off-white and appearing in May — are not as spectacular as its cousin's, but the tree does have a pleasing horizontal form. The pagoda has a relatively brief life span (it can die after 12 or 15 years). In youth it resembles a large shrub, but it eventually grows to about 15 feet and as much or more in width.

■ **GIANT DOGWOOD** (*Cornus contraversa*). This is a fabulous tree that grows into a specimen of mighty presence. A native of China, its habit is to spread broadly. A mature specimen might be 20 feet high but 30 feet or more across.

■ **CORNELIAN-CHERRY DOGWOOD** (*Cornus mas*). This is a shrubby, small tree especially valued for its late-winter flowers, which are small yellow globes about an inch across. It is pest-free and worth planting instead of forsythia.

■ **REDTWIG** *(Cornus alba)* and **YELLOWTWIG** *(C. sericea Flaviramea)* **DOGWOODS**. These varieties are noted for their winter ornament — not the flowers but the stems. They develop a glowing quality in winter that is truly eye-catching, especially when they are used well in a garden design. The variety of the redtwig dogwood usually sold is Sibirica; it grows about eight feet high and five feet across. The yellowtwig dogwood grows as big or bigger.

CULTIVATION

TREE-FORM DOGWOODS (flowering, Kousa, pagoda, giant and Cornelian-cherry) will take full sun or partial shade. Flowering dogwoods, traditionally considered plants of the woodland, often are planted in high shade or on the edge of the forest, because that is the way they grow in nature. The arrival of anthracnose disease has changed this. The flowering dogwood in particular should be planted in a sunny location (six hours of morning sun is desirable). The sunlight will burn off the humidity in which the disease flourishes. The other dogwoods are much less susceptible to the disease, but the same sunny treatment is still preferable.

Place dogwoods in a well-drained but humusy, moisture-retentive soil that is made acidic through liberal use of peat moss and composted oak leaves. It is no use digging a small hole in hard clay and stuffing a dogwood in it. If a building contractor or someone else has done this before you, dig a swale to drain off any standing water and apply an annual layer of leaf mold to build up the soil. Planting ground covers such as liriope or hostas will help keep the roots cool, but there will be greater competition for moisture and nutrients that the gardener must supply.

Dogwoods are among the first plants to wilt in a drought, especially if stressed. Give them a good soaking once or twice a week in the summer. Let the hose trickle at their base (don't use overhead sprinklers). It is best to water in the morning.

These dogwoods as a rule don't need pruning. Remove branches that have died or are rubbing, with a clean cut at the base of the branch. Do not use wound dressing. If you see water spouts, they are a sign of stress. Remove them and address the underlying problem.

Redtwig and yellowtwig dogwoods will take standing water. Like forsythia, they also will benefit from a regimen of selective pruning, which should be done in the spring. Remove one third of the oldest, thickest canes, cutting them with lopping shears at ground level. The brightest color will be in the new canes that emerge. The stems lose their color during the warm months.

Pests and Diseases: In addition to dogwood anthracnose (see box), the flowering dogwood can become infested with dogwood borers. The pagoda dogwood is susceptible to blights, but Kousa dogwoods typically are free of serious problems. Redtwig and yellowtwig dogwoods are prone to twig blights and other diseases. Since they are meant to be pruned heavily each year, however, this is not a problem. They also might get powdery mildew if planted in too shady a spot.[†]

USES IN GARDEN DESIGNS

KOUSA AND FLOWERING dogwoods make great specimen trees for the patio or for other areas close to the house where they will be admired. Giant dogwoods spread so much that they need space. The pagoda tree is less ornamental but still a great specimen, especially as a background tree in large beds and in gardens of native plants. Dogwoods are great for hillsides; their horizontal lines have a pleasing effect against the slope of the land.

The pink-blossomed Rubra variety of flowering dogwood, which has a lot of carmine in it, blends well with

DOGWOOD ANTHRACNOSE

THIS LETHAL fungal blight, also named discula, was first identified in wild-growing populations of flowering dogwood in the Catoctin Mountains of Maryland in the early 1980s. The disease has since spread throughout the region, and neglected trees probably will succumb if untreated. One theory is that the fungus was carried to our shores by the Kousa dogwood, which appears immune to it.

The good news is that the disease can be beaten back with diligent care. The treatment period is from the time the leaves appear in the spring until the start of summer. The following advice comes from Scott Aker, integrated pest management specialist at the National Arboretum:

The fungus thrives in the cool, damp nights of April and May. It appears in the spring as spots on the leaves. They are tan-colored and bordered with a thin purple disc, sometimes the size of a thumbtack, other times consuming almost all the leaf. There is another blight, called septoria, with almost the same symptoms, but it appears in the summer. It is not harmful to the tree.

Dogwood anthracnose is, however, and, unchecked, it will infect a few leaves the first year and then come back the following year, doing progressively more damage. Once the disease gets into the main branches or trunk, it girdles them and the end is nigh.

In the second year, a stressed tree will produce a number of water sprouts. These are fresh, fast-growing stems that emerge directly from the old wood of main branches. They are distinctly different from the regular leaf foliage. The soft tissue of the water sprout is infected by the fungus and allows a swift path into the old wood.

The disease is fought in a number of ways. Trees stressed by drought are particularly vulnerable the following spring, so watering in summer dry spells is essential. Flowering dogwoods, as noted elsewhere, should be planted in sunny locations, with morning sun preferable because the dew is burned off more quickly. But afternoon sun is better than no sun at all. The blight dies once temperatures climb into the 90s, usually in mid-June.

There are two effective treatments for the disease, one mechanical, the other reliant on chemical sprays. Dogwoods at the National Arboretum are maintained simply by diligent pruning of water sprouts, which should be done as soon as they appear. When they are still under an inch long, they can be rubbed out with the fingers. Check for them every weekend until Independence Day.

If you use sprays — Daconil and Banner are two effective fungicides — they must be applied methodically every 10 to 14 days from mid-to-late April until temperatures reach the 90s. One spraying will not counter the disease. Even if you spray, you still should remove water sprouts.

Aker recommends spraying only if you have a particularly valuable, old or sentimental specimen. Many people, of course, do.

purple-leafed plants such as plums and Japanese maples, but it is jarring with the bluer pinks of azaleas, crab apples and tulips.

Redtwig and yellowtwig dogwoods are useful for massing in wilder areas of the garden; they look great next to ponds and lakes or in wet areas where few other plants will grow. But they require full sun and take up a lot of room. They should have a backdrop, either a stand of conifers or a hillside behind them. In winter they will stand out, particularly after a snowfall.

---

†See Appendix for common pest and disease ailments and remedies.

Chapter 10

JAPANESE MAPLES

*J*APANESE MAPLES are among the most prized small to mid-sized trees. In the right location and with a little care, they provide years of enjoyment in every season. These choice trees have drawn the attention of connoisseurs and breeders through the years, resulting in a rich array of varieties suited for almost any setting, even (and especially) the apartment balcony and townhouse patio.

Japanese maples (*Acer palmatum*) fall into two basic categories: weeping, cascading forms (which are like large spreading shrubs, reaching four to six feet high and six to eight feet across) and upright trees (which typically become vase-shaped in maturity, rising to 18 to 25 feet and the same across). The first group is called the threadleaf Japanese maples, or *dissectums*, because the leaves appear to have been cut delicately, like lace. The leaves of upright trees look like hands, some with slender, strap-like fingers (called deeply divided) and others with fatter palms (palmate). One upright, Seiryu, has threadleaf foliage.

Each class comes in dwarf forms, which are particularly suited for containers, rock gardeners or as bonsai. Both threadleafs and uprights have purple-leafed and green varieties. The purple maples tend to turn crimson in the fall, the greens a fiery yellow or orange. Both are spectacular at that time. Many change color, too, as spring turns to summer. Purple-leafed varieties tend to become green with a bronze cast. This is normal, although variation is marked not just between specimens but in the same specimens in different years. Two purple-leafed varieties, an upright named Bloodgood and a threadleaf named Crimson Queen, have thicker petals and keep their color in summer. They are ubiquitous, and other varieties deserve to be tried.

NOTABLE VARIETIES

First, notable threadleaf varieties:

- **CRIMSON QUEEN**. The most popular purple-leafed threadleaf, Crimson Queen is valued for keeping its color in summer. It grows six to eight feet and as broad, and it turns a brilliant scarlet in the fall.

- **FILIGREE**. This variety is green, with tiny golden speckles, and grows to six feet.

- **INABA SHIDARE**. A purple threadleaf that grows upright but with cascading foliage, Inaba Shidare is considered to have the most beautiful leaf of the red *dissectums*. It grows to 9 feet.

- **ORANGEOLA**. This Japanese maple, which rises to six feet, has unusual color and fabulous fall coloration of orange-red.

- **GARNET**. Fast-growing, Garnet's purple leaves can turn to a rich red-orange. It grows to nine feet.

Second, uprights to look for:

- **BLOODGOOD**. This 18-foot tree starts out crimson, turns purple, then reverts to crimson in the fall. It is dependable for the Washington climate.

- **SHOJO NOMURA**. Similar to Bloodgood but slightly smaller (15 feet), it spreads more, has better crotch angles and does not look as stiff.

■ **OSAKAZUKI.** This variety's large, green leaves turn an intense red in fall. It reaches to 20 feet.

■ **ACER PALMATUM.** The green-leafed species from which all others derive, it often is used for root stock. However, it is a wonderful tree in its own right, growing to 20 feet.

Finally, related Asian maples of interest:

■ **PAPERBARK MAPLE** *(Acer griseum)*. Slow-growing and expensive, it has striking, cinnamon-brown, peeling bark, making it a choice specimen for four seasons.

■ **FULLMOON MAPLE** *(Acer japonicum)*. Similar to Japanese maples but with stubbier leaves, fullmoon maples are worth growing. One variety, the Dancing Peacock *(A. japonicum aconitifolium)*, is named for its kaleidoscopic effect in the fall, when its leaves turn crimson, gold, even purple and blue.

■ **AMUR MAPLE** *(Acer ginnala)*. A multi-stemmed small tree, growing to 18 feet, it is not as pretty as the Japanese maple. But it is a graceful and easy big shrub or small tree suited as a patio specimen, border accent or for screening.

■ **TRIDENT MAPLE** *(Acer buergeranum)*. More tree-like, this maple grows to 25 feet. Drought-tolerant once established, it is a good mini-shade tree for the smaller lot.

■ **NIKKO MAPLE** *(Acer nikoense or A. maximowiczianum)*. This is a fine specimen maple, slow-growing and vase-shaped. It rises to 20 feet, and its leaves — unusual in having just three leaflets — turn a muted red in the fall.

USES IN GARDEN DESIGNS

THREADLEAFS are used as specimens in entryway gardens and rock gardens, atop retaining walls, as centerpieces of Japanese-style gardens and near ponds — in short, almost anyplace where they will be seen and savored. They are best used in plant combinations that establish the threadleaf as the star, so you shouldn't pick other specimens that will compete. Instead, select subdued plants that flatter the maple with recessive leaf textures and colors, such as spreading junipers, ivy, liriope, cotoneaster, small ornamental grasses or low-growing ground covers.

It is important to give a Japanese maple a setting that frames and honors the plant. You might choose a dark, natural background, such as yews, hemlocks or hollies, or an artificial one, such as stone, wood or brick. Be careful not to select a variety whose color will clash with unpainted brick. Try to evaluate the color, including the fall color, before selecting. If you inherit a clashing situation, consider painting the brick a neutral off-white, beige or light gray or, with purple-leafed maples, a complementary light yellow. In placing a threadleaf, think of it as a piece of sculpture. This will help you choose the appropriate site.

Upright forms, which attain an imposing stature in a few short years, make superb landscape specimens. They do not produce the same spring show as dogwoods or cherries, but what you give up in April is repaid with months of beauty and leaf color, particularly when the trees are positioned to enjoy the back lighting of the early morning or early evening sun. Consider these trees as alternatives to flowering dogwoods, cherries, crab apples, crape myrtles and deciduous magnolias. Green-leafed maples might not have the same pizzazz as purple-leafed varieties, but they often are favored by those who see a more understated and more satisfying beauty in them.

CULTIVATION

JAPANESE MAPLES GROW in ordinary soil but demand adequate drainage. They will not work in areas with standing water or deep shade. Position them with care, not just aesthetically but horticulturally. They want suf-

MOVING JAPANESE MAPLES

AN EXISTING TREE might be in the way of a proposed addition to the house, unsuited to its current site, or needed as the focal point in a new garden area. Like old azaleas and boxwoods, mature threadleaf Japanese maples are worth transplanting and can be moved successfully. Don't blithely cut down an old specimen: A mature threadleaf maple might sell at a retail nursery for $1,000 or more.

The bigger the tree, the more steps required to move it.

If practical, the tree should be root-pruned at or outside the dripline with a sharp shovel a year before it is to be moved. New feeder roots then form within the circle. The plant must be diligently watered and fed in the months leading up to the transplant, which is best done in mid-to-late fall, after its leaves have dropped but before the ground freezes. When cutting the root ball, take care to stay outside the new root zone, and cut vertically until you are beneath the level of the roots. Then angle the shovel into the bottom of the ball.

The root ball should be wrapped in burlap, which is then knotted at the top and laced like a drum with heavy twine. Smaller plants can be transported on a dolly as long as the soil is not wet, but a mature specimen may weigh hundreds of pounds and is best hoisted onto a tractor cart or the like, with chains laced around the burlap. Never pick up a tree by its trunk.

Horticulturists measure trees by trunk width. A maple with a trunk caliper of more than 1.5 inches is probably best left to a professional to move — the required root ball for such a specimen would have to be 18 inches in diameter and at least as much in depth. A tree with a 2-inch or 2.5-inch caliper obviously would be far bigger and heavier.

If you have a threadleaf maple that you want to sell, call a local retail nursery, a specialist nursery or a landscape architect or designer to elicit interest. Don't expect to get the retail price; as with all retailers, a nursery's asking price includes all manner of overheads, not least the cost of digging up and moving the tree. As a rule, don't deal with strangers who come to your door offering to take your maple (or boxwood or azaleas or paulownia tree) off your hands. Ignore their dire predictions about the effects of the plant on your house, drainpipes, buried utilities or the state of your cat.

ficient sunlight to keep their leaf color bright but not so much that they will suffer from leaf scorch in summer. If they are to go in an exposed site, try giving them three or four hours of afternoon shade in June, July and August. Threadleafs are more likely to be scorched — a condition that kills and browns the edges of leaf lobes. No amount of watering will restore a leaf once it is damaged. If you only have a sunny site, shade the roots with a mulch or ground cover, water more diligently and choose a variety bred for heat tolerance, such as Crimson Queen, Red Dragon, Sunset, Tamukeyama, Bloodgood, Fireglow and Hogyoku.

Japanese maples have shallow roots that dry out easily in the summer. They are worth singling out for special treatment in the hottest season. Those planted in good humus and given a layer of organic mulch will need fewer waterings. Fresh mulch applied in summer, though, actually may form a barrier between water and roots. Move the mulch aside to allow a thorough soaking or, better yet, apply a four-inch layer of leaf mold each April. Do not pile mulch, fresh manure, leaf mold or other material around the bark, which is thin and easily destroyed. The bark also is susceptible to splitting in the winter when its frozen tissue is abruptly thawed by the sun. Apply a tree wrap, a sort of trunk bandage, each November, and remove it each April. A wrap also may protect an upright maple against winter rutting damage from deer. Some maples, particularly threadleafs, will keep their dried foliage in mild winters. This is normal; the old leaves will drop once new buds break in the spring.

Use a balanced fertilizer in April; a fish and kelp feed is highly recommended for its low impact and as a source of micronutrients. Trees in the garden as opposed to containers do not need repeated fertilization, and on no account fertilize after July or with high-nitrogen feeds at any time. Be careful not to get lawn fertilizer in the vicinity. Before purchasing a plant, look for healthy, well-shaped specimens. As with most trees, if angles between branch and trunk crotches are too acute, the tree will be prone to storm damage. Most varieties are grafted onto understock; look for a graft that gives the tree a natural look.

Main Pest: Aphids. Japanese beetles may be a problem on purple-leafed varieties. **Main Diseases:** Japanese maples generally are not troubled by diseases.[†]

PRUNING AND STAKING

CORRECT PRUNING is important to keep Japanese maples looking their best. Such a highly variable plant occasionally will produce aberrant stems and leaves that should be removed. Damaged branches also should be removed; always prune back to the base of a stem, and never attempt to shear a maple. Light pruning can be done at any time — threadleafs benefit from sensitive thinning and shaping once a year — but removal of large stems should be left for a warm day in January while the tree is in dormancy and before the sap rises (maples are heavy "bleeders"). Wait a whole growing season before shaping a plant; it needs all of its leaves in the first season to get established.

Mounding threadleafs with low grafts may need staking to lift the "mop" off the ground. Use a single, 1 x 1 wooden stake close to the trunk, being careful not to damage stems. Tether with plastic tape or twine, never wire. Uprights benefit from conventional staking — two or three stakes arranged like tent pegs, with supporting wires leading to the trunk. Thread the wire through a rubber hose at the point of contact with the trunk.

JAPANESE MAPLES IN CONTAINERS

CERTAIN VARIETIES make excellent container plants, but maples grown this way need some extra care. They should be put in large planters of about 15 gallons. Half-whiskey barrels, concrete planters or custom teak, locust or walnut planters are ideal. Look for containers that are elegant but not overly ornate. Low, broad containers are better than high, narrow ones. Glazed Chinese urns or terra cotta planters may not be frost-proof and will be too heavy to cart indoors in winter.

Avoid plants whose roots are encircling the trunk (called root girdling). Plants should be grown in temporary three- to five-gallon containers for a season or two before transplanting into permanent pots. Make sure that pot-bound plants have their roots scored and butterflied before repotting.

Containers must be well drained. Lay three inches of coarse gravel at the bottom, covered in filter fabric, to speed moisture flow through the soil mix. The soil weight can be minimized with a mix of one part perlite to one part peat moss to one part humus. Leave three to four inches from the top of the soil to the rim of the container to allow room for mulch and watering. Potted maples will need watering at least three times a week in hot, dry summer weather. If you plan to go on vacation, give the plant a good soaking and move the container into the shade.

Pot-grown maples require monthly feeding with a weak solution of low-nitrogen fertilizer. Organic fertilizers are inherently gentle and contain micronutrients to help the plant in the stressed environment of the container.

After four or five seasons, the plant should be root-pruned. Take a sharp hatchet or shovel and slice into the soil about three inches from the edge of the container, moving all around the plant. Lift the maple, soak its trimmed roots in a mild solution of Miracle-Gro, replace the soil mix and replant it. During the summer, try to shield the container from direct afternoon sun.

The following varieties are suited to containers:

COONARA PYGMY
Upright, green-leafed
Grows to 3 feet

GARNET
Threadleaf, purple
6 feet

KAMAGATA
Upright dwarf, green, bronzed
3 feet

RUBY LACE
Threadleaf, purple
3-4 feet

SEIRYU
Upright, green
9 feet

---

†See Appendix for common pest and disease ailments and remedies.

Chapter 11

MAGNOLIAS, CHERRIES AND CRAB APPLES

*M*AGNOLIAS, ORNAMENTAL cherries and crab apples are the three beautifully majestic trees of early spring gardens, each with the power to transform the plainest setting into a magical place. Deciduous magnolias begin to bloom in mid-to-late March, cherries in early April and crab apples in the last weeks of April. Together they help define the period when daffodils and crocuses are abloom but the ground is still bare and the gray days of winter are still fresh in our memories.

I. *Magnolias*

MAGNOLIA CONNOISSEURS, of which there are many, delight in the several species and dozens of varieties of spring-flowering magnolias. The trees differ in flowering period, in eventual size and habit and in the color and form of their blossoms. However, they are all deciduous, have lovely, smooth, silver-gray bark and, with age, become handsome specimens, vase-shaped and arching. In winter, they decorate the landscape with their plump, downy flower buds. You can find a magnolia for virtually any garden setting.

However, the trees bloom early enough that frost damage to flowers is a periodic problem, occurring perhaps once every three years. To minimize this risk, select a later-flowering variety.

NOTABLE VARIETIES

- **SAUCER MAGNOLIA** (*Magnolia x soulangiana*). This is the most common species, the one with sturdy, smooth, silver bark on mature specimens and, in good years, the one absolutely covered in blossoms of white or shades of pink, from rose to purple. The flowers emerging in March and early April are one of the great joys of early spring. Look for two late-season varieties, Brozzonii (a white-purple bi-color) and Verbanica (a white and rose-pink bi-color).

- **STAR MAGNOLIA** (*M. stellata*). The star magnolia's blooms, which appear a little later than saucer magnolia flowers, have strap-like petals that together form little stars. Most varieties are white, but some pink-tinged cultivars are available.

- **THE GIRL MAGNOLIAS.** Introduced by the National Arboretum as later-flowering hybrids, this is a series of shrub-like magnolias that do well in poorer soil conditions. They all bear female names. Eight were introduced, but the most commonly available are Ann, the earliest flowering (early April, with rose-purple blooms), Betty, (soft rose blossoms with purple overtones) and Susan (smaller than the rest, with strong red-purple flowers).

- **MAGNOLIA GALAXY.** This additional National Arboretum introduction is a splendid, tree-form magnolia that is more upright than saucer or star magnolias. It performs well in poorer soil and flowers later to minimize frost damage. Galaxy grows large after several decades, just as star and saucer magnolias do, reaching 25 to 30 feet. Galaxy spreads to about 20 feet, though, compared to 30 feet or more for the other two. You can view all these magnolias at the National Arboretum. A mature specimen of Galaxy is growing near the R Street NE entrance (see Appendix for Public Gardens information).

■ **KOBUS MAGNOLIA** *(Magnolia kobus)*. Look for a variety with the lengthy Latin name of *Magnolia kobus var. stellata Centennial* (not to be confused with *Magnolia stellata*). Centennial is small, growing to just 15 feet, with a lesser or equal spread. It is one of the latest-flowering Asian magnolias (late April) and in most years should not be affected by freezes.

Two later-flowering magnolias are also valuable landscape plants, one small and little known, the other huge and familiar:

■ **SWEETBAY MAGNOLIA** *(Magnolia virginiana)*. The sweetbay is a superb, small native tree that flowers in late spring, after the foliage has grown, and blooms sporadically through the summer. Its leaves are soft and hairy, with a slight blue cast. Its flowers are not overpowering, but its form, foliage and texture make it an elegant specimen. It is semi-evergreen, depending on winter conditions: Trees in protected spots will keep most leaves, while those in outer areas will not. The sweetbay needs acidic and evenly moist, even wet, soil, making it a good candidate for poorly drained areas. It likes a little dappled shade. Conversely, it does not flourish in poor dry sites. In full sun, the soil should be richly amended, and the tree should be watered during dry spells.

■ **SOUTHERN MAGNOLIA** *(Magnolia grandiflora)*. The Southern magnolia is a gorgeous monster. Its leaves are astonishing — like polished leather above, a ruddy down beneath. The flowers are breathtaking — large and waxy, with a lemony fragrance. There are three drawbacks, however, to the Southern magnolia.

First is its size. A mature specimen can reach 60 feet or more and half as much in spread. This makes it wonderful as a lawn specimen for a James River plantation, not so handy for shoehorning into a quarter-acre lot. Second, it is messy. The old, dead leaves seem to drop endlessly, as do the seed cones in the fall. The leaves are too thick to break down on their own (making them poor candidates for the compost pile), so you have to pick them up for some semblance of tidiness. Third, the tree casts dense shade. Few plants, including turfgrass, will grow in its shadow, although chances can be improved if you remove lower branches.

It is possible to grow the Southern magnolia as a huge clipped hedge or against the wall of a building, espaliered so that it might rise 20 feet but stick out just three feet. However, if you do this you are committing yourself and future owners to serious obligations for years to come. Since most people would want professionals to tackle the annual shearing and pruning, there is a financial burden, too. (It is a fabulous way, though, to cover a vast, windowless brick wall.)

If you do grow a Southern magnolia in areas north and west of Washington, make sure to choose a cold-hardy variety such as Edith Bogue.

CULTIVATION

MAGNOLIAS PREFER acidic, organically enriched loam and benefit from a layer of mulch or leaf mold to keep roots moist and cool in summer. They flower best in full sun but perform well, too, in light shade. Planting on the east side of a building will reduce the risk of frost damage to blossoms. Even if flowers are damaged or destroyed by early spring freezes, however, the plants themselves are not injured. Do not try to remove the brown blossoms.

Magnolia roots are fleshy, easy to damage and slow to repair. You must take care when handling and planting a young tree to treat the roots gingerly. You can tease them into a growing pattern with your hands, but don't score or cut them with a blade or shovel. For this reason, it is best to plant magnolias in the early spring, so they have an entire growing season to mend themselves before the onset of winter.

Mindful of this weakness, you should allow magnolias to grow in beds where they will not be disturbed by a lot of soil cultivation (for annuals, for example) or foot traffic. Don't grow them as lawn specimens. Prune them when young to shape them. Mature, overgrown specimens can be opened up through the selective removal of branches. Remove water sprouts as they emerge.

Main Pest: Scales. **Main Disease:** Leaf blight.[†]

USES IN GARDEN DESIGNS

MAGNOLIAS MAKE fabulous specimens, used around the patio or in beds and borders. They are also a useful foundation plant if they can be planted far enough from a wall, eight feet at the least. Be careful that the petal hues don't clash with the building colors. Pinky-orange bricks need to be matched carefully with all flowering plants. If you have the space, a grove of magnolias looks splendid, especially on a hill. The National Arboretum and Green Spring Gardens Park in Alexandria have commendable magnolia collections (see Appendix for Public Gardens information).

II. Ornamental Cherry Trees

WASHINGTON HAS adopted the Japanese flowering cherry as its own. No other plant is as honored here. No other tree can draw the crowds of locals and tourists alike. Those who would like to enjoy ornamental cherries without the bustle can grow their own garden specimens. Cherries do well here. Although they are not long-lived trees, with a little care the best varieties will last 30 years or so, which is long enough for most of us. The Yoshino can live for 50 years or more.

Cherry blossom season is highly variable year to year because of the vagaries of early spring in this region, when a balmy, 75-degree day might be followed by a below-freezing night. The popular Yoshinos bloom in early April, with a second peak 10 to 14 days later with the arrival of the Mount Fuji and Kwanzan cherries. These are among many worthy garden plants, but take heed of mature sizes.

NOTABLE VARIETIES

■ **YOSHINO CHERRY** *(Prunus x yedoensis* Yoshino*)*. The Yoshino is fast-growing and spreading, ultimately reaching 20 to 25 feet in height, with an equal width. This is the classic Tidal Basin plant, with carmine buds opening a blush pink and giving off a delicate perfume.

■ **KWANZAN CHERRY** *(Prunus serrulata* Kwanzan, also known as Kanzan or Hisakura*)*. Upright in youth, this tree eventually grows to 30 feet, with a broad, spreading habit. People love it because it has double flowers and a strong pink color, making it extremely showy. The Yoshino, to my mind, is far more refined.

■ **MT. FUJI** *(Prunus serrulata* Mt. Fuji, also known as Shirotae*)*. This is similar in outline, but the blossoms are semi-double (fewer petals, less conspicuous) and white, though they are large.

■ **WEEPING CHERRIES.** Weeping cherries, which have been selected for their pendant form, generally are grafted onto the trunk of a rootstock cherry. To give the plant a sense of size and age, growers make the graft high, elevating the drooping branches. Unfortunately, in the plant's first years this graft looks awkward and contrived, which it is. Eventually, it will become less noticeable. However, you may want to find a weeping specimen grown on its own roots. Alternatively, some nurseries, particularly topnotch mail-order ones, sell plants with lower grafts. The most common varieties are weeping forms of the Yoshino cherry named Shidare Yoshino (pale pink) and Ivensii (white). Weeping forms of another species, the Higan cherry, are worth seeking out, especially *Prunus subhirtella Pendula* and *P. subhirtella Pendula Rubra,* the latter with stronger, rose-colored blossoms.

There are several other wonderful cherries as well:

■ **CHERRY HALLY JOLIVETTE** *(Prunus x Hally Jolivette)*. This petite hybrid, with a dense form and fine texture, is a superb ornamental plant for the small garden or, indeed, any place suited to a large shrub or small tree, including a foundation bed (see Chapter 14 on bests and worst for more details).

■ **SARGENT CHERRY** *(Prunus sargentii).* This is a large ornamental tree of exceptional year-round beauty. It has single, deep pink blossoms in late April, lustrous green leaves in summer, brilliant fall color and a bark that turns a polished reddish-brown with age. A variety named Columnaris is slimmer and better suited to the smaller garden.

■ **OKAME CHERRY** *(Prunus okame).* An underused, beautiful tree whose narrow, upright habit makes it another choice for the small garden, it flowers early (in March), with carmine pink blooms. The base of the flowers, known as the calyx, is a darker pink color that persists after the petals have dropped, prolonging the ornamental effect until the plant leafs out. The leaves are unusually narrow for a cherry and have a nice orange glow in the fall. This tree also is freer from pests than most cherries.

■ **AUTUMN CHERRY** *(Prunus subhirtella Autumnalis).* Another variety of the Higan cherry, the autumn cherry flowers sporadically in the fall and through the winter, at least on mild days, and then blooms in a larger flush in April. It is upright in form and quite a lovely tree, though not as showy as other flowering cherries. Its off-season blooming is a great conversation piece. The tree should be positioned so you can see it from within your home.

CULTIVATION

CHERRY TREES grow contentedly in ordinary heavy loam as long as the soil drains well. They will flourish in organically enriched soil, but don't fertilize them excessively. Make sure that you soak the roots during periods of drought and especially during the plant's first summer. Place it in full sun or light shade and lay a blanket of mulch, making sure the bottom of the trunk is left untouched. Stake newly planted trees.

People fret for the cherry blossoms when the weather turns cold in late March or early April. Freezes will damage some blossoms, but the far greater peril to the cherry show is a mini-heat wave, which blasts the petals and forces them to drop early. High winds and heavy rains also pose a greater threat than frost. There is nothing you can do to avoid these calamities, which are infrequent.

Main Pests: Eastern tent caterpillars, scales, aphids and borers. **Main Diseases:** Root rot, cankers and leaf spot.†

USES IN GARDEN DESIGNS

POPULAR CHERRY varieties grow larger than usually imagined and should be used as specimens in areas where they have room. Smaller varieties make excellent foundation and patio trees or anchoring plants in the plant border. On large properties, a grove of cherries, adequately spaced, or a single lawn specimen of Sargent's or Higan cherry make for memorable landscape effects.

III. Crab Apples

CRAB APPLE TREES take you on an emotional roller coaster. In bloom, they are plants of unsurpassed beauty. The rest of the year they are sickly and messy. In truth, the crab apple is one of the most attractive large ornamental trees we have. It has beautiful buds, blossoms, leaves, bark patterns and fruit ornament. The key to success lies in choosing the correct variety. Perhaps with no other plant in the garden is this factor so crucial.

Inferior varieties are prone to diseases that cause leaves to turn brown and die almost as soon as they emerge, making the tree sickly and ugly for most of the season. Superior varieties have disease resistance bred into them. Here are those to pick from or avoid:*

VARIETIES FROM WHICH TO PICK

NAME	BUD/FLOWER	FRUIT	HABIT
Adirondack	carmine/white	orange-red	upright, 15 ft.
Ames White	pink/white	yellow	small/rounded
Autumn Glory	red/white	orange-red	upright, 12 ft.
Beauty	rose pink/white	dark red	narrow tree, 24 ft.
Centurion	red/rose-red	cherry red	upright/rounded, 20 ft.
Coral Cascade	red/bluish	white, coral pink	med. weeping, 15 ft.
Donald Wyman	pink/white	red	spreading, 20 ft.
Evelyn	rose-red/rose-red	yellow-red	upright, 20 ft.
Gibbs Golden Gage	pink/white	yellow	rounded, 20 ft.
Harvest Gold	white/white	gold	upright
Henningi	white/white	orange-red	upright/spreading, 25 ft.
Molten Lava	deep red/white	red-orange	small/spreading, 10 ft.
Naragansett	red/blush-white	cherry red	small/rounded, 15 ft.
Professor Sprenger	pink/white	orange-red	upright/spreading
Red Snow	orange-red/blush	bright red	small/arching, 10 ft.
Robinson	crimson/pink	dark red	upright/spreading, 25 ft.
Sparkler	red/red	dark red	small/spreading, 15 ft.
Tina	white/pink-red	red	dwarf, 5 ft.
Weis	pink/pink	red-purple	upright

VARIETIES TO AVOID

The following are highly susceptible to one or more of the four diseases that seriously afflict crab apples and should not be planted in our region:

Almey	Hopa	Red Silver
Crimson Brilliant	*Malus ioensis* and *ioensis*	Royalty
Dorothea	Plena (Bechtel)	*Malus x scheideckeri*
Eleyi	Oekonomierath Echtermayer	Shaker's Gold
E. H. Wilson	Patricia	*Malus sieboldii zumi*
Flame	Pink Perfection	Calocarpa
Golden Gem	Lemoine	Spring Snow
Henry F. Dupont	Radiant	Vanguard
Henrietta Crosby	Red Baron	

*Sources: 1980 survey, Lester P. Nichols, Penn State; 1991 list, Ethel M. Dutky, University of Maryland; *Manual of Woody Landscape Plants*, Michael A. Dirr; *Landscape Plants for the Twenty-First Century*, Erik A. Neumann.

CULTIVATION AND USES

CRAB APPLES grow in ordinary, well-drained and acidic soil and prefer full sun. Be careful not to choose a larger variety if you don't have the room. Many varieties are genetically programmed to bloom lightly one year and heavily the next. This is normal. Don't attempt to fix it.

Don't use as a lawn specimen; the trees cast too much shade. The fruit drop can be messy, which is something to consider if you plan to place a crab apple near a patio or driveway. The crab apple is best used as a border specimen. Place it where it will be seen and admired.

Main Pests: Aphids and borers. **Main Diseases:** Apple scab, cedar apple rust, fireblight and powdery mildew.[†]

[†]See Appendix for common pest and disease ailments and remedies.

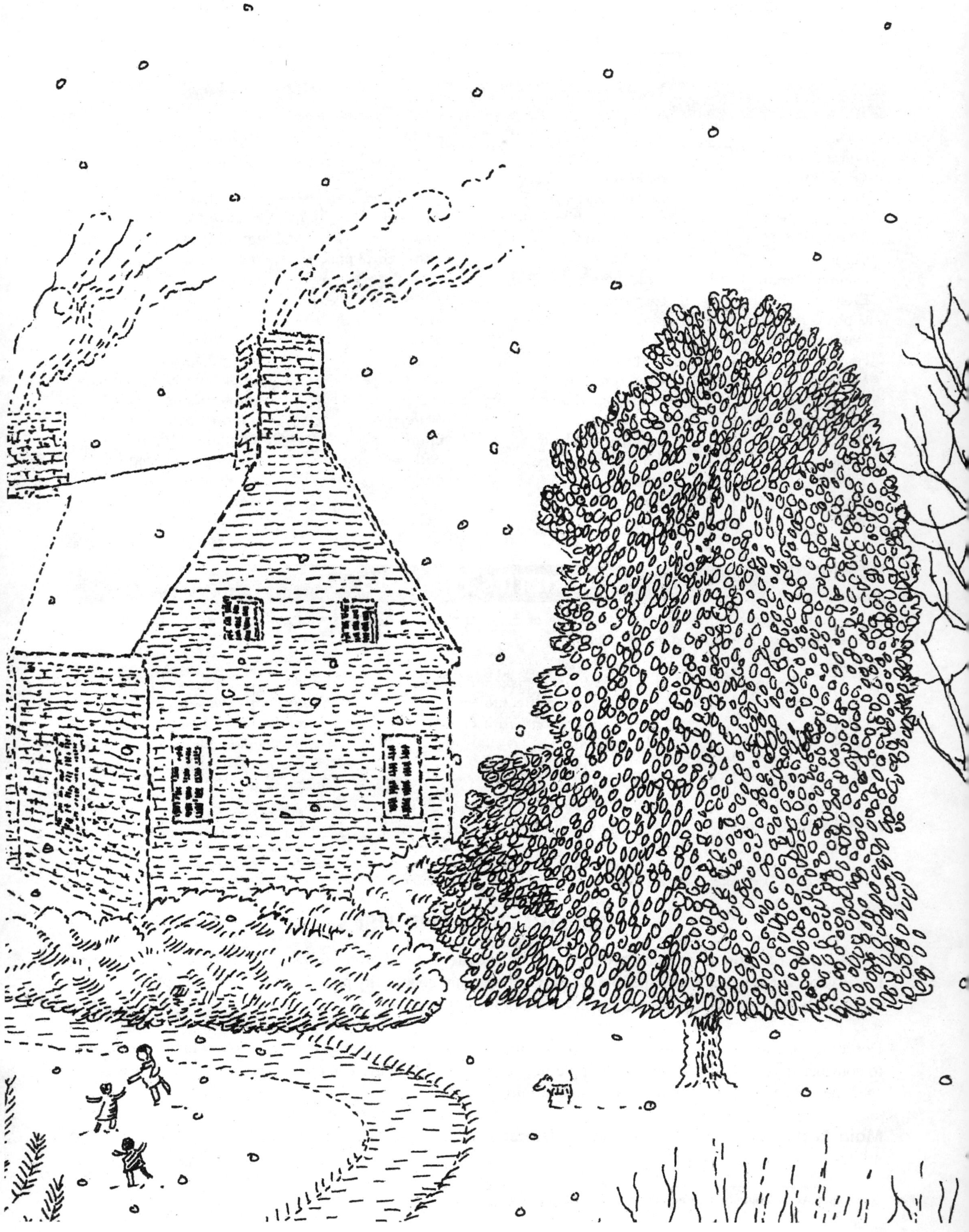

Chapter 12

HOLLIES AND YEWS

$\mathcal{H}$OLLIES AND YEWS are like old friends who are always there to help. In spring they step back to allow softer plants to shine. In summer they stand steadfast against the heat. In winter they are prominent and lovely. Both plants give structure to the garden, in sun or shade. Technically, yews are conifers (see Chapter 13), but they are used and regarded as evergreen shrubs.

I. Hollies

HOLLIES, USED as both tree and shrubs, come in many shapes, sizes and even colors, and a well-chosen variety has a place in many gardens. They make some of the finest sheared hedges in our region. Unclipped, too, they stand as delightful evergreens, with showy, glossy leaves and attractive berries, which mostly are red but also yellow, orange and black, depending on variety. Hollies grow relatively quickly and soon fill their allotted space. You should pay heed to their eventual size, and don't try to squeeze a big holly into a confined area. Generally, only female plants produce berries, so you will have to provide a non-fruiting male in most cases to assure pollination.

NOTABLE VARIETIES

First, large varieties of note:

- **AMERICAN HOLLY** *(Ilex opaca)*. A broad-based pyramidal tree, American hollies grow after 50 years to 40 feet high and 20 feet across. Some people find the leaf dull, and it does suffer in comparison with other hollies. However, this is an attractive native tree with nice silver bark. Some particularly fine varieties are available, bred for better leaf color and form. Look for Jersey Princess (and its pollinator, Jersey Knight), Satyr Hill, Miss Helen and Vera. Xanthocarpa is a yellow-fruited variety. Maryland Dwarf and Clarendon Spreading are two smaller American hollies suited for more modest spaces.

- **ENGLISH HOLLY** *(Ilex aquifolium)*. English hollies arguably are the handsomest of the lot. The variegated versions and their berries are the quintessential motif of Yuletide; the unvariegated ones are a deep and lustrous blue-green. Unfortunately, English hollies do not flourish in our climate: The winters are a tad cold, the summers too warm and humid. The key seems to be to get them through their first two or three seasons with generous mulching and frequent watering. Zone 6 seems better suited than Zone 7. Look for a variety named Lewis, a local, McLean Nurseries introduction. It is a green-leafed female, so you will need a male pollinator; Escort is a good choice. Crispa, another male, is also a fabulous holly. English hollies are more large shrubs than trees here, reaching 15 feet in maturity, not the 60 feet you see in England.

- **KOEHNEANA HOLLY** *(Ilex x koehneana)*. This is a little-known but worthy holly hybrid, with the English and lusterleaf hollies as its parents. It grows to about 20 feet. Look for a female named Agena and its male pollinator, Ajax.

- **FOSTER'S HOLLY** *(Ilex x attenuata Foster No. 2)*. This is a splendid, fine-leafed, conical tree reaching 20 feet or more in maturity. Its narrow habit makes it better for smaller gardens than those above. It doesn't need a mate to fruit.

- **NELLIE R. STEVENS HOLLY** *(Ilex x Nellie R. Stevens)*. A cross between the English and Chinese hollies, the Stevens hybrid is a popular tree that tends to grow larger than many people imagine, as high as 20 feet or more and 15 feet in width. It is a fast grower and distinguished by its glossy leaves. It, too, will set (sterile) berries without a male pollinator, although a nearby male Chinese holly will pollinate and improve the fruit display.

- **BURFORD HOLLY** *(Ilex cornuta Burfordii)*. This is a familiar and much planted holly that has glossy, almost plastic-looking leaves ending in a beak. Although the leaves have smooth sides, they are nonetheless extremely prickly. This is another holly that grows much larger than most people suspect, and it can be trained into a handsome tree. It will grow to 15 feet high as well as wide if it is not pruned. A variety misnamed Dwarf Burford holly *(Burfordii nana)* is slower growing but in time will still reach two-thirds or more the size of Burford holly. Both fruit heavily and don't need pollinators.

Second, medium-sized varieties to look for:

- **JOHN AND LYDIA MORRIS HOLLIES** *(Ilex x John Morris, Ilex x Lydia Morris)*. These male and female hybrids are the result of crosses between Chinese and Perny hollies. They form a dense, vigorous pyramidal shrub, about 10 feet high in maturity, with smallish, lustrous, dark green foliage. Lydia produces red berries. The shubs are beautiful — but exceedingly prickly.

- **MESERVE HOLLIES**. Named after Kathleen Meserve, a Long Island holly breeder who first crossed them, these hybrids are valued for their contained size, attractive leaf and stem color and large, showy fruit. The first series of introductions was called the Blue hollies. Of these, the original varieties of Blue Girl and Blue Boy have been replaced by more compact varieties that require less pruning to shape, although after 10 to 15 years they become large shrubs. Blue Angel is small and slow growing, reaching seven feet at maturity. It has scarlet berries, and its foliage takes on a purple cast in winter. Blue Princess grows to 12 feet at maturity and is valued for its heavy berry set. Blue Stallion, a male pollinator, is more compact than Blue Prince, but it still grows to 12 feet. Meserve also crossed other holly species to produce China Boy and China Girl, valued for their slightly smaller size, compact habit and abundant red fruiting. They grow to 10 feet at maturity.

Finally, small varieties:

- **JAPANESE HOLLY** *(Ilex crenata)*. A few compact varieties of Japanese hollies have been used as fine-textured, small landscape plants suited to use as clipped or unclipped hedging, as foundation plants or in small gardens and rock gardens where the scale must be reduced. The most popular varieties are Helleri, a dwarf growing to three feet, and Convexa, which rises to nine feet but can be clipped to a hedge half that height. Japanese hollies grow in poor soil and so have become the plants of choice in office parks and new subdivisions. Helleri might be used as a substitute for the more finicky and expensive edging boxwood for ornate parterres and knot gardens, but the plant is dull and plain. Its fruits are black and inconspicuous.

- **ROTUNDA HOLLY** *(Ilex cornuta Rotunda)*. This dwarf version of Chinese holly is suited for rock gardens, foundation plantings and small beds. It is unusual in being small but coarse and showy in leaf, giving it a stature beyond its size, which is about 3 feet x 5 feet when mature.

There are also several deciduous hollies. One, common winterberry *(Ilex verticillata)*, is a twiggy native noted for its fruit ornament, with its berries made even showier by the plant's lack of leaves after frost. Winter Red is an improved variety (its male pollinator is Early Male). Breeders at the National Arboretum also crossed winterberry with a wildling found in Japan to produce yet another deciduous holly called *Ilex* Sparkleberry, or Winterberry Sparkleberry. This is a spectacular fall and winter landscape plant (see Chapter 14 on bests and worst for details). All deciduous hollies tolerate wet and poorly drained soil and do best in full sun.

USES IN GARDEN DESIGNS

THE SIZE OF the holly plant and the scale of your garden will dictate a holly's use, but hollies are excellent as screens, hedges or, in the case of larger shrub varieties, as bed or border specimens.

For higher hedges (five to 15 feet), pick American or Burford hollies and plant them four feet apart. For medium-sized hedges (three to six feet), select a Meserve holly planted three feet apart. For small hedges (18 inches to three feet), choose Japanese holly planted two feet apart. You should start training plants when they're young and clip them in early spring, before flowering. You shouldn't trim after August.

Meserve hollies are much in demand because they meet a crying need for a medium-sized evergreen shrub for the home garden, particularly the garden coping with shade.

All make good bed or border plants but not lawn specimens. If you inherit an old American holly that has grown huge at its base, you can remove the lower limbs and incorporate the slimmer plant into a new bed.

CULTIVATION

WHILE HOLLIES grow in ordinary soil, they generally do best in soil that is slightly acidic and evenly moist. Once established, most can withstand drought. Burford and Japanese hollies are particularly tolerant of poor, dry soils. If you are trying to raise an English holly, you must keep the roots shaded, cool and well watered in summer and the plant protected from prevailing winds in winter. Hollies grow in sun or shade. In full shade, though, the fruiting display will fall off greatly, and the plants will become leggy and in need of an annual spring pruning to keep a neat shape.

Main Pests: Spider mites on Japanese hollies, leaf miners on American hollies. **Main Diseases:** Bacterial blight, cankers and stem dieback.[†]

II. Yews

YEWS ARE AVAILABLE either in an upright and large form or as low-growing plants that spread broadly. You have to pick the correct variety for the task assigned. Yews grow slowly — it takes at least five years before they become serviceable hedges — but that slowness makes them dense and elegant. Yews are one of the few needled evergreens that will grow in shade, making them indispensable in the shade garden (see Chapter 22 on shade gardening).

■ **ENGLISH OR COMMON YEW** *(Taxus baccata).* This species is useful for hedging. Unclipped, it will grow into a medium-to-large shrub and can be shaped in youth as a tree. The variety Repandens has a broad, weeping habit, growing three to four feet high but as much as 12 feet across. The Irish yew *(Fastigiata)* is grown in Europe as a tall, upright specimen that, when young, looks like a skinny exclamation point. It will grow here, too, though most people favor an upright American variety named Hick's yew. The golden-leafed form known as Aurea is another popular choice, though its golden foliage looks healthier and more attractive in northern Europe than here because of the different qualities of light. It also grows more slowly.

■ **JAPANESE YEW** *(Taxus cuspidata).* There are several popular varieties of Japanese yew, notably Capitata (a pyramidal tree), Densa (a dwarf variety) and Expansa (which forms into a vase-shaped shrub eight to 10 feet high).

■ **INTERMEDIATE YEW** *(Taxus x intermedia).* This is a hybrid between the English and Japanese yews, with some interesting varieties available. Hicks yew *(Hicksii)* is upright and skinny and a hardier substitute for Irish yew. Hatfield yew *(Hatfieldii)* is a favored large shrub, with especially dense and dark green foliage. Densiformis and Wardii grow low but broad.

CULTIVATION

YEWS PREFER a sandy loam soil that is neutral or slightly alkaline. If you grow them with acid-loving plants such as azaleas and rhododendrons, be careful to give yews their own space and soil. The most critical need is good drainage, and you are better off erring on the side of too much soil amendment than too little. Dig a broad, shallow planting hole and backfill with a thoroughly mixed blend of topsoil, sand and leaf mold or compost. You could add pine mulch and a little limestone to the mix, too. Such a free-draining medium will need watering often to get plants established and to maintain them well during periods of drought. If your ground is low-lying and compacted, you could create high raised beds, though you first should consider alternative plants.

Hedges should be sheared in early spring and again, lightly, after the season's fresh growth has emerged in June. Yews are finely textured, and upright forms don't need shearing to produce attractive hedges. Keep low-growing forms from becoming scraggly by selectively removing entire stems and branches. Don't go overboard: Keep the plant bushy and balanced. If you inherit an oversized, overgrown yew, you can either train it into a tree or saw off the branches to leave stubs 18 to 24 inches long. The plant will regenerate.

Pest and Diseases: While black weevils can be a problem, yews are relatively free of pests and diseases (poor drainage is their biggest killer).[†]

USES IN GARDEN DESIGNS

LOW-GROWING, spreading forms work nicely as woodland plants, ground covers on hillsides, foundation shrubs and rock garden plants. Make sure that you give them the breadth they need, and keep them clear of fallen leaves. Upright forms make good clipped or unclipped hedges, screens, anchor plants for the border or backdrops for flowering or berried shrubs and trees.

[†]See Appendix for common pest and disease ailments and remedies.

Chapter 13

CONIFERS

A CONIFER IS simply a plant that produces cones. Not all evergreens are conifers — hollies and boxwoods, for example, are flowering evergreens, not cone bearers — and not all conifers are evergreen. The vast majority are, but the larch, dawn redwood and bald cypress are conifers that are naked in winter.

Conifers vary is size from the mighty Californian redwood that soars to 300 feet (not exactly for the urban or suburban yard even if it were suited to our climate, which it isn't) to the ground-hugging rug junipers that are the staples of so many gardens. In addition to size, a conifer's habit, disease resistance and pruning traits dictate whether the trees should be used as lawn specimens, border accents, foundation plants, informal screens, clipped hedges, ground covers, rock garden plants or container plants.

A number of common mistakes are made about conifers. There is a belief that if something can be clipped into a cube or a ball, then it should be. Some of the most naturally graceful conifers — hemlocks, yews and upright junipers, for example — suffer this fate. I once saw a line of blue Atlas cedars clipped into a hedge and didn't know whether to laugh or cry.

Another mistake is the view that conifers must be kept in separate assemblies. Sometimes an adventurous person will group Conifer A with Conifer B, but even such an enlightened soul seems unable to integrate conifers with the rest of the garden. You can use the fine textures and unusual colors of conifers to form exciting combinations with other deciduous plants — say, purple-leafed barberry, golden-variegated juniper and blue-leafed *Hosta sieboldiana*. The use of deciduous shrubs, trees, perennials and ground covers seems to restore vitality to conifers. When used alone or with another conifer, conifers become rather artificial and lifeless.

The third pitfall is underestimating the size of conifers, especially those intended as foundation plantings. Overgrown conifers can be opened and lightened by selective pruning, but in many cases even that doesn't work. A number of conifers — white pines, Colorado blue spruces, Norway spruces, Leyland cypresses and cedars — should be planted only on large lots and in locations where they can grow up and out.

A number of conifers are not hardy or will grow poorly in the Washington-area climate. These include Sequoias, Monterey cypress, Italian cypress, larches, firs, white and red spruces and red and ponderosa pines. Similarly, Gray Gleam, Skyrocket and other varieties of the Rocky Mountain juniper *(Juniperus scopulorum)* are sickly trees here, afflicted by a fungal blight and rust; they maintain their healthy appearance only if sprayed preventively with toxic fungicides. The dwarf Alberta spruce is a popular plant because it looks clipped into a little cone, its normal habit. But it often is plagued by spider mites and can look ratty as a result. Think twice before acquiring one.

Main Pests: Hemlock woolly adelgid, mites, scale insects, bagworms and other grubs. **Main Diseases:** Rust and botrytis tip blight.[†]

PRUNING

SOME NEEDLED evergreens take pruning beautifully, while disaster awaits the gardener who blithely shears off the stems of others. Yew, junipers and hemlocks will take shearing as hedges. Others can be trimmed, though timing and technique are important.

As a rule, most conifers should not be pruned. If you find that you have to contain your conifers, it is because they were planted in too small a space or in too much shade. If you feel that you must prune, however, follow these seven rules:

1. Clip yews, junipers, hemlocks, chamaecyparis, Leyland cypress and arborvitae in early spring before new growth appears. A second light shearing, if needed, can be done in early summer.

2. Clip spruces after new growth has appeared, but don't cut old growth. There are no buds on inner branches, and cutting back hard will disfigure or kill the tree. The same applies to pines.

3. Pines produce candles in the spring. These are unfurled bundles of new needles. Before the candles break into needles, remove them, either by hand or with pruning shears. You can remove all or part of the candle, but this is the only pruning pines will take. Most pines will not need this, but it is important to remove the candles of mugo pines to keep the trees bushy and to prevent them from growing too large.

4. Ground-cover junipers in need of thinning should have whole stems removed from the plant crown. Go easy.

5. Overgrown yews can be cut back hard to stumps and will regenerate. This takes three years.

6. When buying a spruce, pine or other conifer for its pyramidal habit, select one with a single central leader. If you have young trees with several leaders, cut back the lesser ones to a lateral branch, leaving a dominant leader.

7. Never prune the leader or "top" conifers, with the exception of the hedging varieties mentioned.

RECOMMENDED VARIETIES

■ **SERBIAN SPRUCE** *(Picea omorika)*. This is a delightful, tall but narrow spruce that is perfect for the small to mid-sized garden. Its finely textured needles are a dark glossy green above and white below. The plant grows slowly — after 20 years it might be 20 feet high and just six to eight feet in width — but it eventually becomes a full-sized conifer.

Use it as a specimen in a winter garden to be viewed from indoors, to break up a monolithic house wall, as a screen in tight quarters, or as the focal point at the end of a long view. There is a pendulous form named (what else?) Pendula whose drooping branches cry out for a dusting of snow. Have your camera ready.

Spruces grow in ordinary soil and full sun or light shade. They will perform better if their roots are lightly top-dressed with leaf mold annually so that surface roots have a cool, moisture-retentive medium in the summer, when the plant is most stressed.

■ **ORIENTAL SPRUCE** *(Picea orientalis)*. This is a bigger version of the Serbian spruce. It can be employed as an impressive and stately lawn specimen or as a large-scale background screen on the far side of an expansive lawn or meadow. Use it in place of white pines, blue spruces or Norway spruces.

The needles here are short and tight and deep green, conveying a fine texture that tempers the size of the plant. After 20 years, expect the tree to reach 25 feet, with a 10-foot spread. In addition to being used as a specimen or as an informal screen, the Oriental spruce forms the perfect backdrop for large ornamental specimens such as crab apples, giant dogwoods, deciduous hollies, Japanese maples, katsura trees and Heritage river birches.

Cultivation is the same as for the Serbian spruce, but select as open a spot as possible. Heavy shade on one side will cause the plant to lose its symmetry.

■ **LACEBARK PINE** *(Pinus bungeana)*. This is another slow-growing evergreen to plant with future generations in mind. A native of China, the lacebark pine is pyramidal in youth. With age, it opens up to reveal a trunk of the most striking bark ornament, mottled in lime greens and tans and browns. It will grow to 30 feet or higher, with branches spreading to 20 feet or more. A prime specimen marks the entrance to the formal boxwood and azalea garden at the National Arboretum (see Appendix for Public Gardens information). Pines prefer full sun and ordinary, well-drained soil.

■ **JAPANESE BLACK PINE** *(Pinus thunbergiana)*. Perfectly at home in smaller gardens, the Japanese black pine offers a superb addition to the informal landscape. It tends to be broad, open and twisted, resembling a bonsai specimen. Don't attempt to tame this tree. Rather, play to its wilder side with plantings of ornamental grasses and perennials of interesting texture. To take the bonsai idea further, the tree can be used as a lone specimen in a gravel-mulched bed framed by the walls or windows of a building.

■ **CANADIAN HEMLOCK** *(Tsuga canadensis)*. In spite of its problems with a bug named woolly adelgid, the Canadian hemlock is one of the most beautiful trees in the garden and deserves to be planted. Its gray-green foliage is fine in texture and handsomely layered, and the tree can be opened at its base to accommodate other woodland plants. This is one of very few conifers that will grow in shady conditions, making it priceless for people with shade gardens.

The Canadian hemlock can be used as a formal or informal hedge, clustered into screens, or dotted about at the edge of a wood, just as it would be in nature. It forms a fine accent plant in a setting of larger conifers or shade trees.

The plant begins as a broad, rounded shrub, growing into a large tree over many years. With sensitive pruning, you can keep it at a desired height and still retain its natural look. It prefers moist, acidic and well-drained soil (add leaf mold and peat moss). These requirements become critical if you grow hemlocks in full sun, which you can do. The plant becomes severely stressed during prolonged droughts and thus should be one of the first landscape plants to receive regular watering. Alas, woolly adelgid is endemic and will show up, but the pest is easily controlled organically.[†]

■ **BLUE ATLAS CEDAR** *(Cedrus atlantica Glauca)*. This tree is only for the most open setting. If you have the space and the vision to plant it today, you will be giving joy still to people in the 22nd century.

The blue atlas cedar grows swiftly in youth, but it doesn't form its broad layered habit for several decades. In maturity it can climb 50 feet high, with a greater spread. This is a more graceful tree than the Deodar cedar and less prone to the central-leader dieback that Deodars suffer in drought conditions. The Cedar of Lebanon, with its thick trunk and horizontal limbs and layered branches, is a choice cedar, too. It rarely is seen in Washington, but specimens have been known to grow here. Some of the best examples of blue atlas cedar are at the Bishop's Garden at Washington National Cathedral (see Public Gardens in Appendix).

A weeping form of blue atlas cedar is a striking plant, producing cascading curtains of icy blue foliage falling from open, wandering limbs. It is so unusual that is must be used carefully and generally granted more space than most people give it.

■ **HINOKI FALSECYPRESS** *(Chamaecyparis obtusa)*. The Hinoki falsecypress has long been favored as an evergreen specimen, and deservedly so. The most commonly planted variety is Nana Gracilis, sometimes wrongly labeled as Nana in the nursery trade. It is a small variety that grows into a six-foot shrub, is loosely pyramidal, and is well suited for use as foundation plants, specimens or patio screens. The scale-like leaves are arranged in flat, dark-green fans. It requires full sun, moist to dry soil and good drainage. (The true Nana variety with which it is confused grows just half an inch a year, making it about as useful as a plant for ant farms.)

- **HICKS YEW** *(Taxus x media Hicksii)*. Yews take about 80 years to turn into splendid specimen trees. Most people don't plant them this way, using them instead as foundation shrubs. These almost always outgrow their spaces, look rather scruffy and eventually are ripped out. One of the best uses for yews is as a hedge, clipped or unclipped. They form living blocks of architecture, great black-green walls of nothingness to enclose and frame inward-looking spaces. Hicks yew is the best variety for this, because it is reliably winter-hardy, has an upright habit, and grows fast for a yew, about eight inches a year. Plant yews three to four feet apart, depending on your patience and budget.

- **DAWN REDWOOD** *(Metasequoia glyptostroboides)*. This is a large, fast-growing and handsome conifer that isn't an evergreen. Its needle-like leaves turn a copper-orange in the fall and drop, leaving a distinctive and attractive winter outline. The branching is symmetrical and pyramidal. With age, the red, flaking bark becomes somewhat fluted and buttressed at the base. This tree has few vices, except that it grows tall, to 70 feet or more, and does not offer total screening in the winter. If you have the room, however, it provides rapid and attractive screening during the three seasons when you are most likely to be outdoors and need it. It is a much better alternative to the Leyland cypress. So far as cultivation goes, it does best in full sun and moist but well-drained soil. For low-lying areas with standing water, substitute the similar bald cypress.

- **YOSHINO JAPANESE CEDAR** *(Cryptomeria japonica Yoshino)*. The Japanese cedar is a delightful conifer, again for larger properties or as high screens in bigger city gardens. It has feathery, cascading foliage and lovely, rugged, red bark. It grows to 60 feet after many decades. The variety Yoshino overcomes the two major flaws of Japanese cedar: It does not suffer from the browning of foliage in winter and the dieback of lower stems. It also is smaller, growing at a rate of a foot a year. Japanese cedar benefits from light shade and deep, moist soil.

---

†See Appendix for common pest and disease ailments and remedies.

Chapter 14

BESTS AND WORSTS

*I*N THE HOPE of pointing gardeners to the most valuable trees and shrubs for our area — and away from those that are unworthy — this chapter reviews both. It contains my picks of 10 each of the best shade trees, patio trees and shrubs. You will find the top 10 conifers in Chapter 13 and top 10 ground covers in Chapter 19. You may have your favorites to add to each list, but the recommended varieties are chosen for their superior performance as much as for their beauty.

Other favorite plants are in later chapters — varieties of roses or irises, for example — but I have reserved these separate top 10 lists for woody plants and ground covers because they form the foundations of any garden.

I. SHADE TREES

Greek philosophers wandered in the groves of great trees, whose shelter and beauty, we are told, induced profound thoughts. Shade trees are the largest building blocks in the garden. They will outlive us, and choosing one is our gift to future generations. They should be selected and placed, therefore, with care and intelligence. In return for their years of service, we must give them room and take care not to injure them. Don't put them close to buildings, near overhead utility lines, anywhere that will experience major excavation in future years (an addition, driveway or septic field, for example) or too close to a neighbor's property.

Some may be grouped (oaks or beeches, for example), but don't plant them in woodland or on the north side of a tall building; they are for full sun. Mostly, choice shade trees should be regarded as giant specimens, to be viewed as the sole plant in a great lawn or within an enclosed garden area, a "room" where we can sit and be in the presence of a great and living thing.

THE 10 BEST

THIS LIST covers trees that are beautiful in every season, long-lived and generally free of serious pests and diseases. The last three are selected for their smaller size, to provide choices for those with less expansive properties. If you still cannot accommodate any of these trees, bring down the scale (but not the function) by selecting from the chapter's patio trees list. This list is not arranged in order of preference. All are winners.

1. BEECH
Both the American and European beech are marvelous trees:

- **AMERICAN BEECH** (*Fagus grandifolia*), related to the oaks, is a tree of rare majesty. With age, its silvery smooth skin becomes furled, and its surface roots form a lace pattern on the ground. Its beautiful leaves are distinctive and heavily veined, turning a golden bronze in the fall. Climbing to 50 feet or higher and broader in its spread, it casts deep shade. It is difficult to impossible to grow anything, including grass, under it, though at Georgetown's Dumbarton Oaks hundreds of chionodoxa, a tiny, blue-flowered spring bulb, have been planted successfully beneath a specimen beech. You will need to place the American beech in a large setting to make the most of it. It needs acidic, moist but well-drained soil and cannot endure soil compaction, so keep it away from driveways.

■ **EUROPEAN BEECH** *(Fagus sylvatica)* is considered even more beautiful than the American species. Smaller, with darker gray bark, its leaves turn color later than its American cousin in the fall. It is not as tolerant of our summer heat, however, and if grown here it should be placed in a site where the roots can wander freely in moist, humusy soil. The purple-leaf beech is a variety of *F. sylvatica* named *Atropunicia*, and the true copper beech is the paler cultivar *Cuprea*. In Washington's summer heat, most trees lose their rich purple color, replacing it with an olive-green cast. There are wonderful specimens at Dumbarton Oaks and at Longwood Gardens in Kennett Square, Pa. (See Public Gardens in Appendix.)

2. BLÀCK TUPELO *(Nyssa sylvatica)*

The tupelo is a native plant that makes a splendid shade tree, especially for naturalized areas. It is one of the stars of the fall garden. It has a rounded crown and horizontal branches and grows to 40 to 50 feet, with a spread of 20 feet or more. The bark is black and blocky, resembling the alligator hide of the persimmon tree, another worthy native that is not quite in the same league as the tupelo. In the fall, the tupelo's leaves turn a brilliant orange-to-scarlet color.

The tree is tap rooted, so buy young trees, preferably those grown in containers rather than field-grown and balled and burlapped. The growth rate is quite slow, about a foot a year when young. It will grow in ordinary soil but prefers deep, enriched, acidic soil, making it a good companion for azaleas, hollies, mountain laurels, pieris and rhododendron. It will take some partial shade.

3. GOLDENRAINTREE *(Koelreuteria paniculata)*

This is a long-favored tree from Asia, valued for its dense, compound foliage, its adaptability to poor soils and its late-summer flowers. It is also somewhat contained, growing to 30 feet, with an equal or greater spread. Its yellow flowers appear in late summer when little else is blooming, and they turn to ornamental lanterns in the fall. The tree has few vices. It is supposed to be a little weak-wooded, and the lanterns do need cleaning up once they drop, so it's probably best not to place the tree next to the patio, swimming pool or pond.

4. JAPANESE ZELKOVA *(Zelkova serrata)*

The vase-shaped zelkova was long regarded as a substitute for the American elm, which was devastated by Dutch elm disease. Now that the National Arboretum has bred a disease-resistant American elm named Valley Forge, it seems only fair that this burden be lifted from the zelkova so that we can enjoy it for what it is — a splendid, relatively fast-growing and trouble-free tree. It is favored for its attractive bark, upright habit and handsome foliage, which resembles the elm's (it is, in fact, a member of the elm family).

The zelkova will grow to 50 feet after several decades, with an equal spread. It adapts to ordinary soil but will do best in a moist, enriched site. It should be kept well watered until it is established, especially through its first two summers. It is hardy north to New York, but young trees are susceptible to frost damage. If you live on higher ground, you may wish to plant in late April. A popular improved variety is Village Green, selected for its vigor, straighter trunk and reliably red fall foliage. Green Vase is another variety worth seeking out.

5. KATSURA *(Cercidiphyllum japonicum)*

An Asian tree introduced in this country in 1865, the katsura is one of the finest specimens of shade tree available. It has heart-like leaves (similar to the redbud's) that quiver in the breeze. They open tinged with purple, turn a clean bright green and, in the fall, become a shining yellow. The trunk is dark and gets shaggy with great age, and the sight of the yellow fall leaves against the black stems and trunk is striking. The trees grow to 40 to 60 feet over many years. The katsura's habit is variable: Male trees are more upright, female trees more spreading. An expert can tell which it is by looking at the flowers in April, but most of us will have to take what comes. Difficult to transplant, the katsura is best bought young and in a container. Some horticulturists recommend planting it in early spring to minimize root stress. It should be in rich but well-drained soil that is slightly acid. A smaller weeping form named Pendula is fast becoming the tree of choice. It is indeed a gorgeous plant, but it would be a shame to fail to use the species plant.

6. WHITE OAK *(Quercus alba)*

One of the truly beautiful native trees, it grows at a medium pace at first, reaching 12 feet or so in its first decade, but then slows down. With age its limbs grow thick and out from its straight, upright trunk, becoming a fabulous specimen. Its mature size is 70 feet high, with a spread of 50 feet or more. The leaves are four to eight inches long, deeply lobed and a blue-green above, paler beneath. The acorn is 3/4-inch in length.

The fall color varies, but it is generally in the muted wines of its species. Like most oaks, it holds its leaves well into fall. It comes alive in the winter, when the light gray bark, arranged into vertical blocks, comes to the fore.

The tree is tap-rooted and resents being moved (it will likely die from the process). That's why you should plant only young trees, preferably container-grown. Washington is full of beautiful specimens, but I fear that we are not replenishing stock lost to storms and development. The tree prefers moist, deep, acidic soil that drains adequately. Once it is established, you should minimize root disturbance.

7. WILLOW OAK *(Quercus phellos)*

A quintessentially southern landscape and street tree that does well in the Washington area, the willow oak has foliage like its namesake but is 10 times the plant. It will rise to 40 feet or more, with a spread of 30 feet, growing rapidly (two feet a year) in youth. A proven street tree like this can take poor soils and stressful urban environments, but the willow oak is beautiful to boot. Its majestic form — straight trunk and rounded crown — is offset by the fine texture of its leaves, which turn a pleasant yellow in the fall. This tree does best in acidic, moist soil but will endure low-lying land given to periodic flooding. Make sure it is well watered during droughts.

Several other native oaks are worth planting. The chestnut oak *(Quercus prinus)* withstands dry and rocky sites. The red oak *(Quercus rubra)* is planted for its fast growth. The similar black oak *(Quercus velutina)* has near-black and furrowed bark on old specimens. (No other oak, however, has quite the bark ornament of the white oak.)

All of the oaks mentioned can be used as lawn specimens or to form an avenue on a larger property. Space them 20 to 25 feet apart.

8. AMERICAN YELLOWWOOD *(Cladrastis lutea)*

A superior and underplanted native beauty, the yellowwood's leaves retain a spring-like freshness and color through the summer and then turn yellow in the fall. In late spring, the tree is covered in panicles of sweetly fragrant white flowers. It is related to wisteria and the locust tree. Yellowwood grows to 30 feet with age, with a spread of as much or more, and prefers ordinary, well-drained soil. As it ages, the bark becomes light gray and smooth and quite attractive in winter. Its trunk and branch crotches tend to be tight, making mature trees prone to storm damage. So select a tree with the most open crotches, and prune out tight ones in youth.

9. GINKGO *(Ginkgo biloba)*

The unique ginkgo, or maidenhair, tree is not small by any means; it grows quickly, and mature specimens can reach 40 to 50 feet. But it does not spread much, and its roots remain contained, so it is a good choice for a narrow site or near a building. The fan-like foliage is a deep green in summer and a brilliant, unrivaled yellow in the fall, remaining free of insect or disease damage. If at all possible, get a male tree. After many years, females produce fruit that is cherished by Asian herbalists but that has a nauseating smell if not gathered.

10. LITTLELEAF LINDEN *(Tilia cordata)*

This choicest of the lindens, with its small, heart-shaped leaves, makes a splendid tree for the home garden. Its attractive, dense foliage casts deep shade, and it remains pleasingly dense and pyramidal in maturity. It grows at a medium rate, 18 inches a year in youth, and after many decades will reach 40 feet high and 20 feet or more in width.

It adapts to poor soil and pollution, but it prefers fertile soil. It is not for swampy areas. Greenspire is a variety to look for, developed for its straight, single trunk and nicely branching habit. Many consider the Crimean linden *(Tilia x euchlora)* an even better tree. It is a hybrid between the littleleaf linden and a species known botanically as *Tilia dasystyla,* but is not as widely available as the littleleaf. Look for a plant that is grown on its own roots; grafted varieties tend to produce unwanted suckers.

The one drawback is that in spring lindens are afflicted by aphids[†], which then produce an unsightly sticky excretion called sooty mold. This isn't sufficient reason to pass over the linden, but plant them away from where you or your automobile might sit.

II. PATIO TREES

THE SMALL, ornamental patio tree gets pride of place in the garden. It is living sculpture, perhaps the single most important plant in most gardens, and thus must be chosen with care. The tree should be beautiful of form and big enough to make a statement but not so big as to overwhelm. It should be interesting in every season, trouble-free and not messy.

A tip: If there is no space around your patio for a tree, lift bricks or flagstones to create a square two to four feet long and wide to accommodate a root ball. For a more dramatic effect, position the tree off center and preferably in a spot where it can be seen from indoors.

Demonstrate your sophistication by avoiding the flowering dogwood and planting one of the following:

THE 10 BEST

1. CHERRY HALLY JOLIVETTE *(Prunus x Hally Jolivette)*
Cherries have their frailties. Prone to insects and diseases, many are short-lived or require excessive attention to keep healthy. Some rise above these problems. One of the best small cherries for patio use is Hally Jolivette, a bushy tree growing and flowering quickly but reaching only 12 to 15 feet, with an equal spread. Its flower buds are pink, then open white. Because the buds do not open all at once, you have an especially long flowering season untroubled by frost. The tree requires full sun, moderately rich soil and good drainage.

2. CRAB APPLE NARAGANSETT *(Malus Naragansett)*
Possibly the finest crab apple ever produced, Naragansett is well suited to the patio border — a small, rounded tree growing to 15 feet with a spread of 10 feet. Practically immune to the disfiguring diseases so prevalent in crab apple varieties, it produces masses of tiny, carmine red blossoms that open to a white tinged with pink. Naragansett sets cherry-red fruit that is ornamental in the fall. It also is small, persistent and not unduly messy: Sweeping up beneath it would be a small price to pay for the year-round beauty of this tree.

Crab apples can be planted in ordinary clay soil, reasonably amended to retain moisture but also well drained, and should sit in full sun or the lightest of shade. Low-lying, wet areas are unsuitable.

3. CRAPE MYRTLE *(Lagerstroemia)*
Once just a twiggy shrub, the crape myrtle has been reinvented through a highly successful breeding program at the National Arboretum. There, the late Dr. Donald Egolf developed cold-hardy, mildew-resistant tree types of splendid ornament — long flowering in the summer, vivid colors in fall and bark patterns that hold interest year round. They want full sun and well-drained soil. Among 20 Egolf introductions, nine are tree forms developed for the home garden. The most popular is Natchez, which is white-flowered with a cinnamon brown bark, but all are worthy.

Crape myrtles can grow as tall as 30 feet after many years, but a height of 15 to 20 feet, with an equal or greater spread, is more typical. In addition to Natchez, look for Biloxi (pale pink flower with dark brown bark); Choctaw (a bright pink with mottled, cinammon-colored bark); Miami (a dark coral pink with dark chestnut brown bark); Muskogee, light lavender with light gray bark); Tuscarora (dark coral pink with light brown bark); Tuskegee (dark pink to red with light gray-tan bark), and Wichita (light magenta with a russet brown to mahogany bark).

4. DECIDUOUS MAGNOLIAS

There are many species and varieties from which to select, but all make fine specimen trees for the patio area. Their only drawback is that in some years, early spring freezes will destroy the fabulous blossoms, although the tree itself is not harmed. Gardeners in protected spots at lower elevations in Zone 7a are better off than those firmly in Zone 6b. You can select a number of later-flowering varieties to minimize this problem. Generally, magnolias prefer acidic, somewhat moist but (with one exception) well-drained sites and flower best in full sun. Buds are best protected from frost, ironically, if the plant is sited out of morning winter sun. The roots are fleshy and don't harden off well before winter, so it is best to plant in the spring.

5. HORNBEAM *(Carpinus)*

The Hornbeam Ellipse at Dumbarton Oaks must be the most photogaphed and beloved arrangement of hornbeams in the world, but the tree is suited, too, for use as a single patio specimen. It is generally free of disease and pests and is not messy. While there is no great floral show, the form, texture and bark ornament are truly wonderful. The beech-like leaves remain attractive throughout the growing season. In winter, the bark and stems are admired for their smooth, sinewy texture and light gray color.

The English hornbeam *(Carpinus betulus)* is considered a better candidate for shearing than the native species *(Carpinus caroliniana)*, and it certainly is larger and less shrub-like. The most common variety is Fastigiata. It isn't as narrowly upright as its name suggests, but it is less spreading than the straight species and better suited to smaller properties. The American hornbeam in particular develops a muscular fluting to its stems. Fall color can be quite spectacular on the American species, but it varies by plants. Hornbeams resent root disturbance, and mature specimens are not reliably moved. They also dislike flooding, preferring moist but well-drained soil. They will take dryer conditions once established. Place them in full sun or partial shade, and plant container-grown trees, preferably in the spring.

6. JAPANESE MAPLE *(Acer palmatum)*

Upright forms of Japanese maples (not the mounding threadleafs) and other ornamental maples make fabulous patio specimens. One of the most attractive is the straight species *Acer palmatum*, which is a green-leafed variety of understated beauty. It grows to 20 feet. Other maples to consider are the paperbark maple *(Acer griseum)*, whose peeling, cinnamon bark makes the tree interesting year round. The bark of three-flower maple *(Acer triflorum)* also peels, though to a lesser extent, and it, too, is a superior ornamental tree, growing to 20 feet. It has great fall color (see Chapter 10 for cultivation).

7. JAPANESE SNOWBELL *(Styrax japonicus)*

The Japanese snowbell is another valuable all-round tree that's untroubled by pests and disease. It begins life dense and pyramidal but soon becomes slender and open, with wide horizontal branching. With age, it will grow to 20 feet and at least as much in spread. Careful pruning when it is young can keep the side branches growing where they are wanted. Its flowers are borne conspicuously on clusters of dangling white bells in May. In winter, it is admired for its smooth gray bark and the interesting zig-zag line of the stems. A new variety named Emerald Pagoda, with larger, glossier leaves, is worth seeking out.

(The American snowbell *(Styrax americanus)* is a medium-sized shrub of rhododendron culture and use. The fragrant snowbell *(Styrax obassia)* is another Asian species forming a larger shrub that blooms in June. It is a handsome and useful plant but not the same as the Japanese snowbell.)

8. JAPANESE STEWARTIA *(Stewartia pseudocamellia)*

The stewartias are superior landscape specimens, lovely in every aspect: branching habit, proportion, leaf, flower and, above all, bark ornament. With age, they are mottled in striking russets, tans and khakis. The favored species is the Japanese stewartia. The Korean stewartia *(Stewartia koreana)* is a little smaller and more upright and has slightly larger, flatter blooms. Both are terrific, with handsome red and orange fall color.

Like hornbeams, they are best put in as young, container-grown plants. If you buy balled and burlapped trees, handle the root ball gently; be careful not to injure, bruise or cut the roots when planting. Stewartias need humusy, acidic soil and benefit from a little afternoon shade. They resent baking heat and drought, and you should do your best to provide ample mulch (leaf mold of oak is perfect) and keep the tree watered in dry periods. The attention will be repaid a thousandfold.

9. SILVERBELL *(Halesia)*

An elegant native tree for semi-shady conditions, the silverbell is underused and little known, but you can help correct that. It is grown for its handsome form and its pretty, bell-like flowers, which appear in early spring dangling in clusters on bare stems. It is not troubled by pests or disease, but it demands a rhododendron-like culture — preferring a little shade, and insisting on lots of evenly moist, organically enriched soil on the acidic side. Amending the soil to provide this is a small price to pay for years of reward.

There are two versions to choose from. The more common is the Carolina silverbell *(Halesia carolina)*, but look, too, for the two-winged silverbell, or snowdrop tree *(Halesia diptera)*. The latter should be of a variety named magniflora, developed for its prolific flowering. Both species grow to 25 to 30 feet in maturity, with a spread of about 20 feet.

10. SOURWOOD TREE *(Oxydendron aboreum)*

One of the most beautiful plants in the garden, the sourwood tree grows after many decades into a small shade tree, but because it is a slow grower (gaining only a foot a year), it serves as a terrific patio specimen. It is of ornamental interest in every season but truly shines in the fall, when the pendulous foliage turns from deep green to a range of incredible hues, often ruby red but tinged with purple.

Its racemes of heather-like flowers appear as a great lacy covering in the summer, and the seedpods persist as terrific fall ornament. The bark is dark and furrowed. Like the halesia, it is a native plant that will take semi-shade and needs rich, acidic soil. It colors best in full sun, and keep it watered until established and during periods of drought.

III. SHRUBS

THE SHRUBS selected here are ornamental year-round, generally free of pests and disease, and will flourish even if you have little gardening expertise. Flowering is but one virtue taken into account, and the one azalea mentioned is not of the sort commonly imagined.

THE 10 BEST

1. BUTTERCUP WINTERHAZEL *(Corylopsis pauciflora)*

This is an attractive, small specimen shrub valued for its fragrant pendants of lemon-yellow flowers in late winter. It forms a neat mound, rising to five feet in maturity, with an equal spread. Flowering with early daffodils and bulbous irises, it carries the garden at a time when other beauties are hibernating. Corylopsis takes full sun or, preferably, light shade in an enriched soil. Try to place it in a sheltered corner to protect blooms from possible freezes.

2. DOUBLEFILE VIBURNUM SHASTA *(Viburnum plicatum tomentosum Shasta)*

Despite its long Latin name, this plant is very much worth getting to know. Virtually all viburnums make terrific garden plants — great flowers, nice habit, attractive berries and good fall color — but shasta stands out for its striking horizontal branching and its flowers. The blooms appear in May, pure white and arranged to look as if they are floating above the leaves. The plant grows to six feet (short for a viburnum) and twice that in breadth. Plant it on slopes and in a space where it can be viewed from above.

The plant is surface-rooted and should grow in enriched, well-drained loam that retains moisture. The ideal spot is one where the plant will receive light, dappled shade in the afternoon. It will grow in full sun, but this makes the soil and watering requirements critical. In too deep a shade, its striking form and flower show will suffer. This is generally true of viburnums.

3. FOTHERGILLA

This woodland shrub comes in two basic versions, both similar except for size. Large fothergilla *(Fothergilla major)* grows to about six feet or more in height, with an equal spread. Dwarf fothergilla *(Fothergilla gardenii)* grows to half that size. The dwarf is useful in small gardens or tight corners, the bigger version where the scale needs to be enlarged. They should be used as accent plants in the foundation bed or garden borders, beside woodland trails and in small groupings. If you're looking for an alternative to the rhododendron or azalea, this is it.

The flowers, sweetly scented bottlebrush blooms, appear in April, before the foliage emerges. The leaves are attractive, and they are clean throughout the summer, but it is in the fall when the shrub excels. In November, it is a kaleidoscope of color — lime greens, yellow, oranges and scarlets.

The fothergillas are native woodland plants, meaning that they have specific growing requirements. They demand acidic, loamy soil on the lighter side. The soil must be moist but well drained, and the plants prefer some shading from the afternoon summer sun. If they are placed too far into shade, the fall color will not be as strong, though they still would be worth growing. Water during dry spells, and be careful not to allow peat moss used in planting to dry out. Do not prune or (heaven forfend) clip.

4. FRINGE TREE *(Chionanthus virginicus)*

This is another deciduous native plant deserving much greater appreciation and use. The fringe tree is a big shrub, growing in time to 12 feet or higher and with an equal spread. This makes it a large specimen in the smaller property or useful as a screen or informal hedge in bigger properties. It is also valuable as an anchoring background shrub in the mixed border. In other words, it's a splendid alternative to the lilac, though much more open and airy in habit.

The fringe tree is covered with highly distinctive flowers in May, white tassels as long as six inches (male plants have showier blooms). They appear before the leaves are fully mature. After the tree flowers, the leaves grow to eight inches and remain green and attractive until fall. Blue berries ripen in late summer, but birds soon eat them. The fringe tree prefers acidic, evenly moist soil and a sunny location. Water it in the summer, especially when it is young.

5. HEAVENLY BAMBOO *(Nandina domestica)*

The foliage carries a passing resemblance to bamboo, but nandina is not an invasive grass. Rather, it is an extremely well-behaved, upright evergreen shrub of year-round interest and ornament. Though overplanted, this shrub is still fresh and beautiful to the eye. It has graceful, arrowhead leaves, a fine texture and attractive, conspicuous clusters of red berries. The foliage and stems often are tinged red, becoming more so in fall and winter. In harsh winters, the plant may drop its leaves, but don't assume that the bare stems are dead; they often refoliate in time.

Nandina grows to six feet in height, but because it is at most only half that in width, three or four make a valuable screen in tight quarters — around air conditioning units or trash can areas and in balcony gardens (in containers), as well as between properties. If planted close to a building, nandina often doesn't get enough rainwater and should be watered periodically, especially when young. It requires full sun to partial shade.

6. JAPANESE BARBERRY *(Berberis thunbergii var. atropurpurea)*

The Japanese barberry is planted a great deal — and with good reason. The purple-leafed barberry is delicate in texture and form yet as tough as nails, withstanding the rigors of the Washington-area summer. The regular shrub grows to four or five feet, with an equal or greater spread. It is useful as an accent in the shrub border. One of the most popular cultivars is a dwarf form named Crimson Pygmy, which grows to just two feet. This makes it valuable massed as a ground cover, especially on a difficult, out-of-the-way slope. Rose Glow is an interesting, full-sized variety whose purple leaves are streaked and mottled a rose pink.

The small yellow flowers of Japanese barberry are not conspicuous, but they are astonishingly beautiful and turn into bright red berries in the fall, revealed as the leaves gradually fall. Many people plant this as a low hedge, either informally or rigidly clipped. The plant deserves to be used, too, as an accent in the border: It combines beautifully with feathery, lime-green conifers or yellow-leafed plants such as spireas, or in a color scheme featuring grays, whites and silvers.

Barberry has nasty thorns and is not for high-traffic areas. It grows in ordinary soil in full sun and dislikes damp places. Water it during its first summer.

7. OAKLEAF HYDRANGEA *(Hydrangea quercifolia)*

This is not for formal gardens, but it is an aristocrat of the shade and naturalistic garden. The oakleaf hydrangea is named for its large, oak-like leaves, which grow slowly but steadily for weeks in the spring. They are presented ornamentally in an open and layered habit, turning an attractive maroon in the fall. In June, tall, showy panicles of white flowers appear, and their decoration persists as the flowers dry and turn rose-colored and brown. The bark, which peels with age, is a bright cinnamon color that is of great winter interest.

In 10 years, the plant will grow to seven feet high and as much across. It is useful as a large border shrub beneath shade trees, for massing on larger properties, or for brightening dark corners. Like most woodland shrubs, the oakleaf hydrangea prefers to grow in light shade and organically enriched soil that retains moisture but drains well. In deep shade, its habit will become leggy and flowering will diminish, but it is still worth growing provided you can supply enough moisture for shrub and trees alike. In full sun, the need for humusy soil and a good layer of mulch becomes critical, as does a commitment to summer watering to avoid wilting.

8. ROYAL AZALEA *(Rhododendron schlippenbachii)*

A prince among azaleas, the royal azalea differs from conventional azaleas in a number of ways: It is deciduous, the leaves are large, and they turn fabulous colors in the fall. The flowers, pale pink and sweetly fragrant, emerge with new leaves. They are abundant but not in freakish profusion. The stems are an attractive smooth gray in winter, and the plant in time grows to six feet, with an equal spread. The royal azalea deserves to be used as a specimen in the mixed border or, on larger properties, massed in small groups near paths. It does best in high or partial shade, and it prefers organically enriched soil that retains moisture. It is worth seeking out or special ordering (see Specialty Plant Sources in Appendix).

9. WINTERBERRY SPARKLEBERRY *(Ilex Sparkleberry)*

This is a deciduous holly grown for its stunning winter effect. Hundreds of cherry-red berries appear on naked, arching stems. If birds do not eat them all, the berries persist until early spring, remaining ornamental through daffodil and crocus season. With age, the shrub will grow to about 10 feet and develop an equal spread. On larger properties, it can be massed in the background. When it is set against a high informal hedge of conifers, its berries can be admired from afar.

It grows in ordinary clay soil in full sun or light shade and will take swampy conditions, making it a terrific addition to difficult, waterlogged areas. Sparkleberry is a female; you will need a male pollinator named Apollo for the fruit to appear. With the help of bees, one Apollo will pollinate a whole harem of Sparkleberry.

10. WITCH HAZEL *(Hamamelis x intermedia)*

Witch hazels are wonderful plants, and there are a number of native and Asian species and hybrids from which to select. They flower in the fall through early spring, depending on species, and the most popular, with good reason, are crosses of the Chinese and Japanese witch hazels that flower in mid-to-late winter. They are untroubled by pests or disease, have handsome veined and wavy leaves and turn attractive colors in the fall. Among these, the favored variety is Arnold Promise. It is one of the bright, yellow-flowering versions. Others of note include Diane (copper-red) and Jelena (red-orange). The reds are not as eye-catching from afar as Arnold Promise (a consideration when the plant is viewed from indoors), but their fall color is better and they tend to cleanse themselves of their dead leaves. Arnold Promise is reluctant to let go of its leaves, distracting the flower show. (The fastidious gardener, however, simply can pluck off the dried foliage.) The witch hazel takes full sun or light shade in amended, well-drained, humusy and acidic soil.

IV. 10 PLANTS TO AVOID

Here's a list of common plants best avoided. Some have fleeting ornamental merit, others are disease-ridden, and still others simply grow too large for the typical garden. Most are planted too much. The inclusion of the flowering dogwood (whose beauty understandably evokes deep attachments) and perhaps a couple of others will provoke disagreement, even outrage, but gardening is difficult enough with bulletproof plants. We should not make it even harder.

I have not put crab apples, rhododendrons or azaleas on my hit list, but read Chapters 6 and 11 before selecting one. Most bamboo shouldn't be planted into the ground, even with barriers; eradicating it will be a chore passed on to neighbors and successive owners. Container-grown bamboo is fine and provides useful screening in the tight quarters of the townhouse patio or apartment balcony.

I assume that nobody would purposefully plant the misnamed tree-of-heaven *(Ailanthus)*, and stay away from the mulberry, both the true common mulberry *(Morus alba)* and the related paper mulberry *(Broussonetia papyriferia)*. They are fast-growing weeds with devilish root systems. I have not included any shrubs or, as noted earlier, any perennials: Any mistakes with them are far easier to rectify. Do, however, stop planting loosestrife *(Lythrum)*. This once-favored perennial is choking native wetlands and doesn't need any encouragement from the home gardener. Here goes:

1. COLORADO BLUE SPRUCE *(Picea pungens glauca)*

Not a bad conifer in itself (though there are better), it often is totally misused as a border or lawn plant without any regard to its mature size. It grows 60 feet high and has a 20-foot spread. That is an area of 1,200 square feet: You could put a vegetable garden in that space and keep a family of four in fresh food from April to

November. Please, choose this tree only if you have a couple of acres or more, and then place it away from the house as an accent plant with other large trees.

Alternatives: See list in this chapter on best conifers.

2. EASTERN WHITE PINE *(Pinus strobus)*

This is another handsome conifer badly misused over the years. It provides quick screening at first. But the lower branches rise with the tree, and you lose that screening effect. You then are stuck with giants growing into each other, linebackers attempting a pas de deux. It will grow to 60 feet or more, with a 25-foot spread. Reserve it as a background plant in large, sweeping landscapes.

Alternatives: Dwarf clones of white pine such as compacta, nana or contorta.

3. FLOWERING DOGWOOD *(Cornus florida)*

Flowering dogwoods always have been rather fussy, requiring rich, deep, acidic soil that is evenly moist and well drained, a site that is protected from the full blast of the summer sun and a watering commitment in droughts. Now that the discula, or dogwood anthracnose, is endemic, the only way we can keep these plants alive in the long term is through a management program that is unrealistic for most people.

Alternatives: Kousa dogwood, Pagoda dogwood, Giant dogwood, Eastern redbud, Little Girl magnolias, Washington Hawthorn, cherry Hally Jolivette or magnolia Centennial or magnolia Galaxy.

4. LEYLAND CYPRESS *(X Cupressocyparis leylandii)*

In the space of 15 years, this tree has gone from being a prized landscape conifer to a ubiquitous screen plant. Nurserymen love it — it grows three feet a year — and homeowners like it for the same reason. After five years, however, you will pay a heavy price. The tree consumes your property. In maturity, it will grow to 60 feet, with a spread of 15 feet. A grouping of three could take up half the backyard. Even if you had the room, it would shade out the lawn, the perennial beds, the rose garden and the flowering ornamental trees and turn your house into a dark abode fit only for Gothic romance. The tree has two cultural problems: Its root system is small compared to its vigorous top growth, and it keels over in storms, particularly when there is heavy snow and ice and the ground is saturated. It also gets a fungal blight that can be devastating, and this may be more prevalent on trees that have been sheared into hedges. The Leyland cypress has had its day in suburbia. Let's move on.

Alternatives: See list of 10 best conifers in this chapter and privacy techniques in Chapter 1.

5. LOMBARDY BLACK POPLAR *(Populus nigra Italica)*

Fast-growing, upright and perhaps recalling the romantic landscapes of France for the first month or two, this tree soon is overtaken by the rigors of the North American ecosystem. It is plagued by ailments, notably a canker disease, and even if it survives you will want to put it out of its misery. It is a dreadful weed.

Alternatives: Possibly the Eastern Cottonwood *(Populus deltoides)*, the upright English oak *(Quercus robur Fastigiata)* and the ginkgo.

6. SIBERIAN ELM *(Ulmus pumila)*

Fast-growing and tolerant of poor soils, the Siberian elm is perhaps the ugliest, messiest, sickliest — in sum, most worthless — plant in the garden. Do not plant it unless you like trees that have no ornament in any season, require constant raking, have running sores and remain close to death but never quite close enough. It should not be confused with the Chinese or lacebark elm *(Ulmus parviflora)*, which is not the most trouble-free shade tree but which has nice lacy foliage and a pleasing, flaking bark in maturity. Check the Latin name before you buy — sometimes the dreaded Siberian elm is sold as the other article.

Alternatives: Anything but *Ulmus pumila.*

7. SILK-TREE OR MIMOSA *(Albizia julibrissin)*

This is a vase-shaped weed growing to 20 feet or more in height and as much across. Some people like it for the tropical effects of its acacia-like leaves and muddy pink flowers, but it really is a tree of little value or virtue. It has no ornament outside its flowering period (if, that is, you admire the blooms). It sets seed with a vengeance, and it is soft-wooded and poorly formed, its branches coming together at a weak point. Fortunately, it is afflicted with a wilt disease that usually is fatal.

Alternatives: Crab apples, cherries or magnolias.

8. SILVER MAPLE *(Acer saccharinum)*

Planted by homebuilders because it is cheap and grows fast, the silver maple is a monster in the confines of suburbia, growing 70 feet high and 50 feet across. The surface roots are invasive, seeking out and choking drain pipes and robbing owners and neighbors of the ability to plant anything in its proximity. The tree is weak-wooded and poses a threat to property in summer storms. It looks all right in the countryside, in a grove at the far end of a swampy field, but not where humans live in any density. Speaking of inferior maples, stay away from Norway maples, even purple leafed-varieties. They are coarse, dense and greedy, although silver maples are worse.

Alternatives: Red maple, sugar maple and trees listed in this chapter as among the 10 best shade trees or conifers.

9. WEEPING WILLOW *(Salix alba)*

For precisely the same reasons as for the silver maple, the weeping willow should not be planted anywhere but in a rural or semi-rural property next to water. Granted, no other plant quite evokes the haunting beauty of the weeping willow, and its lime green flush of leaves in March is one of the earliest and surest signs of spring. But it simply is incompatible with the small to moderate-sized yards that abound in our area.

Alternatives: Weeping cherry, limber pine var. *Pendula* and the crab apple Coral Cascade.

10. WHITE BIRCH *(Betula species)*

This list includes the Paper Birch *(Betula papyrifera)* and the European White Birch *(Betula pendula)*. Ill suited to the rigors of the Mid-Atlantic region, these beautiful northern trees become stressed in our summers and then succumb, slowly and painfully, to the bronze birch borer.

Alternatives: The river birch Heritage is a much-loved replacement, although its peeling bark is apricot rather than bone white.

---

†See Appendix for common pest and disease ailments and remedies.

Section 3

THE PLANT PALETTE

Chapter 15

PERENNIALS

*E*verybody loves gifts that keep on giving. That's why the perennials that grow and flower through the season, die back to their roots each winter and emerge again each spring are so popular. Indeed, they are changing the face of gardening in America. Since the early 1980s, perennials have been central to the shift away from static, formal gardens of foundation shrubs and bedding plants to places of dynamic beauty that evoke nature, even on the city balcony.

While annuals sound their single notes for a season, perennials provide ultimately more satisfying crescendos, peaks and decrescendos and then begin again. They bloom at different times and come in seemingly endless varieties, sizes, habits, flowering forms and colors. The six-inch-high creeping phlox of April is a perennial, as is the seven-foot-high joe-pye weed that blooms in September.

Little wonder that sales of perennials at local nurseries and through mail-order catalogues have burgeoned. Where once the nursery's perennial section consisted of hostas wrapped in tarpaper or peonies in pots, whole areas now are devoted to hundreds of perennials and their newfound herbaceous partners, the ornamental grasses.

Annuals certainly have their place, and many are beautiful, but the recurring costs make them more expensive in the long run, and they usually require more watering, fertilizing, deadheading and staking. Perennials, of course, generally don't flower as long, though some do bloom for weeks or months. But you should keep in mind other traits as well, from leaf ornament and plant form to overall texture and even fall color.

This chapter first explores such perennial favorites as irises, peonies and daylilies, turns to perennials of value in poor, dry soils or especially damp areas, and finally commends 20 best bets for the Washington-area garden. While space does not permit every worthy perennial to be discussed, the nearly 50 included here are proven components of splendid gardens. Such popular perennials as hostas, ferns and other ornamental flowers that thrive in the shade, moreover, can be found in Chapter 22 on shade gardens.

I. Bearded Irises

THE BEAUTIFUL IRIS that blooms in May in the Washington-area garden is the tall bearded variety — tall because its stems rise to 27 inches and higher, bearded because the petals that grow horizontally and then bend down (called falls) have hairy tufts at their base. (The petals that stand upright are the standards.) The tall bearded is the queen of irises — large, showy, ruffled and unmatched in range and color combinations.

Other types of bearded irises grow smaller and flower earlier — dwarfs, which grow to 15 inches, and medians, which grow to 27 inches — and are useful when you want to reduce the planting scale or hasten the flowering season. Some bearded iris varieties re-bloom in September, and watering them during summer droughts encourages optimum repeat performances.

There are so many worthy varieties of bearded irises that listing a few would be of little value. Seeing them would be far more useful. Iris fancier Richard Sparling, of 18016 Lafayette Drive, in Olney, Md., has a labeled display garden of dwarf, median, tall bearded, species and beardless irises that hits its peak from late April to early June. Call first before visiting: (301) 774-4151. In deciding which varieties you might want to grow, look for other qualities beyond color. The plant should be vigorous, with stout, fleshy leaves. The petals should feel thick and waxy. The standards should be upright and no larger than the falls. And, as with daylilies, those with the most buds and low branching will produce more flowers and present them better. Avoid unnamed varieties, except those at iris society sales, which can be counted on to do well locally.

CULTIVATION

BEARDED IRISES ARE not difficult to grow, but they are a little demanding. A bit of light shade in the afternoon is all right, but the irises need at least six hours of full sun. Partial shade is undesirable and full shade out of the question.

The plant grows from a hard rhizome that is closer to a stem than a root (the roots grow under it), so it can't be buried deeply. It should be planted so that after the soil has been watered and settles, the rhizome's top is slightly exposed. You can't lay heavy mulch over bearded irises, which is one reason why they don't mix well with other perennials, and don't allow other plants to engulf the rhizome as the season progresses. The rhizome must be kept dry and airy to prevent rotting.

During the first season and especially the first early spring, diligently weed the iris bed — pull the weeds by hand when they are young — to prevent them from choking the plants. Soak the ground first and wait an hour, and be careful again not to harm the rhizomes.

Once the irises have bloomed, do not cut the leaves into a clipped fan, which northern gardeners do to get more sun on the rhizome. If leaves have turned brown or are diseased, remove the individual blade. Do remove the flower stem after bloom.

The soil must be worked so that it drains freely. Rhizomes planted in wet clay will rot. Set plants 18 inches to 24 inches apart or you will end up having to divide the plant after a season or two.

Once clumps get crowded, flowering diminishes and disease risks increase. The plants should be lifted, divided and replanted every third or fourth year. Dig up the entire clump and separate the new rhizomes. Irises should be divided in July. New rhizomes should be planted by early fall to allow root development before winter. Later planting probably will affect flowering the next year and increase chances of winter rot. Work bone meal into the soil at planting, and feed the iris lightly in early spring, as the fans emerge, and again in early summer, after bloom. Do not use a fertilizer high in nitrogen, and make sure that lawn fertilizer does not scatter or leach into iris beds.

Main Pests: Borers and aphids. **Main Diseases:** Soft rot and leaf spot.†

USES IN GARDEN DESIGNS

BEARDED IRISES ARE one of the few plants that look good lined up like soldiers in a narrow bed. Planting at the base of a masonry retaining or building wall is an ideal way of presenting them and giving the rhizomes the baking they want. The special cultural needs, as noted, make the bearded iris difficult but not impossible to grow in a bed or border with other plants. If you do use them with other plants, make sure that the irises have room to breathe, even if that leaves something of a gap in the bed later in the season.

II. Beardless Irises

WITH THE REVOLUTION in perennials, irises known as beardless varieties — particularly Siberian and Japanese irises — have caught on. Generally, they are easier to grow and to place with other garden plants, though they are not as showy as the tall bearded.

■ **SIBERIAN IRIS** *(Iris siberica).* Siberian irises grow into clumps of finely bladed leaves capped with masses of flowers in late May and into June, blooming with the roses and clematis. The flowers typically are in a range of blue-indigos and violets, though some are whites or bi-colors, and they have beautiful petal markings. Even out of bloom, the plant has great ornamental value: tall, narrow, vertical blades, three feet high, that would be a perfect foil and companion to a range of other plants, including cranesbills, hostas, peonies, shrub roses, larkspur, foxgloves and small to medium shrubs.

Siberian irises are not as good as bearded types as cut flowers and have a narrower color range, but they are far easier to integrate into flower borders and do not need dividing as often. They do ask for a sunny site, or light dappled shade, and prefer soil that's organically enriched so that it's moisture-retentive. They also will take wetter soils. They should be watered regularly in their first season and, once established, during dry spells. A diluted, low-nitrogren feed should be applied in April and again in late May. Divide them in late summer or early fall.

■ **JAPANESE IRIS** *(Iris ensata).* Japanese irises are revered in their native land, and it is easy to see why. The summer flowers are big but delicate, like giant butterflies floating on air. They typically are six inches wide but can be as broad as 10 inches. The netting and veining of the petals on certain varieties is unlike anything else in the flower world.

Japanese irises flower later than Siberians, in June and July, and have easily provided growing needs. They prefer slightly acid, humusy soil and a sunny location and cannot get enough moisture during growing months, from April to October. Indeed, they will flourish in standing water. Aha, you say, just the plant for that boggy area. Well, maybe. The rub is that they cannot abide standing water in winter, when they are dormant. That is a season (along with spring) when high-water tables manifest themselves in our gardens. So pick your site carefully and work in much leaf mold and peat moss. The Japanese iris grows to four feet and 18 inches across and should be lifted and divided every three to four years.

There are also three wild species of iris that are well suited to bogs, the edges of ponds and low-lying wet areas, but they can self-seed prodigiously and become invasive. (It is possible to cut off the seedpods before they ripen and split.) The flag irises are particularly useful for the rural property with a pond. Wild irises bloom in May and into June:

■ **YELLOW FLAG IRIS** *(Iris pseudacorus).* From Europe, this variety reaches three feet or higher. It is a wonderful accent plant for the pond vista, especially a variegated form *(Variegata)* with a yellow stripe along its blade-like leaves (the stripe tends to fade as the season progresses). A variety named *Gigantea* grows to ceiling height.

■ **BLUE FLAG IRIS** *(Iris versicolor).* This is the homegrown version. It is blue with yellow blotches. Some types have more red in the flower: Kermesina (red-purple) and Rosea (pink).

■ **VIRGINIA IRIS** *(Iris virginica).* Another American species, this one is similar to Blue Flag but not as heavily branched and at about its northern range in the Washington area. Alba is a white form, and Giant Blue is (of course) blue with larger flowers.

Pests and Diseases: Slugs can be a problem, but beardless irises otherwise are generally free of ailments.[†]

III. Peonies

THE LARGE SILKY FLOWERS of the peony are one of the stars of the late spring garden. The plant also deserves to be employed as a low hedge or as part of a broader garden composition, but use it with restraint. A single plant can steal the show in a bed by a patio or path, or it can serve as a front-of-the-border accent in a larger bed or border. Peonies come in soft pastel colors, ranging from white to creamy pink to lemon yellows, or in much stronger carmines, magentas and hot pinks. Most popular garden varieties are doubles — dozens of ruffled petals with no discernible center — that are bred to be eye-catching and long-lasting. But there also are poppy-like, single-flowered types with pronounced decorative stamens, such as Japanese and Anemone peonies, as well as an intermediate group of semi-doubles.

The other great garden peony is the tree peony. It is not really a tree but a spreading shrub that grows slowly over decades: One that is six feet or more across is a treasure indeed. Single-flowered varieties are sublime. The blooms are like huge silk confections, six or more inches across, and they bloom earlier than herbaceous peonies, in late April. This is a plant that should be carefully sited as a border specimen and then left to do its thing. Plant in the fall in rich, well-drained soil that is neutral to slightly alkaline. It will perform in light shade. Like dogwoods and blueberries, it shouldn't be neglected in a drought. Top-dress with a low-nitrogen fertilizer in late March and again after flowering. Try not to crowd it with overbearing bulbs or azaleas; the tree peony deserves to be savored in reverent solitude.

The Japanese peony *(Paeonia japonica)* is the most self-effacing of the species — small, white, cup-shaped — but with the remarkable quality of liking shade. Introduced into the United States by Pennsylvanian Barry Yinger, it is a wonderful woodland plant and deserves wider use.

CULTIVATION

THE REGULAR herbaceous garden peony is essentially a northern plant, and it will flower longer and retain its color more if given a little dappled shade in the early afternoon. However, it is not a plant for the shade garden and will take full sun if that is what is available. Do not plant in the shadow of young trees that will grow bigger and shadier. Rather, find a spot where shade conditions are not likely to change materially.

Peonies are best planted in the fall. Since peonies are heavy feeders and long-lived, the planting hole must be well excavated and backfilled with enriched humus thoroughly mixed with bone meal and a cup or two of pulverized limestone. You will see tiny buds at the union of the old stems and the crown of the plant. The roots should be planted so the buds are under soil, but by no more than two inches. Any deeper and flowering will be harmed.

Double-flowered peonies are so heavy after spring rains that they are guaranteed to flop over. Singles aren't quite as prone to flopping, but chances are high that they will do so anyway. Staking after stems have fallen is never as successful as staking beforehand. Peony stems are best staked individually. In April, use discreet green wire stakes with top hoops that can be positioned under the flower bud as it develops. Don't spear the roots.

Peonies resent disturbances. They should be lifted and divided only if they were planted too low or are in too much shade and their flowering has suffered.

Main Pest: No serious pests. Ants drawn to bud secretions do no harm. **Main Disease:** Botrytis.[†]

IV. Daylilies

LONG BEFORE other perennials became wildly popular, the daylily could be found in the hearts and gardens of Americans. Although the species originated in Asia, it is easy to understand why its garden varieties have been adopted with singular enthusiasm here. The plant grows famously from Louisiana to Maine, shrugs off pests and disease and lends itself to easy hybridizing. Indeed, nearly 40,000 new varieties have been registered in the past 60 years, and countless others have been created and discarded by home breeders. Despite this, there still are no true white or blue daylilies, but there are dozens of superior varieties of almost every size, shape, habit and flowering period.

The daylily bears a close resemblance to the true lily, but it is an entirely different plant. (Lilies are known botanically as *Lilium*, daylilies as *Hemerocallis*). Lilies keep their individual blooms for a week or more, while daylily flowers live for less than a day. But there are so many of them — 20, 30 or even 40 per stem — that the overall flowering period typically is four to five weeks per plant. Some bloom at night, depending on their bloodlines, but the vast majority crack open overnight, are fully open by first light, and last until the late afternoon or early evening.

Colors range from pastels to primary yellows, reds and oranges as well as apricots, lavenders, melons, maroons, greens, pinks, deep crimsons, and pinks and yellows just this side of white. Many are blends with two, three or four hues per blossom. A gardener with a good eye will look to all the colors in selecting companion plants for daylilies.

There are three basic types of daylily, classified by whether they keep their leaves in winter: Dormant, semi-evergreen, and evergreen. Dormant types, which are deciduous and thus reliably winter-hardy here, should be the sort selected first by the novice gardener. Semi-evergreens will survive most winters with protection. Evergreens might be all right in the sheltered Georgetown garden, but in Leesburg, Va., you would be taking your chances.

The daylily began as a trumpet-shaped flower but has since been bred to take on a number of other forms as well. Triangle, Recurve, Circular and Flared tend to have broad, overlapping petals that bend back sharply. Spider, Orchid and Pinwheel are among the forms with narrower petals. Daylilies also are classified by the markings of the flowers.

Beginners should steer clear of expensive novelty plants: All the beauty of the daylily is captured in old favorites at down-to-earth prices. The National Capital Daylily Club has developed a list of 61 recommended varieties for the beginner (sizes are for the height of the flower-bearing stalk, called a scape, that rises above the foliage). Following are two dozen of them:

YELLOW
Suzie Wong (24 inches, early mid-season)
Stella De Oro (18 inches, early, repeat bloomer)
Frozen Jade (28 inches, mid-season, night bloomer, fragrant)
Mary Todd (26 inches, early, semi-evergreen)
Buttered Popcorn (32 inches, mid-season, fragrant)

CREAM TO WHITE
So Lovely (30 inches, mid-season, semi-evergreen)

PINK TO PEACH
Lake Norman Sunset (26 inches, mid-season, repeat, fragrant)
Persian Market (32 inches, mid-season, repeat, evergreen, fragrant)
Peach Fairy (26 inches, mid-season)
Ruffled Apricot (28 inches, early mid-season, fragrant)
Serenity Morgan (22 inches, early mid-season, repeat, semi-evergreen, fragrant)
Tender Love (22 inches, late)

PURPLE TO LAVENDER
Hamlet (18 inches, early mid-season, fragrant)
Metaphor (22 inches, early mid-season, fragrant)
Glorious Temptation (28 inches, mid-season)
Chicago Knobby (22 inches, early mid-season, semi-evergreen)

ORANGE
Jim Cooper (30 inches, early mid-season, repeat)
Jersey Spider (48 inches, late season, repeat till frost)

RED
Lord Camden (18 inches, mid-season)
Ed Murray (30 inches, mid-season)
Pardon Me (18 inches, mid-season, repeat)
Oriental Ruby (34 inches, late, repeat)
Apple Tart (28 inches, early mid-season, repeat, night bloomer)
Christmas Is (26 inches, early mid-season, repeat)

SELECTING DAYLILIES

THE SMARTEST WAY to pick daylilies is to view them in bloom, particularly in the company of experts. Our region has a number of daylily display gardens, including the National Arboretum, River Farm and Meadowlark Gardens (see list of public gardens in Appendix). In addition, the National Capital Daylily Club and the Northern Virginia Daylily Society organize tours of daylily gardens during high season in early July. In judging a daylily, consider the following in addition to flower colors and forms you like:

- **NUMBER OF BUDS PER SCAPE.** You will want at least 20 to assure an extended season.

- **LOW BRANCHING.** Scapes should be branched so that flowers are well presented, not crowded.

- **PETAL SUBSTANCE.** Petals should be thick and waxy, the better to withstand afternoon heat and humidity. Varieties with thin petals, like the tawny lily, turn to black mush under the July sun.

- **PROPORTION.** The flowers' size and height should be in proportion to the plant's overall stature.

- **FOLIAGE.** The leaves, an important ornamental characteristic, should look glossy and handsome.

- **COMPANIONS.** Daylilies deserve to grow with other beauties, so note the plant associations you like.

CULTIVATION

DAYLILIES HAVE a reputation for being easy to grow, and they are. They withstand a little flood and a lot of drought, have few pests and diseases worth worrying about and perform despite neglect. However, they truly will flourish if you take the trouble to follow a few basic steps.

The biggest single need is for water, especially during the critical growing period. A good soaking once or twice a week as the buds develop in June will ensure many blooms. A continued schedule of watering into July and August will prolong the blooming period and encourage re-blooming plants to set new buds. Watering is more important than feeding the plants. As with most plants, daylilies respond to good soil. Light, humusy earth that is mulched also will retain the moisture they crave, reducing your watering burdens.

For each plant prepare a hole 12 inches across and six inches deep, mixing the dirt with generous amounts of dried, rotted cow manure, peat moss, bone meal and, if the soil is particularly heavy, some builder's sand. Make sure that the entire clump of tubers is spread out, gently, and buried, remembering that the soil will settle a couple of inches after watering. Allow three feet between daylilies. If you plant too closely, you will make work for yourself in a season or two when they will have to be lifted and replanted. Bare-rooted daylilies purchased in the spring should be planted by the end of April. You will not get decent blooming until the following year.

Every four years or so, when you notice crowding and reduced flower show, you should dig up your daylilies, cut the foliage back to six inches from the crowns and pull or cut apart the clumps, guided by the leaf clusters, or fans. This dividing should occur in late summer, after blooming. You can then replant divisions in the same location, find other spots for the remainder, or give them to friends and relatives. The bare tubers should be replanted within a day or two, and they should not be allowed to dry out. Soak them overnight in a weak solution of Miracle-Gro. Try not to divide later than early October. The new tubers need a period of root development in the fall to avoid winter rot. Late-blooming varieties should be divided in early spring.

PERENNIALS FOR THE DRY GARDEN

INEVITABLY, THERE are garden areas that have poor, dry soil, that are in full sun in July and August and that will not be pampered. Yet these beds need not be eyesores. There are generally pest-free and disease-free perennials that will take the abuse and, planted with similarly ironclad ground covers and ornamental grasses, can still produce a landscape of interest and beauty. They may need watering, however, to get established over their first season. Look for the following:

- **GOLDENROD** *(Solidago)*. Goldenrod grows to one to five feet (depending on variety), producing yellow flowers in later summer. Some consider this a weed, but there are lovely cultivars to choose from. It often is confused, inexplicably, with ragweed.
- **SEDUM** *(Sedum)* Another late-summer bloomer, the fleshy sedum looks great massed in the company of creeping junipers, St. John's-Wort and dwarf grasses and in front of and between shrubs. Look for Autumn Joy, Ruby Glow and Brilliant.
- **YARROW** *(Achillea)*. Yarrow is a little like Queen Anne's lace but with tighter, yellow flower heads and ferny foliage. As beautiful as it is tough, yarrow, which flowers for several weeks in early summer, deserves to be planted en masse. Varieties to look for: Coronation Gold, Gold Plate and Hope (Hoffnung).
- **RUDBECKIA**. Related to the black-eyed Susan (which is short-lived), rudbeckia's best variety is Goldsturm. Though used a lot, it is a wonderful, tough, long-blooming summer flower.

- **PURPLE CONEFLOWER** *(Echinacea purpurea)*. This falls in the same category as rudbeckia. It may be a little trite, but it is marvelous for those difficult summer beds.
- **GAURA LINDHEIMERI**. This is an underused native plant that is great for hot, dry spots. It sends up weeks of flower spikes with attractive, small white blooms.
- **FALSE INDIGO** *(Baptisia australis)*. False indigo grows like a shrub, with pretty blue-green leaves and dark, indigo flowers clustered along showy spikes.
- **PLUME POPPY** *(Macleaya cordata)*. This is an upright, back-of-the-border, summer bloomer.
- **PENSTEMON BARBATUS**. A useful if short-lived native plant, this species is noted for attracting hummingbirds. Look for an award-winning variety named Husker's Red.
- **ROSE SUNDROP** *(Oenothera speciosa)*. Pink-flowering and low-growing, *oenothera* can do too well, becoming invasive. It is useful as a fill-in plant in hot corners or on embankments.

FULL-SUN PERENNIALS FOR DAMP PLACES

- **ROSE MALLOW** *(Hibiscus moscheutos)*. A large, showy hibiscus, this variety emerges in mid-to-late summer — with flowers the size of dinner plates.
- **GOOSENECK LOOSESTRIFE** *(Lysimachia clethroides)*. This forms attractive clumps, about three feet high, with long-blooming white inflorescences in mid-summer. It can be invasive.
- **MINTS** *(Mentha)*. There are many mints from which to select. Popular varieties include spearmint *(mentha spicata)*, peppermint *(M. x piperita)* and pineapple mint *(M. suaveolens variegata)*.
- **JOE-PYE WEED.** *(Eupatorium purpureum)*. Fabulous for the naturalistic garden, it is noted for drawing butterflies. It grows tall and flowers in late summer. Look for named cultivars.
- **DEER GRASS** *(Rhexia virginica)*. A swampland plant, deer grass grows on upright stems to 18 inches and blooms in late summer. The flowers are rose pink.
- **TURTLEHEAD** *(Chelone obliqua)*. The native turtlehead, a late-season, pink-flowering perennial, benefits from some shade in the afternoon.

- **CARDINAL FLOWER** *(Lobelia cardinalis)*. Growing four feet high and capped with nodding bell flowers in rich scarlet hues, the cardinal flower is another useful native plant for attracting wildlife, particularly hummingbirds.
- **NEW YORK IRONWEED** *(Vernonia noveborancensis)*. A willing native for low-lying meadows, this plant flowers in late summer on five-foot stems. It makes a good companion to other natives and is not for formal gardens.
- **CUTLEAF CONEFLOWER** *(Rudbeckia laciniata)*. This is another late-flowering native plant suited to natural plantings. It is tall — growing to six feet or higher. Another species, *R. nitida*, is a good substitute. Look for Goldquelle.
- **KNOTWEED.** *(Polygonum)*. Two knotweed species are planted by connoisseurs afflicted with damp soil, Firetail *(Polygonum amplexicaule)* and Superbum *(P. bistorta)*. Both will take partial shade, too. They are distinguished by their showy, bottlebrush flowers borne on long stems above leathery foliage. Superbum flowers in early summer, Firetail in late summer.

20 BEST BETS FOR WASHINGTON GARDENS

The following perennials were picked for their ease of care, pest resistance, long flowering period and beauty:

1. ALUMROOT *(Heuchera x brizoides)*
Height: 18-30 inches. Spacing: 18 inches.
Color: Pink, red, white. Full sun or partial shade.
Sometimes called coral bells after a popular red-flowering species *(Heucher sanguinea)*, alumroots today are offered as a series of hybrids grown for both their clusters of delicate flowers, borne on long stalks, and their attractive leaves. One variety, Palace Purple, is valued for its maple-like foliage. Alumroots require enriched but well-drained soil and prefer a little shelter from the afternoon sun.

2. BARRENWORTS, BISHOP'S HATS OR EPIMEDIUM *(Epimedium)*
Height: 9 to 18 inches.
Spacing: 12 to 18 inches.
Color: Yellows and whites.
Full or partial shade.
This wonderful plant flowers in spring but is grown chiefly for its foliage, shaped like a bishop's miter and fresh and dainty all year. It is one of the few plants that do well in dry shade. Look for a hybrid called rubrum whose lime-green leaves are tinged rose-red.

3. BEEBALM, OR WILD BERGAMOT *(Monarda)*
Height: 3 feet. Spacing: 18 to 24 inches.
Color: Reds, violets, lavenders, pinks.
Full sun or partial shade
Beebalm, grown for its summer stands of crimson red flowers *(Monarda didyma)*, is renowned for attracting butterflies and hummingbirds. Another native species, *Monarda fistulosa,* has gray-green leaves and subdued purple flowers. Both are somewhat wild-looking perennials that, though not for specimen use, are great stalwarts of summer gardens. They prefer moist soil but will grow contently in dry soil, especially if shielded from afternoon sun. Look for a mildew-resistant dwarf variety named Petite Delight.

4. BUGLEWEED *(Ajuga reptans)*
Height: 6 inches. Spacing: 12 inches.
Color: Electric blue. Sun or shade.
This low-growing foliage variety is valuable as a fill-in plant in difficult sites, including under trees. It produces its breathtaking flower spikes in early spring.

5. CARYOPTERIS, OR BLUEBEARD *(Caryopteris x cladonensis)*
Height: 24 inches. Spacing: 36 inches
Color: Blue to Indigo. Full sun.
This shrubby herb, treated as a herbaceous perennial (i.e., cut back in winter), is an extremely useful late-summer plant, grown as much for its silver leaves and mounded form as for its attractive and somewhat showy flower clusters. Valuable as a border specimen or for massing, it prefers well-drained soil.

6. CATMINT *(Nepeta spp.)*
Height: 1-3 feet, based on variety.
Spacing: 1-3 feet. Color: Blue. Full sun.
Reminiscent of lavender, gray-leafed catmints are great foils for other plants and for grouping. They bloom for weeks on end starting in June. Blue Wonder is a compact variety suited for smaller spaces. Six Hills Giant is the largest variety and best suited to Washington's humid summers.

7. CRANESBILL *(Geranium)*
Height: 12-24 inches. Spacing: 18-24 inches.
Color: Magenta, pink, blue, violet, white.
Full sun or partial shade.
Cranesbills, or hardy geraniums, form lovely mounds of cutleaf foliage. Most bloom from mid-to-late spring and early summer, though some flower in late summer. Popular varieties include Johnson's Blue (violet blue), Ingwersen's Variety (pale pink), Claridge Druce (rose pink) and *Geranium sanguineum striatum* (light pink).

8. DAYLILIES *(Hemerocallis)*
Height: 18 to 36 inches.
Spacing: 24-36 inches
Color: Virtually all except pure white and blue.
See daylilies section in this chapter.

9. HELLEBORE *(Helleborus)*
Height: 12-24 inches. Spacing: 24 inches.
Color: White, maroon, chartreuse.
Partial to full shade.

Many types are available, with varieties of three species most commonly planted: the lenten rose *(Helleborus orientalis)*, the Christmas rose *(Helleborus niger)* and the misnamed stinking hellebore *(Helleborus foetidus)*. Varieties are likely to increase as these plants become more popular. With handsome evergreen leaves, they are valued for their off-season, mid-to-late winter flowers — large, nodding bells often in bloom in the snow. These are good hosta substitutes. They prefer a well-drained, loamy soil that's not too acidic. Water during dry spells.

10. JAPANESE ANEMONE
(Anemone x hybrida)
Height: 2-3 feet. Spacing: 2 feet.
Color: Whites and pinks with yellow centers.
Partial shade.

The maple-like leaves grow throughout the season. Beautiful blooms then emerge from late summer to early fall, with the September flowering making it indispensable. Popular varieties: Honorine Jobert (white), September Charm (pink) and Alba (white). Related species: *Anemone tomentosa* (August flowering) and *Anemone vitifolia*, whose leaves resemble those of the grape.

11. ORANGE CONEFLOWER
(Rudbeckia fulgida)
Height: 2 feet. Spacing: 18 inches.
Color: Golden yellow. Full sun.

Large, bright daisies with black centers, these are superior cousins to the wild-growing black-eyed Susan. The favored variety is Goldsturm. This is an extremely valuable plant, flowering in August and September when garden color is sparse.

12. PINKS *(Dianthus)*
Height: 12-18 inches. Spacing: 12-18 inches.
Color: White, shades of pink, crimson,
magenta, often marked with "eye."
Full sun or partial shade.

There are dozens of ancient (and modern) varieties of garden pinks, all valued for their fragrant and colorful late-spring blooms, easy to place with other perennials. Out of bloom, they also are highly ornamental as evergreen buns or mats of leaves in a range

of colors, including blue-green and silver. They generally are free of pests but must be planted in free-draining soil to avoid crown rots.

13. PURPLE CONEFLOWER
(Echinacea purpurea)
Height: 3-4 feet. Spacing: 2 feet.
Color: Rose-lavender. Full sun.

These are huge, daisy-like flowers that bloom in early to mid-summer, with petals radiating from a bronze-orange disc. They are showy, carefree and happy in the narrowest of beds, but they are not for damp soil. Look for a new, award-winning variety named Magnus.

14. RUSSIAN SAGE *(Perovskia atriplicifolia)*
Height: 3 to 5 feet. Spacing: 24 inches
Color: Lavender-blue.

This is a popular and delightful perennial prized for its feathery silver foliage, haze of blue flowers and ease of care. The top growth should be cut back hard in winter. It is a great companion to grasses, rudbeckias, daylilies and almost anything else that likes the heat. Be sure to give the plant some room; it always grows larger than you think.

15. SAGE *(Salvia)*

This is an extremely diverse and useful group that includes the sage used in cooking *(Salvia officinalis)* and the Victoria sage that brings spring freshness and color all summer and into fall. Sages generally prefer full sun (a little shade is okay) and well-drained soil that isn't overly rich.

■ SALVIA X SUPERBA
Height: 2-3 feet. Spacing: 2 feet.
Color: Violet blue or purple, by variety.

This plant's attractive flower-spikes bloom for several weeks in June and July, making it a wonderful companion to landscape roses, early daylilies, achilleas and cranesbills. Superior varieties: East Friesland (Ostfriesland), May Night (Mainacht) and, for smaller effect, Blue Queen.

■ MEALY CUP SAGE *(Salvia farinacea)*
Height: 18 inches-3 feet.
Spacing: 18 inches. Color: Blue

While this tender perennial is not hardy in the Washington garden, it is worth growing for its long blooming period. Once established, it re-seeds freely. It is handsome en masse on a sunny hillside or as a single plant with trailing ivy in a container. Victoria and Blue Bedder are worthy picks.

■ SALVIA ARGENTEA
Height: 2-3 feet.
Spacing: 24 inches. Color: White
Short-lived but extremely showy and unique, this sage has large, soft leaves low to the ground and is covered in silver hairs that give it a sheen. The blooms should be removed as they emerge to keep the leaf ornament. This variety is a great foil for other sun-loving plants.

■ SALVIA GAURANITICA
Height: 3 to 5 feet.
Spacing: 24 inches. Color: Indigo
A terrific late-season bloomer, tall salvia is useful in the mixed border. It goes well with asters and chrysanthemums. It is not hardy here and should be grown as an annual, and it needs staking.

16. SIBERIAN BUGLOSS
(Brunnera macrophylla)
Height: 18 inches. Spacing: 24 inches.
Color: Blue. Full or partial shade.
The bugloss produces its airy blue flowers in spring, and then its heart-shaped leaves grow into showy clumps. This is a valuable plant for small beds or as a ground cover on a larger scale. It self-seeds and spreads when contented (i.e., in moist, rich soil).

17. SIBERIAN IRIS *(Iris siberica)*
Height: 24 to 36 inches. Spacing: 24 inches
Colors: Blue, white, violet, mauve, purple.
This delightful plant is useful for damp spots and as an accent in border plantings. Its late May/early June flowers are exquisite, but its sword-like foliage is of interest all season (see iris section).

18. SPEEDWELL *(Veronica)*
Height: 1 to 6 feet, by variety.
Spacing: 12 to 18 inches.
Color: Blues, pinks, whites, violets.
Full sun or partial shade.
This is a valuable, long-flowering summer perennial. Smaller and dwarf varieties are useful as vertical accents in mixed borders, while taller types — *Veronica longiflora* and the native Bowman's Root *(Veronica virginicum)* — do best in the back of the border. Speedwell prefers ordinary, well-drained soil that is neither too poor and dry nor too rich and wet.

19. SWEET WOODRUFF *(Galium odoratum)*
Height: 6 to 12 inches. Spacing: 12 inches.
Color: White, but grown chiefly for foliage.
Partial to full shade.
This ground cover is an attractive alternative to the ubiquitous English ivy and pachysandra. The plant prefers rich soil and should be watered in dry spells.

20. TICKSEED, OR COREOPSIS *(Coreopsis)*
Height: 18 inches-2 feet. Spacing: 18 inches.
Color: Pale yellows, golden yellows and rose.
Full sun to partial shade.
There are two types of this early summer-to-fall bloomer: tall, larger-flowered *C. grandiflora*, useful for perennial beds or wildflower meadows, and low-growing, mounding threadleafs *(C. verticillata)*, great as fill-ins around larger perennials and small shrubs. Moonbeam (pale yellow) is the best known. Zagreb (a stronger yellow) is lower growing. *C. rosea* is similarly low-growing but pink with yellow-green centers. It tolerates wetter soils.

DIVIDE AND CONQUER

MOST PERENNIALS will need dividing, in some cases after just two years (as with certain daisies) but usually in their fourth or fifth season (as with daylilies and coreopsis). Digging up a mature clump of perennials, separating it into segments with new stems and roots and discarding the old core is an effective way to keep plants vigorous, free-flowering and disease-free. Since one old plant can generate four or five new plants, it is also an inexpensive and rewarding method of expanding your plant stock and sharing the surplus with others.

You will know when a perennial needs dividing by its crowded look and the diminishing number and size of its flowers. Generally, early fall is the best time to divide, after the season's growth and before the winter halts root development of young divisions. Remember not to try dividing a plant while it is still in the ground.

Different plants have different structures. Some have roots leading to stems, others rhizomes or tubers between the stems and the roots proper. Whichever kind you are working with, look for the little nubs, or "eyes," near the crown that will become the new stems of the following spring, and dissect the plant so that one or more nub is left intact on each division.

Some clumps are best separated gingerly by hand, while others need encouragement with a sharp penknife. Some perennials have thick, fibrous roots and require much effort to split them up. Many books advise you do this with two gardening forks placed back to back. But most people do not have two gardening forks. Split them instead with a hatchet or cleaver, being careful to keep stems (and fingers) intact.

Know where you are going to put your new babies before delivery, and be prepared to plant them and give them a good soaking within a few hours. If you can't plant them for a day, soak them overnight (but no longer) in a bucket of water with a solution of Miracle-Gro or its equivalent diluted to half strength.

STAKING

IF PERENNIALS need staking, consider whether they are worth growing. There are many superior perennials that don't require staking. Some are worth the effort, notably peonies, asters, garden phlox and *salvia guaranitica*. Often, like asters, the plant simply needs twine tied around its outer stems to keep the stalks from slumping to the ground. Tall, skinny plants such as oriental poppies may need tying to a bamboo cane, driven a foot into the ground. Yet others, like peonies, will prefer a cage of wire or twine to grow up into.

If you decide that a plant needs staking, the best time to do it is before the stems are beaten down by wind and rain or, better yet, just as the plant begins its spring growth. A perennial that is staked after it has grown leggy and become battered never looks as natural or attractive as one staked preventively. Typically, a perennial that grows to three feet or higher may need staking.

To avoid plants becoming leggy, place them in sufficient sunlight and deadhead the first flush of blossoms once they finish flowering.

---

†See Appendix for common pest and disease ailments and remedies.

Chapter 16

ANNUALS

*A*NNUALS ARE powerful temptations, sort of the gardening equivalent of romantic flings. Many are beautiful and fun, easy flowers that bloom for months, and they can quickly consume time and money. They should be used as flings, as splashes of color and form here and there, not as the mainstays of the garden. Indeed, a landscape composed principally of annuals would not be so much a garden as an ultimately unsatisfying series of fleeting flower beds, one swath of plants this season, another the next and mostly barrenness in winter.

You shouldn't buy annuals on impulse (yes, easier said than done). Instead, map out plants you want and how you will use them before the season starts. Traditionally, annuals have been employed as separate bedding and edging plants, but there is no reason why you cannot mix them with perennials, grasses, ground covers or shrubs. Reserve pockets for annuals in borders and beds, and tuck them into places where bulbs or other spring plants have come and gone.

Think of annuals in other ways as well. They are wonderful in containers on patios and decks and in hanging baskets. Annual vines, which grow quickly, make flamboyant and shady covers for arbors and arches. Some annuals, like zinnias or tender salvias, are perfect additions to gardens designed to draw butterflies, hummingbirds and other wondrous creatures. Others, like sunflowers, are ideal for children, who can watch a single seed grow into an adorable giant.

So use annuals freely as highlights, especially for mid-to-late summer, but not to fill a void in your imagination for a year-round garden.

If you want to avoid the extra time and expense of annuals, you can substitute similar perennials in a number of cases. Rather than buying and planting black-eyed Susans every year, for example, you can use rudbeckia Goldsturm, a related perennial. Instead of the annual Margeurite daisy you can pick the similar and perennial shasta daisy. (For alternatives to annuals in general, refer to chapters on perennials, ornamental grasses, herbs, shade gardens, hillside and rock gardens and natural gardens.)

Technically, some plants are misidentified as annuals. In a tropical climate or a greenhouse, the geranium is a perennial, the lantana a shrub. Caladiums are tropical bulbs, and the moonflower is a tender perennial vine. A true annual grows from seed, flowers, sets seed and dies all in one season, no matter its hardiness. This distinction is important only if you want to lift tender and tropical plants in October to winter over. Candidates include cannas, dahlias, mandevilla, elephant's ear, lantana and caladiums. With true annuals, you can collect seed to sow the next spring, though many hybrids are genetically unstable and may not be the same plant you had the year before.

NOTABLE VARIETIES

THERE ARE MANY annuals from which to choose, but these are some you might especially want to consider for our area:

■ **SUNFLOWERS** *(Helianthus)*. Sunflowers come in an array of sizes, flower forms and colors. Smaller varieties, which grow to about four feet, are much easier to place with other plants. Taller ones make great screens in sunny corners of large lots.

- **SPIDER LILY** *(Cleome)*. This is a wondrous and bizarre-looking plant — tall, feathery and well suited to filling gaps in mixed borders from mid-summer to frost. It comes in lilacs, whites and pinks.

- **COSMOS.** In rich hues of magentas and purples and pastel pink, rose and white, the cosmos bloom's beauty is enhanced by its lacy green foliage.

- **PANSIES.** Pansies are available in an extraordinary range of colors, and an inventive gardener can create breathtaking combinations. Most people plant them in early March; the heat effectively ruins them by June, when they should be pulled. Alternatively, this is one annual that can be planted in October and enjoyed through the winter. In cold and snowy winters, they will look flattened and beaten back, but in early spring they will bounce back and make a robust display.

- **GERANIUM** *(Pelargonium)*. Look for varieties whose leaf markings and variegations are as ornamental (well, nearly) as the flowers. The flower colors range from strong reds and pinks to softer hues, including white.

- **MARIGOLDS** *(Tagetes)*. Ungainly and strongly colored, the marigold is useful for sustaining ornament through the dog days of summer. French marigolds are more attractive to my mind than the taller and double-flowered African varieties. A striped, red-and-yellow variety of French marigold named Pinwheel is worth seeking out. A carefully chosen marigold, massed, looks good at the feet of orange-flowering cannas.

- **HOLLYHOCKS** *(Alcea rosea)*. Plant seedlings or grow your own from seed started indoors in mid-February. Hollyhocks are the quintessential spiky cottage flower, though they are more sickly in our area than in cooler climates. Taller types should be staked when first planted.

- **ZINNIAS.** Like marigolds, some zinnias are fairer than others, though they all tend to be garish and challenging to use well with other plants. The main problem is powdery mildew, which turns the leaves an unsightly gray. Plant zinnias in full sun, don't water the leaves, and try a homemade solution of baking soda and water or an organic fungicide to control the disease. My favorite variety is *Zinnia angustifolia,* which has lacy leaves and tiny, marigold-type flowers floating above them. It is a great summer border plant.

ANNUALS FOR SHADE. Many people seem to believe that the only annual for shade is impatiens. This is a wonderful plant for difficult, shadowy sites, but so are others. Consider these: flowering tobacco, geranium, nasturtium, forget-me-nots, petunias, Johnny-jump-ups, coleus, foxgloves, elephant's ear and caladium.

ANNUALS FOR CONTAINERS. A number of annuals work well in containers. They include geranium, petunias, pansies, nasturtiums, alyssum, verbenas, lantanas, purple pennisetum grass, nierembergia, ornamental peppers and portulaca.

ANNUAL VINES. Most annual vines are prolific and need a secure support. Some, such as the scarlet runner bean and purple hyacinth bean, become truly massive and must be well anchored to a sturdy structure. Look for moonflower, whose white trumpets open at night, the several species and varieties of morning glories, and cardinal climber, which lures hummingbirds.

MONSTERS. Several annuals grow into gorgeous monsters. In addition to the popular sunflowers and cannas, you might want to try elephant's ear *(Colocasia antiquorum),* the cardoon *(Cynara cardunculus)* and the castor bean *(Ricinus communis),* which has huge palmate leaves and fuzzy, red seed husks. (The seeds, though, are poisonous, so be careful not to let anybody ingest them).

CULTIVATION

AS A RULE, annuals increase the maintenance pitch of the garden. Their three basic needs are watering, fertilizing and deadheading of spent flowers to promote repeat blooming. Of the three, watering is the most important. Annuals are shallow-rooted and don't need as much tilth as perennials, but giving them deep soil will reduce watering demands. You also should mulch, though not too thickly (so you don't provide too much of a slug habitat).

Deadheading demands differ by plant. Impatiens keep coming without removal of spent flowers, but marigolds, geraniums, zinnias, petunias and pansies all respond markedly to deadheading.

Annuals need a little fertilizer to perform their best, but don't go overboard. Work bone meal or a slow-release granular fertilizer formulated for annuals into the bed before planting. Once the plants are established, use a soluble fertilizer at recommended or diluted rates. Annuals prefer fertilizers high in phosphate but low in nitrogen. If your annuals are close to shrubs and trees, don't inadvertently fertilize those woody plants, especially after August. If you cannot keep the annual fertilizers from the other plants, use slow-release fertilizer stakes for the annuals.

SEEDS OR SEEDLINGS? The idea of starting your own annuals from seed has great appeal. You save lots of money, produce large quantities of plants, and earn a thrill from your green-thumbed virtuosity. In practice, however, the effort can be fraught with frustration, and it is easier and possibly cheaper to buy seedlings.

The two most compelling reasons to start seeds indoors are (1) to get varieties not offered locally at retail outlets and (2) to provide a jump-start so that the annuals flower in time for summer. Most gardeners, however, will find the varieties they want at local garden centers, regional retail nurseries and weekend farmers' markets. In addition, most annuals don't need to be started indoors in the Washington area, given our region's generous outdoor growing season of five to six months or more between spring and fall frosts.

Seeds begun indoors require the right equipment, including proper growing lights, and fastidious care, from repotting to hardening off of plants. This is not hard and can be fun if you want to make a hobby of it, but for those wishing simply to get their hands on annuals, it is easier to let others worry about these chores.

That said, it is important to buy seedlings wisely. Shop early in the season (not too early for tender annuals), in May and June, before young plants become pot-bound and stressed. Look for short, bushy and healthy looking seedlings with plenty of unopened buds. Buy the smallest plants you can, in six-packs or flats. There is no point in paying through the nose for a mature annual. You will achieve the same plant in your own garden in a matter of weeks.

Some annuals can be sown directly into the garden. Cosmos and sunflowers are good examples. But the soil must be warm (at least 70 degrees) and prepared well first, and you must mist the area once or twice a day until the seeds germinate and the plants are established. You will still have to thin seedlings and keep weeds at bay.

Pests and Diseases: Aphids, mites, caterpillars, wilts and blights affect annuals. But since most annuals love to be pruned, you can simply remove affected flowers and foliage without doing harm.

Chapter 17

BULBS

*T*HERE IS ONLY one thing more uplifting than spying a clump of daffodils under the gray skies of March: the anticipation of such a sight in the grayer months of January and February.

The glorious and dependable early bulbs — snowdrops, winter aconite, the first daffodils, glory-of-the-snow, crocuses — herald the start of another gardening year. Waves of other spring bulbs follow until the deliciously gaudy parrot tulips tell us that spring is winding up and that the scent of roses soon will be in the air. Some summer bulbs, particularly lilies, are full of the heady romance of years past, while others, such as summer-flowering alliums, open our minds to new possibilities. In the autumn, fall-flowering crocuses and colchicums are poignant reminders of the quiet beauty of the late-season garden and the need to prepare for another spring.

Bulbs are particularly useful for the beginner, because they are virtually foolproof. As the gardener becomes more confident in knowing and growing them, they can be used to stunning effect with other plants or by themselves.

Our love affair with bulbs can only intensify in years to come. As enlightened gardeners move away from one-season, spring-flowering shrubs and trees in search of a four-season garden, the spring show will, by definition, diminish. Spring bulbs will fill that gap more than ever.

I. Daffodils

IF THE GARDENER were restricted to five plants (not five bulbs), daffodils would have to be on the list. They are cheery, nostalgic, virtually free of disease and pests, inexpensive, perennial, diverse, great as cut flowers, successful for beginners, endlessly engaging for the experienced — the perfect plant.

There is needless confusion about the name of these plants. Some call them daffodils, others jonquils, yet others narcissus. Jonquil is a traditional Southern term for daffodils simply because the daffodil species that grew well and naturalized in the South's heat was the jonquil, known botanically as *Narcissus jonquilla*. Jonquils remain great daffodils, with lots of small, fragrant flowers and the virtue of enjoying the Washington summer, but they make up just one of 12 official daffodil classes, or divisions. *Narcissus* is the Latin name and useful for identifying species of wild daffodils and their hybrids. Unless you crave taxonomic precision (and who doesn't?), use the word daffodil.

Daffodils are a metaphor for gardening: What at first seems a rather simple deal turns into an endless journey down numerous fascinating paths. The yellow King Alfred trumpets lead to the large-cupped Ice Follies, which lead to the red-rimmed, bone-white poet daffodils, which lead to the nodding triandrus and so on. The flowers have many uses over many weeks, beginning with the Early Sensation in late February and lasting into May with the poets. Miniatures and smaller types can be employed in rock gardens and small beds or in nooks and crannies of great trees. Novelty daffodils can be exalted as princes, while mixes of naturalizing daffodils are the yeoman stock, dancing through meadows and woods and riverbanks in some timeless vernal rite.

The Washington gardener is blessed with a complete array of daffodils: We can grow the northern types epitomized by the trumpet daffodils as well as the warm-climate daffodils such as jonquils and tazettas.

VARIETIES AND USES

IT IS NOT CRITICAL to know a great deal about the plant to grow daffodils or any other bulb. Plant bulbs in the fall, don't worry about them, and they will delight you sometime in the spring. The following advice, however, is aimed at getting the most out of the plant. Anyone with a remote interest in daffodils would do well to attend the Washington Daffodil Society's annual show in April, when each variety is clearly presented and experts can answer questions. You will find many new and expensive cultivars on display — there is an active international trade among top breeders — but it is not necessary to acquire these novelties to have fine daffodils. Many inexpensive, tried-and-true daffodils will satisfy the most discerning gardener, although exposure to the novelties has been known to induce a mania in many fanciers.

The daffodil world divides the bulbs into 12 classes:

- **TRUMPET DAFFODILS.** These are the robust early-to-mid-season daffs that everyone knows, distinguished by their long cup. The most recognized is King Alfred, which actually is likely to be a substituted cultivar named Dutch Master. It is yellow, the flower tends to look skyward, and it grows to 20 inches. Other popular trumpets: Early Sensation (yellow, one of the first to bloom, in February, 12 inches); Spellbinder (an unusual mid-season plant with chartreuse petals and a trumpet that whitens with age, 18 inches); Unsurpassable (yellow, to 22 inches, big-flowered, early to mid-season), and Mount Hood (16 inches, mid-season, the classic white trumpet).

- **LARGE-CUPPED DAFFODILS.** Brent Heath, a daffodil guru from Gloucester, Va., calls these the workhorses of the daffodil world, good for bedding, picking, naturalizing, forcing and showing. Stalwart varieties include Carlton, (two-toned yellow, to 20 inches, fragrant, early mid-season); Ice Follies (creamy white petals, flat, crinkled yellow cup, to 18 inches, early mid-season), and Salome (white petals, pinkish cup, to 18 inches, late mid-season). Other worthy large-cupped varieties include many of the pink-cupped ones so much in vogue. Among these try Coquille (late mid-season, 16 inches); Eastern Dawn (petals swept back a little and the cup an apricot pink, stronger at the rim, late mid-season, to 16 inches); Romance (white, orange-pink cup, to 18 inches, late mid-season), and Rosy Wonder (white with the cup ringed with a broad band of pink, to 18 inches, late mid-season).

  Still other large-cupped worthies: Redhill (white with a fiery orange cup, to 18 inches, late mid-season); Filly (white, superb form, to 18 inches, mid-season); and Brackenhurst (similar in form but with petals a primrose yellow, orange cup, 18 inches, early mid-season).

- **SMALL-CUPPED DAFFODILS.** This is a small group (in number, not height) but good as part of a naturalizing mix. They grow to 18 inches. Some of the orange-cupped varieties — Edna Earl (late mid-season), Verger (late season) and Barret Browning (early season) — recall the poet daffodils but bloom two weeks or more earlier. Also try Birma (golden yellow with orange cup, early); Angel (white and large-flowered, early), and Sabine Hay (deep yellow-orange with orange-red cup, late mid-season).

- **DOUBLE DAFFODILS.** These are mutations of established varieties in which the cup has produced a cluster of petals, some resembling roses. With the extra petals producing a bigger show, doubles are catching on with the public. Most are sweetly fragrant. I find them freakish and best suited to naturalizing mixes. The extra petals catch more wind and rain, making them a little top heavy. Worthy varieties include Abba, (white with orange segments, to 18 inches, early mid-season); Cheerfulness (creamy white with yellow flecks, to 16 inches), and Unique (white and gold, to 18 inches, with strong stems that make them a good bet against the wind).

- **TRIANDRUS DAFFODILS.** These and the next class are really worth getting to know. Triandrus have two or more pendulous blooms per stem, swept-back petals and a sweet fragrance. They are useful for semi-shady areas, returning reliably each year. They tend to be short and are wonderful in small beds, next to

BULBS IN CONTAINERS

GARDENERS WITH small patios or balconies can have all the magic of spring bulbs by growing them in containers. Follow the same planting, soil preparation and fertilizing regimen as for garden bulbs. However, the container must be well drained. Place gravel at the bottom of the pot, position landscape filter cloth above the gravel, and then use a potting mix of one part sand, one part perlite, one part peat moss, one part topsoil. Mix thoroughly, adding a dry, balanced organic fertilizer and a little dolomitic limestone. You must have a large container to minimize the risk of bulbs freezing and thawing; a half whiskey barrel works well (drill drainage holes if necessary). If you live in an apartment, check restrictions on balcony weight and watering.

If a container is large, you can plant minor bulbs above the major ones. Grape hyacinths, with their delicate foliage, are great candidates for this. You have to make sure that your main show of tulips or daffodils blooms late enough to coincide with the grape hyacinths, which flower in mid-to-late April. You also should plant an early-season bulb, a small cyclamineus daffodil or a Kaufmanniana or early species tulip.

If the container is less than 24 inches in diameter, insulate it with bales of straw or, if you can stand to look at it, bubble wrap.

paths and in containers. Varieties of note include Ice Wings, (pure white, to 12 inches, early mid-season); Thalia (also white but larger and more ruffled and open than Ice Wings, to 18 inches); Liberty Bells (medium yellow, to 14 inches, late mid-season), and Tuesday's Child (similar to Thalia but with cups that are lemon yellow, to 16 inches, late mid-season).

■ **CYCLAMINEUS DAFFODILS.** So named because they are supposed to resemble cyclamen, they are far more appealing. They are similar to triandrus in their nodding flowers and swept-back petals, but they are smaller, shorter and among the earliest to bloom. They are terrific for rock gardens and small borders, next to the patio and in containers. Varieties to try: February Gold (yellow petals, orange cup, to 14 inches, very early); Foundling (clear white, pointed petals with rose-pink cup, to 12 inches, late mid-season); Jack Snipe (white with clear yellow, fringed cup, a miniature to 10 inches, mid-season); Peeping Tom (bright yellow with very long trumpet, to 14 inches, early mid-season); Beryl (light yellow with orange-yellow cup, a fabulous miniature with a small cup and oversized petals, to nine inches); Surfside (an elegant plant with white petals and a soft yellow cup, lightening with age, to 14 inches, mid-season).

■ **JONQUILLA DAFFODILS.** The daffodils of the Deep South, they demand hot, dry conditions, especially during their summer dormancy. They thus are good candidates for planting next to heat-blasted city walkways and south-facing masonry walls and in the poor, dry soil of sunny hillsides. Don't expect them to flourish in woodland shade. They tend to be tall and bear two to five flowers per stem. They are all sweetly scented and deserve to be picked and brought indoors. Favorites include Dickcissel (a yellow bi-color, to 16 inches, early mid-season); Trevithian (deep yellow, to 18 inches, early mid-season); Bell Song (white with pink cup, to 14 inches, late), and Suzy (a lovely variety with yellow petals and a flat orange cup, to 17 inches, mid-season).

■ **TAZETTA DAFFODILS.** Originally from the Middle East, they sulk in the North but do well in the Washington garden. Paperwhites are a member of this class and speak to their characteristics: prolific clusters of small flowers with a pungent fragrance. Tazettas are the one class that can be planted late due to their minimal winter chilling requirements. Look for these: Avalanche (an heirloom variety with trusses of small flowers, white petals and butter-yellow cups, to 18 inches, mid-season); Cragford (white with small orange cups, to 14 inches, early mid-season), and Scarlet Gem (soft yellow petals with red-orange cups, to 16 inches, late mid-season).

FORCING BULBS

TRICKING BULBS into blooming out of season is a way of getting the bright beauty and fragrance of the spring bulb into the home in mid-winter, when you need it most. Forcing, however, is a bit like brewing one's own beer: The result is great but the effort seems hardly worth it, especially since you can buy winter potted bulbs that someone else has gone to the trouble of chilling.

If you wish to force daffodils or tulips, look to the catalogs in early summer, select varieties suited to forcing, and ask the catalog companies to send you your bulbs as soon as they get them in September, not with regular shipments in October. Put them dry in the crisper of your refrigerator until mid-October, when the soil temperature outside is low enough to begin root formation. Pot them up and bury the pots in ventilated cold frames or raised beds that are heavily mulched, making sure that they are watered first. The protective blanket is vital in preventing the bulbs from freezing and thawing.

Six to eight weeks later, pull the pots and look to see a mat of roots at the bottom. The bulbs are then ready to bring indoors, where they should be kept watered as the top growth develops and placed near a bright window facing south or west. The plant will bloom indoors in two to three weeks. You will be lucky to have anything before Christmas, but successive plantings will produce cheery blooms through January and February. You can do the same with hyacinths, crocuses (if kept in a cool room indoors), snowdrops, muscari and glory-of-the-snow.

Paperwhite narcissi and amaryllis do not need this chilling preparation, which is why they are favorite indoor bulbs for winter. Amaryllis takes six to eight weeks to bloom, paperwhites three to five. If either is in too much shade, it will grow long and flop over, so give them as much light as possible, and be ready to stake them if necessary. Paperwhites look pretty growing in nothing but a bowl of water mulched with polished river stones, but their roots will have no anchorage, so the plant may well tip over. A sandy potting mix will give them better footing.

- **POETICUS DAFFODILS.** These are the poet daffodils, though Wordsworth didn't have this sort in mind when he penned his ode to the narcissus. He might have gone into an artistic stupor if he had: This limited but uplifting daffodil group produces flowers of heavenly beauty. They are sturdy, tall, reliably perennial and with petals of the purest white, a collar for the small, red-rimmed cup. They all bloom late, into May. Usually only four varieties can be found, of which Acteae, which grows to 16 inches, is the most available. The species is also available (see below). The other varieties are Cantabile, Felindre and Milan. They have more green in the cup than Acteae but otherwise are indistinguishable to most people. Pheasant's Eye is the nickname of the species, *Narcissus poeticus recurvus*. It's still around and worth growing.

- **SPECIES DAFFODILS.** These are the originals from which all others were bred. They are a diverse lot, useful in numerous ways. Dating back centuries (many were favorites in early American gardens), they are valid additions to any period garden. Many are small or miniatures, valuable in rock gardens and herb gardens as well as in containers and window boxes. Notable examples:

Narcissus bulbocodium conspicuus. A big name for a cute little thing, this also is called the Hoop Petticoat daffodil because of its ballooning cup (to six inches, mid-season).

N. odorus is a yellow *jonquilla* hybrid that blooms very early and is fragrant (to 12 inches). Its double-flowered version, *N. odorus plenus*, known commonly as Queen Anne's double jonquil, has delightful, rosebud-like flowers.

Butter and Eggs *(N. telamonius plenus)*. This looks like a small, golden trumpet, except that the trumpet is doubled inside (to 14 inches, blooms early).

Rip Van Winkle *(N. pumilus var. plenus)* is another striking species mutant, with petals and cups formed into a golden starburst on a miniature plant (to six inches, mid-season).

In case you are counting, there are two more daffodils divisions, one where the cup is split, the other a catchall class for everything that isn't in the others.

CULTIVATION

EXAMINE DAFFODIL bulbs well before buying or planting. They should be free of mold and insects, and they also should be firm. They can have a little give, but soft bulbs are no good. Size does count. The larger the bulb the more and the sturdier the blooms. With daffodils, this means not only larger bulbs but bulbs with one, two, even three offsets attached to the main bulb. Trumpet bulbs with one offset might be three inches across, while a tiny species daffodil might be just an inch across. "Topsize" is a designation bandied about by bulb retailers, but there is no industry standard for the term, so go by actual stated bulb size, usually measured by the circumference in centimeters. If you are buying a discounted batch for naturalizing, as with lilies, you should expect slightly smaller bulbs.

Large daffodils should be planted deeply, to eight inches. There is no sugarcoating the fact that this is a thankless chore in the fall, but the reward will be years of glorious springs. If your soil is good and worked well, use a bulb planter; otherwise, loosen the soil with a gardening fork and then excavate using a sharp shovel. In heavy clay soil you can plant a little shallower, but use the opportunity to lighten the soil with humus, gypsum, sand and peat moss. Don't plant in low-lying wet areas; bulbs must be kept dry during the summer and moist but not wet the rest of the year.

Daffodils do not start producing roots until the soil temperature dips below 60 degrees, around early to mid-October in Washington, so there is little point in getting them in earlier. But there is a penalty in delaying too long — in reduced root growth and in being stuck with the last of the season's bulb crop, meaning smaller, picked-over bulbs that are out of the ground longer than desired.

In January and February, some people get worked up at the sight of budding daffodils and tulips, worried that unseasonably warm winter days will prompt flowering and that subsequent cold spells will cause damage. Hard freezes (but not light frosts) will harm opened flowers, but the alarm is mostly unfounded. The plants will regulate themselves, slowing down if the weather turns frigid and keeping the blooms protected in their buds. Do not mulch or provide other protection at this point; it will only increase chances of premature growth and then freeze damage.

All bulbs need watering when they are planted to initiate root growth. They also need to be watered when they are growing throughout the spring, especially in dry years. Beds containing spring-flowering bulbs should not be deeply watered in the summer; this is when the bulb goes dormant and needs protection against rotting. If you know that your bulb beds will be regularly and heavily irrigated in the summer, lift the bulbs, store them in onion bags in a closet and replant them in the fall.

Fertilizing is important for optimum performance. Bone meal supplemented with potassium (wood ash is a good source) should be worked into the soil at planting time, along with other soil lighteners. Or use a proprietary bulb formulation. Mix the nutrients well and avoid direct contact between bulb and fertilizer. A granular, high-nitrogen fertilizer should be avoided. Bulbs benefit from a little limestone worked into the planting mix, especially those of tazettas and triandrus daffodils. Once the tips emerge in late winter, soak the ground with a water-soluble 5-10-20 fertilizer. Do not fertilize after the flower buds have formed.

When daffodil bulbs peter out, it usually is not so much because they are crowded but because they have insufficient nutrients. Before going to the trouble of lifting and dividing, feed them once in the fall and again in late winter as described above. They should flower again in spring.

Main Pests: Daffodil bulbs are poisonous, and rodents leave them alone. A fly maggot will visit bulbs on rare occasions. As a rule, deer also do not eat daffodils, making daffs good candidates for the outer suburban and rural garden. However, deer lured to the garden by other plants do tread on daffodils and damage them. **Main Diseases:** Most fungal diseases are evident in storage, and a reputable supplier will sell only clean, disease-free stock.

II. Tulips

ANY PLANT THAT CAN raise the pulse rate of the usually sanguine Dutch — and even cause the Tulip Mania of the 1630s, when prices soared to the equivalent of $25,000 to $50,000 a bulb in today's terms — must be a magical flower indeed. It is easy to understand the passion generated by these blossoms. The sight in late April of single late tulips, with their tall, plump goblets flowering under the filtered canopy of the dogwood, is a delight. The Washington garden at that moment is known the world over, and tulips do much to make it that way.

We are lucky to have a long spring season and a transitional climate that allows us to grow the full range of tulips and to enjoy them over many weeks. Few parts of the country are so blessed. However, people in deer territory may have severe problems with disappearing tulips.

VARIETIES

HORTICULTURISTS GROUP tulips into 15 divisions. Having a sense of where a given variety fits in the tulip world will help meet the gardener's needs for color, size, blooming period and use.

- **SINGLE EARLY TULIPS.** These are cup-shaped with shortish stems, typically 12 to 16 inches. Their compactness suits them to the blustery days of late March to early April when they flower. Several tend to have "flames" on their exterior petals (good for forcing and container growing). Some varieties date back to the 18th and 19th centuries, making them useful for period gardens. Varieties of note: Apricot Beauty (salmon, somewhat fragrant); Couleur Cardinal (scarlet flushed with purple); Keizerskroon (red and yellow bi-color, dates to 1750); Prinses Irene (orange with purple flame); General de Wet (gold, flecked orange, fragrant), and White Cascade.

- **DOUBLE EARLY TULIPS.** These are also early season bulbs but with double flowers. Varieties of note: Fringed Beauty (ruddy orange fringed yellow); Monte Carlo (yellow, fragrant); Schoonoord (white, fragrant); Peach Blossom (deep rose with cream-colored flames); Electra (cherry red, fragrant); Mr. Van der Hoef (golden yellow), and Abba (red with scarlet flames, fragrant).

- **TRIUMPH TULIPS.** Blooming in Washington in mid-April, these grow to 18 to 20 inches. With a classic cup, triumphs are rather showy and are given to softer colors. The petal shape is of a pointed arch. Grouped together, they create a pleasant, scalloped profile to the top of the bloom. Sound varieties: Douglas Bader (china-rose fading to white at edges, named for a World War II British flying ace); Peerless Pink; Washington (bright yellow with red flame); Peer Gynt (deep pink edged in silvery pink); Bastogne (red with contrasting purple anthers); two near-black cultivars, Negrita (purple) and John Giant (red); Rosalie (bluish pink), and, among the whites, Pax, Snowstar and White Dream (yellow anthers).

- **DARWIN HYBRIDS.** Flowering in late April, these are large and robust tulips, growing to 30 inches. They are good for forcing. They often come in primary colors with a black base inside the flower, forming a striking contrast. (For varieties, see box on perennial tulips).

- **SINGLE LATE TULIPS.** This is the workhorse of the mid-spring garden, but it is a thoroughbred. Largest in flower size and tall — they, too, grow to 30 inches — single lates come in a vast range of cultivars that should appeal to everyone. The class encompasses the old categories of Darwin and Cottage tulips. The flower tends to be elongated and distinctly rectangular in profile. Favorite cultivars include Anne Frank

THE PERENNIAL TULIP

ONE OF THE FEW complaints about tulips is that they don't come back every year, or if they do the show is weak. The fault is not so much with the tulips as with our expectations. The tradeoff for ornament in highly bred varieties is longevity. Treat them as annuals; they certainly are inexpensive enough to be within most people's reach, and you will not be disappointed.

However, it is possible to get tulips to return, or to increase the chances that they will return, by selecting certain varieties and treating them well. Species or botanical tulips, though not as showy as the hybrids, are more willing to return. In addition, cultivars of three species — Fosteriana, Kaufmanniana, and Greigii — are more likely to reappear, at least for a few years.

Popular Fosteriana cultivars include Red, Pink, Orange and White Emperor, Princeps and Yellow Purissima. Kaufmanniana varieties include Gluck, Ancilla, Shakespeare and a medley of music geniuses: Chopin, Berlioz, Fritz Kreisler and Franz Lehar. For Gregii tulips, consider Red Riding Hood, Cape Cod, Plaisir and Grand Prestige.

Darwin Hybrids have Fosteriana and Kaufmanniana ancestry and are more likely than other hybrid types to return each spring. Popular varieties include Ad Rem, Apeldoorn, Beauty of Apeldoorn, Golden Apeldoorn, Elizabeth Arden and Golden Parade. The late Henry Mitchell of *The Washington Post*, a legendary garden writer, loved Jewel of Spring (soft yellow with fine red edge), derived from another fine Darwin Hybrid named Gudoshnik (cream tinged with pink).

Open, enriched and free-draining soil is particularly important for perennial tulips, as are a sunny site and freedom from plant competition. Try to plant as deeply as possible while still providing drainage — eight or nine inches is not too much. A balanced fertilizer should be applied in liquid form during the spring growing season. Avoid high-nitrogen fertilizers. Some gardeners feel the chances of tulips returning regularly are enhanced if the bulbs are lifted once the foliage has died back in late spring and stored in a cool, dry place, to be replanted in October.

(white); Queen of the Night (deep purple, almost black); Halcro (raspberry-red pink); Pink Supreme (deep salmon pink); Queen of Bartigons (glowing salmon pink), and Sorbet (white with carmine-red flames).

In addition, a number of single lates called tetraploids have been genetically altered to increase petal substance and flower longevity. This is worth noting in the Washington garden, where occasional early heat waves in late April to early May can blast the last of the tulips and daffodils. Tetraploids retain more color and substance in the heat. Among these bulbs are some old favorites, including Maureen (ivory white), Menton (china rose), Mrs. John T. Scheepers (huge, golden yellow) and Renown (carmine red).

■ **LILY FLOWERED TULIPS.** These tulips share a distinctive large flower with pointed petals that flare outward. Another late-season class, they grow to 18 to 24 inches. Many gardeners adore their graceful look. Cultivars include Mona Lisa (creamy yellow with red flame); West Point (bright primrose yellow); China Pink (bluish pink); Elegant Lady (creamy yellow with a blush of pink), and Queen of Sheba (red, edged in golden orange).

■ **FRINGED TULIPS.** Fringed tulips have needle-like fringes at the tops of their petals, as if edged with tiny crystals. From 16 to 24 inches tall, they are another late-season class. Varieties include Hamilton (deep yellow with heavy fringe); Madison Garden (carmine red with yellow-pink fringe); Aleppo (raspberry with apricot fringe); Swan Wings (white with black anthers); Burgundy Lace (burgundy red edged white); Maja (golden yellow with a bronze cast to base), and Fringed Beauty (vermilion edged gold with a black base).

■ **VIRIDIFLORA, OR GREEN TULIPS.** This is another small, late-season and gently freakish class of tulips, grouped by the green flame extending up the outer petal. They are wonderful for arrangements; the flash of green can be matched to such plants as viburnum mopheads. They grow to 20 inches. Popular varieties, all with apple green bands, include Golden Artist (golden yellow, pink blend); Angel (off-white); Spring Green (yellow-ivory); Greenland or Groenland (rose pink), and Esperanto (rose, green-yellow blend).

■ **REMBRANDT**. These are the "broken" tulips with streaking or feathering on outside petals, which actually is caused by a virus. These tulips were all the rage in 17th century Holland, where the Old Masters painted them. One variety in particular, *Semper Augustus*, helped spawn the Tulip Mania of the 1630s. This class is likely to be phased out due to restrictions on diseased bulbs. They should not be planted where you or your neighbors grow lilies. Other non-viral cultivars in different classes have similar flaming without the disease.

■ **PARROT**. The name comes from the gyrations of the immature petals, which are supposed to resemble parrot beaks. The tulips are just as colorful as the birds, and they don't talk back. Among the latest to flower, in May, they grow to 24 inches. As the flowers mature, they open almost flat, presenting a large surface to the elements. They can be damaged in storms, but the risk is worth it. Parrots are one of the few garden flowers that manages to look wildly exotic without losing any dignity. The petals are flamed and deeply incised to look like silken feathers. Varieties include Flaming Parrot (primrose yellow with scarlet flames); Black Parrot (deep purple); White Parrot (pure white with apple green streaks); Apricot Parrot (apricot salmon with pink stripe, fragrant), and Estella Rijnveld (deep red flamed creamy white).

■ **DOUBLE LATE, OR PEONY.** These are graceful, lacy tulips that also grow late, into May, when the canopy has filled out and the garden tends to be shadier. They do indeed resemble peonies and are often fragrant. They look especially effective in dappled light. Like the parrots, they are vulnerable to rainstorms and thundershowers, but the risk is again worth taking. Double lates are 18 to 24 inches. The most popular variety is Angelique (pale pink with darker flush), followed closely by Mount Tacoma (white, sometimes with green markings). The two look lovely together. Other varieties worth trying: Carnaval de Nice (white with showy scarlet flames, tiny cream margins on leaves); Gold Medal (deep yellow), and Maywonder (deep rose).

■ **KAUFMANNIANA**. These hybrids flower early and grow low, six to nine inches, and are useful for rock gardens, small borders, containers and other spaces that won't overpower them. The flowers deserve to be observed and enjoyed: Their pointed petals open flat on sunny early spring days, exposing the inner petal, often colored differently at its base, or throat. Contented bulbs will come back year after year. In addition to varieties listed in the perennial tulips box, Heart's Delight is treasured for its medley of colors (exterior carmine pink, interior rose with yellow throat).

■ **FOSTERIANA**. This is another early-flowering type, with stems up to 24 inches, but many are far shorter. They are known for bright primary colors and big flowers, though some may view the bloom as out of scale with the rest of the plant. (See perennial tulips box.)

■ **GREIGII**. In addition to their value as perennials, Greigiis flower early and are noted for their strikingly ornamental foliage with its reddish stippling. (See box for varieties).

■ **SPECIES**. The last division is the species tulips, generally small plants, some multi-flowered, with pointed petals that open flat. This makes them great companions for other small bulbs such as grape hyacinth, squill, glory-of-the-snow, miniature daffodils and crocuses, as well as for early spring wildflowers such as Virginia bluebells, trilliums, foamflowers, ajuga, aubretia and creeping phlox. They are perfect for the historic garden.

Many species and their hybrids are available. Buy from a reliable source, and look for certification that the bulbs have been propagated and not collected wild.

Early-blooming species and varieties include *Tulipa polychroma* (white tinged pink), *T. pulchella Liliput* (deep red) and other *pulchella* cultivars, plus *T. maximowiczii* (orange-red). Mid-season choices: *T. batalinii* (buff yellow) and its varieties, *T. chrysantha* (yellow and red), *T. clusiana* Cynthia (candy-striped yellow and red), and *T. linifolia* (scarlet with black base). Late varieties, flowering well into May: *T. kurdica* (orange and red), *T. wilsoniana* (vermilion red) and *T. vvedenskyi,* or Tangerine Beauty (bright red with orange flames).

CULTIVATION

TULIPS SHOULD BE planted deeply (six to eight inches) in soil that has been amended to an even greater depth to assure good drainage and the delivery of oxygen and nutrients to the bulbs. Plant bulbs four to six inches apart, with the tip, or nose, skyward. Try to prepare a whole bed rather than inserting in single holes made by a bulb planter. If no new bed is available, clear free areas within existing beds to receive clumps of tulips. You will need at least 10 of the same variety to make a statement. If space is limited, tulips can be grown in containers (see box on page 135).

Tulips are best planted in late October to early November (after the first frost or two is perfectly acceptable). The bulbs need cool soil to start producing their roots. Late-season tulips can go in as late as December as long as the soil can be worked, but early-season types must grow more of their roots in the fall and thus should be set no later than mid-November. With early or late types, wait until the ground freezes before laying mulch, so the bulbs are properly chilled.

Use a penknife — not fingernails — to remove, carefully, the skin surrounding the bulb if you have a variety where the flaky covering seems to constrict the bottom of the bulb (the basal plate where the roots emerge). This is particularly needed on a variety named Preston's Fusilier, says horticulturist Peter J. Schenk, Jr. of Alexandria, Va., as well as on bulbs used for forcing in pots.

Tulips do best in a sunny site and will grow hopelessly leggy where it is too shady. For heavy clay soil, amendments include sand and well-rotted humus. Flowers will be stronger and last longer if the soil is then well blended with bone meal and a low-nitrogen fertilizer, preferably organic and high in potash (wood ash or New Jersey greensand are good sources of potash). A slow-release granular fertilizer, applied atop the soil but beneath the mulch once the tips emerge, will see the bulb through the season. Do not allow grains to touch the foliage. Perennial tulips must have good summer drainage; they will not work in a bed that is heavily irrigated come July. You also should remove the flower head, but not the stalk, once the petals drop. Cut off the leaves once they begin to age and turn yellow. Annual tulips, meaning most of them, simply can be dug up with a fork in late May and fed to the compost pile. The cloud has a silver lining: You don't have to fret about untidy foliage for weeks after the bloom is done.

USES IN GARDEN DESIGNS

TULIPS ARE MORE FORMAL in character than daffodils and aren't as well suited to the large, sweeping naturalistic garden. However, the species tulips, sometimes called botanicals, are quite different in character from the showy garden hybrids and are superb for small-scale gardens near the house, for rock gardens, at the foot of hills and in other areas where a natural look is sought.

While tulips make terrific container plants, they come into their own as colorful plantings in perennial beds, mixed borders, path-side beds and amid foundation shrubbery. They prefer little competition and thus are not suited for the base of trees and shrubs with mats of surface roots, such as maples, crape myrtles and forsythias, or beneath vigorous ground covers. They are extremely useful in decorating beds before they fill in with herbaceous plants.

Plant tulips in soil that can be dug each fall without damaging existing plantings, including dormant perennial bulbs such as daffodils and snowdrops. Larger tulips planted in blocks in rectangular beds look splendid, especially in the city garden, but avoid planting in rows. The most common mistake with tulips is not planting enough of them. If you buy 10 bulbs, do not attempt to cover a quarter-acre with them. Buy 20 and plant them in a generous clump some three feet across, in a position that will been seen.

If you are planning a garden party for the spring, tulips more than any other plant will dress up the garden for the occasion. Single lates normally can be counted on to be in bloom in the third and fourth week of April. Hedge your bets with additional plantings of Darwin hybrids and triumphs for a delayed tulip season and parrots and double lates for an early one. Schenk offers this tip: Many people want a symmetric look, but one side of the garden is shadier than the other. Select early and late varieties of the same color (white and medium pink are easy to match), and plant the early varieties in the shady area and the late one on the sunny side.

Dramatic color combinations lend great drama, but be sure that the mix is of the same type of tulip so that the flowering is simultaneous. The gardener eyeing the spring garden party can save money by buying mixtures instead of named varieties. For an unusual and classy effect, try a pastel mixture of single lates.

Tulips make great cut flowers, especially single lates, double lates, parrots, viridifloras and Rembrandts. Remember that tulips continue to grow once cut; it is impossible to keep them from moving about in an arrangement, and that is their charm. If you have sunny areas you can set aside, establish a cutting garden (you can sow summer annuals once the tulips are pulled). In a bed just 5 x 10 feet, it is possible to grow between 200 and 400 tulips, depending on spacing.

Main Pests: Deer (they regard tulips as ice cream), squirrels, slugs and voles. **Main Disease:** Tulip fire.[†]

III. Lilies

LILIES ARE AMONG the most beautiful flowers in the garden — showy, colorful, often heavily scented and full of nostalgic qualities. It is possible to have lilies from late May to frost time, with the main season occurring in June, July and early August. Lilies are rather like roses: They do well in the Washington area so long as they receive proper care, including a program of spraying. Those who want lily flowers without the effort or use of chemical sprays would be better off planting daylilies, which are related but not the genuine article.

Like most highly popular garden plants, lilies have been hybridized heavily, with offerings growing vaster each year. The Washington gardener is most likely to have success with Asiatic hybrids, an early-to-mid-season group that is often, but incorrectly, lumped together as the Tiger Lily. That is but one Asiatic species and not the best representative. It was considered a fabulous lily a century ago, but it has since been surpassed by Asiatic variants of better color, form, petal substance and disease resistance.

The lily comes with certain limitations: Its long springtime growth heightens the anticipation of the flower, but once the bloom is over the lily is not decorative. Even in flower the habit is spindly, and the plant benefits from its ankles being hidden by ground covers, large perennials or small shrubs. In addition to the need for chemical sprays, soil preparation is onerous. Yet for all that the lily deserves to be grown. It is one of the few spring-fresh plants to carry the garden through the difficult summer months. The flower itself is one of life's treasures.

VARIETIES OF NOTE

THE NORTH AMERICAN Lily Society has 10 divisions, or official classifications, for lilies:

■ **ASIATIC HYBRIDS:** These are the most familiar garden varieties. They have the broadest color range of any lily type and include pastel shades. Short as lilies go, they reach a maximum height of about four feet and bloom in June. Depending on variety, the flowers either face to the sky or outward or dangle like bells. They are among the easiest lilies to grow, favored by beginners and hobbyists alike. The Potomac Lily Society recommends the following as particularly good for the Washington area, identified by shapes:

Upright Flowering: Cherished (rose pink), Chinook (pastel orange), Connecticut King (yellow), Enchantment (red), Kismet (orange), Mount Blanc (cream to white), Sterling Star (cream to white) and Unique, (pink bi-color). *Outward Facing:* Scuetzenlisl. *Pendant:* Connecticut Yankee (orange), Tiger Babies. A number of smaller hybrids are suited for the city garden or container growing, including Golden Pixie, a yellow upright, Pixie Flame, an orange-red upright, and Elf, a pendant form that is pink and grows to three feet.

■ **TIGER LILY** The true tiger lily is a species known botanically as *Lilium lancifolium*, growing to six feet or more. The smallish orange-red flowers are marked with black-purple streaks, and the plant is as tough as it is scentless. It forms baby bulbs, which are black in the crotch of leaf stalks. It is not the most beautiful lily, and there is another reason for giving it a pass: It harbors lily virus and will likely infect finer varieties.

■ **TRUMPET AND AURELIAN HYBRIDS.** Flowering as Asiatic Hybrids wind down, these form the classic lily image: a trumpet flower, slightly nodding, arranged in a whorl on tall stalks. The image is derived from the regal lily, with its white flower and heady perfume, but its successors also come in different flower clusters and forms: blooms that are flared or bowl-shaped, pendant or shaped like sunbursts or stars. Trumpets grow to six feet or more and need staking to withstand summer storms. The local society recommends the following varieties:

Trumpet: Black Dragon (white, dark reverse), Golden Splendor (deep yellow), Pink Perfection (pink), Copper King (orange with maroon reverse), Mabel Violet (pink) and the regal lily, *Lilium regale* (white with yellow center). *Flare and Sunburst:* Lady Ann (cream, with apricot center), White Henryi (white with orange center) and Thunderbolt (apricot).

■ **ORIENTAL HYBRIDS:** These are the most coveted of all lilies, the sort seen in expensive flower arrangements. Large, velvety, richly colored and sublimely marked, they are also sweetly fragrant. Heights generally vary from four to six feet, with taller ones again needing staking. As a rule, Orientals resent the heat and humidity of Washington summers and are more susceptible to virus than Asiatics and Trumpets. If you grow them, it is important to get topflight named varieties that are certified free of virus, and they fare better planted in fall rather than the following spring. The local society suggests the following varieties, again identified by terms for the shape of their flowers:

Bowl-Shaped: Casablanca (white). *Flowers Flat:* Imperial Silver (white), Stargazer (carmine, suited to container growing), Imperial Crimson (crimson). *Recurved:* Journey's End (carmine). Another to try is Miss Rio, an early-season pink cultivar that grows to just 18 inches. Washington gardeners also report success with Grand Commander (white with red blotches) and Uchida (red with white edge and black spots).

In recent years, breeders have developed a new class of hybrids between trumpets and Orientals that produce flowers of immense size. These may prove the best lily with Oriental blood for our region. One of the early crosses is named Black Beauty.

A number of other lilies are very much worth noting:

■ **SPECIOSUM LILY.** This native of Japan grows well in the Washington-area garden and is valuable for extending the lily season into the fall. Two forms are commonly grown, both generous with their blooms: Rubrum, with red flowers, Album with white.

■ **MADONNA.** Botanists call it *Lilium candidum*. It is an early-season and long-beloved species with flowers of pure white. The Christian church has long used it as a symbol of purity. But in the garden it is easily blemished by botrytis blight. Madonna can be grown with great success in the Washington area, but it has unusual requirements: It must be planted early, in September, to a depth of just one inch in soil that is sweet, certainly no lower in pH than 6.5. It would make a good companion for such other lime-lovers as lavender, irises and boxwood.

■ **GOLDBAND.** This is another late-season Japanese lily with huge, bowl-shaped and outward-facing flowers marked with a golden yellow band along the white petals. The most vigorous form, is *Lilium auratum var. platyphyllum*, can grow as high as 12 feet.

■ **EASTER LILY.** Easter Lilies are forced into bloom early in the greenhouse as pot plants for Easter and Passover. Once enjoyed indoors, they can be planted outside, though they should go in a protected spot with plenty of mulch. Chances of the plant making it are about even. When planting, cut off flower heads before they form seed capsules, but leave the foliage intact — advice that holds for all lilies. Easter Lilies should bloom the next year, but be aware that they usually are prone to viruses. Breeders have developed hybrids between the Easter lily, *Lilium longiflorum*, and the Asiatic species *L. auratum*. These so-called L.A. Hybrids, with large blooms and great petal substance, have caused a stir in the lily world.

■ **MARTAGON LILIES.** The species, from Europe, is sometimes hard to find, which is fortunate, because it also is hard to grow here. Martagon Hybrids are lovely edge-of-woodland plants, tall with whorled leaves and small Turk's-cap flowers, but they tend not to thrive. They are also susceptible to the soil-borne fungus fusarium. Try them if you are adventurous.

■ **NATIVE LILIES.** Ironically, native lilies are difficult to get and to grow. The one most likely to succeed is the Canada Lily, *L. canadense,* which climbs to six feet, again with whorled leaves and small, bell-shaped flowers in reds and yellows. This is one of the few lilies to prefer damp soil.

USES IN GARDEN DESIGNS

LILIES HAVE a variety of uses — in mixed borders, in beds on the edges of woodland (with reasonable sunlight), by heavily traveled paths and in confined spaces that are not shaded. Their drainage and good soil requirements make them excellent candidates for pot growing. Since lilies, particularly those with pastel colors, prefer a little shading from the early afternoon sun, pot culture allows you to move them into the optimum position. For containers, look for shorter varieties that do not need staking.

Lilies also make great cut flowers, long-lasting, fragrant and beautiful. If you have room for a cut-flower garden, plant lilies six inches apart and separate the rows by 36 inches. A monoculture of lilies, however, will increase the chance of diseases spreading among them, so a cut-flower garden needs a commitment of regular feeding, watering and spraying to minimize problems.

CULTIVATION

FIRST AND FOREMOST, lilies demand soil that is heavily worked and freely drained. It is no use putting a lily bulb in heavy clay soil or even in a hole that has been backfilled with sand or peat. The whole area must be prepared. If this is not possible, plant in raised beds that have been amended. Remember that fluffy new beds settle to about half their original height.

Lilies, when happy, will expand their clumps over the years, so plant bulbs at least a foot apart. Most lilies are planted at a depth of four inches, but the soil must be worked another eight inches or so below this so that the roots are free to grow. Typical amendments include sand or perlite and lots of peat and other humus. Add bone meal to the mix but not granular fertilizer — that should be applied as a top dressing at the time of planting or in early spring for established plants. Go easy on nitrogen. Unlike other bulbs, lilies are never fully dormant and thus must be handled more carefully. They are best planted in the fall; late winter or early spring is the secondary choice. Bulbs planted too late are weakened and will not bloom as well, if at all, the first year. Look for bulbs that have a healthy root system and avoid those with none. Lilies are not tulips.

Plant hygiene is a must here. Do not plant bulbs with blackened scales, and take out those that show signs of basal rot or viral infection. Water only their feet — a sprinkler will spread botrytis from one lily to the rest.

Generally, only lilies that grow above four feet — taller varieties of trumpets, Orientals and Madonnas, for example — need staking. Use a six-foot bamboo stake, pushed a foot into the ground in spring, when the new growth can be seen. Be careful not to spear the underground bulb. Tie with twine or landscape ties.

A Tip: Avoid discounted bulbs of poor size and condition, especially those sold in the spring. Traditionally, American-grown bulbs are the most reliably disease-free. To see lilies, watch for local shows in early summer, particularly the annual show of the Potomac Lily Society. Members have access to superior bulbs ordered in the fall.

Main Pests: Aphids and slugs. **Main Diseases:** Botrytis leaf blight, basal rot (which is similar to root rot) and viruses.[†]

IV. Other Bulbs

THE MINOR-BULB PALETTE once was restricted to snowdrops and crocuses. The adventurous gardener will discover here a whole new world of bulbs, mostly perennial, that bring down the scale of the garden and enliven it at the same time. Woodland floors coated with anemones, small daffodils or squill or sunny banks of daffodils, crocuses and glory-of-the-snow are a sight to behold in March and early April. The smallest bulbs should be planted generously. Here are some of my favorites, listed in bloom sequence:

■ **SNOWDROPS** *(Galanthus)*. How can something this fragile lift the yoke of winter? Yet it does, year after year, multiplying along the way. Plant them three inches deep and five to six inches apart and leave undisturbed. These are among the most likely bulbs to have been collected wild from their native Asia Minor, so seek a supplier willing to certify non-wild stock.

■ **WINTER ACONITE** *(Eranthis hyemalis)*. Its primrose yellow buttercups, presented on leafy crowns, poke up gladly above the snow, the stalk extending in an amusing way over the early months of the year. These are cheery and underused bulbs. They are sometimes difficult to establish. Once ensconced, they are prone to migrate by seed. Let them wander.

■ **BULBOUS IRISES.** Not to be confused with the giants of late spring, these small bulbous irises are charming March heralds of the season ahead. Two species and varieties are most popular here: *Iris danfordiae*, with primrose yellow flowers, and *Iris reticulata*, whose many varieties range in color from sky blue to deep purple. They sometimes are called rock garden irises, because their tiny scale is suited to small beds. Plant them four inches deep and leave them alone. They will come back.

■ **DUTCH IRISES.** Blooming in late May, these bulbs are tall but dainty and the sort used freely in florist's arrangements. They cannot be counted on to return year after year, so treat them as annuals and use them in the cutting garden.

■ **CROCUSES.** These fabulous harbingers of spring come in two basic varieties. Species, or bunch flowering, crocuses are the smaller and bloom first, in early March. Lavenders, purples, yellows and bi-colors abound. The best type for the lawn, these delightful bulbs also are particularly suited to rock gardens, tubs, small beds and intimate locations. They grow to four inches and should be planted about as deeply and as far apart. The second type, the large flowering crocus, or *C. vernus* hybrids, grow to six inches and flower about two weeks later, making more of a statement. Popular varieties include Jeanne d'Arc (pure white), Enchantress (lavender) and Purpurea (strong purple). Squirrels love crocuses even more than they love tulips, especially when crocuses are first planted in the fall.

DON'T MOW THE BULBS

CLUMPS OF EARLY daffodils look fabulous in the meadow setting of the large lawn, as do glory-of-the-snow, Siberian squill, snowdrops and crocuses. In March, before the grass has greened up, these splashes of color are blissfully welcome. But as all good gardeners know, mowing over the leaves after the blooms are spent would be disastrous for these perennials. The leaves feed the bulbs and their babies, forming underground in the spring. Come early April, though, the lawn is asking for that first brisk cut. What's a tidy gardener to do?

Do not braid the foliage or bend and tie it. Though pretty in magazine pictures, this practice is bad news for the plant. Tie whole clumps loosely to get the leaves off the surrounding grass, where they can mat and kill the turf. You do not have to wait the full eight weeks or so for the leaves to die and yellow before mowing them, however, especially if you feed the bulbs once in the fall and again as they emerge in late winter. Do not mow too neatly around the leaves; you will spoil the rustic effect if each clump is shaped like a perfect kidney or ameba.

An alternative is to set aside a certain area of the garden for spring bulbs, somewhat out of the way and preferably lightly wooded, and then have other parts of the garden succeed it as an attention grabber. Crab apples and azaleas, for example, are bound to redirect the eye.

- **ANEMONES.** These ancient and beguiling beauties are a must in the woodland garden. Their capacity to carpet our forest floors makes them one of the joys of early April. Anemone bulbs (actually tubers) are odd, wizened things. It is hard to tell which side is up and even harder to imagine that such ugly things can produce such beautiful and delicate plants.

  Plant them the same as crocuses. The most common variety is the Grecian windflower *(Anemone blanda)*. This is a delight, though to me the magenta color of some varieties is too strong for the season and off-putting. Chose whites (White Splendour) and soft pinks (Rosea or Radar). The Italian windflower *(A. apennina)* is hard to find but well worth the search: It is a soft powder blue (some varieties are white or light lavender) and looks stunning at the foot of columns of hardwoods. Like the winter aconite, it is wont to travel.

  The tall, bright and cheerful anemones seen so much in florist shops and European marketplaces are not winter-hardy here except in sheltered Zone 7 gardens, but they can be grown as an annual if planted in mid-to-late March. They will bloom in June. They are called Anemone Giants or Poppy-Flowered Anemones and are known botanically as *A. coronaria*. Da Caen types are single and preferred by many gardeners to the showier, double, St. Brigid varieties.

- **GLORY-OF-THE-SNOW AND SQUILL.** Glory-of-the-snow *(Chionodoxa)* is well worth getting to know. Plant a few dozen bulbs four inches deep and four inches apart in a location that is sunny in spring and they will not only return each year but multiply by self-seeding. A species named *C. gigantea* has larger flowers than the classic *C. luciliae*. I prefer the latter with its smaller flowers, up to 10 on each stem, colored a cerulean blue with white center. Siberian squill *(Scilla siberica)* behaves much the same as glory-of-the-snow, producing a wonderful blue carpet in March before trees leaf out. The squill is a deeper blue, and it can take more shade than its twin. Plant to the same depth and with the same spacing.

- **HYACINTHS.** Some hyacinth colors are magnificent — the pale blue of Delft Blue, the navy blue of Blue Jacket, the deep purple of Blue Magic, the deep, clear yellow of City of Haarlem — and the fragrance is sweet and overpowering. But the hyacinth has been so highly bred that the individual beauty of each flower has been lost. Breeders call the inflorescence a truss, but it is more like a stump. The hybrid hyacinth thus is difficult to place in beds and borders. It might prove pleasing to use a mix of interesting colors (say, whites, blues and pinks), to grow the bulbs in containers, or to force them indoors in glass forcing jars that reveal the interesting root growth. A few grains of activated carbon will keep the water in the jar clear.

In the garden, I prefer the ancient varieties called Roman hyacinths: They might have just eight flowers on each spike, each a little trumpet waiting to be admired. They bloom early, are fragrant, and are much easier to place with other spring bulbs and among low-growing ground covers. Unlike their flashy cousins, they also will come back yearly.

■ **CAMASSIA.** There is a dearth of worthy native bulbs, but this is among the best. Two types typically are offered, *Camassia quamash* (sometimes known as *C. esculenta*) and *C. leichtlinii*. Both come in blue or white varieties, but the first blooms earlier in May and is shorter, its flower spike rising to about 24 inches. The later-flowering *C. leichtlinii* can grow to 36 inches. Both are found along stream banks in the wild. They should not be permitted to dry out during the critical spring growing and flowering season. Other indigenous bulbs — in addition to heirloom varieties of daffodils and tulips that could be considered native — include certain varieties of *arisaemas* (jack-in-the-pulpit), trillium, a few alliums, fritillaries and lilies, Louisiana irises and *I. cristata*.

■ *FRITILLARIA.* This is an often overlooked but splendid genus of spring bulbs, at home in shadier gardens. Most are of European or Asian origin (though some West Coast natives now are becoming popular). Exotics have been grown here for so long, though, that it would be churlish not to regard them as homegrown.

The showiest member of the clan is the Crown Imperial *(Fritillaria imperialis)*. It is a classic oddity, with a ring of nodding flowers hanging from a tuft of foliage at the top of a three-foot to four-foot stem. The usual varieties are either hot orange or yellow. The bulb blooms with the last of the tulips, but it is somewhat difficult to place, given its form and color (and smell, which is not pleasant). Still, it is a wonderful thing.

The Checkered Lily, or Guinea Hen flower *(F. mealigris)*, blooms at the same time but is more demure and quite unlike its cousin. This delightful fritillary has nodding flowers with purple checks and grows to 12 inches or so. It is a plant for damp woodland but not waterlogged clay. Another charming fritillary for filtered light is the *F. pallidiflora*. It grows to 15 inches with pendant, light-greenish-yellow flowers.

The Persian fritillary *(F. persica)* has been planted in America since Colonial times, but is only now being rediscovered. Unlike the Crown Imperial or the Checkered Lily, it is tall with clusters of small flower bells hanging like tassels from distinctive blue-green foliage. The striking blooms are a deep, dusky, plum color. A late-season bulb, it would go well with late tulips in harmonious pinks, whites or rose reds or with complementary shades of yellow or chartreuse. Fritillaries can take a season or two to get established, so don't write them off if they don't flower well the first spring. Once ensconced, a contented *F. persica* will outlive the gardener who plants it.

Fritillary bulbs are perishable and should be planted as soon as you get them; avoid any that you suspect have been sitting for a while. Large ones are planted deeply, to seven inches, down with the tulips. Smaller ones are planted at four to five inches. Don't lift and divide.

■ **ALLIUMS.** An onion is an allium. If you let an onion go to seed, a globe of dusky white flowers emerges atop its stalk. Ornamental alliums take this trait a step further, producing flowers of extraordinary color, form and longevity in spring and early summer. Purple, violet, blue, white and even yellow, the blooms might be as small as chives' (another member of the tribe) or as big as a softball. The largest is the *A. schubertii*, which has inflorescences a foot across, resembling a huge violet firework. They flower for as long as three weeks, and some remain ornamental dried on the stalk. They are reliably perennial, disease-free and unmolested by rodents. Here are some of the best:

Allium moly. This is an ancient, small species growing to 12 inches, with clusters of golden yellow blooms. Great for the rock garden or the border, it blooms in early June.

Neapolitanum. This flowers early, in April, in loose clusters, or umbels. The flowers, a bright white, would be a valuable companion to such early-flowering plants as *Phlox divaricata*, muscari and pansies.

A. flatunense. This is a violet-flowered allium with tallish stems growing to 30 inches, a four-inch flower head and thick, leathery leaves. It blooms around Memorial Day. The most common variety is Purple Sensation.

A. christophii. Also known as Star of Persia (and separately as *albopilosum*), its flower head is composed of tiny, star-like blossoms arranged in a huge sphere that is lower to the ground than other giant alliums. It thus is easier to tie in visually to ground covers. This is a great plant for the arid garden, and its flower heads remain ornamental after they have dried. This allium, like the *A. schubertii,* is terrific for dried flower arrangements.

A. giganteum (Giant Allium). This is for gardeners wishing to make a statement (proclamation might be a better word). It is enormous, a six-inch globe of purple rising as high as five feet on sturdy green stems. It blooms in early June. Despite its individual stature, it looks best when used in plant groups. Allow at least two feet between bulbs.

A. sphaerocephalon. This is Drumstick Allium, a splendid fill-in plant for the early summer border or decorative herb garden. It is a worthy accent in a leafy border at the edge of woods, mixed, for example, with hostas, oakleaf hydrangeas, ferns and other textural plants. There is a fair bit of blue in its purple-violet flower heads, and while it would go well with roses of a harmonious hue, it grates with carmines and magentas.

A. flavum (Small Yellow Onion). This is another allium with primrose yellow blossoms in loose clusters. It flowers a bit later than *A. moly* and, at 18 inches, is half again as tall.

A. tuberosum. The rear-guard allium, this flowers in late summer on stems that climb to 24 inches. The umbels are white and about two inches across. The bulb is hard to find, but it is worth seeking out. It makes a fresh-looking accent plant in the late-season garden.

Main Pests: Occasional slugs for bulbous irises, occasional aphids for Dutch irises and late-flowering alliums. Squirrels munch crocus bulbs and blossoms (for their stamens). **Main Disease:** *Fritillaria* are susceptible to bulb rot unless planted in well-drained soil.[†]

FALL-FLOWERING BULBS

IT COMES AS A PLEASANT shock to the new gardener to find crocus-like blooms in September and October. This is not a result of global warming but a natural part of the life of these bulbs. Some bloom naked, growing leaves in winter and spring after the flowers have come and gone. (The grape hyacinth, by contrast, leafs out in autumn and flowers the following spring).

Here are fall-flowering bulbs of note:

■ **COLCHICUMS.** Also named Autumn Crocus, its brightly colored flowers emerge in late summer to early fall, rising as high as 12 inches. They usually are a violet-pink (Album is white) that looks splendid in the season's low, clear light. Slow to multiply, they also tend to be expensive.

■ **FALL-FLOWERING CROCUS.** These are true crocuses, nine species that flower in autumn. The most famous, *Crocus sativus*, gives us the herb saffron. Plant it for its beauty, not for the saffron, which comes from the dried stigmas. It takes tens of thousands of plants to yield a decent amount of the seasoning.

■ **STERNBERGIA.** This has golden yellow, crocus-like chalices on tall stems and blooms in October. It is a wonderful coda to the bulb year.

More than with any other bulbs, all of these fall bloomers must be planted with an eye on the clock. They cannot be shipped until late summer, so they must be planted as soon as you receive them. Crocuses should be planted at two to three inches deep and four inches apart, colchicums at five inches down and eight inches apart, and sternbergia at six inches deep and six inches apart.

All do well in ordinary soil so long as it is not heavy and wet, and they prefer a sunny site. Don't place them where they will be blanketed with falling leaves and, please, don't point an activated leaf blower at them.

Main Pest: Squirrels munch fall-flowering crocuses as well as spring ones.

---

†See Appendix for common pest and disease ailments and remedies.

Chapter 18

ORNAMENTAL GRASSES

*A*LONG WITH PERENNIALS, the wide popularity of ornamental grasses in recent years has changed our notion of what a garden should be — looser, freer, more natural, less demanding and kinder to the environment. The forms and textures of grasses, particularly the larger ones, are delights, especially when massed and played against ground covers and groupings of perennials.

Grasses are among the few garden plants that flourish through the dog days, hitting their stride in August when other plants are spent or wilted. As the days grow longer, the grasses' inflorescences swell with seeds and change to the colors of the harvest — wheat, raspberry, pumpkin. With the frost, the grasses themselves change to these glorious earth tones and, once winter arrives, they remain as bleached arrangements in the garden.

Ornamental grasses thus have helped us draw so much more out of our gardens year round. They flesh out the late-season garden in the same way perennials like peonies, columbines, phloxes and pinks do in the spring. Used in conjunction with late-season perennials such as perovskia, rudbeckia and sedums — as well as fall-colored shrubs and small trees — grasses bestow a character to the garden that is entirely different in the last half of the year from the first. The English cottage garden gives way to the American prairie. Both are delicious, both have their day.

NOTABLE VARIETIES

■ **MISCANTHUS.** There are several species, ranging in height from three to 12 feet, all with long, ribbed blades, an arching or upright habit and exquisite flower heads. Giant Chinese silver grass *(Miscanthus floridulus)* grows to ceiling height and above. Maiden grass *(Miscanthus sinensis Gracillimus)* has the finest blades; though it grows to six feet, it remains upright and delicate. Morning Light is distinguished by its reddish-bronze seed heads. Purple silver grass *(Miscanthus sinensis purpurescens)* grows to five feet, with blades that turn fiery copper in fall. Autumn Red, growing just three to four feet, is useful in small gardens.

■ **PENNISETUM.** The sweetest *pennisetum* is fountain grass *(Pennisetum alopecuroides)*, a cascading mound of grass with foxtail plumes of seed heads arching gracefully above the foliage. There are many varieties, including dwarf versions that grow to just 12 inches, though the regular height is closer to four feet. Purple fountain grass *(Pennisetum setaceum Atrosanguineum)* is an upright grass with a purple cast to its leaves and seed heads, but it is an annual in Zone 6 and 7.

■ **CALAMAGROSTIS.** Feather reed grass *(Calamagrostis acutiflora stricta)* is one of the most handsome and versatile ornamental grasses, growing to six feet in a skinny, vertical clump. The seed heads are particularly handsome, turning wheat-colored in late summer.

■ **MOLINIA.** The purple moor grass *(Molinia caerulea arundinacea)* is one of the most elegant of the group, forming two-foot-high clumps of foliage from which long, slender stems emerge and grow to seven feet. They are decorated with transparent seed heads with a haze of purple-brown and gold colors. A variety named Windspiel was selected for its vigor.

- **PANICUM.** Switch grass *(Panicum virgatum)* is another beautiful plant valued for the way it stiffens and displays its seed heads after the frost. In late summer, its unique flower heads float above the cascading green foliage. Several improved varieties have superior ornament: Heavy Metal, Cloud Nine, Pathfinder and Rehbraun, the last being smaller, with reddish fall color.

- **HAKONECHLOA.** The hakone grass *(Hakonechloa macra)* is a stupendous, low-growing and cascading foliage plant. A variety named *H. macra aureola* has a golden, variegated form that is showier en masse (see cultivation).

- **CHASMANTHIUM.** Northern sea oats *(Chasmanthium latifolium)* is a low-growing, small grass best massed in partial shade. It is distinguished by its flat and showy seed head, pendant on arching stems.

- **PHALARIS.** Ribbon grass *(Phalaris arundinacea picta)* has a bad reputation as being invasive, but it is precisely that vigor under stress that makes it an ideal ornamental ground cover for dry shade, second homes and other places where it will be abused and neglected. It is heavily variegated, with vertical white stripes, making it shine in the darkness of the shade garden.

CULTIVATION

MOST GRASSES do best in ordinary soil in full sun, at least if the ground is adequately drained. Both the Northern sea oats and the *hakonechloa*, particularly the variegated variety, demand relief from the afternoon sun and do best in an enriched, moist soil. Ribbon grass will take sun or shade; in too rich a soil, it will become invasive. Although the other grasses endure drought, you should water them when they are young to help them develop a good root system. Also, some grasses, especially miscanthus, will brown out at the bottom if not watered during dry spells.

Miscanthus, pennisetum and Northern sea oats self-seed prodigiously. You should be prepared to scout in spring for seedlings, which should be pulled (or grown on in pots and planted elsewhere), or remove the seed heads in the fall before the seed is released.

In time, the miscanthus roots will grow out in a concentric ring, leaving the center empty. It should then be lifted and divided. Some gardeners keep the expansion of the giant *miscanthus* in check by using a sharp ax to chip away at the outer shoots in spring. Another method is to use a five-gallon plastic bucket, saw one-third off the bottom, including the base. Bury what is left of the pail — essentially a collar — and plant the *miscanthus* within it.

Grasses are best planted in the spring. They tend to get pot-bound, so you should score and butterfly the roots before planting. The one essential chore with ornamental grasses is to cut them back low to the ground in late winter, before new shoots emerge. Use a string trimmer or sharp hedge shears.

Remarkably free of pests and diseases, ornamental grasses do not need chemical sprays to flourish.

USES IN GARDEN DESIGNS

GRASSES COME in so many sizes and shapes that they can be used just like shrubs, perennials and annuals: as doorway specimens, border accents, screens, ground covers, mass plantings, embankment plantings and container plants. They are particularly useful in small town gardens for providing high screens quickly without taking up much space. *Miscanthus* and *calamagrostis* are highly prized in this regard. Their adaptability to container plantings make them ideal screens for decks and balconies, provided there is enough sunlight. Grasses are a flower arranger's delight.

Chapter 19

GROUND COVERS

*L*ET OTHER PLANTS be prima donnas — ground covers are the chorus, and a handy chorus at that. You can plant them in place of lawns, possibly in shade or on hillsides where it's impossible to grow turf. You can use them as interludes in garden beds or to form woodland floors. You can employ them to suppress weeds or prevent soil erosion, two of their principal functions.

But ground covers also can be beautiful in their own right. Their individual structures are lost by planting them en masse, so look instead for the overall foliage effect and, to a lesser degree, the flower show. As an added benefit, ground covers generally are free of pests and diseases or are bred to survive with them.

The three most common ground covers are English ivy, vinca (periwinkle) and pachysandra. They are handsome enough and can be put to good use, though everyone else has them. Also, ivy can smother trees and gutters and needs watching. They are all evergreen and attractive in winter as well as summer. However, ground covers need not be evergreen and static. They can grow and change with the seasons, and good candidates include many tough perennials, ferns, grasses and even deciduous shrubs, as well as new kinds of roses. Certain of these ground covers remain interesting in the winter, and they can be used in conjunction with evergreen ground covers such as cotoneaster, creeping juniper and sweetbox.

NOTABLE VARIETIES

THE FOLLOWING varieties are as much an attempt to get you to think about different plants as ground covers as to push specific ones, though all are worthy.

A. LARGE AREAS IN FULL SUN

■ **THE BONICA ROSE.** Bonica was a watershed rose, introduced in the 1980s as the first of a rose series developed as low-maintenance ground covers. Others have since been introduced, but Bonica is still a champ, especially with its larger-flowering successor named Royal Bonica.

Bonica plants are vigorous, reaching three to five feet high and four feet across. Their blossoms are double, medium pink and so abundant that after they emerge in a big flush in early June, they return in waves to the end of the season. Bonica is disease-resistant but not entirely immune from blackspot. It's so tough, though, that you simply can take hedging shears to tired stems, cutting them to nine or 12 inches, and they'll produce fresh growth and new bloom. Bonica takes ordinary soil and full sun. Water the plants in the first summer to let them get established. It is unnecessary to spray these roses. To keep beds tidy and roses lower, cut them back in late winter with shears. If Bonica is too large for your ground cover site, lower-growing landscape roses are available.

Buy Bonica in one-gallon or two-gallon containers and set the plants four feet apart. You will need six plants per 100 square feet. At first the bed will look incredibly sparse, but by the second summer the gaps will be filled. Mulch between plants until then.

■ **AARON'S BEARD** (*Hypericum calycinum*). This plant has so many common names that you should look for it by its Latin name. *Hypericum*, growing about 18 inches high, spreads by underground stems, making it use-

SAVING MONEY

BECAUSE MANY plants are needed, buying ground covers represents a sizable investment. In the long run, the cost of installing perennial or woody ground covers is recouped in reduced recurring expenses for maintaining lawns, buying annuals or mulching constantly (ground cover sites do need initial mulching). But there are other ways to save money short of propagating your own plants or pursuing the standard shopping tactic of pressing for discounts for volume purchases.

Many popular plants can be bought cheaply at farmer's markets. If you buy from a retail nursery, get the smallest size of the plant available (measured by the size of the container). You may have to wait an extra year for the plant to attain mature size, but so what?

Another approach is to buy plugs. These are newly propagated plants sold in two-inch to three-inch pots. They usually are prepared by wholesale growers to sell to retailers, who then grow them on. But it is possible to find wholesale nurseries that will sell plugs directly, or to buy them from a retail nursery that will sell them at a fraction of the cost of regular potted plants. You will again have to wait one to three seasons longer to see the effects, but the savings can be substantial.

You will need to buy mulch. The cheapest bulk source is leaf mold or leaf mulch from local governments that sell it. However, is it not screened for trash and may not be available at certain times of year. A bulk delivery of mulch is cheaper than buying by the bag if you have a large area to cover.

ful for controlling erosion. The medium-to-fine-textured leaves stay fresh throughout the year. In summer, the plant produces large, buttercup-yellow flowers with long decorative stamens. They bloom, on and off, through the summer. The leaves' underside has a blue cast, often tinged with maroon in the fall. *Hypericum* loses many leaves in harsh winters, but it will regenerate in spring and flower again in summer.

You can tidy and rejuvenate these plants, too, with a good haircut in early March (don't prune after August). *Hypericum* also takes light shade. Water it during droughts. Buy plants in quart to gallon containers and set them two feet apart. You will need 25 per 100 square feet.

- **SPIREA GOLD FLAME** (*Spiraea x bumalda* Gold Flame). One of the most attractive of the low-growing spireas, Gold Flame forms a neat mound, making it a good candidate for planting en masse. In summer it has lime-green foliage and small clusters of long-lasting, deep-pink flowers. It is a deciduous shrub growing to three feet and as much in width. Young foliage is red. Prune to tidy it in late winter. Buy it in gallon containers and space the plants three feet apart in loamy soil that is well drained. You will need 11 plants per 100 square feet.

B. Small Areas in Full Sun

- **MOONBEAM THREADLEAF COREOPSIS** (*Coreopsis verticillata Moonbeam*). A popular, low-growing and neatly mounded perennial, Moonbeam coreopsis makes a mass of tiny, lemon-yellow, daisy-like flowers that are unstoppable. It is one of the easiest and most willing plants in the garden, and its popularity does nothing to diminish its value. It is a good companion to a host of other small shrubs, perennials and grasses and valuable as a late-season plant teamed with sedums, Japanese anemones, grasses and asters. Its texture is fine. It grows to 18 inches and as much in width. Buy it in pint-sized to gallon-sized containers and plant 18 inches apart it a sunny, well-drained site. You will need nine plants per 20 square feet.

- **PLUMBAGO** (*Ceratostigma plumaginoides*). Another unlikely looking workhorse, *ceratostigma* is a spreading, deciduous perennial with delicate leaves and clusters of violet-blue flowers — not a carpet of them, but a steady bouquet for much of the season. (It grows low, but you shouldn't think it is a weakling.) It doesn't appear until mid-to-late spring, and some impatient types think in early May that it is dead. But

PLANTING GROUND COVERS

THE BEST TIME to plant ground covers is in early fall or early spring, but most plants can be installed almost anytime provided they receive adequate watering until they are established.

First, allot sufficient time for this chore. You cannot put in 100 plants during half time of a football game. Second, site preparation is onerous but necessary for the success of the project and may take two to three Saturday mornings. This is what should be done:

STEP 1: Kill existing turf, weeds and other vegetation by spraying with an all-purpose herbicide containing glyphosate, following label directions carefully. Then wait two weeks.

STEP 2: Use a sharp shovel to skim off the dead top growth. Cultivate the soil with a garden fork, or rent a rototiller or the services of someone who has one. Blend in soil amendments, rake the ground smooth and wait another week.

STEP 3: If the soil is covered in tiny weed seedlings, use a sharp hoe for light cultivation of the top half-inch. Lay the mulch now, to a depth of three inches. This is an essential barrier against the weed seeds in the ground. Plant the ground covers through the mulch, making sure the root crowns of the plants are at the soil line, not the mulch level. Firm the soil and the mulch around the plants and push the mulch away slightly from the stem of the plant. Water regularly for the first 12 weeks, and pull any weeds while they are young.

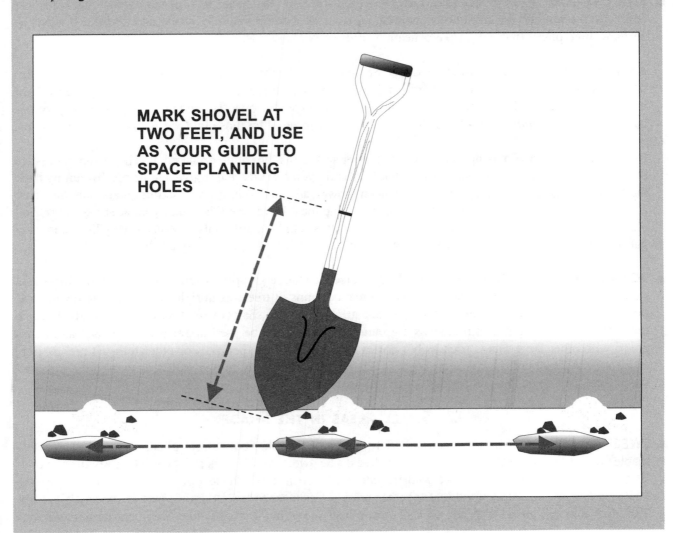

MARK SHOVEL AT TWO FEET, AND USE AS YOUR GUIDE TO SPACE PLANTING HOLES

it will indeed appear, and about eight weeks after first emerging it will produce the first of its flowers and then bloom on and off until the frost. In fall the leaves are burnished with copper.

Its late appearance makes it a perfect bedfellow for daffodil, allium, snowdrops, scilla and other perennial bulbs. You wouldn't want to disturb *ceratostigma* each year, however, to dig and plant tulips. It grows to 12 inches and will take light shade. Buy it from quart containers and space 12 inches apart. You will need 20 per 20 square feet.

C. Large Areas in the Shade

- **BIGROOT CRANESBILL** *(Geranium macrorrhizum)*. This is one of the true geraniums, a hardy perennial that should not be confused with the summer container plant that is not winter-hardy outdoors in our climate. Several cranesbill species and varieties are of immense value outside, particularly the bigroot cranesbill: Once established, it endures dry conditions, flowers unusually well for a shade plant and forms a dense mat, pushing out any weeds. Its foliage is fragrant, especially when bruised. Its flowers, which emerge in spring, range from light pink to magenta and white. Deadheading will encourage later re-blooming.

This plant prefers light-to-moderate shade to dense shade and will grow happily in average soil, provided it is not wet. Water occasionally in its first year. It grows to 18 inches, with an equal or greater spread. Buy in one-gallon or two-gallon containers and space 24 inches apart. You will need 25 plants per 100 square feet.

- **BLUE LILY-TURF** *(Liriope muscari)*. Liriope is God's gift for the steam bath of summer. It has vigor and beauty in the most trying conditions, including the dreadful combination of shade and dryness. It is one of perhaps three plants that will thrive beneath a silver or Norway maple.

A variety named Big Blue grows to two feet. Some people like the variegated form, *Variegata*. I find it inferior to the plain green version, less hardy and less vigorous. Moreover, the greens seem to capture sunlight in their slender dark blades and throw it back at you from the shadows. Though not as big, a second species named *Liriope spicata* is more cold-hardy and may be preferred by those in Zone 6 and at high elevations.

In late summer liriope puts up pale lavender flower spikes that are quite ornamental. They support clusters of shiny black berries that persist into winter. In March, you can tidy and rejuvenate liriope by cutting back the foliage. Some brave souls do this with a lawn mower, adjusted to its highest setting (make sure the blade is sharp). The miniature version, useful when the scale must be reduced, is actually another closely related plant named Mondo Grass *(Ophiopogon japonicus)*. It is reliably hardy only to Zone 7. Buy liriope in half-gallon to one-gallon pots and space 18 inches apart. You'll need 44 per 100 square feet.

- **ROYAL FERN** *(Osmunda regalis)*. One of the choicest of the large upright ferns, the royal fern works as a shrub in a shady corner. But massed between great columns of trees, its upright form, delicate texture and rich green color create an ethereal atmosphere, particularly when shafts of light play on the fronds. It might reach five feet in height or more, so as a ground cover it should be used in generous expanses and juxtaposed with other large plants such as big hostas, aruncus, astilbes, petasites or other ferns. It prefers rich, moist soil and will endure wet feet, but it is not for dry shade. Buy in one-gallon or two-gallon pots and space three feet apart. You will need 11 per 100 square feet.

D. Small Areas in the Shade

- **SWEET WOODRUFF** *(Galium odoratum)*. This is one of the other bulletproof plants either for the foot of maples or for less shaded and more inviting areas. The sweet woodruff is a delicate, fine-textured, woodland ground cover whose leaves are whorled into small green stars. Clusters of small white flowers top the leaves in late spring. Bloom and leaf together bring a freshness to the gloomiest part of the shade garden. The plant is small, growing to just six inches or a little more, but it spreads like fire in optimum conditions (moist and rich soil), and it is content if not boisterous in drier, ordinary soil. Buy in four-inch pots and plant 10 inches apart. You will need 29 per 20 square feet.

■ **BUGLEWEED** *(Ajuga reptans)*. Bugleweed's rosettes of glossy, evergreen leaves form thick mats, often with striking coloring and markings. Generally low-growing, bugleweed is used solely for its leaf ornament. However, in the spring it puts forth dozens of flower spikes covered in tiny gentian blue blossoms. The effect is startling, especially in combination with pink-flowering dianthus or bleeding heart or with the white plumes of foamflower. Bugleweed fans should keep an eye out for two varieties — Burgundy Glow and Bronze Beauty — that are quite different and quite beautiful. They grow to just six inches (out of bloom) and spread quickly. Buy in four-inch pots and plant 12 inches apart. You will need 20 per 20 square feet.

Chapter 20

ROSES

ANY GARDENERS are bewitched by roses. They try them, enjoy the first flush of bloom around Memorial Day — and then watch the plants go into sorry decline in our climate. Love turns to hate. The roses get the shove, and the gardener ends up with pangs of wistfulness and regret each time someone else's roses are glimpsed in bloom.

It doesn't have to be this way. Modern roses do need care and, just as important, some forethought. But you can enjoy them year after year with minimal work if you make a commitment. Many folk, however, don't have that will (or the inclination to use the chemical sprays needed in some instances), so the rose as a treasured garden plant has lost its sheen with the gardening public. While other aspects of gardening have exploded in the past 25 years, rose sales generally have been flat. Why fuss with roses when you can have weeks of color and interest from perennials?

Yet there remains something alluring, almost irresistible, about the majestic rose: layer after layer of unfurling buds, the silky petals in the richest of colors, the heavenly fragrance.

Rose growers have recognized this ambivalence and are developing new varieties expressly for the hard-pressed professional with little time for gardening but with a lingering yearning for the plant all the same. Breeders have achieved remarkable things: near-constant flowering, hundreds of blooms per bush, winter-hardy plants that perform even in the face of almost total neglect. There are now whole classes of landscape roses less suited to producing the pristine blooms of the flower show but more able to survive the rigors of the Washington climate and to integrate with other plants. There is also a resurgent interest in old garden roses, beloved for their form and scent, and in such hybrids as the David Austin English roses that seek to combine the virtues of modern and heirloom varieties. Climbing roses, moreover, bestow a precious, romantic quality to the garden, add ornament to small city gardens and deserve greater use in general.

MODERN ROSES

THIS IS THE TERM given to the hybrid tea rose, the floribundas and the grandifloras. The hybrid tea has relatively few flowers, but its large, well-displayed blooms on long stems makes it perfect for cutting. The floribundas are shorter and bushier and yield many more flowers, albeit smaller ones. The grandifloras, a cross between the two, are marked by large blossoms and hybrid vigor, easily growing to five feet or higher. The hybrid tea is the most common, and all three are used similarly, although the floribunda is best suited to massing by single variety or as a rose hedge.

"Modern" is a relative term in rose history. The first hybrid tea, La France, was introduced in 1867. By the turn of the century, the model for formal rose gardens to show off the flowers was well established in the private estates and public parks of Europe and North America.

The rose garden of Everyman was — and in most people's minds still is — a rectangular or circular bed or two devoted solely to roses, perhaps in the front lawn, perhaps along the driveway or as foundation plantings.

There's good reason to keep roses separate like this. The soil and site requirements for a whole collection can be met in one place. The roses, once planted, can be maintained more conveniently when they are together. And, aesthetically, these roses are hard to place with other garden plants. They are bred principally for the flower — for its size, color, form and petal substance. The overall plant habit is upright and twiggy and very much secondary.

This doesn't mean that modern roses are ugly. The ones that have made it to the public, and particularly those that have been awarded the rose "Oscar" — the All America Rose Selection — are the cream of the crop, selected for superior habit, foliage, flower height and presentation, balance and plant symmetry. But even the most graceful modern roses look a little stiff and are best kept together in small collections rather than forced into beds with other plants. "Small" is the key word for new gardeners. Start with three or five or seven — enough for a rose bed but not so many that you are overwhelmed by their demands.

Don't buy rose varieties on impulse. Don't go to a garden center in May or June when container-grown roses are in full bloom and fall prey to your weaknesses. It is essential to buy a variety that has proved itself in the difficult Washington climate and that is resistant to blackspot. Buying potted roses shipped from California or Oregon or elsewhere will yield no clue to their performance here. (It is fine to indulge at a garden center in rose season, but do your homework first and go with a list of pre-selected varieties.)

You can assess the local performance of roses by visiting rose display gardens in early summer, when they are at peak bloom. Return in August to see if favored varieties are still presentable or disfigured by disease. The roses probably will have been sprayed against blackspot, but this visit at the most stressful time of year is still a good measure of the flower's resistance. In addition, the American Rose Society puts out the *Handbook for Selecting Roses*, with rankings based on trials held across the country. Other sources of information are spring lectures given by rosarians at botanical gardens and parks in the region. Also, in June and September local rose society chapters hold shows where members can be quizzed about superior varieties. Look for show and lecture announcements in *The Washington Post*.

PLANTING AND CARE

MANY GARDENERS BROWSE through rose catalogs over the winter and order plants from mail-order nurseries, to arrive in March. They are shipped as two-year-old, bare-rooted plants, which new gardeners tend to find a little unsettling. How can this mass of twigs be full of vibrant blooms in a matter of weeks? Well, it will be, especially if you prepare the planting beds properly. Remember, though, that it will take two or three seasons for roses to reach their flowering peak; don't expect too much the first year.

SPACING
Roses shouldn't be crowded in our climate. Place smaller floribundas about 30 inches apart, hybrid teas 30 to 36 inches apart and grandifloras at least 36 inches apart, all staggered in alternating rows. Select a site with good air circulation — higher ground away from buildings, fences and hedges — and one that receives a mimimum of six hours of direct sunlight daily. The optimum spot will receive some shade from mid-afternoon on.

Roses must have soil that is slightly acidic (pH 5.5 to 6.5), moisture-retentive and well drained. This means plenty of well-rotted manure, peat moss, a little sand and good topsoil. The hole should be at least 18 inches deep and 24 inches in diameter. If you are planting several different roses, go to the extra trouble of preparing the entire bed. Discard excavated clay if it is too heavy to mix with the amendments. Bare-root plants are installed in early spring, often when waterlogged soil should not be worked. Place and secure a plastic sheet over your new rose bed before the roses arrive to keep the ground dry enough to handle.

DRAINAGE
Pour water into the hole. If it doesn't go away after several hours, you have a problem. You could go to the trouble of installing a drainpipe and placing raised beds on top, but it is generally easier to find a better-drained site. Hillsides can be converted into rose beds with the use of terraces retained with boards, landscape timbers or stone walls. Don't wait for your roses to arrive before doing this.

SUGGESTED MODERN ROSES FOR THE WASHINGTON GARDEN

HYBRID TEAS

Electron (deep pink)
Las Vegas (ruddy orange-yellow bicolor)
Olympiad (red)
Sheer Bliss (pink)
Mikado (red)
Peace (white, yellow, rose mix)
Yankee Doodle (yellow orange with apricot pink centers)

Oklahoma (dark red)
Mister Lincoln (dark red)
Dainty Bess (pink, single flower)
Double Delight (red-white blend)
Garden Party (white)
Just Joey (orange blend)

FLORIBUNDAS

Europeana (red, semi-double)
Iceberg (white, Zone 7)
Gruss an Aachen (light pink, takes some shade)
Saratoga (white)

GRANDIFLORAS

Queen Elizabeth (pink)
Aquarius (light pink)
New Year (orange)

PREPARATION

Soak the bare-root roses overnight in a pail of slightly tepid water, adding a soluble, balanced fertilizer at half strength. Some gardeners put in a couple of tablespoons of chlorine bleach to kill any bugs or fungi. If you cannot plant the next day, heel in the roots in a temporary bed and water, but don't keep them there for more than a few days. The object is to keep the roots buried so they don't dry out. Check daily to make sure no animal has dug up the plants or that the soil hasn't been washed away in a storm.

PLANTING

Before planting, remove roots and stems that are cut or damaged. In the base of the planting hole, fashion a mound of soil, on which the roots will sit and spread out and down (picture an octopus atop a rock). Backfill with material that has been thoroughly mixed, including with it a cup of bone meal or other organic fertilizer, and tamp down gently with your hands. When the hole is filled, pour in water gently and wait several minutes. The soil will have settled. Add more material until it forms a mound, which will take two or three inches more with successive waterings. The bud union — the swelling in the stem where the top has been grafted onto the roots — should be planted just above soil level in Zone 7 and just below soil level in Zone 6. Once you have set the roses correctly, dress the entire bed with a two-inch layer of mulch, but be careful not to mound the mulch against the rose stems.

Container-grown roses are planted the same way, except that you won't need to make a little dome for the roots. It is important to remove the container as delicately as possible (some people remove the base and then cut it away in place) to minimize stress at a time when the plant is in leaf.

Roses shipped in cardboard boxes and smothered in wax (often sold in hardware stores) are all right. But examine them for disease, damage or dieback before purchasing, and plant them as soon as they arrive on the shelves. Roses that are left for weeks and begin to grow in that condition will become severely stressed. Don't try to remove the wax; it will melt in the sun in time. Select only disease-resistant varieties.

Roses come in three grades, according to size and vigor: No.1, No. 1½ and No. 2. Always get No. 1 grade when possible and No. 1½ only if you are desperate for a given variety. Avoid No. 2. The money you save is not worth it; roses in our climate need all the head start they can get.

WATERING

Roses are thirsty and should receive the equivalent of an inch of water a week during the growing season. Water the roots with a pail or watering can to avoid getting the leaves wet. Be diligent about watering, especially during periods of drought. Drought-stressed roses are more susceptible to ailments and pests, and flower size and production will fall off.

FERTILIZING

Roses are heavy feeders. However, apart from slow-release organic fertilizers worked into the planting hole, new rose bushes should not be fertilized until after their first cycle of blooms is complete. Slow-release granular fertilizers are best. Push back the mulch, scatter the correct amount over the root zone and replace the mulch. Soluble fertilizers could encourage blackspot if placed on leaves. Stop feeding around Labor Day so that the bushes have a chance to harden off before winter.

PRUNING

Modern roses need pruning to remain vigorous, healthy and floriferous. The main pruning, in fact the only pruning if you so desire, should occur in late winter, as the buds swell on the stems. If the buds have broken, you can still prune. Long-handled lopping shears are much more effective at this heavy pruning than hand-held pruners, which require too much effort to cut through thick canes and place your hands close to thorns.

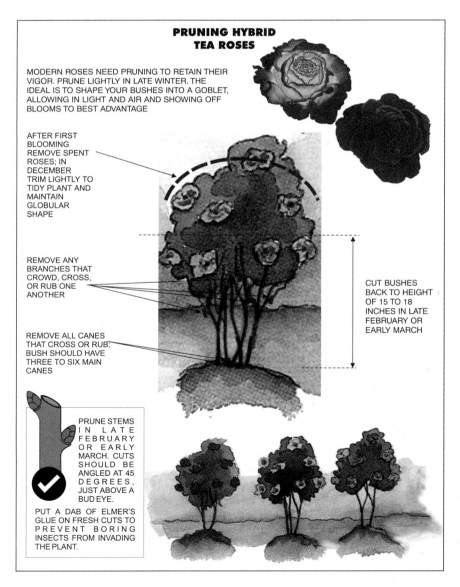

PRUNING HYBRID TEA ROSES

MODERN ROSES NEED PRUNING TO RETAIN THEIR VIGOR. PRUNE LIGHTLY IN LATE WINTER. THE IDEAL IS TO SHAPE YOUR BUSHES INTO A GOBLET, ALLOWING IN LIGHT AND AIR AND SHOWING OFF BLOOMS TO BEST ADVANTAGE

AFTER FIRST BLOOMING REMOVE SPENT ROSES; IN DECEMBER TRIM LIGHTLY TO TIDY PLANT AND MAINTAIN GLOBULAR SHAPE

REMOVE ANY BRANCHES THAT CROWD, CROSS, OR RUB ONE ANOTHER

REMOVE ALL CANES THAT CROSS OR RUB; BUSH SHOULD HAVE THREE TO SIX MAIN CANES

CUT BUSHES BACK TO HEIGHT OF 15 TO 18 INCHES IN LATE FEBRUARY OR EARLY MARCH

PRUNE STEMS IN LATE FEBRUARY OR EARLY MARCH. CUTS SHOULD BE ANGLED AT 45 DEGREES, JUST ABOVE A BUD EYE.

PUT A DAB OF ELMER'S GLUE ON FRESH CUTS TO PREVENT BORING INSECTS FROM INVADING THE PLANT.

You should do a light pruning in December to tidy up the plant and the main pruning in late February or early March. Rose bushes should not be cut back hard in our climate; don't go below 15 to 18 inches. Ideally, the bush will come through the surgery with three to six canes, each about two feet high, with an open center and new buds on the outside of the plant.

Remove all wood that is blackened by winter freeze damage. Always cut canes back sufficiently to healthy pith, which should be the lightest beige, not brown. Cuts should be clean, and angled at 45 degrees above a bud eye. This is the tiny red nub appearing at various points on a stem. The buds, if possible, should be facing out so that the new growth moves away from inside of the bush. If two canes are crossing or rubbing, remove the one that least fulfills this optimum goblet shape. Take out canes that grow inward. On bare fresh cuts, squeeze a generous dab of Elmer's Glue. This will stop boring insects from entering the plant.

THE HIGGINS METHOD OF BEATING BLACKSPOT

■ Select varieties that have proved resistant. Avoid yellow-blooming roses.

■ Place in a sunny site where air moves freely. An air-conditioning unit often provides a breeze when it is most needed.

■ Avoid proximity to bodies of water.

■ Provide optimum growing conditions, especially well-worked soil.

■ Prune to keep the rose bush open in the center.

■ Mulch to prevent rainwater from splashing up onto leaves.

■ Water the roots, never the foliage. Use a watering can, not a garden hose or, God forbid, an overhead sprinkler.

■ Do not water after 2 p.m.

■ As soon as foliage has unfurled in late March, spray with Funginex every two weeks in a pump sprayer. Set the nozzle to a fine mist and work from the base upward, coating the underside of leaves first. Spray in the morning. If there is no sign of blackspot by July, cut back to monthly spraying.

■ Between April and August, spray monthly, in the mornings, with a foliar feed of fish and seaweed emulsion. Avoid squirting the blooms. Some concoctions really smell foul; don't use them five minutes before the bridge club arrives.

■ Patrol the rose garden at least once a week. Handpick leaves at the first signs of blackspot, before they turn yellow. Pick up any fallen leaves. Put all infected material in a plastic bag and throw it out.

After the first blooming cycle in June, remove spent roses down to just above the first five-leaflet leaf; new flowering stems will emerge from the leaf axils and will begin to bloom in late August. In milder areas, gardeners can expect a third blooming sequence before freezes kill the buds.

Here's how to handle the debris of pruning. Get a spool of bare wire and, with wire-cutting pliers, cut three six-foot lengths. Place them parallel on the ground, about a foot apart. Twist an eye into the end of each wire. Cut the rose canes into four-foot lengths and place them lengthwise across the wires. Once you have enough for a bundle, thread each wire through the eyes and pull tight, twisting to tie off. Throw out the bundles; do not try to recycle them as mulch or compost.

Wear a long apron, long-sleeved jacket and suede gardening gloves for this work, no matter how warm it is. Roses have vicious thorns.

Main Pests: Aphids, Japanese beetles, spider mites, leafhoppers, whitefly, greenworm and deer. **Main Diseases:** Blackspot (see box), rose decline, rust, fireblight and powdery mildew.[†]

SHRUB ROSES

THIS IS A catchall phrase for classes of roses that are tough, undemanding and suited for more utilitarian roles. Most have been developed since the 1970s for American gardeners who don't want to fuss with roses. Some will look bad if not sprayed, but generally they can survive with little care once established, and they don't need pruning or deadheading, although the old foliage should be cut back in late winter. (A shearing is fine, but you don't have to worry about shaping individual plants.) They grow on their own roots, so if they are killed by freezes they will grow back true to variety.

The individual blossoms generally are not as attractive as modern roses, but there are many more of them in near-continuous waves of color during the growing season. They are not reliably fragrant. Many are much less appealing to deer than modern roses.

Depending on height and scale desired, these shrubs can be used as ground covers, for slopes, as hedging or simply as sturdy border plants. For ground covers on small and medium-sized areas, pick roses that grow no higher than three feet. The House of Meilland in France, the Kordes family in Germany and David Austin in England have developed many of these shrub roses:

VARIETY	COLOR	HEIGHT & WIDTH
Bonica and Royal Bonica	pink	3-5 feet x 4 feet
Alba Meidiland	white	4 feet x 5 feet
Red Meidiland	red with yellow stamens; flowers single or semi-double	3 feet x 5 feet
Sevillana	red	4 feet x 3 feet
Scarlet Meidiland	red	4 feet x 5 feet
Cherry Meidiland	strong carmine red; single flowers	5 feet x 5 feet
The Fairy	pink	3 feet x 4 feet

RUGOSAS

UNFAIRLY ASSIGNED as beach roses because of their salt and wind tolerance, the rugosas are one of the most beautiful and rugged of all garden plants, and the fragrance of the single and semi-double flowers is beyond description. Most have highly ornamental fruit or hips in the fall, and, to allow them to form, should not be deadheaded. Rugosas typically grow 5 feet x 5 feet and come in a range of soft, blue-tinted pinks, crimsons and magentas as well as whites. My favorites are Sarah van Fleet, Frau Dagmar Hartopp, White Grootendorst, Hansa (double) and Roseraie de L'Hay (semi-double, few hips).

ENGLISH ROSES BY DAVID AUSTIN

THESE HAVE BEEN developed to capture the sumptuous colors, forms and fragrances of old garden roses but with modern virtues of contained bushes that bloom more than once in a season. Some varieties do well in the region, others struggle to get established, and yet others do too well — they become huge. Local gardeners also report differences in the performance of the same variety. It is a matter of trial and error. Try the following: Abraham Darby, Gertrude Jekyll, Leander, the Countryman, Othello and Graham Thomas.

Rosarian Clair G. Martin, author of *100 English Roses for the American Garden,* offers a great tip for dealing with English Roses that get out of hand. At pruning time in late winter, thin the shrub so that five or six of the plant's longest canes — some might be 10 feet long — are left. Then tie each one back on itself to form a coronet. This causes buds to break that otherwise wouldn't, so the roses are smothered in flowers come summer. Good candidates, he says, include Brother Cadfael, Charles Austin, Gertrude Jekyll, Graham Thomas, Jayne Austin and the Countryman.

OLD GARDEN ROSES

OLD GARDEN ROSES are also known as heritage and antique roses. All modern roses trace their bloodlines to these old roses, which fell from grace when the Victorians became entranced by the hybrid tea. They also were discounted because many bloom only once and are too big for small gardens. Happily, people have been rediscovering these beauties. They are wonderful additions to the garden, with fragrances that modern roses can't come close to matching. They grow for the most part on their own rootstock, making them more winter-hardy. They also are less prone to diseases and resistant to deer. There are many good reasons to reserve at least one spot in the garden for antique roses. Think of them as a large flowering shrub, such as forsythia, lilac or viburnum. There are many from which to choose:

NOISETTES
Tall, needing support of fence or wall. Pastel colors and heady scent.
Champney's Pink Cluster
Blush Noisette
Mme Alfred Carriere (Zone 7)

BOURBONS
Large, sprawling shrubs with free-flowering blooms in rich pinks and deep reds.
Mme Isaac Periere
Zepherine Drouhin

CENTIFOLIAS
Classic cabbage rose.
Chapeau de Napoleon
Fantin-Latour

GALLICAS
Ancient, vigorous shrubs that are extremely cold-hardy and blessed with masses of blooms in strong reds and pinks.
Hippolyte
Cardinal de Richelieu
Charles de Mills
Belle de Crecy
Tuscany

MOSS ROSES
Named for furry covering to stems and buds.
Little Gem
General Kleber
Alfred de Dalmas

ALBAS
Not all white, some in pinks.
Maxima
Mme Plantier
Maiden's Blush
Konigin von Danemark

HYBRID MUSKS
Developed early this century, the ones listed are among the most exquisite roses in the garden.
Buff Beauty (big shrub)
Moonlight (treat as small climber)
Ballerina

DAMASKS
Mme Hardy

CLIMBING ROSES

These need support: arbors, bowers, pergolas, sheds, arches or walls. There are many places for them to rest if you look about. Look for beds that are too shady for other roses; if they grow up into sunlight, they will work. Try to position the climber so you see it from the south or the west, where most of the flowering will occur. Suggested varieties: New Dawn, White Dawn, Dublin Bay, Dortmund, Alberic Barbier and American Pillar.

Pests and Diseases: Climbing and English roses share the modern rose's pest and disease problems, but other roses are much less prone to them.

---

†See Appendix for common pest and disease ailments and remedies.

Chapter 21

DAHLIAS AND MUMS

*O*LD FAVORITES with a continued place in the garden, dahlias and chrysanthemums provide color and beauty when the garden most needs refreshment — in late summer and into fall for dahlias, in fall for mums.

Both plants have been grown in isolation in the past, but new varieties and new thinking should bring them into association with other specimens. Because hobbyists raise the plants for show, a culture has emerged suggesting that they are hard to grow. It might be difficult to produce flawless blooms of show quality, but both dahlias and mums can be grown well by anyone, though they probably are not for the organic gardener.

I. Dahlias

TO MANY, the quintessential dahlia is bright yellow or red and the size of a dinner plate, with literally hundreds of petals. This is the Giant, or AA, dahlia. But 180 years of breeding have produced hundreds of other types and many more cultivars.

Dahlias are divided into 17 flower forms — from formal decoratives, cactus and pompon to anemone, collarette and single — and nine sizes. The sizes range from the tiny Mignon Singles (less than two inches in diameter) to the Large, or A, flowers (eight to 10 inches across) to the Giants that exceed 10 inches and sometimes 15 inches. It is telling that a flower classified here as Small (four to six inches in diameter) would be deemed huge if it were a rose or a camellia.

With the vast number of types and varieties, listing a handful would be of little value. Remember, though, that larger is not always better. Some of the most exquisite dahlias are quite small, particularly waterlily, pompon and cactus varieties and those with two-colored petals. Whatever type you prefer, it is essential to buy tubers identified by the plant's exact size, habit and flower color, so you will know where to place it.

Bush-type dahlias grow about four feet high and as much across (with some help from the gardener), and they are the easiest and most useful to integrate into the late-summer border. Exhibition types are stiffer, more upright in form, always need staking, and can be placed at the back of a sunny bed to provide valuable height. Those intended for exhibition, or for cutting, are best grown in their own beds. Side yards are a good location, providing there is enough sun.

Dahlias also are great as container plants on patios and balconies, but you will have to be diligent about watering and feeding them. Dahlias are tuberous herbs from Central America, related to sunflowers. They are not hardy in Washington and will not survive winters in the ground. However, they can be lifted in the fall, divided, stored and replanted in spring.

CULTIVATION

IN SPITE OF their variety, all dahlias require the same basic culture. They grow swiftly and vigorously and so need even and large amounts of moisture and nutrients. This is best achieved by planting them in raised beds with enriched soil high in organic matter. When working the bed in early spring, try to mix in large amounts of compost and organic fertilizers, such as greensand or fish and seaweed meal, and supplement this afterward with low-nitrogen inorganic fertilizers. Use either granular fertilizer, tilled into the soil at a rate of 10 pounds per 100 square feet, or the same amount of a slow-release fertilizer like Osmocote, gently raked into the top of the soil after the bed has been prepared. The flowers still will need feeding in the summer. Dahlias should be given a root zone of at least three feet across, and avoid treading in that zone once the tuber is planted.

The soil should be worked to a depth of at least eight inches: The dahlia is planted four inches deep in the Washington area and is later mulched when the weather turns hot. Pine bark chips are preferred over shredded hardwood, which often harbors slugs and earwigs.

The tubers can be started indoors in April or planted directly into the ground after frost danger has passed, usually early to mid-May. Tubers begun indoors will have a better chance of avoiding destruction by cutworms and slugs. If slugs are a problem, you may have to use slug pellets around young dahlias after you set them out. You also may need metal cages (tomato cages with netting work well) in areas afflicted with deer or rabbits. Organic gardeners can control slugs by handpicking, with beer traps that drown them in the brew, or with a powder (diatomaceous earth) consisting of minuscule shell shards that cut mollusks.

If you do start tubers indoors, place them in an aluminum baking pan with holes cut for drainage. Fill the pan with sterile potting mix, without soil, and cover it with newspapers. Place the pan in a warm area away from direct sunlight, and keep the soil medium moist but not wet. Once the tubers have sprouted, remove the blanket of newspaper and wait for the plant to develop its first pair of leaves. Harden off the plants by placing the pan outdoors during the day. Keep it out of direct sunlight, and bring it in at night.

TRANSPLANTING

Transplant the seedlings into the bed on a cloudy day in early to mid-May (hot direct sun will stress the plant and delay its growth). If your tuber has produced two shoots, pull off the weaker one.

If you are planting dahlias in their own beds, set them 30 inches apart in rows that are at least three feet wide. Fifteen to 20 plants will yield an ample supply for cutting, with Small varieties producing far more blooms than Large and Giant dahlias.

When the plant has two to four sets of leaves (four for smaller-flowering varieties), remove the tip of the shoot. This is essential for flower production. Lateral branches then will emerge from the leaf nodes. As they grow, they will produce three to five flower buds — one at the tip and a pair at the first and possibly the second leaf branches or nodes. Remove all of them except the one at the tip of the branch. If you don't, you will have weaker, smaller flowers that will not bloom at the same time, making the stem useless as a cut flower. You still will have plenty of flowers.

Once a flower has bloomed, cut it off, and more side branches will develop. Repeat the winnowing of lateral buds from these secondary branches. With bedding dahlias, you should remove the growth tip to promote bushiness, but it is not necessary to remove the lateral flower buds when they appear.

Dahlias that grow above three feet (most varieties) should be staked. Use a sturdy bamboo cane and plunge it nine to 12 inches deep (don't spear the tuber). Tie the plant with plastic tape or loose twine, being careful not to choke the dahlia stem. In mid-to-late summer, when the dahlia buds begin to grow and swell, feed the plant every two weeks with a water-soluble fertilizer low in nitrogen (look for formulations of 10-20-30, 10-60-10 or 5-50-17). Stop fertilizing by the second week of September if you are planning to lift and store the tubers; any additional growth will encourage winter root rot.

Dahlias are best watered at their base to keep fungal diseases off leaves. Give the plant a good soaking every five to seven days in high summer. If plants wilt, you can and should recharge them by watering the leaves.

LIFTING AND STORING

Lifting and storing dahlias is a time-consuming chore, but it is an inexpensive way to expand your dahlia stock as well as to assure a supply of varieties you love. In mid-October, cut back the dahlia plant so the stalk is four to six inches above the ground. Cover the hole in the top of the cane with a lid of aluminum foil to prevent rainwater from rotting the roots. In mid-November, or before a hard freeze, lift the tubers carefully with a garden fork.

You will notice four or five tubers emanating from the base of the stalk. By leaving the cluster in the ground, you have allowed time for tiny buds to develop close to the stalk. These are next year's stems. Indoors, with a firm base and a sharp knife, separate the individual tubers, making sure each has at least one bud. Place each tuber in a one-gallon plastic food bag with two cups of dry vermiculite. Then put the sealed bags into brown shopping bags and store in a cool, dry place (a lightly heated garage is ideal) where temperatures will not freeze or exceed 50 degrees.

Check monthly through the winter. Roots that have begun to rot should be discarded. In late March or early April, sprinkle some water into the bags and move them to a warm location to promote bud development.

In the summer, heavy rains might cause the backs of petals to turn brown. Dark oranges and reds get bleached by direct sun and will last longer if shaded. To guard against sunlight and storms, some hobbyists shield prized blooms with umbrellas attached to their own stakes. This is a sign of advanced dahlia mania.

Main Pests: Slugs, aphids, spider mites, cutworms, deer and rabbits. **Main Diseases:** Powdery mildew and viruses.[†]

USES IN GARDEN DESIGNS

DWARF OR BEDDING dahlias offer great massed form and color in the late summer/early fall border. They bloom with sedums, Japanese anemones, crape myrtles, hostas, *ceratostigma* and coreopsis as well as with ornamental grasses. They also work well with sunny annuals, such as marigolds, lantana, annual salvias, flowering tobacco and zinnias. Even dark-colored dahlias tend to have rich hues, so you have to anticipate color clashes. Some dahlias have purple leaves, which are particularly effective with other purple, silver-leafed or blue-flowering plants. Consider the annual purple pennisetum grass and silver-leafed artemesias or senecios, as well as the blue-flowering *ceratostigma*, perovskia or caryopteris.

If you are using exhibition-type dahlias at the back of a border, remember that the larger the flower, the taller the plant. Contented plants will rise to four to six feet and will need staking. Some gardeners like to stake before planting so they can get the stake as close as possible to the tuber without fear of damage.

II. *Chrysanthemums*

CHRYSANTHEMUMS FALL into three distinct classes: the ubiquitous common garden mum of the fall, the exhibition, or disbud, types grown by fanciers, and dependable and worthy perennials, including shasta and Marguerite daisies, suited to flower borders and cottage gardens.

CULTIVATION

THE GARDEN mum purchased in bud or flower in late summer and enjoyed to mid-fall is an easy plant that requires little or no special care when treated as an annual and discarded in November. Smaller varieties, growing to 18 inches, are known as cushion mums. Taller ones are called garden hardy mums. You should water these garden mums once they dry out. Some taller ones may need staking. Use a bamboo cane to support a tie strapped discreetly and not too tightly around the outer stems. The plants do not need fertilizing or pinching back: The grower has done this for you. (If you want to keep these mums, see box on saving garden mums.)

CAN I SAVE MY GARDEN MUMS?
SHOULD I PLANT THE POTTED MUMS?

CHRYSANTHEMUMS ARE so colorful and bushy in October that the overriding desire is to keep them. The universal cry is: Can I? The answer: Yes — but it's probably not worth the trouble.

The garden mum will survive most winters (though early, hard freezes as well as the freezing or thawing of non-mulched mums will kill the plants). Remove the old top growth and allow new shoots to emerge in March. However, the mum is genetically unstable, and one year's flower color and plant habit are not guaranteed the next year. Old plants also become magnets for insects and disease, the most serious of which probably is the soil-borne, worm-like nematode that destroys plant roots and is ineradicable.

In April, you can lift the plant and use a knife or trowel to take the youngest, outermost growth — a division with roots, stem and leaves intact — and plant that in a sunny spot. One plant will yield several more, a good way to increase stock for free. Local growers fear, though, that these divisions will attract pests, too. So after they take stem cuttings in March or April, they grow them indoors, under lights. This is easy once you have the equipment: a bench and seedling trays under a fluorescent lamp, or a custom-built seedling trolley. Take three-inch stem cuttings, dip them in rooting hormone and grow them in a potting mix. Don't water, but mist the cuttings two or three times a day. They will root in about two weeks.

Members of local chrysanthemum societies do this work for you, selling rooted cuttings at various locations in the metropolitan area, usually on the third weekend of May.

If you grow divisions or new cuttings, you still should pinch back the plants to encourage bushiness and flowering (see cultivation section).

Potted chrysanthemums also can be forced into flower in the greenhouse. They then can be planted out and, with proper care, will re-bloom the same year. The problem is that the plant may need shading to induce flowering in October before frosts and freezes. This must be done in early August for two weeks. At 7 p.m., place a black plastic trash bag over the plant, anchor the bag with pegs or bricks and remove it 12 hours later. If your neighbor catches you at it, plead insanity.

Both disbud and perennial mums are planted in the spring. They will do well in ordinary, well-drained soil. Disbud types are grown the same way as dahlias, in their own enriched beds. In smaller gardens, you can raise show-quality mums in eight-inch nursery pots made of black plastic.

Perennials should be spaced 18 inches apart in beds and borders. Disbuds, which grow taller but narrower, can be set 12 inches apart. Mums have shallow roots and should not be planted too deeply.

If you want to raise disbud types for cutting or showing, here's the regimen: Mulch with buckwheat hulls or pine needles (shredded hardwood will foster slugs). Fertilize every two weeks with a balanced, soluble fertilizer. Water as needed, but keep the foliage as dry as possible.

In June, you should start a program of pinching back the plant, similar to what's done with dahlias. When plants are about five inches high, remove the top half-inch of the tip. The lateral shoots then will grow. They, too, should be pinched back. If new laterals have appeared by mid-July or so, pinch back a third and last time. If you pinch back after that, you will lose flowers for the fall.

Some of the most interesting chrysanthemums, including spiders, quills and some incurves, flower late in the season. They can be enjoyed into November if you place a floating row cover over them on frosty nights.[1]

---

[1] A floating row cover is a spun-fiber cloth that forms a barrier against light frosts and insects while letting in both light and water. It also is sold as Reemay cloth.

Main Pests of Disbuds: Aphids, cutworms, slugs, earwigs, caterpillars, mites, thrips, mealy bugs and nematodes. **Main Diseases:** Fusarium wilt, powdery mildew and a fungus-induced browning of petals caused by rain. (Perennials are not as prone to these pests and diseases, and common mums planted in September and discarded in November are not in the garden long enough to develop serious problems.) [†]

NOTABLE PERENNIALS

WHILE COMMON garden mums require little elucidation and disbud mums should be viewed at fall shows, perennial mums deserve a bit more discussion. Several worthy perennials are long-flowering and good for cutting as well as for borders and beds. As a rule, they are not as hard to raise. Preferring full sun and soil that drains freely, they will flower longer and better with regular deadheading of spent blooms and monthly feedings with a balanced fertilizer.

■ **OXEYE DAISY** (*C. leucanthemum*). A low-growing perennial, it sends up white daisies with yellow centers on tall, wiry stems, blooming for weeks in early summer. Use it as a front-of-the-border accent plant with daylilies, Siberian irises and lilies, to brighten a bed of evergreens, or as a welcoming clump at a doorway or along an entrance path. It also is effective at the base of a climbing rose, to hide the lower canes.

■ **SHASTA DAISY** (*C. x superbum*). One of the easiest plants in the summer garden, the shasta daisy is an enduring favorite. It, too, has yellow-eyed, white flowers. A number of varieties are available, some dwarf, others with double flowers. Shasta daisies will take partial shade at the expense of flowering. Plants are not long-lived, and lifting and dividing every other year is recommended.

■ **NIPPON DAISY** (*C. nipponicum*). Flowering in the fall, this grows about two feet high and as much in width. It has pretty, fleshy green leaves and produces its yellow-eyed, white daisies late in the season. It is valuable for sustaining late-season interest in the garden, along with sedums, ornamental grasses, Japanese anemones, liriope and other glories of the back-to-school period. However, it grows leggy and is best planted behind a bushier plant. Tolerant of salt air, it is also useful as a seaside plant. Similarly, this makes it handy along a walkway that might be salted in the winter.

■ **FEVERFEW** (*C. parthenium*). Old-fashioned and somewhat dull, feverfew is nevertheless a grand old herb valued for its long blooming period in August and September, its ferny foliage and its button-like blossoms. Lift and divide the plants each spring.

■ **CHRYSANTHEMUM CLARA CURTIS** (*C. x rubellum or C. zawadskii*). This variety is valued for its attractive rose-pink daisies in the early fall, blooming with (and a great companion to) asters.

■ **MARGUERITE DAISY** (*Chrysanthemum frutescens*). Not hardy in our area and thus used as an annual here, it grows into a robust plant three feet high and as much across. It has clusters of white, yellow and pink daisies about two inches across.

■ **CHRYSANTHEMUM PACIFICUM.** This is a relatively new but stunning late-season perennial. It is grown for its beautiful green leaves, notched, clustered and defined by the thinnest margin of silver, as if laid in by a jeweler. It flowers into frost. It is a marvelous ground cover for hot, sunny sites.

[†]See Appendix for common pest and disease ailments and remedies.

Section 4

SPECIAL GARDENS

Chapter 22

SHADE GARDENS

*W*E ARE PROGRAMMED to believe that if our properties are cast in shadow, something is wrong with our gardens and, by extension, with us. We are second-class gardeners, sentenced for our sins to a life of pachysandra and periwinkle.

With a little forethought, however, the shade garden can be transformed into a lush paradise and a welcome shelter from the baking sun of high summer. You don't have to restrict your plant repertoire to accomplish this. You have to alter it, remembering all the while that it is changing lines and textures, in varying forms and contrasts, that a garden reaches its most interesting state.

Indeed, think of how nature constructs its forests. Redbuds, mountain laurels, rhododendrons and azaleas grow at the edge of the wood. Hollies, hemlocks and viburnums grace the deeper shade. Ferns cover embankments. Trilliums, may apples and other ground covers sweep across the woodland floor. Wet-soil species such as ostrich ferns and turtlehead line tiny streams, and lone specimens such as jack-in-the-pulpit emerge at given spots. There can be no doubt that beauty grows in the shade.

TYPES OF SHADE

GARDENS, LIKE WOODS, have different types of shade, often in the same terrain:

- **PARTIAL SHADE.** The term applies to areas that are sunny for part or most of summer mornings but shielded by trees and shrubs or structures the rest of the day. This is space for both sun-loving and shade plants. You may have to test what does well for you. If you do, you should include northern plants that are for sunny conditions but that at our latitude benefit from some relief from afternoon sun, perhaps lilacs, roses, Japanese maples or camellias.

- **DAPPLED OR LIGHT SHADE.** These areas are in near-constant shadow — but light, filtered shadow provided by trees with small, fine leaves, such as black and honey locusts, willow oaks, katsuras, golden raintrees, ginkgos, tulip poplars, pines, dogwoods and crape myrtles.

- **HIGH SHADE.** This is nirvana in the shade garden, a place where old shade trees such as oaks, tulip poplars and hickories provide a high canopy. The light reaching the ground is filtered but bright, making it ideal for flowering trees and shrubs that need a slight sun screen — azaleas, tree peonies, rhododendrons, pieris, stewartias, dogwoods or redbuds.

- **FULL SHADE.** This is the toughest garden shade — unremitting darkness, caused by vegetation or buildings or both. But, as you will see, the darkness almost always can be relieved and a garden made.

A FIVE-STEP TRANSFORMATION

You can create a shade garden from an overgrown wooded lot in five steps. It would be disingenuous to say five easy steps, but the tasks are quite achievable if the will is there:

1. **THINNING OUT THE WOODLOT.** The thicker the stand of trees, the more you should remove. Noted shade gardener Judy Springer of Great Falls, Va., estimates that she took down almost half of her own

shade trees, though none of her garden's woodland feel has been lost. You may be tempted to save every tree and thin out the canopy, but that is more expensive in the long run, since it will have to be done by professionals every three or four years. When you plan to remove trees, pick a company at a quiet time of year, say late fall, when the firm is in need of work.

In deciding which trees to fell, start with those that are damaged, diseased or in decline. Then remove those that cast the deepest shade and have bullying root systems, especially maples, sycamores, beeches and Southern magnolias. Next, if two trees are too close, remove the lesser specimen (try to keep all oaks). Have stumps ground out in areas where you intend to place woodland ground covers, perennials, bulbs and the like. Where you expect to put shrubs, the stumps can remain; indeed, they will add to the naturalistic intent. Thin out dense shrubs and trees, but keep the natural look of the plants. If your shade is cast by a tall fence or building wall, paint the surface white or a light hue to draw in and reflect the light. Similarly, to brighten dark corners use light-colored plants such as caladiums, astilbes, aruncus and lamiastrum.

2. **BUILDING A PATH AND OTHER FEATURES.** The shade garden is not simply for viewing — it is for discovery. Thus, think hard about where a path should go, and imagine it being framed and guided by a delicate ground cover like foamflower, a large shrub like viburnum and hefty clumps of camellias. Woodland paths should have lots of curves, and you can maximize the space with a trail that doubles back on itself. The earth's contours and the position of trees will help suggest where the path should go. If you have an existing path, consider improving it. If the land is flat, consider building berms or small hills to create the effect of an upland wood. A hill will channel the path and bring plants up to eye level.

If you have the room, you may want a clearing, or glade, in the center of the wood, planted with azaleas and ferns. Even if you don't have a great deal of space, consider creating a midpoint that is different. Place a bench there and perhaps an arbor draped in climbing hydrangea, though not a pond. Ponds are unwise in woods. The shade precludes the prettiest aquatic plants, and you will battle constantly to keep leaves and twigs out of the water. On a hilly site, though, you could build a recirculating waterfall or a series of cascading pools. Use the path to bolster your design ideas. Make it narrow in particularly shady spots, broader and more spacious in more open areas.

You will need paving material to keep your feet from getting muddy and to delineate the path. Red brick is classy and textural, but it is expensive, requires skill to lay and is a bit artificial. You shouldn't use concrete or asphalt. The simplest material is mulch, but that needs regular replacing. Shredded hardwood looks good but is messy and breaks down quickly, especially if you maintain a watering schedule. Wood chips are more durable but not as attractive. Judy Springer feels that she has found the answer: a dark brown stone called crusher run, available at local quarries and stone yards. It consists of tiny shards that pack together when compressed, so they stay put and don't spread into woodland beds. The stone, laid to a depth of two to three inches, does not decay or become muddy, no matter how moist the environment. The initial expense of the stone is higher than mulch, but the long-term costs are much lower, and the path is more useful. Assuming the path is three feet wide and the material spread two inches deep, you will need a cubic yard of crusher run for each 50 feet of path.

3. **IMPROVING THE SOIL.** A natural wood takes decades to create a rich organic base, or duff. You need to speed the process, because most shade plants want soil that's evenly moist and cool and drains reasonably well. They also compete with tree roots for water and nourishment. In beds, work in at least 12 inches of leaf mulch or leaf mold. Some also add peat moss for the acidity needed by many woodland plants. Springer, fearing peat moss' depletion in northern bogs where it's harvested, substitutes finely chipped pine bark mulch or an even finer version called Virginia Fines. Also add a little Osmocote, a slow-release balanced fertilizer, to counteract the mulch's tendency to draw nitrogen from soil as it decays. This will damage surface roots of some trees and shrubs at first, but the enriched soil will foster rapid re-growth.

4. **IRRIGATING.** You may think that shade and enriched soil would be enough to keep the woodland earth moist, and in a natural setting it would be. But you will be planting the forest floor with some shrubs, ground covers and perennials. They can't keep pace with trees, which in summer draw hundreds of gallons a day through their systems. In thickly canopied shade gardens, moreover, surprisingly little rain makes it to the floor. In short, you will likely need to irrigate.

Don't try to lug a hose in and out of the garden; that time-consuming chore invariably does damage to the plants. At a minimum, you should have a garden hose just in the shade garden, hooking it into the regular hose when needed. Judy Springer rented a ditch-digging machine and laid one-inch plastic pipes a few inches deep. They emerge at strategic points as bibbs. From these, she runs soaker hoses in beds, sprinklers on three-foot stands, and other sprinklers mounted on tree trunks, the highest at 15 feet. By elevating sprinklers, you achieve greater coverage and also get above clumps of shrubs that otherwise would impede the water sprays. Irrigating the woodland garden makes the difference between plants just hanging on or flourishing. Some gardeners double the standard watering quantity in shade gardens. If they give sunny beds an inch of water a week, they apply two inches in the shade (measured with a coffee can set in the sprinkled area). Springer says that she merely keeps an eye on her Japanese painted ferns. The fronds start to wilt when the ground dries out.

5. **CHOOSING PLANTS.** In a shade garden, where you want to enjoy a restful environment, it is unwise to use too many different plants. Rather, pick a limited variety, with some used en masse.

A good number of small trees for shady areas already have been noted here or examined more fully elsewhere — redbud, stewartia, Japanese maple, pagoda dogwood, witch hazels, hemlocks, American hornbeam, magnolia and Japanese spicebush *(Lindera obtusilosa)*, to cite just some. The same holds for such shrubs as fothergilla, hydrangeas, yew, viburnums, hollies, pieris, rhododendrons, mountain laurels, azaleas, cotoneaster and others. However, it is worth looking a bit more at three of the most popular or valuable elements of shade gardens: ferns and hostas and other perennials.

I. Hostas

HOSTAS ARE grown for their foliage ornament, though many varieties have flower spikes with bold decorative effect, especially when planted en masse. Some varieties, such as Gold Standard, Royal Standard and Love Pat, are suited to deep shade, but generally hostas perform best in partial, dappled or high shade.[1]

Hostas fall into two simple color categories — green and other. Collectors prize chartreuse or near-blue or variegated hostas, but plain green plants are valuable providers of recessive texture against which fancier ones can be seen (in moderation). As for design, hostas come in three broad classes:

1. Smaller, more narrow-leafed varieties such as *Hosta lancifolia* lend themselves to mass planting — as woodland drifts, around the bases of trees and even as ground covers.

2. Hostas with showy flower displays also deserve to be massed so that the flowers (often sweetly fragrant, as with the Royal Standard and Honeybells) form their own striking effect. Larger varieties, with oversized and often richly green or blue-green leaves, should be treated as specimen shrubs, given pride of place. Specimen varieties include Hosta Krossa Regal, *H. sieboldiana* and Sum and Substance.

3. The third kind falls in between — medium-sized, leafy hostas best used with other plants as part of a thoughtful composition of leaf textures. They work well, for example, with daylilies, astilbes, hellebores, kirengoshima, bigleaf goldenray *(Ligularia dentata)* and bergenia, as well as with broadleaf evergreens.

---

[1] It is possible to place hostas in a sunny position, but you must select certain varieties and make sure that they are in light, moisture-retentive soil and well mulched. They take several seasons to mature and should not be lifted and divided unless they are clearly crowded and unproductive.

These hostas are ideal for shady corners of the garden needing a sensitive touch — at the woodland edge, alongside a passageway or at the foot of a hill.

You can spend large sums for novelty hostas, but there are some tried-and-true favorites available at down-to-earth prices. The American Hosta Society polls members on favorites and lists the top 20. This is one of the annual versions (all great plants, most old standards):

1. Sum and Substance
2. Great Expectations
3. *Hosta fluctuans Variegated*
4. Gold Standard
5. Frances Williams
6. *H. montana Aureo-marginata*
7. Patriot
8. Krossa Regal
9. Paul's Glory
10. Love Pat
11. Halcyon
12. Blue Angel
13. *H. tokudama Aureo-nebulosa*
14. Golden Tiara
15. *H. sieboldiana Elegans*
16. Sun Power
17. Francee
18. On Stage
19. Regal Splendor
20. Fragrant Bouquet

Main Pests: Deer and slugs. **Diseases:** Hostas don't suffer from serious diseases.[†]

II. *Perennials for Shade Gardens*

MANY OTHER perennials do well in the shade garden. Large retail nurseries have whole areas reserved for them, growing under shade cloth. Also, you should visit public gardens to see what is flourishing in the shade. The following are particularly worthy:

- **VIRGINIA BLUEBELL** (*Mertensia virginica*). This is a handsome native plant suited to the damp shade garden, but add lots of leaf mold to the soil. It flowers in April and May.

- **MAY APPLE** (*Podophyllum peltatum*). A showy native ground cover, may apple is one of the delights of the spring woodland garden. It is a deceptively big plant, with leaves a foot across, and a colony needs room to spread. It is great at the feet of woodland shrubs and goatsbeard.

- **GOATSBEARD** (*Aruncus dioicus*). Resembling an oversized astilbe, goatsbeard is an underused perennial that thrives in moist, semi-shaded conditions. It can be used as a specimen in the smaller garden or en masse on larger properties.

- **ASTILBE.** With their decorative, lacy foliage and plumes of flowers, astilbes make fine perennials for shade — except that they resent wet soil during their winter dormancy. This can be fixed if you raise up damp spots with plenty of organic matter. Astilbes look best in a group of at least five (if you have the room). The pinks and reds, sometimes hard to place, can be dramatic, and you can't go wrong with white varieties.

- **DEAD NETTLE** (*Lamium*). This member of the mint family comes in many attractive varieties suited to massing in the moist woodland setting. It is mainly a foliage plant, and silver-leafed and variegated varieties are useful for brightening garden dark spots. Look for Beacon Silver.

- **CORYDALIS LUTEA.** This is a finely textured plant for shade, with lots of tiny yellow flowers. Amend the soil as with astilbes.

- **EUPHORBIA PALUSTRIS.** Difficult to find but worth seeking out, this perennial has shrub-like qualities, mounding to three feet, and is superb in habit and texture. It is best massed. It also is marginally hardy in our area, so mulch after cutting back the foliage in late fall.

■ **JAPANESE BUTTERBUR** *(Petasites japonicus)*. A large, spreading plant with huge, lotus-like leaves, butterbur also is valuable in wet spots where little else grows. It needs lots of room and, once established, is hard to eradicate. The leaves can be three feet across. A larger form, *giganteus*, has even bigger leaves. It is a good background plant for the banks of a large pond, the U.S. version of the gunnera that is so popular in England but that is not reliably hardy here.

■ **WILD GINGER** *(Asarum)*. A terrific, low-growing foliage plant for light to deep shade, wild ginger is well suited to small gardens and shady nooks in larger ones. The most common type is the glossy-leafed European wild ginger, but look for interesting native species, too.

Pests and Diseases: Shade-loving perennials generally are free of pests and diseases, except for slugs that can damage dead nettle and wild ginger.[†]

III. Ferns

FERNS LEND a dignified air of naturalism to shade gardens. Pre-historic specimens that predate conifers and flowering plants, they are our direct link to the primeval beginnings of life on earth.

In most cases, ferns flourish in light to medium shade. In large woodland settings, they are best employed in blocks, linking large shrubs such as rhododendrons or hollies and hiding the ankles of such smaller trees as dogwoods, redbuds and young hemlocks. Ferns should be used in shade as ornamental grasses are in full sun, blocks of one variety separated from similar varieties by other ground covers or shrubs. Dissimilar ferns — for example, the upright cinnamon fern next to the lower-growing Christmas fern — can be placed cheek by jowl. If you have wet, poorly drained soil, ferns could be the answer to your prayers, especially the royal and ostrich ferns. In areas of unyielding dry shade, consider the hay-scented fern planted with liriope, epimediums and Japanese ribbon grass.

The ferns noted here, all hardy, will survive year round in the garden, some as evergreens but most as deciduous plants:[2]

LARGE FERNS

LARGE FERNS form striking ornaments. They tend to be upright and are best seen when backlit by the early morning or late afternoon sun. Use them to cover large areas under shade trees or to line damp swales and streams.

■ **OSTRICH FERN** *(Matteuccia pensylvanica* or *M struthiopteris)*. Sometimes called the shuttlecock fern, it spreads by interconnecting, submerged stems called stolons. In wet years, its arching fronds can grow to five feet or longer. This is essentially a northern plant, and in the hotter parts of our region it should be given deep shade unless it is in constantly moist soil, when it will take more sun. Place it in enriched soil, mulched with leaf mold. When happy, it will spread vigorously. It is easy to lift and divide. Simply use a fork to dig up a young shuttlecock as it forms from a parent plant, cutting the stolon between them.

■ **ROYAL FERN** *(Osmunda regalis)*. The royal fern has the same stature and growing needs as the ostrich fern (although it readily takes hotter climes), but its leaf structure is far more complex and finely textured, making it easier to place with other woodland plants.

■ **INTERRUPTED FERN** *(Osmunda claytoniana)*. The interrupted fern is so named because the fronds bearing the spores are a darker color and seem to interrupt the foliage. It grows from two to five feet, depending on moisture, so in drier sites it would qualify as a mid-sized fern.

---

[2]Varieties such as the Boston and staghorn fern are tender ferns that will not survive outdoors in the colder months in our area, though they can adorn a shaded terrace or balcony in the summer.

■ **GIANT WOOD FERN** *(Dryopteris goldiana)*. The arching fronds of this deciduous native species have a classic fern shape, and the plant makes attractive clumps in light to full shade. It grows to four feet. A number of species of wood ferns make beautiful garden plants, retaining their leaves in mild winters and growing in a range of sizes. They do best in moist soil.

■ **MALE FERN** *(Dryopteris filix-mas)*. The male fern has a lovely upright spreading quality and feathery foliage and would make a perfect single accent plant in smaller borders as well as a classy ground cover in the woods. It grows to four feet.

MEDIUM-SIZED FERNS

THESE FERNS ARE defined by the spaces around them. In an open woodland setting, they have a smaller presence than in a narrow bed by the house. The suggested species are easy to grow and commonly available:

■ **MAIDENHAIR FERN** *(Adiantum pedatum)*. This has singularly beautiful fronds presented on striking black stems. Beads of dew and rainwater sit like jewels on the foliage, whose sprays are 12 to 18 inches across or more. This fern deserves to be used in small groups in places where it can been seen and enjoyed. Place it in evenly moist soil and partial to full shade.

■ **CINNAMON FERN** *(Osmunda cinnamomea)*. Somewhat smaller than other *osmunda* species, the cinammon fern is another delightful resident of garden areas that get light to full shade and evenly moist, humusy soil with a slightly acidic pH. The fern is named for the bright orange-brown fertile fronds that it displays in summer.

■ **CHRISTMAS FERN** *(Polystichum acrostichoides)*. The plant, an evergreen native, was used by early settlers as Christmas decorations (hence its name). It does get a little flattened and tired by winter snows, but its leathery, glossy leaves look splendid for most of the year. It grows in thick clumps and spreads by rhizomes, so it is easy to lift and divide. It is another fern that likes rhododendron conditions — evenly moist, acidic, organically enriched soil that is well drained — although it will take more shade than rhododendrons and azaleas.

■ **HAY-SCENTED FERN** *(Dennstaedtia punctilobula)*. This native plant is the bamboo of the fern world, beautiful but invasive. If you have large areas to cover, or difficult sites with thin soils, the hay-scented fern is a terrific plant. The fronds are wispy, upright, up to 30 inches long, and wonderful at catching the light behind them. One of the few ferns that will grow in open sunny sites without a lot of moisture, it also is valuable for dry shade. It will need watering until it is established. Because of its vigorous spreading habit, it can be spaced farther apart than other ferns, and there is no need to buy excessive amounts.

■ **BRISTLE FERN** *(Polystichum polyblepharum)*. A little harder to find, this fern is worth seeking out. It grows to two feet, with arching, glossy and dark evergreen leaves that are exceedingly fine in texture. It prefers partial shade and evenly moist soil.

SMALL FERNS

SMALL AND small-to-medium ferns look terrific in dark corners, set off by the architecture of mossy brick terraces or wooden fences. They are extremely effective in instilling a sense of far-off wilderness in the smallest city garden.

■ **JAPANESE PAINTED FERN** *(Athyrium niponicum var. Pictum)*. It's a big Latin name for a small fellow, but the Japanese painted fern is a great plant. It has striking hues: silver-tipped leaves and the most intense purple-violet stems. The smart gardener will use it with flowering plants that pick up the colors of the veins, such as creeping phlox, *aubretia*, bulbous irises, blue *ceratostigma* or pansies. This fern does best in light shade and prefers moist but well-drained soil. In a contented spot, the fern will continue to produce fronds for most of the season, always looking fresh. It grows 8 to 12 inches or so in height.

■ **COMMON POLYPODY** (*Polypodium vulgare*). Sometimes difficult to get established, this is the cute little fern that appears in rock crevices of its own accord. Transplanted volunteers rarely succeed, but pot-grown plants will work in evenly moist soil and in shady corners.

■ **UPSIDE DOWN FERN** (*Arachniodes standishii*). This is a fine, feathery semi-evergreen that grows 12 inches and sometimes twice that long. It prefers light shade and evenly moist soil. Its leaflets, known as pinna, are interestingly and beautifully arranged.

Ferns should be spaced two, three or four feet apart, depending on mature size and spread. The number of plants needed for a given area is the same as for ground covers (see Chapter 19). Ferns are particularly fragile in spring and should be treated gently, especially since this is the best season to plant them. Fern leaves, or fronds, are brittle, easily broken and will not tolerate human feet: You shouldn't line a path with them as if they were thyme or chamomile.

Pests and Diseases. Ferns generally are untroubled by diseases and pests, including deer. Slugs can be a problem in the spring, when the young, unfurling stems, or croziers, appear.[†]

[†]See Appendix for common pest and disease ailments and remedies.

Chapter 23

HILLSIDE AND ROCK GARDENS

PEOPLE OFTEN DISMISS hillsides as places for gardens, but slopes make for far more engaging and dramatic terrains than flat sites, and adding a path and artful plantings can produce spectacular results. Hilly sites are prized, moreover, for rock gardens, another subject covered here.

Creating a garden on a slope is more complex than doing so on a flat site. Of the additional factors you must consider, patience probably is the most important, for a site cannot be changed in one fell swoop. Hills need to be improved one shovelful at a time. You might ask: Why bother? Because land is precious, especially to the gardener, and hills are exceptional garden sites. Just because land slopes doesn't mean that it should be wasted.

Usually, the hillside starts off covered with junk-tree seedlings, brambles and weeds, with areas that are scoured by erosion. In repairing the land, you should think first as an engineer, second as a designer and third as a gardener.

1. THE ENGINEER

FIRST, CHECK and correct soil erosion. You will need to replace earth that has been washed away and then cover the bare hill with a three-inch layer of shredded hardwood mulch. If storm water continues to wash away soil, clear away the mulch, regrade the soil and use lengths of burlap (sold in rolls like fabric) for soil retention. Peg the burlap, and then lay the mulch atop it.

Lop off the top growth of unwanted trees, vines and shrubs, and spray herbaceous weeds with glyphosate. You shouldn't dig up the roots or work large areas of soil. The roots, even when dead, hold the topsoil together. Cover them with mulch and continue to chop back emerging top growth until you are ready to plant. In addition, you may need to fix a drainage problem, particularly if the hill is above your house (for drainage techniques, see Chapter 3 on preparing your land).

2. THE DESIGNER

THROUGH THE CENTURIES, designers have fashioned gardens from slopes in two basic ways. One is to create a series of descending terraces, buttressed by retaining walls, and then lay upon these verdant gardens of symmetry and order. The second is to form an artificial but natural-looking garden, crafted without major earth-working and following the hill's existing contours.

The second approach is far better for the suburban home. It not only avoids the considerable expense of constructing walls, but it produces a garden more attuned to its setting. The suburban lot is an awkward hybrid between city and country but one that generally takes naturalistic landscaping much easier than formal designs. The formal garden, with its reliance on architecture and symmetry, can look strange in a suburban context and is rarely done with the quality of craftsmanship and materials needed to pull it off.

With a hillside garden, you still need both a place to sit and a flat area around the house from which to enjoy the landscape. If the hill is above the house, you may have to build a retaining wall into the slope to make room for a patio or deck. If it is below the house, you have the easier option of building a deck supported by stilts.

Chances are that you will plant one kind of garden on a hill below your home, another kind on a hill above it. If the house is perched above and set back from the street, the front yard is little more than an embankment that you notice, briefly, as you hurry from the street to the front door. You should not dismiss the space — it will set the tone for the whole property — but you are not likely to linger in the area or use and view it a great deal, so there is little point in making a major landscape investment there. Rather, employ ground covers and low-maintenance shrubs.

On the other hand, if the hillside is behind or to the side of your home, you are likely to use and view it more often, and thus you should pay much greater attention to it. As with wooded lots, you will get the most out of it if you build a path that draws you into the space.

3. THE GARDENER

WHEN YOU PLANT, take a mattock and chop into the hill about a foot above the planting hole. Use that soil, along with some amendments, to create a small terrace for the plant. Pack the soil with your hands and lay mulch to prevent erosion. If you are planting in areas you have stabilized with burlap, cut an X into the material and plant through it. In time, the burlap will rot away.

In areas where you want to put a small grouping of plants, or on slopes that are particularly steep, you can create mini-terraces retained by stone walls stacked dry. They might be just six to 12 inches high and three to six feet long. They need not be pretty or expertly crafted. In time the vegetation will cover them.

Just as you create cut-and-fill pockets for plants, you can do the same for the hillside path. A path that goes from side to side with switchbacks will be easier to traverse than one that goes up and down, and it will offer more places to build plant beds. The path can be of mulch or gravel, though at some points you may have to build a flight of stairs using large, flat landscape stones. Try to get them delivered uphill of the job. At parlous points, you also may need to put in a hand railing.

Hillside plantings still need to be arranged into a pleasing composition using the same principles discussed in Chapter 1. In addition, certain plants can be used to break up the line of the slope and make for a more inter-

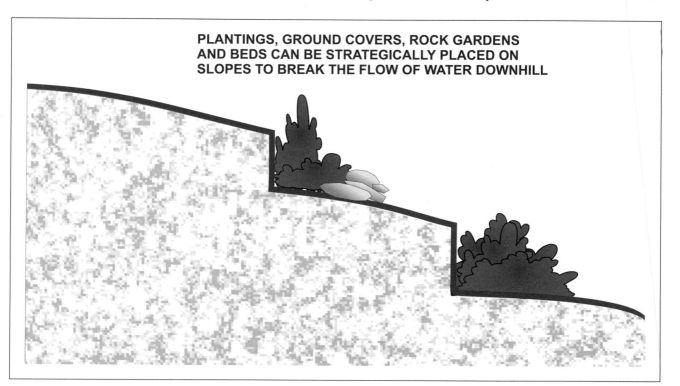

PLANTINGS, GROUND COVERS, ROCK GARDENS AND BEDS CAN BE STRATEGICALLY PLACED ON SLOPES TO BREAK THE FLOW OF WATER DOWNHILL

esting arrangement, especially plants with spreading and layered habits, including low-growing yews, junipers, bottlebrush buckeyes, pagoda and kousa dogwoods, shasta or shoshoni viburnums, spreading-form crab apples such as Tina or Sparkler and mugo pines.

Mounding plants will mimic the cresting nature of the terrain and produce some interesting shadows. Look for such specimens as threadleaf Japanese maples, cotoneaster, winter jasmine, forsythia, pennisetum grass and hostas. As an accent, select a vertical plant or two like a Hicks yew, miscanthus grass or a dwarf conifer. Plants that demand a dark background to show off their flowers, fruit or bark find the perfect backdrop in the hill. Candidates include winterberry holly, shasta viburnum, witch hazels and leatherleaf mahonia.

If you are looking down on the plants, choose some that are ornamental from above — hydrangeas, kousa dogwoods, spireas, pieris, nandina, leatherleaf mahonia, threadleaf falsecypress, callicarpa or shrub roses. On the other hand, if you are looking up to the plants, select those that are showy from below — halesia, styrax, witch hazel, corylopsis, fringe tree, pennisetum, northern sea oats or daylilies.

A hill facing north or east will be colder and shadier, especially if buildings and trees sit atop it. Conversely, a slope facing south or west, with little or no shade, will be a more stressful plant environment. Slopes, of course, provide strong drainage, so the soil tends to be dry; in such circumstances, the plants will bake. Thus it is important to keep the site mulched and the plants watered, especially during their first year. You also should pick plants that can take these adverse conditions. Remember that some ground covers, such as liriope and bigroot cranesbill, thrive in dry conditions and also are valued for thick roots systems that hold soil together for erosion control (see Chapter 19 on ground covers). Other plants to consider: creeping juniper, sedums, the cactus opuntia, cotoneasters, bugleweed, barberry and Russian olive. The good news is slopes in full sun warm up first in spring and are splendid sites for spring-flowering bulbs.

ROCK GARDENS

ROCK GARDENS have captured the gardener's imagination since the early Victorian period as a way of recreating natural rock outcroppings and their plant colonies. It is difficult to explain the magic of such a place. Perhaps it's the enchanting paradox of frail-looking plants in a rugged setting, or the way rock gardens force us to observe plants closely. Whatever the allure, the rock garden is one landscape form that has never fallen from grace.

Attractive landscape features in their own right, they are also a plantsman's delight, a place to grow unusual species that peak in the spring but that can bloom every month of the year. Rock garden plants are petite — you can pack a lot of specimens into a small area. At its purest, rock gardening involves the use of alpine plants that grow at high elevations. True alpine plants don't work in the Washington climate, but many rock garden plants of similar habit and character will grow here with a little help.

Most rock garden enthusiasts would give their eyeteeth for a hilly site: they usually are forced instead to go to the trouble and expense of building a berm and trying to blend it into its surroundings (dwarf conifers make convincing frames). The hill gardener will still have to haul in rock and soil amendments, but the basic landform is already there. Try to use local stone for your rock garden — gneiss, sandstone or schist. An exotic stone such as lava rock looks out of place. If your hill does not already have boulders, you will need to arrange for their delivery and placement on your site.

Donald Humphrey, a noted rock garden specialist from Falls Church, Va., prefers to use smaller chunks of Virginia fieldstone and then create two or three terraces retained by the stones. At first the arrangement looks like an old ruined wall, but Humphrey says that it mimics the layers of rock found in nature. The stones usually weigh 50 pounds or less and can be carried or wheeled to the site without heavy equipment. In stacking courses of stone atop each other, use plenty of sandy loam, not only to bed the stones but to create pockets of soil for plants. Also, Humphrey says, any gaps in the wall will become havens for slugs, which feast on choice specimens.

THE SUNNY ROCK GARDEN. In full sun, fill areas around the stones with a mixture of sand, loam and compost, to a depth of at least 12 inches. This is essential to provide the drainage the plants need. Then mulch the rock garden with a light gravel. This makes weeding easy and keeps the roots cooler in summer. It also ties together the garden visually. A hill converted to a rock garden should not have problems with erosion because the soil is so well drained.

Rock gardening introduces even experienced gardeners to a world of new plants, or at least miniature versions of familiar ones. Humphrey notes that you can plant a convincing rock garden using dwarf varieties of three garden favorites — pinks *(Dianthus)*, columbine and phlox — as well as hens-and-chicks, sedums and other common, low-growing succulents. But most rock garden plants must be obtained from specialty nurseries, especially once the bug has bitten. The rock gardeners will discover a whole new world of anemones, daffodils, species tulips, irises (both dwarf bearded and bulbous), alyssum, dwarf composites, drabas and campanulas.

Once established, the plants will only need occasional watering during periods of drought.

THE SHADY ROCK GARDEN. In shade, the rock garden is a different animal. The soil mix will have to be richer, with more humus to retain a degree of moisture. It must still drain freely. The plant palette changes, with the use of such specimens as trilliums, rue anemone, trout lilies, dodecatheons, a dwarf mounding jasmine called *Jasminum parkeri,* dwarf rhododendrons and azaleas, foamflower, *Phlox divaricata* and wood ferns.

To get more ideas, you might want to visit the model rock garden on display at Green Spring Gardens Park in Alexandria, Va. Also, look for notices in *The Washington Post* of American Rock Garden Society meetings and plant sales (see Appendix for information on both public gardens and plant societies).

Chapter 24

WATER GARDENS

OR THOSE DRAWN to water gardening, ponds have become all the rage, and with good reason. Ornamental ponds — with lilies or lotuses, fish, fountains or falls — often become the soul of the garden, a place of wonder and life. Once the pleasures of the rich, ponds now are available to everyone, thanks to modern technology.

The path to pond nirvana, though, is not always easy. Ponds are laborious and somewhat costly to install. They demand considerable care, and even then fish die and algae grow and raccoons do their worst. Is a pond still worth it? Absolutely, especially if you adhere to some basics of design and take steps to avoid needless problems.

DESIGN

■ **LOCATION.** A pond should be placed prominently, as a centerpiece of the garden, and on a site that receives at least five hours of direct sunlight. Choose a spot close to the house, preferably where the pond can be viewed from inside and definitely where those sitting outside can see it, perhaps next to a terrace or below a deck.

■ **SIZE.** Be as generous as possible with proportions (unless you are putting a container water garden on a small patio, a delightful way to enhance a city garden). A big pond will match the scale of its surroundings, will allow you to use more plants over the years, and actually will be easier to maintain than a smaller one, mainly because it will be less prone to rapid temperature changes.

■ **CONGRUITY.** Make sure the pond fits well in its setting. Unless you are especially artistic with rock and plant placement, opt for a geometric or formal pond shape rather than an irregular, naturalistic one. If you fashion a pond into a square, rectangle, oval, diamond, circle or semicircle, you can repeat the shape in near-by paving, planting beds, even decorative motifs. Don't worry about a pond looking too formal: Water plants soon soften the edges.

PRECAUTIONS

Taking some precautionary steps can save you from later grief:

■ **SAFETY.** Safety comes first. Ponds and unsupervised toddlers don't mix. If you have a small child, you should either hold off building a pond for a while — probably the wise course — or put an attractive fence around the pond, following local fencing codes. Second, ponds that have pumps for fountains or falls obviously need electricity; local codes dictate minimum distances between water and power source as well as the use of certain circuit breakers. Third, avoid digging where there are buried utility lines.

■ **THE RIGHT CONDITIONS.** Pick a place that's relatively flat, so it's easier to create a level pond, and a spot that's away from large trees, especially deciduous shade trees: You don't want leaf-filled water. You also shouldn't have turf around a pond, unless the ground slopes steeply away: Lawn chemicals contaminate ponds. Nor should you place a pond in a low-lying wet spot. If you do, it's likely to receive chemical runoff from surrounding land — and if the water table gets too high, the pond liner may rise up, damaging or dislodging the pond.

- **DRAINAGE.** Create swales around the pond to handle storm overflows, and don't allow any overflow to head toward the house.

- **PESTS.** Raccoons are common and destructive pests. To help give the edge to the fish, provide them with water at least 30 inches deep (remember that this may affect fencing requirements) and hideaways, such as cinder blocks or pipes into which they can scurry. Move marginal plants[1] that might attract raccoons away from the water's edge. If bullfrogs or turtles show up, be prepared for them to snack on some of your fish as well; regular frogs will be no problem.

- **WATER QUALITY.** You need to make the pond water safe for fish, which not only provide beauty but which feast on mosquito larvae.

INSTALLATION

ONCE, PONDS WERE made from concrete basins. They cracked and leaked. Then came flexible liners made of thin plastic. They ripped and grew brittle in the sun. People wept and gnashed their teeth, and, lo, the powers that be took pity and provided EPDM, a synthetic rubber.[2]

EPDM is a blessing for today's ponds (and you can use it to line any old, leaky, concrete pond you may have inherited). Pick thick EPDM — 45 mil — and don't get the kind made for roofs: It's deadly for fish.

First, of course, you need to dig your hole, which shouldn't be any shallower than 14 inches. The digging is no small undertaking in our clay subsoil. You'll need mattocks, a place to deposit excavated dirt and a strong back. If the pond is sizable — say, more than 50 square feet — you may want to hire an excavator, assuming machinery can get to the spot.

You then must remove stones and roots and other objects and lay a three-inch layer of sand to create a level floor. Use a builder's flexible tape to measure the pond at its widest and longest points, leaving six inches all around for the pond lip. On the wall of the pond, put padding beneath the liner (carpet padding or old carpeting will do).

Next, the earth has to be formed so that the top of the pond is perfectly level. Put in a stake at the pond's highest point and string a line to the lower side. A line level will indicate how much trimming of the high end and filling of the low end is needed to achieve a horizontal pond lip. If you install a preformed fiberglass pond, the three-inch leveling course of sand at the base of the hole is critical in accomplishing a level top.

FOUNTAINS, FALLS AND FISH

THERE ARE TWO ways to have water in motion in your pond. You can buy a pump-driven fountain, or you can build a second reservoir above the main pond for a waterfall. A waterfall, too, requires a pump, to take water to the higher level, plus a lined spillway through which the water courses. The pump size will depend on the height of the upper pond and the distance from the main pond.

If you feel adventurous and decide to build a series of cascading pools, make sure that the main pond is considerably larger than the upper ones. Otherwise, the main pond's water level will drop markedly once you run the pump, or it will flood when the pump is turned off.

While most pond plants should not be where water hits or disturbs them, falls and fountains can be placed anywhere with fish. To stock the pond with fish, count on one inch of fish per square foot of surface area. Thus a pond that is 10 feet square (100 square feet) will take up to 25 four-inch fish or 17 six-inch fish. Fish repro-

---

[1] Marginal plants grow in mud, with their roots in water.
[2] EPDM stands for Ethylene Propylene Diene Monomer.

duce, so give away babies to friends with ponds. You shouldn't release them into rivers or streams, where they may upset the ecological balance or introduce diseases to native fish.

Koi, beautiful fish that grow large, are not for small ponds. Pool-quality koi from the United States or Israel are quite affordable. Show-quality koi from Japan are expensive, and fish hobbyists who collect them tend to tune out other aspects of aquatic gardening, especially since large fish eat aquatic plants. Consider, instead, various goldfish, especially comets: They are attractive and inexpensive, and if one succumbs to disease or a raccoon, you won't be out there committing hara-kiri.

Feed fish once the water temperature rises above 45 degrees, and stop feeding when it drops back to that temperature. It is better for the health of the fish and the pond to underfeed than to overfeed them. If you see large numbers of mosquito larvae, you can stop feeding the fish; they'll do fine on their own. The fish also will find their own food when you are on vacation. What you have to do for the fish, however, is ensure the quality of the water. Here, you should keep four items in mind:

1. **MUNICIPAL WATER.** Town water contains chlorine, chloramine and other additives that will kill fish, so you have to use chemical buffers before stocking the pond. If you top off the pond with the garden hose, as most people do, add neutralizing chemicals each time you do this.

2. **FILTERS.** A pond with an optimum balance of fish life, scavengers (snails and tadpoles) and submerged aquatic plants will keep the water naturally cleaned of ammonia and other toxins. However, a filter will assure the best water quality. Biological filters outside the pond, using beneficial bacteria to eat the bad stuff, are less work and more effective than in-pond mechanical filters. But they take several weeks to become charged with microbes.

3. **ALGAE.** All ponds become clouded with algae. Algae are unsightly and clog filters, which are ineffective against them. There are two ways to get rid of algae. If aquatic plants cover 60 percent of the water surface, they will crowd out and kill the algae; this will take four to six weeks, and you shouldn't try to hurry the process. Alternatively (or as a supplement), you can run your water through an ultraviolet filter.

4. **NEUTRAL pH.** The fish need water with a roughly neutral pH. Large stones in and around the pond will raise the pH for the first few months. Use acidifiers as needed. If possible, don't use sedimentary rock for ponds.

PLANTS

YOU CAN FILL your pond with an array of wonderful plants:

■ **WATERLILIES.** These are the most attractive and hardworking of aquatic plants. They come in two basic types — the hardy lily and the tropical lily — each with dozens of varieties.

The hardy lily, which sits on the water, comes in shades of white (with yellow stamens), pink, yellow, apricot and red. It opens in mid-morning and closes in late afternoon. If you work outside the home and have normal hours, you may miss the show, except on weekends. Tropical lilies are held aloft on stems, blooming in exotic colors, including violet blue and magenta. Most flower in the evening, but there are day-blooming tropicals, too (and they are scented). Tropicals need more sunlight (preferably at least six hours) than hardy lilies (five hours).

Both hardy and tender tropical lilies require six to 18 inches of water over the root crown, and keep them away from waterfalls and fountains. Plant them in plastic containers in ordinary soil, mulched with two inches of gravel. Slow-release pellet fertilizers will help them perform their best. Also, their pads turn yellow and black when they fade; cut them off, being careful not to nick emerging stems.

- **LOTUS PLANTS.** Lotus plants are beautiful but somewhat difficult. The tubers can be planted only in spring, and you must take care not to damage the growing tip. Lotuses need lots of direct sunlight and still water and, once established, can become invasive in earthen ponds.

- **FLOATING PLANTS.** You also can pick from a number of floating plants, the most famous of which is the water hyacinth, with its fleshy leaves and lavender blossoms. It is good for crowding out algae and providing habitat for fish. Other candidates include the water lettuce or good old duckweed.

- **SUBMERGED PLANTS.** These are vital for reducing nutrients to starve the algae. Common types include parrot's feather, anacharis and hornwort.

- **MARGINAL PLANTS.** Marginals provide a fabulous way of integrating a pond with the surrounding land. They all grow in shallow water and can be invasive. My favorites include the yellow flag iris, the blue water iris, pickerel weed, arrowhead, horsetail and thalia. There are a number of enticing tropical marginals, too, including taros, papyrus and calla lilies.

Don't grow marginals in pots on a pond shelf: Raccoons will knock them over. Rather, between the shelf and the pond proper, stack fieldstones to form a wall. In the area behind the wall, dump ordinary clay soil, into which you can set the plants. To prevent the soil from silting the pond, lay filter fabric on the soil side of the wall and cover the soil with a two-inch mulch of gravel.

In winter, tropical lilies and other tender plants must be lifted and stored in a cool place or discarded. Hardy plants want to be in deeper water to prevent roots from freezing. You shouldn't let the water freeze for long periods. An electric de-icing device will keep an area open. A large waterfall that moves 1,200 gallons of water an hour also will keep a pond from freezing over.

BOG GARDENS

YOU CAN GROW many wet-meadow and pond-margin aquatic plants in their own ornamental bog, using an adjoining fishpond as a reservoir to keep the outlying ground moist. If you already have land that is almost always waterlogged and where nothing else will grow, a bog garden can turn this negative into a positive. Bury a sheet of flexible pond liner to prevent the site from drying out during high-summer dry spells, and then plant the aforementioned marginals or other species: Japanese butterbur, joe-pye weed, ferns, ligularias, skunk cabbage, astilbes, turtlehead or moisture-loving sedges. Several shrubs take periodically wet soil, including myrica, willows *(Salix)*, inkberry, redtwig dogwood and arrowwood viburnum.

True bog plants, many of which are insect-eaters, are fascinating to the botanist, but they must be grown in a separate garden because they demand poor, acidic soil. Plant them in a mixture of sand and peat moss and keep them moist. There are several beautiful species and hybrids of the pitcher plant *(sarracenia)*. Other candidates include native irises *(I. versicolor, I. virginica, and I. verna)*, a relative of the gentian named *Sabatia campanulata,* and swamp pink *(Helonias bullata)*. Among native bog orchids, consider *Calopogon pallidus, Calopogon tuberosus* and the *Pogonio ophioglossoides.*

Chapter 25

NATURAL GARDENS

*G*ARDENERS ONCE worked blithely outside the natural ecology, or tried to, by reaching for highly toxic chemicals to attack every pest and disease. It's clear today that some pest populations have been winning the battle, while we have been shooting ourselves in the foot. What those pests have gotten over time are immunities to the chemicals. What we have gotten are health perils, polluted waterways, endangered wildlife and the loss of some beneficial bugs.

Realizing this, more than a few gardeners have set out to become stewards of the land. This is not just a matter of their growing interest in freer, more natural gardens, in ornamental grasses and ferns, in sharply reduced chemicals or disease-resistant plants. Many gardeners have ventured deeper into the wilderness and found a richness they never had imagined.

WILDFLOWER MEADOWS

THE MOST POPULAR expression of this natural garden is the yearning for an instant wildflower meadow where toxins are banished, plants take care of themselves and butterflies hover above a season-long haze of floral color. This seems to be the first image of naturalistic gardening that comes to people's minds. It should be the last.

You can create a wildflower meadow (or a miniature version of one), but it's not as simple or as easy as wildflower seed companies would have you believe. You cannot open a can of seed, sprinkle it on the ground like fairy dust and expect an immediate, enduring and self-sustaining meadow.

Naturally, you can't lay the seed on an existing lawn. You wouldn't be able to mow the grass, and the turf would quickly crowd out emerging seedlings. Seed must be sown in bare, well-prepared soil. So if you want to use your lawn for a wildflower meadow, you must skim off the layer of turf, making sure to remove all grass roots and weeds. If you pick an overgrown corner of the yard, perhaps bare or weedy ground with the odd junk bush or two, you must dig out all shrub roots and weeds. Either way, it's a major job.

Most seed mixes, moreover, are all or mainly annuals, plants such as cosmos, sunflowers and poppies that do not reliably re-seed. Hence you may get a pleasing show the first year, but afterward the meadow will become an unsustainable weed patch. So don't attempt to replace your whole lawn with a wildflower meadow until you've first experimented on a smaller scale.

RECOMMENDED METHOD. A wildflower meadow site must be sunny and well drained. (Check with your local government or homeowner association to see if there are any restrictions against such meadows.) To replicate a real meadow, you may need an acre or more, but there is no minimum size. Indeed, gardeners on small properties can have just a taste of such a meadow with plantings along open-fence lines or in corners of the yard.

If you plan a big meadow, don't throw away the lawn mower. You still will want to cut a swath, not only as a way of moving through the garden but also to announce to your neighbors that this untidiness is deliberate. The path should be winding, not straight. Nature has no straight paths.

Once the ground has been cleared, you should till to eight inches. Amend the soil to fix any extremes of pH, and create a loam, but don't add lots of enriched humus; wildflowers thrive in poorer soil. Water and allow the thousands of weed seeds to germinate. Once they are one to two inches high, spray with glyphosate — yes, you've still got to use a chemical to start with — and repeat the spraying in two weeks. Till the soil once more, but this time at the shallowest tiller setting. Then rake and spread the seed. By buying a series of named varieties rather than a mix, you can scatter drifts of like flowers, as they would appear in nature.

As an alternative labor-saving approach, you can lay sheets of newspapers over the existing clay subsoil and heap loam on top of them to a depth of 12 inches (it will settle). You then sow the seeds. This method may require the delivery of topsoil.

If you are creating a meadow of annuals, collect the seeds from the first season's plants in the fall (store them in a cool, dry place) and mow the meadow in late winter. In April, cultivate the top two inches again and sow seeds directly, using the collected seeds as well as newly ordered packets.

A PERENNIAL MEADOW. No matter how much weed killing you do at the outset, weeds will return and bully out the annuals. That's one reason why many seasoned meadow makers eschew annuals. Instead, they plant perennials and grasses, installing them as started plants, not from seed. Whether you cultivate existing soil or use the newspaper-and-new-soil method, plant the perennials after the bed has been prepared and lightly mulched to keep weeds back. This approach is more costly and labor intensive, but it will give you a long-lasting, low-maintenance meadow.

If you want a meadow solely of native plants, pick from the perennials and grasses noted in the accompanying native plant lists. Some mail-order nurseries sell young divisions of perennials and grasses as plugs or tubes, reducing the cost of the plant stock. Farmer's markets are another source of low-cost plants. Most perennials will not flower in their first season, so scatter annual seed among them for a show the first year.

NATIVE PLANTS

THE INCREASED interest in naturalistic plantings has led, inevitably, to a desire to use only native plants. In taking this route, you might give up showy hybrid color and vigor, but you will get a fascinating, educational collection of plants native to the United States. Purists, moreover, employ only plants that are native to our region.

Employing wild plants doesn't mean that you can ignore design principles. In some respects, they become more important, given the relaxed habit of some of these plants. Visit some model native plant gardens in the region: Fern Valley at the National Arboretum, the Winkler Botanical Preserve in Alexandria, Va., and Mt. Cuba Center near Wilmington, Del. (see Appendix section on public gardens). Look at how the gardens are arranged and try to present similarly natural plantings yourself. A native rhododendron might be a lone shrub in front of a stand of viburnums. A small and curious woodland native such as jack-in-the-pulpit might be found as a single specimen. A group of trillium might form a large drift on either side of a woodland path.

Here are some of the most useful and beautiful native plants for the home garden, most based on a list compiled by Brenda Skarphol, native plant specialist and horticulturist at Green Spring Gardens Park in Alexandria. All are native to the eastern United States, and most are native to the Mid-Atlantic region. (The ♣ symbol indicates that the plant requires or adapts to shade, and named varieties have superior qualities to the species plant.)

SHADE TREES

American yellowwood (Cladrastis lutea)
Bald cypress (Taxodium distichum)
Bigleaf magnolia (Magnolia macrophylla) ▲
Bitternut hickory (Carya cordiformis)
Black oak (Quercus velutina)
Black tupelo or sour gum (Nyssa sylvatica)
Chestnut oak (Quercus prinus)
Kentucky coffee tree (Gymnocladus dioica)
Mockernut hickory (Carya tomentosa)
Pecan (Carya illinoinensis)
Pignut hickory (Carya glabra)
Pin oak (Quercus palustris)
Red maple. October Glory or
   Red Sunset (Acer rubrum)

Red oak (Quercus rubra)
River birch Heritage (Betula nigra)
Scarlet oak (Quercus coccinea)
Shagbark hickory (Carya ovata) ▲
Sugar maple. Bonfire, Green Mountain
   or Legacy (Acer saccharum)
Swamp white oak (Quercus bicolor)
Sweet gum (Liquidambar styraciflua).
   The variety Rotundiloba does not have
   the messy seed pods.
Tulip tree (Liriodendron tulipifera) ▲
White oak (Quercus alba)
Willow oak (Quercus phellos)
Yellow buckeye (Aesculus flava) ▲

ORNAMENTAL TREES

American holly (Ilex opaca) ▲
American hornbeam (Carpinus caroliniana) ▲
Carolina silverbell (Halesia teraptera) ▲
Eastern redbud (Cercis canadensis) ▲
Pagoda dogwood (Cornus alternifolia) ▲
Serviceberries (Amelanchier species) ▲
Silky stewartia (Stewartia malacodendron) ▲

Snakebark maple (Acer pensylvanicum) ▲
Sourwood (Oxydendron arboreum) ▲
Southern magnolia (Magnolia grandiflora)
Sweetbay magnolia (Magnolia virginiana)▲
Umbrella magnolia (Magnolia tripetala)
Washington hawthorn (Crataegus phaenopyrum)
Winter King hawthorn (Crataegus viridis)
   Winter King

CONIFERS

Carolina hemlock (Tsuga caroliniana) ▲
Eastern arborvitae (Thuja occidentalis)
Eastern hemlock (Tsuga canadensis) ▲

Eastern red cedar (Juniperus virginiana) Corcorcor
Eastern white pine (Pinus strobus)
Loblolly pine (P. taeda)

SHRUBS

American beautyberry (Callicarpa americana)
American elder (Sambucus canadensis) ▲
Azaleas, various deciduous
   (Rhododendron arborescens, calendulaceum,
   canescens, periclymenoides, prinophyllum
   and viscosum) ▲
Blackhaw viburnum (Viburnum prunifolium) ▲
Bottlebrush buckeye (Aesculus parviflora) ▲
Coast leucothoe (Leocothoe axillaris) ▲
Devil's walking stick (Aralia spinosa) ▲
Dwarf fothergilla (F. gardenii) ▲
Fringetree (Chionanthus virginicus) ▲
Inkberry (Ilex glabra) Compacta ▲
Large forthergilla (Fothergilla major) ▲
Mountain laurel (Kalmia latifolia) ▲

Oakleaf hydrangea (H. quercifolia) ▲
Red chokeberry (Aronia arbutifolia)
Redosier dogwood (Cornus stolonifera)
Rosebay rhododendron (Rhododendron maximum) ▲
Sandra witchhazel (Hamamelis vernalis Sandra) ▲
Smooth hydrangea (H. arborescens) ▲
Southern blackhaw viburnum (V. rufidulum) ▲
Spicebush (Lindera benzoin) ▲
Staghorn sumac (Rhus typhina)
Summersweet (Clethra alnifolia) ▲
Virginia sweetspire (Itea virginica)
   Henry's Garnet ▲
Winterberry (Ilex verticillata)
Witchhazel (Hamamelis virginiana) ▲

FERNS

Broad beech fern *(Phegopteris hexagonoptera)* ♠
Christmas fern *(Polystichum acrostichoides)* ♠
Cinnamon fern *(Osmunda cinnamomea)* ♠
Hay-scented fern *(Dennstaedtia punctilobula)* ♠
Maidenhair fern *(Adiantum pedatum)* ♠
Netted chain fern *(Woodwardia areolata)* ♠

New York fern *(Parathelypteris novaboracensis)* ♠
Ostrich fern *(Matteuccia struthiopteris)* ♠
Royal fern *(Osmunda regalis)* ♠
Sensitive fern *(Onoclea sensibilis)* ♠
Wood ferns *(Dryopteris goldiana, ludoviciana, marginalis)* ♠

PERENNIALS

Alumroot *(Heuchera americana, H. villosa)* ♠
Asters *(Aster divaricatus,* ♠ *lateriflorus novae-angliae, oblongifolius, spectabilis)*
Beebalm *(Monarda didyma, fistulosa)* ♠
Black snakeroot *(Cimicifuga racemosa)* ♠
Blazing star *(Liatris spicata)* Kobold
Bloodroot *(Sanguinaria canadensis)* ♠
Blue star *(Amsonia tabernaemontana)* ♠
Boltonia *(Boltonia asteroides)*
Cardinal flower *(Lobelia cardinalis, siphilitica)* ♠
Columbine *(Aquilegia canadensis)* ♠
Coreopsis
Cup plant *(Silphium perfoliatum)*
False goatsbeard *(Astilbe biternata)* ♠
False Solomon's-seal *(Smilacina racemosa)*♠
False sunflower *(Heliopsis helianthoides)*
Flowering spurge *(Euphorbia corollata)*
Goatsbeard *(Aruncus dioicus)* ♠
Goldenrod *(Solidago rugosa Fireworks, S. spacelata Golden Fleece)*
Hardy hibiscus *(Hibiscus militaris, moscheutos)*
Jack-in-the-pulpit *(Arisaema triphyllum)* ♠

Joe-pye weed *(Eupatorium purpureum)* ♠
Meadow rue *(Thalictrum pubescens)* ♠
New York ironweed *(Vernonia noveboracensis)*
Obedient plant *(Physostegia virginiana)*
Orange coneflower *(Rudbeckia fulgida)*
Penstemon *(Penstemon digitalis)* Husker Red
Phloxes *(Phlox divaricata,*♠ *glaberrima,* ♠ *paniculata, stolonifera* ♠ *)*
Purple coneflower *(Echinacea purpurea)*
Small Solomon's-seal *(Polygonatum biflorum)* ♠
Soapwort gentian *(Gentiana saponaria)* ♠
Spikenard *(Aralia racemosa)*
Swamp sunflower *(Helianthus angustifolius)*
Tall white violet *(Viola canadensis)* ♠
Turtlehead *(Chelone obliqua)* ♠
Verbena *(Verbena canadensis)*
Virginia bluebells *(Mertensia virginica)*
Wild bleeding heart *(Dicentra eximia)* ♠
Wild geranium *(Geranium maculatum)*
Wild indigo *(Baptisia australis)*
Yellow wood poppy *(Stylophorum diphyllum)* ♠

GRASSES, SEDGES AND RUSHES

Bottlebrush grass *(Elymus hystrix)* ♠
Gray's sedge *(Carex grayi)*
Hairy woodrush *(Luzula acuminata)*
Indian grass *(Sorhastrum nutans)* Sioux Blue
Little bluestem *(Schizachyrium escoparium)*

Prairie dropseed *(Sporobolus heterolepsis)*
River oats *(Chasmanthium latifolium)* ♠
Sedge *(Carex pensylvanica)*
Sugarcane plume grass *(Erianthus giganteus)*
Switch grass *(Panicum virgatum)*

AQUATIC PLANTS

Arrowhead *(Sagittaria latifolia)*
Bog lily *(Crinum americanum)*
Bog rosemary *(Andromeda polifolia)*
Blue flag *(Iris versicolor)*
Horsetail *(Equisetum species)*
Lizard's tail *(Saururus cernuus)*
Louisiana iris *(Iris species)*

Marsh marigold *(Caltha palustris)*
Pickerel rush *(Pontederia cordata)*
Pitcher plant *(Sarracenia species)*
Skunk cabbage *(Symplocarpus foetidus)*
Sneezeweed *(Helenium autumnale)*
Wild calla *(Calla palustris)*
Yellow lotus *(Nelumbo lutea)*

NATURAL HABITAT GARDENS

WE ARE BLESSED with a rich diversity of insect, bird and animal life in the garden — sometimes too rich. Many gardeners have embraced one or more of these living things and built natural habitat gardens. They pick plants not necessarily for their beauty but for how they support the creatures they love.

They plant flowers that provide nectar and pollen for insects, including butterflies and honeybees, as well as for hummingbirds. They grow fruit to feed birds and mammals. They provide water that draws a host of creatures. They develop thick shrubs and collections of plants as a hedgerow to provide shelter from predators and the elements. A minority of habitat gardeners even support certain animals, such as raccoons and deer, that are serious pests for most of us. It's not clear that all of their neighbors feel the same way as they do, so you might check with others before encouraging such animals in your community.

Low-lying wetlands can be planted with moisture-loving vegetation such as joe-pye weed, ironweed, jewelweed, inkberry, myrica and hardy hibiscus. Another approach to natural habitat gardening is to allow the lawn to revert to a meadow (with your assistance) next to hedgerows. To minimize friction with neighbors, advocates suggest two courses: Keep areas around the house tidy and mowed, and let the neighbors know what you are doing.

A HABITAT POND. The most important element of a habitat garden is a reliable source of drinking and bathing water, especially in summer. Habitat ponds are created the same way as ornamental ponds (see Chapter 24 on water gardens), but with one major difference: One side of the habitat pond is not deep. Rather, it has a ramp, or beach (mulched with pebbles to below the water line). This way, birds, butterflies and small mammals can drink and bathe in shallow water. The beach can be framed by marginal plants to integrate the pond into the landscape.

Such a naturalistic pond will lure turtles, raccoons and an array of birds, possibly including herons, so provide fish in your pond with the kinds of hideaways noted in Chapter 24. If your fish losses are high, consider buying fish raised at pet shops to feed other animals. These feeder fish are inexpensive and winter-hardy.

SHELTER. The second most important feature of the habitat garden is shelter, a place where birds in particular can thrive, safe from predators and protected in winter. You can use property lines and remote corners to establish a hedgerow where birds, amphibians, rabbits and other cuddly creatures can live and move in relative safety.

Pyracantha make fabulous sheltering spots for birds, but habitat gardeners often see plant conservation as part of their mission and so use native plants. Consider such plants as native roses, blackberries, elderberries, sumac, winterberry and buttonbush. Native plant societies have developed full lists of hedgerow plants.

HUMMINGBIRDS. Hummingbirds occupy a special place is many people's heart. Pretty, energetic and fascinating, these birds will grow quite used to human presence if you provide them, year after year, with an abundance of hummer-friendly plants.

Hummingbirds need plants rich in nectar and tubular in form. They are drawn to red flowers but will feed from others. If you plant some of the following, chances are good that hummingbirds will be part of your summer life: Columbine, trumpet creeper, coralbells, honeysuckles, penstemons, cardinal flowers, phlox, salvias, flowering tobaccos, impatiens, geraniums and morning glories.

Hummingbird feeders are effective, and they are good alternatives if you live in the city, but, for the health of the birds, you must keep them clean and supply the correct dilution of sugar water.

BUTTERFLY GARDENS. People once caught butterflies in nets, gassed them and pinned them for study. Now, we enjoy them alive and well, flitting from flower to flower. Butterflies are a direct indication of a garden's health. One where pesticides are used liberally will have far fewer butterflies than one where organic precepts are followed.

Serious butterfly gardeners put out rotting fruit for red admirals, mourning cloaks and commas, or create drinking areas where all butterflies, especially swallowtails, alight and sup. You can do this by burying a plastic pan and filling it with sand, keeping it moist. If you have a habitat pond or bog garden, this won't be needed.

You don't have to go to great lengths to enjoy these lovely creatures, and you don't need a commercial butterfly house; while pretty, such houses appear to be notoriously unattractive to butterflies. All you have to do is chose from among more than two dozen basic flowers that are magnets for a range of butterflies and closely related skippers. Many of the plants are not native, but if you employ them, expect to see such handsome insects as swallowtails, monarchs, fritillaries, hairstreaks, blues, painted ladies and an array of skippers.

BUTTERFLY-LURING PLANTS

Asters	Goldenrods	Lilacs	Verbena
Butterfly bush	Heliopsis	Marigolds	Viburnums
Butterfly weed	Impatiens	Monarda	Violets
Cardinal flower	Joe-pye weed	Phlox	Yarrow
Columbines	Lantana	Purple coneflower	Zinnias
Crape myrtles	Lavender	Rudbeckias	
Daylilies	Liatris	Sedums	

You can take butterfly gardening a step farther by employing plants where the caterpillars feed and live, including parsley, rue, spicebush, pipevine, viburnums and birches.

Section 5

THE EDIBLE GARDEN

Chapter 26

VEGETABLES

*A*NYONE WHO has grown one knows the difference in taste between a plump, warm tomato just off the vine and the blander version found in the market. Imagine the same leap in flavor in virtually every garden vegetable — lettuce, sweet peppers, cucumbers, beans, squash and much more — and you begin to understand why such gardening is so rewarding. Once you've feasted on a row of vegetables from your own land, it's hard to go back to those other rows of wire baskets and fluorescent lights.

Just-picked freshness is not the only advantage over commercial vegetables. At home you can enrich your soil to ensure the tastiest produce, and you can choose from numerous varieties with their own special mix of flavors. If you have environmental and health concerns, you can be sure that no pesticides are used, that your vegetables carry no food-borne diseases or that they haven't been genetically altered. In the end, you will have a sense of accomplishment and self-reliance, a hint of what our farming forebears felt at harvest time. Some will tell you that this alone makes the vegetables taste better.

We are not, of course, the same as our agricultural ancestors, and the nature of most vegetable gardens has changed. They generally are smaller, and each vegetable must earn its space. Few of us have the expanses to accommodate such crops as sweet corn, melons or cabbage. We therefore look for quality rather than quantity. We are not so much farmers today as gourmet growers, concentrating on salad greens, beets or radishes, spinach, peppers or carrots, beans, shallots or those succulent tomatoes.[1]

This low-investment, high-yield credo is not carved in stone. Some gardeners are drawn to more demanding or more space-consuming produce once they have tried the easy stuff. I, for one, raise onions and rhubarb because they remind me of the English allotment, or community, gardens of my youth, and I grow potatoes and peas despite the small size of my garden. For me, just one or two meals of fresh potatoes are worth the trouble, and fresh peas are a sheer delight.

Here, then, is how to create and cultivate a vegetable garden, plus a menu of plants from which to choose (including some for the more venturesome or those with more land).

CREATING A VEGETABLE GARDEN

CHOOSE A SPOT in full sun. While lettuce, carrots and beets can be grown in light shade, most food plants need six hours of direct sunlight to yield sufficient harvests. If possible, you also should pick a plot where your starter garden can be enlarged as your desires and skills grow.

A small but good garden size to begin with is 16 feet x 20 feet. This will allow for three beds, each four feet wide, running the garden's 20-foot length. Each bed will accommodate two or three planting rows, depending on the vegetables you choose — carrots and beets, for example, need less shoulder room than tomatoes and eggplants — and whether you stagger plants to extract more space. Thus you can grow six to nine vegetables in the beds (or more if you plant more than one vegetable per row).

You also will have room for four paths, each 12 inches wide, beside the beds. These catwalks are a must for all the work you do, since you cannot tread in planted beds without compressing the soil and damaging the plants.

---

[1]The tomato, originally from South America, is botanically a fruit, specifically a berry, but it is commonly treated as a vegetable.

RAISED BED VEGETABLE GARDEN FRAMED WITH LANDSCAPE TIMBERS

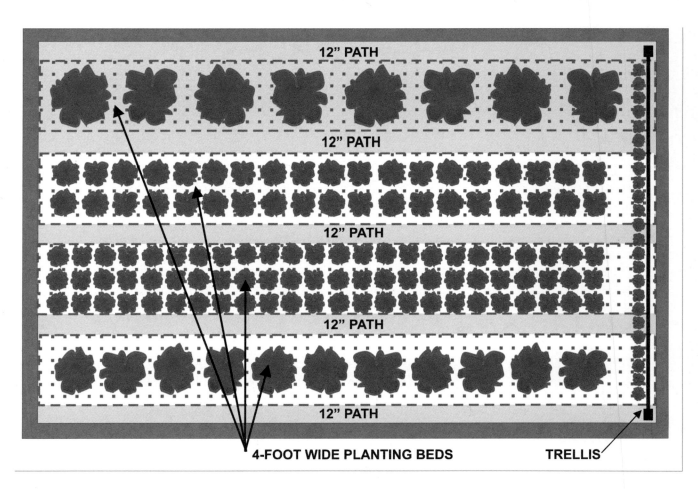

12" PATH

12" PATH

12" PATH

12" PATH

12" PATH

4-FOOT WIDE PLANTING BEDS   **TRELLIS**

Sand and gravel are good for the catwalks. It's unwise to use mulch, which harbors slugs, or grass, which is impossible to mow and edge.

The garden will need enriched, well-drained soil, at least eight inches deep. This is the fuel that fires the plot. If your soil is poor and unimproved, your plants are likely to be stunted, sickly and less productive. Many gardeners create a raised bed, simply mounding the soil or retaining it. Pressure-treated timbers appear safe to use as retainers, though iron edging is slimmer and more efficient. Railroad ties and old utility poles often have been infused with creosote, a wood preservative; to be on the safe side, they are better avoided.

In late fall, mark out the plot, lay the retaining timbers if you want them, and weed and turn the soil. Weeding is essential: In the race for life between weeds and vegetable seedlings, the weeds will win. Next, add compost, humus and topsoil. Don't add much, if any, peat moss — it will make the soil too acidic — and avoid composts made from human sewage sludge, which contain heavy metals. (In March, when you are ready to put in cool-season plants, you should weed and turn the soil again, adding more amendments if needed to bulk up the beds. In ensuing years, you should keep building up the soil, preferably with your own compost.)

If you live in deer or rabbit country, you would do well to put up a wire fence at the outset with 4 x 4, pressure-treated posts. Make the fence six feet high to preclude the deer. Clad the lower third with chicken wire (the bottom few inches should be buried and turned out, away from the garden, to keep burrowing animals at bay, especially the rabbits). You will need a gate wide enough for your wheelbarrow. Make sure that the gate fits tightly and that you remember to keep it closed.

Finally, you will need supports for vining plants, either in beds or at a garden edge, where you will be able to grow more vegetables. Supports are especially important for small gardens, where there's no room to let climbers sprawl. Place the supports at the garden's north or east side, so the vining plants don't create afternoon shade for lower-growing vegetables.

Every gardener seems to prefer particular supports, ranging from simple stakes to elaborate trellises. Whatever you choose, the smart approach is to over-design the support: It's too late to discover halfway through the season that your tomato stakes aren't strong enough. Peas, which climb to just four feet, will be content on nylon netting strung taut on bamboo stakes. But other vining crops, such as tomatoes, runner and pole beans and winter squash, will grow heavy and leafy and collapse on all but the sturdiest supports. Here are some choices:

■ **WIRE CAGES.** Wire cages sold in spring for tomato plants are of limited value with the indeterminate varieties (those continuing to grow and produce throughout the season) that many people plant, which can attain a height of six feet or more. If you want tomato cages, buy the largest ones you can find. Some people use smaller cages for peppers.

■ **STAKES.** You can use wooden or metal stakes for tomatoes, to which you loosely attach the vine with soft twine or cloth (not wire ties) as it grows. Stakes should be at least six feet high, so they can be driven a foot into the ground for anchorage. Some hardware stores sell metal posts (used for barbed wire fencing) with a triangular plate near the bottom that acts as a subsurface anchor. These are useful not only for garden tomatoes but for those grown in large containers.

■ **TEPEES.** For pole beans, the simplest, most effective support is a tepee made from four sturdy bamboo stakes, tied at the top. Press the stakes several inches into the ground before tying. You should use eight-foot lengths, which are hard to find, but you can cut your own poles.

■ **TRELLISES.** A popular trellis, particularly for beans, is made of 2 x 2 posts, eight feet high. Set the two posts two feet into the ground, from 10 to 20 feet apart, and support them with staked guy wire and wooden braces. Using eyehooks, string wire across the tops and bottoms of the posts, and then tie twine between the wires. The beans grow nicely on the twine (see illustration). The trellis can be dismantled at season's end or left as a permanent structure.

You can grow tomatoes on the trellis, but training them requires fastidious pruning, and they cannot be raised in the same spot for too long: Tomatoes should be rotated every two years to prevent a buildup of soil-borne disease. The trellis also can be used for such crops as squash, cucumbers and zucchini, at least with proper pruning.

If you have a trellis with cross members of bamboo or thicker wood, it may become a favored perch for blue jays and crows. Commercial plastic trellises may be strong enough for some plants but not for others.

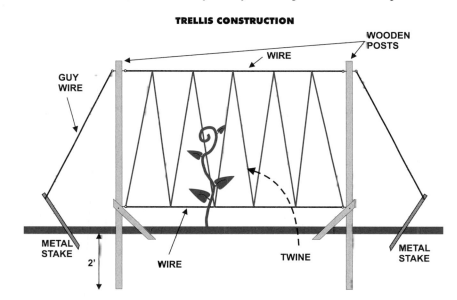

TRELLIS CONSTRUCTION

GENERAL CULTIVATION

EACH VEGETABLE is grown in its own way, but there are a few universal cultivation needs:

■ **THINNING.** Thinning vegetable seedlings may seem like a difficult and counterproductive step, but you have to be ruthless to prevent mature vegetables from becoming crowded and stunted. Instead of pulling the seedlings, which can dislodge their neighbors, snip them with scissors. Lettuce, mesclun, onion, turnip, spinach and beet thinnings can be used in salads or sandwiches.

■ **WATERING.** Have a garden hose or, better yet, a hose bibb close to the garden. Temporary soaker hoses are helpful, but you don't want any permanent form of irrigation pipes in the garden, since the soil must be worked after each harvest. Seeds and seedlings should be misted daily, with the hose nozzle adjusted to its finest spray. In high summer, if possible, water crops daily in the mornings. Certain summer plants, such as peppers, cucumbers and tomatoes, particularly should not be allowed to dry out.

■ **MULCHING.** If you cannot water daily, you will have to mulch the beds, despite the fact that mulch tends to harbor slugs. Mulches are useful in late fall to protect overwintering onions, leeks, garlic and parsnips. Some observers advise you to lay a black plastic mulch over cultivated soil, through which seedlings are planted. In our climate, however, the plastic warms the soil and causes the seedlings to grow quickly at first, and they then become stressed by insufficient water and nutrients. They will either die or produce poorly. On soil that you are trying to build up, lay newspaper covered by straw, and work the material into the soil after harvest.

A MENU OF VEGETABLES

ASPARAGUS. Asparagus is a perennial, and it is not for the small garden. It requires its own bed or plot — one that is 12 feet x 10 feet will produce a reasonable harvest — amended with a good deal of compost. You will need 20 plants for a garden that size. You should plant rootstock in early spring spaced at 18 inches, in narrow trenches that are four feet apart. Keep the soil weeded, cut back top growth in November, and mulch for the winter. Don't harvest the first year — you will weaken the plants. The second year you can cut larger spears for two weeks, but you will have to wait until the third spring for a full yield. Pull or cut spears when they are six to eight inches tall, and harvest for eight weeks. The spears can be frozen, but you would be daft not to eat them fresh.

■ **Varieties:** Chose male plants, especially disease-resistant Jersey Knight Improved.

■ **Main Pest:** Asparagus beetles, which appear with the spears in spring. The larva is a gray-green grub, the adult a blue-black beetle with a red area behind its head. Both feed on foliage, doing great damage. Spray with an organic insecticide such as pyrethrin. Slugs can be a problem in spring. [†]

BEANS. Beans grow as either little bushes in rows or tall vines on trellises or tepees. Bush beans are more convenient and mature quickly, but pole beans are more productive. Sow bush beans after mid-May and plant new rows every three weeks to assure a continuous harvest. Stop sowing by mid-August. An inoculant coated on the seeds will increase yield in soil where beans have not been grown before.

Beans eaten with their pods — string or snap beans — should be picked young, just as the beans swell. Shell beans, including favas and limas, are eaten after the pod has begun to shrivel but before the bean has hardened. Dried beans — stored and used for winter stews — are harvested after the pod has turned brown. Pull whole plants and store them indoors in a shed or basement until the pods begin to split. Shell the beans and store them in airtight jars to prevent mold. With scarlet runner beans, you can pick them as young pods (remove the string and cut into strips before steaming) or let them grow and dry on the vine.

- **Varieties:**

  String or Snap Bean. Most varieties today are stringless and disease-resistant. Yellow versions are called wax beans. Popular varieties include Roma II (bush), Blue Lake (bush or pole), Romano (pole), Contender (bush) and Tendercrop (bush).

  Filet or Harricot Verts. These are the slender, tender gourmet bush beans that must be harvested continuously and young. Varieties include Nickel, Triomphe de Farcy and Vernandon.

  Lima Beans. Available in pole or bush varieties, limas need warm soil to germinate, so wait until mid-to-late May to sow. Look for King of the Garden (pole) and Fordhook (bush).

  Fava Beans. A spring crop, favas are the ne plus ultra of gourmet beans. They are hard to raise, though, because it may get too hot in May before the beans are ready for harvest. You can take your chances or, in early October, sow an overwintering variety for the next spring and mulch heavily.

  Dried Beans. All are bush types. Look for Jacob's Cattle, Yellow Eye and Cannelone.

  Runner Beans. Many people love these as ornamental plants, especially since they attract hummingbirds in late summer. In our region, sow them in June, so the scarlet flowers appear in late summer once temperatures have cooled (the flowers abort above 90 degrees). Varieties include Lady Di, Fergie and Painted Lady, which has variegated pink-and-white blossoms.

- **Main Pests:** Mexican bean beetle, whose orange eggs can be handpicked on the underside of leaves, and the flea beetle. Both can be kept off bush beans with floating row covers. Use a lightweight cover in summer, a heavier cloth in fall; the latter also will extend the harvest. **Main Disease:** Fungal blights afflict beans in poorly drained, heavy soil.[†]

BEETS. Beets are not difficult to grow as long as your soil is light and rich, another reason to have raised beds. Sow one crop in April, to enjoy in mid-to-late June, and another in July, to harvest in September and October. The seeds come in natural clusters, so they must be thinned when they first emerge and again as they grow. Mature plants should be spaced four inches apart. Harvest when the beets are two to three inches in diameter, typically 50 to 70 days after they germinate. If you wait too long, especially in summer's heat, the beets will get woody and lose sweetness.

- **Varieties:** Big Red, Albina Vereduna and Chiogga (which has a striped center).

- **Pests and Diseases:** Usually no serious ones.

BROCCOLI. Many gardeners feel that the broccoli yield — one floret cluster and some side buds after the first harvest — is hardly worth the effort. But if you love fresh broccoli, plant seedlings 18 inches apart from late March to late April and again from late July to mid-August. Broccoli and its ilk (cabbages, Brussels sprouts and cauliflower) prefer evenly moist but well-drained soil. Keep an eye on the emerging head, which matures about two months after planting. If you wait too long, the buds will swell and flower.

- **Varieties:** Broccoli can be started from seed, but most people buy started plants. This is convenient and shortens the growing season — critical in spring in the race to beat the heat — but limits the selection. For spring planting, try to find transplants of such early-season varieties as Early Emerald, Packman, Green Comet and Green Duke. For later planting, use Green Comet again.

- **Main Pests:** Larvae of cabbage maggot fly and cabbage white butterfly, plus aphids.[†] Cover young plants with a floating row cover to exclude the pests.

Broccoli Raab is a related but different plant, actually a mustard green. It, too, is grown in the two cool seasons of spring and fall but raised for its stems and young leaves. Grow it from seed.

CABBAGE. With a little care, cabbages grow well in our area, but their space needs — 24 inches between plants, more with larger varieties — require bigger plots. All cabbage family crops should be rotated regularly to avoid a buildup of soil pathogens. Feed plants with a balanced, slow-release organic fertilizer, but follow directions carefully: Excessive fertilization, along with other stressful conditions such as drought or flooding, may prevent the cabbage from forming a head. Instead it will bolt (send up a flower stem) and be useless. Most people buy transplants, setting them out from mid-March to early April for the early-season crop and from early July to mid-August for a fall crop. You can start them from seed indoors in a light, soilless mix four to six weeks before they are to go into the garden. Wait until the maturity date (typically 60 days with an early-season variety, 75 days for a main season and 85 days for a late-season variety) and harvest when the head feels firm. Ornamental cabbages and kale are planted for winter decoration. Use them that way, not for eating.

- **Varieties:** If you can find them, grow Dynamo and Stonehead, both early-season, disease-resistant varieties. Dynamo is a baby variety for smaller gardens.

- **Pests and Diseases:** Same as broccoli, except cabbage larvae have many more hiding places on cabbages. Using a floating row cover.

As interest in international cuisine grows, so does the following for Chinese cabbage varieties. They rarely are available as transplants and thus must be started from seed. This isn't a problem, since they reach maturity faster than traditional cabbages. Spring varieties such as Napa, Kasumi and China Pride are started indoors in late February or early March and set out by their fourth week. Fall-grown varieties, such as Jade Pagoda, Michihli and Monument, are sown directly into the garden in July. Pak Choi is a related plant, best grown as a fall crop here. Sow seeds directly and successively from early July to late August.

CARROTS. For successful seed germination and root development, carrots need light, deep, sandy soil. Sow directly into the soil after the last frost. Baby carrots can be sown in blocks, but larger carrots are best in rows. Cover the furrows with a soilless mix to mark them and to aid germination. It is important to mist seeds during this period. Block-sown baby carrots don't need thinning, but others do. Thin initially with a scissors and again once the carrots have reached an edible size. Carrots left in the ground too long after maturity get woody. Sow again in late July and August for a fall crop. Avoid heavy nitrogen feeds.

- **Varieties:** Select fast-maturing varieties in the spring. For fall, any variety should be successful provided the garden has good tilth. Do grow baby carrots, which are the most succulent.

- **Main Pests:** Carrots can attract a number of pests, including carrot weevils and carrot rust fly, but these are uncommon and can be controlled with organic insecticides or floating row covers.

CUCUMBERS. Cucumbers are a warm-season crop grown in rows, mounds (hills) or on trellises. Well-drained and evenly moist soil is a must. Sow successively at two-week intervals between early May and late June. The first cucumbers should be ready to pick by late July. Some varieties are sold with male and female plants, while others bear first male and then female flowers on the same vine. The harvest window for cucumbers is just two to three weeks. Take slicing cucumbers when they are five to eight inches long, picklers when they are two to three inches. Make sure to pick them before they get too big and old, lest fruiting falls off and the old cukes are misshapen and bitter. If you have planned correctly, one cucumber plant will be coming into harvest as another wanes.

- **Varieties:** You can get a wide range of slicing and pickling cucumbers as well as the French cornichons, or gherkins, pickled for crudité. The overriding factor in picking a variety is multiple resistance to fungal and viral diseases.

■ **Main Pest and Disease:** Cucumber beetles, which chew the plant, and the wilt disease they carry. A summer-weight floating row cover is a good non-toxic solution, but it should be lifted once flowers appear to allow insect pollination. Cucumber mosaic virus is another problem. Pick resistant varieties.

EGGPLANT. Eggplant loves sun and hates cold. Buy transplants and set them out in mid-May, once the soil has warmed. If you start from seed, you will have to sow indoors in early to mid-April. Pinch young plants to develop a bushy habit. Heavy feeders, eggplants should be side-dressed with a balanced fertilizer monthly as they develop, flower and fruit. The plant normally takes about 70 days to mature, but harvest them before they are fully developed and while the skin is still glossy. This will promote continued fruiting and give you the tastiest eggplants.

■ **Varieties:** In addition to the familiar bulbous eggplant, slender Asian varieties are excellent. They mature earlier and generally are more prolific. Of these, Ichiban is highly recommended.

■ **Main Pests:** Flea beetles, though lacebugs and leafhoppers can be troublesome.[†] All can be countered with a summer-weight floating row cover. **Main Disease:** Wilt. To avoid it, don't plant in the same spot year after year or where tomatoes or potatoes were grown in the preceding three years.

GARLIC. Sow cloves in October, pointed end up and one to two inches deep. Space them three inches apart in close, double rows. Garlic and other members of the onion family (leeks, onions, chives and shallots) prefer a sandy loam that is slightly acidic or neutral, so work wood ashes and a little pulverized limestone into the bed. Some gardeners lay mulch over the garlic to bring it safely through the winter. It then grows vigorously through spring and is harvested at the beginning of summer when the top growth has died. Pull and eat fresh or cure for keeping by allowing bulbs to dry in a well-ventilated room for several days, turning them occasionally. To prevent rot, be careful not to drop or damage bulbs.

■ **Varieties:** Specialty nurseries offer an array of garlics, from mild to hot, white to mauve (see Appendix for Specialty Plant Sources). Otherwise, grow cloves separated from supermarket bulbs.

■ **Pests and Diseases:** Generally free of diseases as long as the soil is well drained. Do keep watered, however, especially in May and June as the bulbs form.

LEEKS. Leeks are another long-season, onion family crop. Buy them as sets (try farmers' markets) or sow seeds indoors under lights in February, setting them out in spring when they are eight inches tall. Spacing them four inches apart, use a dibble or dowel to make the hole and bury them to their necks. As they mature, hill them up to keep the bottom stalks blanched, but be careful not to damage them. Leeks don't store well. Once mature, dig them as needed (they shouldn't be pulled). You can direct-seed a fall crop in late summer, but you will have to thin the seedlings.

■ **Varieties:** Try King Richard, Otina or Titan for spring growing, Blue Solaise for fall harvests.

■ **Pests and Diseases:** None that are serious.

LETTUCE AND OTHER SALAD GREENS. Lettuce and most other salad greens are grown in spring and again in early fall. They are virtually foolproof, growing fast and even taking some shade, but they require even moisture and detest drought. Don't try to grow through high summer: They will bolt and turn bitter. Save some seed to sow again in August for a fall crop. Lettuces look most attractive in single or double rows, and seedlings can be thinned regularly to avoid crowding and used for salads. You also can snip off leaves so the plant continues to produce. Start from seed rather than buying seedlings.

■ **Varieties:** Looseleafs are the easiest to grow and harvest, making the best cutting lettuces. Cos (romaine) varieties extend the spring season a bit. Butterhead varieties are sweet and delicious but grow bitter with heat. Iceberg (properly crisphead lettuce) is a bust this far south.

- **Pests and Diseases:** Slugs can be a problem.[†]

Mesclun is a loose term for a variety of salad greens that typically includes lettuce varieties along with endives, pak choi, kale, arugula and chervil. Italian-inspired versions usually include chicories. The seeds are block sown, and the greens should be snipped when the leaves are young, three to four inches, before they turn bitter. Mesclun is great for container gardens on patios and balconies.

ONIONS. We live on the cusp so far as onions are concerned. Long-day onions (the pungent storing type) will bulb up here, but not into the giants of New England, where summer days are longer and cool nights shorter. The classic southern sweet onion, the Vidalia, is a short-day plant that bulbs at the wrong time for our climate. Nonetheless, if you select the right varieties and treat them well, onions can do nicely in our area. You can, for example, grow Walla Wallas, sweet, non-storage onions similar to Vidalias.

Onions need well-drained soil that's on the sandy side and organically rich, with a neutral pH (don't use peat moss). They should be watered often, especially as they mature in late May through June. Storage onions must be properly cured. When top growth begins to fade in early July, lift the onions, but let them bake in the garden sun for several days. Then put them in a well-ventilated, dark room (an attic with a fan is a good place) for a week or two. Only then remove the vestiges of the tops, and leave one to two inches of the stalk. Do not nick or bruise the bulbs.

Onion sets are young onions sold in early spring, usually as simply yellows, whites or reds. These are easy and little fuss, but they are hard to get to bulb, and you often end up with bunching onions by default.

For seeds, order by variety in late winter, but don't direct-seed into the garden: You won't be able to distinguish between emerging onions and weeds. Instead, start seeds indoors under lights in late February and set out seedlings in April. Plant in rows for ease of weeding. Alternatively, you can buy named seedlings (as opposed to unidentified sets) from mail-order nurseries (see Appendix for Specialty Plant Sources). With Walla Wallas, you can direct-seed them in late August or early September (when weeds are not as big a deal as in spring) and let them overwinter with a protection of mulch. They will bulb up the next spring. Harvest them when the top growth withers in late June. You also can buy this variety as a seedling in early spring.

- **Varieties:** In addition to Walla Walla, try Copra, a long-day variety, and Norstar, an early-season variety. Both have been proved locally.

- **Main Pests:** The onion root maggot, which is serious but uncommon. If you have had trouble with it, use a floating row cover to exclude the fly. Aphids also can be a problem.[†]

PEAS. The garden pea was the favorite vegetable of Thomas Jefferson, who of course had the room and free labor to grow it. For a decent harvest, you must devote much space to vines and be prepared to harvest them at their convenience, not yours. On balance, the trouble is worth it. The pea is sown in March and harvested in June. The aim is to get the peas to produce as soon as possible, before pre-summer heat halts the yield. In some years, the pea harvest is a bust because winter lingers too long and the soil is too wet and cold to work and sow. Again, raised beds with good tilth can make the difference. Vines are brittle and easily broken, so handle them with care.

A trellis or fence lets you make the best use of space and raise taller, more prolific varieties. My own bamboo frames clad in stretch nylon netting are four feet high. I plant double, staggered rows; 15 to 20 feet of trellising are needed for a decent harvest. One seed packet is insufficient; buy three, and for fun select different varieties. Harvest them when pods have swelled and you can feel the peas inside, but don't wait too long or the peas will get starchy. Check daily in June: Prompt harvesting will promote additional yield. Petit-pois varieties are harvested when the peas are smaller. Children, of course, love to take their share, but do supervise to ensure that they don't pull out a whole vine or tread on the garden beds.

■ **Varieties:** Vining varieties are the most productive, but grow dwarf or bush peas if you don't want to go to the trouble of building a support:

English, or garden, peas. In years when winter is prolonged, plant short-season varieties like Knight, Daybreak or a bush type called Improved Laxton's Progress. In regular years, Wando and Lincoln are good heat-tolerant varieties for our region.

Snap Peas. These were developed so the pod could be eaten as well, increasing the bulk of food from the plant. Almost all have a string that must be removed before cooking. Seeds may rot in cold, wet soil. Varieties of note include Sugar Snap, Super Sugar Mel and Sugar Daddy, which is stringless.

Snow Peas. Snow peas are grown for their flat, edible pods, not for the seeds. Vigilance is a must in early June: Pods left too long become twisted and inferior, swollen by seeds. Varieties to try include Oregon Giant, Little Sweetie (stringless) and Sugar Pod 2.

■ **Main Pests:** Crows might eat emerging seedlings; sow more if they do. Squirrels and chipmunks, which are tough to fence out, might eat pea pods. Aphids can smother new growth.†

PEPPERS. Peppers, a warm-season vegetable, are valuable for smaller plots. Hot peppers are far more successful in our climate than bell peppers, which tend to be grudging in their vitality and output. The production shuts down naturally if you allow bells to ripen to red, which you want to do for the sweetest, most nutritious peppers. Bell peppers dislike the unremitting heat of high summer. Provide some shade with a summer-weight floating row cover. Also, bell peppers shouldn't be planted with hot peppers that bloom concurrently; bees may cross-pollinate and cause the sweet pepper to develop a bite. Whichever sort you grow, mix bone meal into the soil for calcium and Epsom salts for magnesium. Unless you are good at it, don't raise peppers from seed (a chore that must be done indoors under lights for a relatively long period). Instead, buy and set out transplants in late May, once the soil has warmed. Try planting on a cloudy day, and don't let the plant wilt. Erratic watering and particularly wilting will seriously set back the plant. Taller varieties may need staking or wire cages.

■ **Varieties:** For bell types, look for Bell Boy, Bell Tower, Yellow Belle, Gypsy and Golden Summer. For hot peppers, try Cayenne, Habanero, Jalapeno and Super Chile Hybrid.

■ **Pests and Diseases:** Viruses and bacterial disease, often carried by aphids, can stunt or kill plants.†

POTATOES. Though fresh potatoes are a joy, they are not for smaller gardens. Fingerling types are a gourmet delight, and new potatoes are so good that you still may be tempted to grow them at least once. Potatoes are planted in a medium to light loam in mid-to-late March. The richer the soil, the better and bigger the crop. Cut small seed potatoes into halves or thirds (the object is to leave on each piece one to three buds from which stems will sprout). Place these in a dark, well-ventilated room for three days for the cuts to callus. Plant in rows four inches deep and 18 to 24 inches apart. When the stems are young, begin to hill soil around them, to just below the lowest set of leaves. The potatoes form in these mounds: They must be kept covered in soil to prevent sunlight from turning them green and toxic. New potatoes can be retrieved — gingerly — from growing plants, or you can lift whole plants for the young spuds, which are the size of eggs. Otherwise, just leave the potato plant to mature. New potatoes should be ready by June, mature ones once the top growth withers in late July.

■ **Varieties:** For fingerlings, look for Austrian Crescent, French Fingerling or Rose Finn Apple. For whites, try Anoka or White Rose; for reds, Red Norland or Sangle; and for yellows, Yukon Gold, Yellow Finn or German Butterball.

- **Main Pest:** The Colorado potato beetle, which is striped yellow and black, with a pinkish-red larva. Handpick adults; spray larva with Bt. **Main Diseases:** Viruses and bacteria that cause leaves to wither and die. You must plant seed potatoes that are certified as disease-free. Also, do not grow in the same earth as last season's crops of tomatoes, eggplants, potatoes or peppers.

PUMPKINS. A form of winter squash, pumpkins are grown as trailing vines. This is not a plant for anything but large lots or unused sunny slopes. On flat or sloped beds, you will need to add large amounts of leaf mold, rotted manure and compost. Vines need rich, loose soil for the trailing stems to form roots. Each pumpkin hill is formed from a mound in the center of a square measuring 10 feet on each side. The aim is to get vines to trail on all sides, from the center out. In late May, once the soil has warmed, sow six seeds per hill, thinning them out to the three strongest once seedlings emerge. Pumpkins need lots of water as well as nutrients; a slow soil soaking is preferable to overhead sprinkling, to reduce the chances of powdery mildew. If you can't avoid getting leaves wet, water in the morning, not at night. Pumpkins take more than three months to mature. Be prepared to give them frequent care and attention from June to September and October. For the largest specimens, disbud flowers and cut back vines once chosen pumpkins have developed.

- **Varieties:** For large Halloween pumpkins, try Prizewinner or Connecticut Field. Small Sugar is not as big but is hefty enough and excellent for pies. Hobbyists have grown pumpkins exceeding 1,000 pounds, all using seed from Dill's Atlantic Giant. Giant pumpkins will never attain that size here because of our shorter summer days and our heat and humidity. The Washington record was set in 1997 by Joe Mills of Falls Church, Va., with a pumpkin weighing more than 400 pounds. Among small varieties that fit on one hand, try Sweetie Pie, Baby Boo (white skinned) and Spooktacular.

- **Main Pests:** Squash-vine borer, a moth worm that tunnels into vines and eventually kills them. It often is found at the base of main stems. You can spray or dust an insecticide, but to avoid killing bees, don't use it when flowers are in bloom. If you spy holes where worms have entered, cut out the insects with a sharp razor. Mound earth or place masking tape over the wound (don't encircle the stem). Deer and raccoons should be fenced out. **Main Disease:** Powdery mildew is a serious ailment, often worse in dry spells.†

RADISHES. Radishes are grown from seed sown directly into the garden in rows. Start planting in early March, and sow successively for a continuous harvest from April to June. They will need thinning once, maybe twice, so that they are two to three inches apart. Use the thinnings in salads. Save seed for a second sowing in mid-to-late August for a fall crop. (Radishes don't do well in summer, turning hot and woody.) Their rapid germination and growth — they mature 25 to 35 days after sprouting — make them ideal for children to grow. They are choice for just a few days, so don't let them get old. Radishes that are not harvested shoot up to about three feet and produce lovely white and lavender flowers that turn into fleshy pods. The pods are supposed to be edible, but you would have to be ravenous to eat them.

- **Varieties:** Look for Cherry Belle, Sparkler and Red Devil. Oriental Daikon is rubbery when large; try it pickled.

- **Main Pest:** A root maggot. Use a floating row cover to keep the fly at bay. If you have had serious maggot damage, don't plant radishes in that spot for a couple of seasons.

SQUASH. Most people grow summer squash, including zucchini, though winter squash is less troubled by disease and considered tastier by many squash lovers. Most varieties are bushy rather than vining, but they still need space and are best grown on little hills like pumpkins. A hill of two or three plants will need two to three feet in each direction. Sow seeds directly in late May, once the soil has warmed. Then sow another crop in mid-

June and a third in early July to assure a constant fresh supply or to compensate for any early crop failure. However, don't go overboard: There are only so many friends and co-workers who will take your harvest glut. Harvest when vegetables are young; they form quickly and should be policed daily in season. You should be able to nick the skin with your thumbnail. If you can't, the vegetable is too old.

■ **Varieties:**

Summer Squash. Sunbar, Fortune, Goldbar (straightnecks), Sundance and Supersett (crooknecks).

Pattypan-Scallop Squashes. Peter Pan, Sunburst and Scallopini.

Zucchini. Gold Rush (yellow), Aristocrat and Revenue. (For Revenue, try Stokes Seeds of Buffalo, N.Y. See Appendix for Specialty Plant Sources).

Winter Squash. Other than pumpkin varieties, there are acorn, Hubbards (best storing), Butternut and Buttercup types. As with pumpkins, these vines ripen through the season and are harvested by mid-October.

■ **Main Pests:** Same as for pumpkins. However, the squash plant's smaller size makes it easier to use a floating row cover to exclude the squash-vine borer. Remove the cover when the plant is in flower, to allow pollination and fruiting. **Main Diseases:** Viral and bacterial diseases, including wilts. Select disease-resistant varieties, and keep them well fed and watered.

TOMATOES. The virtues of the tomato are well known to everyone from the apartment dweller with a sunny balcony to the suburban homeowner with room for half a dozen types. In growing them, you first need to choose between determinates and indeterminates. Determinate varieties reach a certain size and yield their fruit in one flush, dying when tomatoes mature. These are useful for container-grown patio tomatoes, because they stay within bounds and don't need staking. They are valuable, too, for canning, since you get the whole crop at once. Indeterminates keep growing and fruiting, most until the first frost. They not only yield more over time, but they generally taste better. They do, however, become unruly and unkempt. If you raise tomatoes on a trellis, remove the lateral stems as they appear at leaf stalk joints (axils) to keep the vine growing with some semblance of order.

You can grow your own from seed or buy started plants at many outlets. Avoid plants that are available too early in the season or that have been sitting around and become potbound and stressed. If you can't find a variety you want at a nursery, garden center or hardware store, look for it at a weekend farmers' market. Modern hybrids are no less tasty than heirloom varieties and in some respects are often more disease resistant. However, only open-pollinated varieties will yield seed that will grow true the following season. Seed can be grown indoors, with young plants hardened off and set out, or sown directly into sun-warmed, well-drained soil, in early to mid-May. Seedlings will produce earlier, in July, and should be set deeply when planted: Roots will develop along the buried stem, producing a stronger plant.

Tomatoes are hungry and thirsty vines, so water often, especially during dry spells. But don't overfeed them, especially with nitrogen-rich fertilizers. You should work some bone meal into the soil, along with a fertilizer formulated for tomatoes. Side-dress with a slow-release fertilizer once flowers appear.

Container-grown tomatoes need a pot that's at least 18 inches in diameter, so it doesn't dry out too quickly. Make sure that you have some topsoil in the mix: A potting soil mix will be too light and won't hold enough water for exceptionally hot days. Don't be afraid to grow tall, vining, interdeterminate types in pots. Just place a four-foot stake in the container or grow the plant on the railing of a balcony or deck, tying stems loosely with twine. Alternatively, you can mount a trellis and train the potted tomato onto it.

■ **Varieties:**

Hybrids. Better Boy, Big Beef and Beefmaster are all first-rate, disease-resistant beefsteak varieties. Carmello is a highly praised French hybrid, as is Dona. Other proven varieties include Enchantment and Flavor King Hybrid. Celebrity is an excellent determinate type.

Heirlooms. Brandywine is the classic favorite. Others include Old Flame, an old beefsteak variety, Valencia (orange), also large and productive, Mortgage Lifter, Costoluto Genovese (determinate) and Large Red.

Cherry Types: These often are the most vigorous and productive. Red Cherry and Sweet Million grow well in our heat. Other good choices are Sun Gold (orange), an early hybrid, and Green-Cape (yellow-green). With currant varieties, hundreds of tiny tomatoes form on huge vines. Currants are a lot of work to harvest, but they keep children entertained for hours and are very tasty. The unruly vines are apt to return from seed, year after year, without bidding.

■ **Main Pests and Diseases:** Tomato hornworms, huge but well camouflaged, can be destructive, but only if you have few plants and many caterpillars. Don't kill those with rice-like eggs on their backs; they are about to undergo death by a parasitic wasp, whose numbers then will multiply. If mockingbirds or squirrels are near, they will help themselves to some tomatoes; there should be enough to share. Stinkbugs should be handpicked and destroyed. Uneven watering fosters blossom-end rot or causes fruit to crack.

---

†See Appendix for common pest and disease ailments that are not specific to particular vegetables.

Chapter 27

HERBS

ERBS CAN BE GROWN almost anywhere by anyone. Once you've tasted fresh basil or rosemary or other herbs from your garden (or deck or balcony), you're likely to swear off dried herbs — or even fresh-cut ones — from the market. After initial modest investments in pots, soil mixes and seedlings, moreover, you'll save money and have fun in the process.

Herbs not only excite the palate, and they not only are used for teas, potpourris and medicinal purposes, but they are visual treats as well. Some, such as lavender, chives and beebalm, are valued for their flowers, but herbs mostly are exceptionally beautiful foliage plants. They come in a range of textures (from the fineness of chives or thyme to the coarseness of comfrey or horseradish) and colors (yellow, blue, silver, purple, gray, gold and a shade or two of green). Even the most haphazard collections can look wonderful, and those assembled with a little thought can be a joy.

Herbs are grown in four ways: (1) in containers on patios and balconies, (2) in beds with other garden plants, (3) in their own ornamental herb gardens, and (4) indoors near a window or under lights. The herbaholic, of course, may grow them all four ways.

1. HERBS IN CONTAINERS

POT-GROWN HERBS are ideal. You can place them close to the kitchen where they are needed, readily move them into or out of the sun, or use them to decorate outdoor sitting areas. Herbs also happen to love containers. Most common herbs are fussy about having excellent drainage, and you can make sure that they get it by raising them in clay pots, half whiskey barrels, plastic containers, wooden planters, faux-lead troughs or whatever strikes your fancy.

Whichever container you chose, it not only should have good drainage but be large enough not to dry out on a summer's afternoon. It is unwise to consider anything with less than a 12-inch-diameter or the equivalent for rectangular planters.

A word about terra cotta pots: They look fabulous and lend an elegant Mediterranean air to the patio, but because they are porous they dry out quickly. This creates a commitment in high summer to water once and sometimes twice a day to keep herbs from wilting. Also, terra cotta pots are prone to cracking if left outdoors in winter. This means that you either have to grow annual herbs alone, empty the pot in October and store it dry or bring in all the pots at that time, no matter how heavy or cumbersome some might be.

You may wish to consider high-quality, plastic look-alikes, which are lighter, can be left outdoors year round and will not dry out as quickly, even though the sun's rays will destroy them in three years or so. Glazed Chinese pots, which are not frost-proof, are unsuited to growing herbs. Planters of concrete, stone or wood are best.

If you are going away for, say, two weeks in August, water the herb garden heavily in the days leading to your departure and cut back half the top growth in the case of basil, mint, rue, cilantro, oregano and parsley. Then put the containers where they will be in afternoon shade. If you lose some herbs, there's sufficient time to replant with seedlings for the remaining six to eight weeks of the growing season after Labor Day.

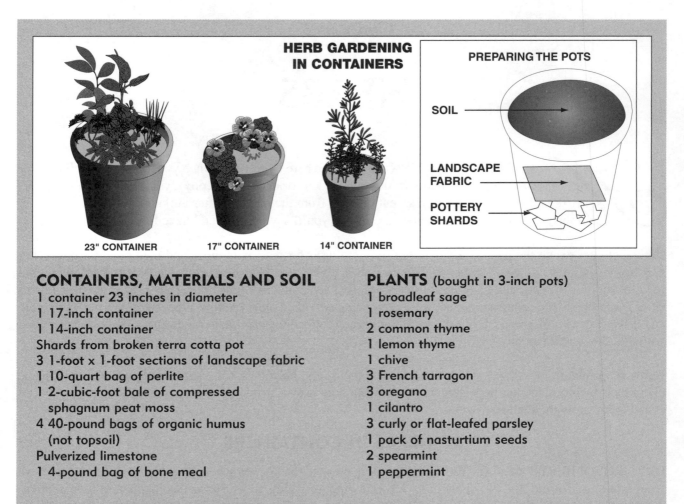

CONTAINERS, MATERIALS AND SOIL

1 container 23 inches in diameter
1 17-inch container
1 14-inch container
Shards from broken terra cotta pot
3 1-foot x 1-foot sections of landscape fabric
1 10-quart bag of perlite
1 2-cubic-foot bale of compressed
   sphagnum peat moss
4 40-pound bags of organic humus
   (not topsoil)
Pulverized limestone
1 4-pound bag of bone meal

PLANTS (bought in 3-inch pots)

1 broadleaf sage
1 rosemary
2 common thyme
1 lemon thyme
1 chive
3 French tarragon
3 oregano
1 cilantro
3 curly or flat-leafed parsley
1 pack of nasturtium seeds
2 spearmint
1 peppermint

Make sure each pot has a drainage hole. Place a layer of shards at the bottom and cover it with the filter fabric to prevent the soil mix from washing away.

In a wheelbarrow or large trash can, mix (dry and by volume) one part sphagnum peat moss to two parts humus to one part perlite. Add two cups of bone meal and one cup of limestone for each container. Mix thoroughly, using a shovel, trowel or your hands. Fill the containers with the soil, but leave two inches below the rim level to permit watering.

23-Inch Container
The container will seem big and the plants small, but don't fret: By summer the balance will be redressed. Place the sage and sweet basil in the back (they grow the tallest), giving them room. Group the oregano in the center. Place the tarragon at the front alongside the parsley. Squeeze the cilantro and chives into available pockets. At season's end, plant the sage in the garden or use it in the container for another season. Bring the chives in for winter use, and harvest the tarragon or keep it for another season. The oregano can be left. The parsley will survive the first few frosts. Lift the cilantro and replace it in spring.

17-Inch Container
Position the mints in a triangle toward the center, but with plenty of space between them. On the outer rim, sow the nasturtium seeds: The nasturtium will grow to trail over the edges. This container should be fertilized at half the frequency of the others but watered a little more. It will take partial shade. Indeed, the plants will prefer this in July and August.

14-Inch Container
Stick the rosemary in the center and the thyme plants near the rim, equally spaced. The whole container can be brought indoors in winter and set out again in spring. It will do best indoors in a bright but cool room. Mist it there occasionally, but water it sparingly.

2. HERBS IN GARDEN BEDS

SOME COMMON HERBS are wonderful ornamental plants in their own right and deserve to be used as part of the decorative landscape. Sticking herbs with other plants is a time-honored method of making room in tight gardens for favored culinary, medicinal or aromatic plants. Finding candidates is easy:

■ **LAVENDERS.** These make an attractive informal hedge (or low-clipped hedge) and look great in beds bordering patios. Lavender's silver-gray foliage can be played against greens, whites, purples and blues.

■ **THYME.** Culinary varieties of thyme are more upright than low-growing mat forms, but either can be used as a small-scale ground cover or planted in and around stairs.

■ **CHIVES.** Chives have fine, upright, green foliage and produce small, rose-purple flowers in late spring.

■ **BEEBALM.** Once used for making tea, beebalm now is more renowned for its summer flower display of scarlet-red blooms that attract butterflies and hummingbirds.

■ **SAGE.** Used in beds and borders, sage is a handsome, medium-to-coarse-leafed, shrubby herb that combines well with lavenders, cranesbill, campanula, coreopsis, columbine, perovskia and many other small-to-medium-sized perennials that like sun or partial shade. Some varieties are a light gray-green, others silver gray, still others purple-leafed.

■ **RUE.** Rue is a fine-textured jewel with a unique leaf structure. Interesting season-long, it deserves to be used in prominent and cozy settings with spring-flowering bulbs, small-to-medium-sized perennials and small shrubs. Its distinct blue cast works well with orange or yellow flowering plants, including pot marigolds (*calendulas*), geum and coreopsis.

■ **FENNEL.** Fennel grows tall and might need staking, but its fine, feathery foliage adds substantial interest to beds. Use in the middle or back of a border. Bronze fennel, with its purple-brown cast, goes well with yellow-flowering irises, helianthus, coreopsis, daylilies, peonies and tulips.

■ **MINT.** Mint is a valuable foliage plant for poorly drained areas and takes partial-to-medium shade. There are many varieties, but you should be mindful that the more vigorous ones will take over garden beds. If you plant them with other perennials, keep them in containers, sunken and masked by a thin layer of mulch.

3. HERBS IN THEIR OWN GARDEN

THE HERB GARDEN, an ancient tradition, was a fixture of every monastery garden in the Middle Ages. Magazines today are full of modern recreations, often beautifully crafted with expertly laid brick paving, a spherical sun dial in the center, neatly clipped low hedges of boxwood or lavender, and not a leaf out of place.

Hedges look quite nice, but they will commit you to both the expense of the plants and the burden of maintaining them. If that is fine with you, good candidates for herb bed edging include edging box, lavender, hyssop, santolina, germander or winter savory. The hedges must be clipped two or three times each growing season to keep them neat, and you'll need some spare plants elsewhere in the garden to lift and fill in gaps in the hedge when some plants there inevitably die. Importantly, though, you can create the effect of the herb garden without this expense and bother. Consider these tips:

a. **SCALE.** Don't make the herb garden too big. Herbs are small plants when young, and in too large an area the beds will lose their structure. Also, weeding becomes a chore. Consider a garden 10 feet or 12 feet square, which will let you use landscape timbers sold in those lengths, avoiding the need to saw them. Access paths should be 18 inches wide, to maximize bed space.

b. DEFINITION. Your herb garden will need definition. Its edges should be framed and the herb beds arranged in a geometric shape. The landscape timbers will frame the garden and raise it up, allowing for the amendments needed for light, well-draining soil. The timbers also will let you create a flat, terraced garden on a sloping site. Where beds abut paths, mark edges with a row of cobblestones. You also can define the garden with three-foot picket fencing. This lends a Colonial air and keeps rabbits and cats out without impeding airflow to the plants. (You may have to staple inconspicuous wire or black plastic netting around the fencing for pest control).

c. PAVING. Brick or flagstone paths, laid on a two-inch bed of sand, are excellent. Alternatively, you can use pea gravel, laid to a depth of three inches on compacted soil. Use filter fabric as a weed blocker beneath the gravel. The gravel is less expensive than stone or brick, but it can be a nuisance to keep out of herb beds. Don't try to use turfgrass for paths.

d. SOIL. Use a 50-50 mix of organic matter and coarse sand to a depth of 12 inches.

e. HEIGHT. Herb gardens look better with some vertical elements. Some people use roses, rosemary or other plant standards trained up into a lollipop on a stick, or some sort of topiary. These need high maintenance and are not recommended for the casual gardener. In the center of the garden, place a sundial or birdbath on a pedestal. Tall herbs such as rosemary, lavender, sweet basil and fennel add their own height. In addition, you can throw in a clay "prop" or two: a bee skep, an olive oil jar or strawberry pots.

4. HERBS INDOORS

INDOOR GARDENING, the hardest on herb and gardener alike, usually is done only to get both through the winter safely. Herbs that grow quickly from seed are ideal candidates for indoors: sweet basil, cilantro, chives (seed or bulbs), curly and Italian flat parsley, oregano, chervil and dill. Some tender herbs — rosemary, bay and scented geraniums, for example — are brought indoors to survive the winter and can be discreetly harvested at the same time, but don't water or feed them too much. This is the period for them to rest.

HARVESTING AND MAINTENANCE

NEW GARDENERS sometimes get into a tizzy about when to start harvesting herbs. Obviously, you have to wait for new plants to get over transplant shock and establish themselves, which takes about three or four weeks. Once they start putting out new growth, it is safe to take leaves and whole stems. Herbs not only tolerate this; they need it to grow bushy and to delay flowering and setting seed. Oils are at their strongest before flowering, so keep pinching back and being greedy.

Herb gardens need a fair degree of maintenance. It is impossible to keep them looking or behaving as you might wish. Some herbs have short life cycles, others fail to get established, still others do too well, outgrowing their bounds. Go with the flow. Be prepared to replace some plants each spring and to try new ones. That's part of the fun.

Pests and Diseases: Herbs tend to be trouble-free. The oils that give them taste and fragrance seem to discourage many insects (lavender and wormwood, remember, are used to repel moths in closets). Lavender, thyme and rosemary are prone to fungal rots and blights if grown in wet, heavy soil or in shade. Rosemary can get scale. Leafhoppers and whitefly can appear, but they don't warrant fighting unless they arrive in large numbers.[†] Needless to say, don't use chemical insecticides or herbicides, including systemic pesticides, around herbs for the table. Sometimes a large green-and-black-hooped caterpillar feasts on parsley or rue. This becomes the beautiful black swallowtail butterfly and would be a crime to kill.

A GALLERY OF POPULAR HERBS

BASIL, SWEET (Annual)
Height: 36-48 inches. **Soil:** Well-drained but evenly moist. **Full sun to partial shade.**
Sow seeds or plant seedlings in May and again in early August. Pinch back to promote bushiness and delay flowering. Leggy, floriferous plants should be pulled and replanted in mid-summer.
Use fresh for salads, pestos and other sauces, soups, meat dishes and pastas. Can be dried or frozen for winter use.

CHAMOMILE, ROMAN (Perennial)
Height: 6-12 inches. **Soil:** Well-drained but evenly moist. **Full sun to partial shade.**
Plant seedlings or divisions in spring. Chamomile is attractive in containers or near paths, where the occasional misplaced foot will bring out the plant's apple-like aroma.
Harvest flower heads to dry and use especially for teas and potpourris.

CHIVES (Perennial)
Height: 16 inches. **Soil:** Average to moist.
Full sun to partial shade.
Plant seedlings or divisions in spring. Cut back foliage after flowering, in part to prevent self-seeding. In early winter, after chives have gone into cold dormancy, lift a clump, pot it up, cut back the foliage and bring it indoors, where it will re-sprout obligingly for the cook.
Use as garnish and flavoring for soups, fish, eggs and vegetables.

CILANTRO, OR CORIANDER (Annual)
Height: 12 inches. **Soil:** Well-drained.
Full sun to partial shade.
Sow seeds or plant seedlings in spring, then successively. Cilantro goes to seed (bolts) in summer; use in spring and fall. Young foliage resembles flat-leaf parsley and is best harvested at that stage. Most of the piquancy of cilantro, though, is in the stems. Taste falls off after mature, finer foliage and white flowers appear, so keep the cycle going with younger plants.
Use especially in Indian, Thai and other Asian dishes. Fabulous finely chopped on fresh tomato slices.

DILL (Annual)
Height: 36 inches. **Soil:** Well-drained. **Full sun.**
Sow seeds in May, then successively. Harvest foliage and seeds.
Use for fish dishes, pickling cucumbers and garnish or flavoring for soups, potato salad and dips.

FENNEL (Biennial)
Height: To 5 feet. **Soil:** Well-drained but moist.
Full sun.
Harvest stalks and foliage. In its second season, it will flower and set seed. Harvest the seed as well, using some to propagate new plants.
Eat fresh in salads or with cooked dishes.

LAVENDERS (Perennial)
Height: 2-3 feet. **Soil:** Well-drained. **Full sun.**
Most people grow English lavender (*Lavandula angustifolia*) varieties such as Munstead, Lady and the slightly smaller Hidcote, for closer spaces and rock gardens. Look for *Lavandula x intermedia* hybrids. One, Grosso, is larger and more vigorous than English lavender, with bigger leaves and silver foliage that better decorate winter gardens. Spanish lavender (*Lavandula stoechas*), an heirloom variety, flowers with tiny purple pennants above violet florets and is hardy only to Zone 7b; bring it in for winter. French lavender (*Lavandula dentata*), with lovely serrated foliage, is not winter-hardy here.

Lavenders sulk and die in heavy clay soil. When planting, excavate whole areas and replenish with a mix of sand and composted humus, plus a generous dose of lime. Lavenders need frequent watering at first, but once established they prefer drier soil. Mulch with a light-colored sand (not salt-ridden beach sand) or tiny gravel called chicken grit. This will reflect sunlight and burn off moisture on leaves. Prune every few years. In early March, cut back to above buds breaking on lower part of the stem. Don't prune after mid-March: You'll risk killing the plant.

If you plan to dry it, cut stalks as flowers break open and color up, and tie in bundles. Dry in a well-ventilated, dark area. You'll miss the season's full flower show, but cutting stems encourages re-blooming in fall. Also remove spikes after flowering to promote re-bloom.
Use for potpourris or moth repellents.

MINTS (Perennial)
Height: 24-36 inches. Soil: Evenly moist to periodically wet. Full sun to partial-medium shade.
Cut stems to use and to encourage bushiness. Mints make great container plants, especially a collection chosen from the many available types — peppermint, spearmint, apple mint and low-growing Corsican mint, among others. Lift and divide when clumps get crowded.
Use especially to flavor and decorate cold drinks, in Middle East dishes and for mint jelly or sauce for lamb.

NASTURTIUM (Annual)
Height: Trailing, to 4 feet. Soil: Well-drained and sandy. Full sun or partial shade.
Sow seeds on the edges of containers or garden beds in early spring. Keep slugs off emerging seedlings. Nasturtium should not be grown in heavily enriched soil — you'll get many leaves but few flowers — but the soil should be open and light to let roots go deep, assuring better performance in high summer.
Harvest young leaves and flowers for salads.

OREGANO (Perennial or Annual)
Height: 12-24 inches. Soil: Well-drained and non-acidic. Full sun to light afternoon shade.
Common oregano (*Origanum vulgare*), a leggy, plant, is not the best flavored but is hard as nails. Lower-growing, more compact sweet marjoram (*Origanum majorana*) is better tasting and more often used in the kitchen, but it usually is not hardy in our region and must be grown as an annual. Plant seedlings in May. Other notable culinary varieties: Italian oregano, or hardy marjoram (*Origanum x majoricum*), and Greek oregano (*Origanum vulgare subspecies hirtum*). Oreganos have many common names, so identify by Latin names.
Use for pizza, pasta sauces, meat dishes and seafood.

PARSLEY (Biennial)
Height: 18 inches. Soil: Well-drained, evenly moist. Full sun to partial shade; protect from afternoon sun.
Fresh parsley has a piquancy all its own. Plant young seedlings in April. Harvest outer stems and leaves. Parsley will give usable leaves until New Year's, so don't pull in October. In its second year, it flowers and dies. You can harvest seeds and re-grow plants, but it's easier to treat it as an annual,

lifting in winter, replanting in spring. Italian, or flat-leaf, parsley resembles cilantro and is considered a gourmet delicacy.
Use chopped leaves in an array of dishes.

ROSEMARY (Perennial)
Height: 36 inches. Soil: Average, well-drained; add lime. Full sun; shield from northern winter wind.
In our region, rosemary won't develop into large evergreen shrubs. Gardeners in Greater Washington and to the south and east should try the two hardiest varieties, Arp and Hill Hardy. Arp isn't the tastiest or handsomest. An unnamed variety likely will be tender, but it will be prettier and taste better. No-names can be grown outdoors for several years, but eventually a frigid winter will kill them. Just replace them or bring them in for winter. Keep in a bright, cool, humid room with good ventilation. If you have many plants, you may need growing lamps, fans and a humidifier You'll then have to harden them off in March for a couple of weeks, taking them out in daytime, bringing them in at night. Plant rosemary beside a well-traveled spot. Gently grasp the foliage and smell the oils.
Use for meat, fish and vegetable dishes.

RUE (Perennial)
Height: 18 to 24 inches. Soil: Average, well-drained. Full sun.
This semi-evergreen actually has little herbal utility, and its oils cause some people to break out into a rash. But its fine leaves and distinctive blue coloring make it a magnificent foil for other plants.

SAGE (Perennial)
Height: 24 inches. Soil: Average, well-drained. Full sun.
Culinary, or broadleaf, sage (*Salvia officinalis*) grows into a shrub-like, mounding specimen that's as beautiful as it is tasty. A bulky plant, it should be used to anchor beds and other smaller plants. One sage plant should suffice. Types range from the traditional silver-green-leafed variety to others with golden, purple and even tri-colored foliage. Tri-coloreds are not as cold-hardy but should endure all but the worst Mid-Atlantic winters. Sage is short-lived anyway and should be replanted every third year. Pineapple and other fruit-scented sages are not hardy and should be grown as annuals.
Use fresh or dried, especially in stuffings and sausages.

TARRAGON (Perennial)
Height: 36 inches. **Soil:** Average, well-drained.
Sun, but some afternoon shade in high summer.
French tarragon is grown from cuttings, or divisions, and forms wispy strands of glossy green leaves. It is short-lived and should be harvested freely and often. Divide every two years to promote longevity.
Use fresh sprigs for salads, roast chicken, tomato sauces and soups, and put in processed vinegar.

THYMES (Perennial)
Height: 3-12 inches. **Soil:** Sandy, well drained.
Full sun.
Common thyme *(Thymus vulgaris)* is favored for eating. Its several varieties include English and French thyme. Lemon thyme *(Thymus x citriodorus)* is both attractive and tasty, with a citrus-like piquancy. Woolly thyme *(Thymus pseudolanuginosus)*, mother-of-thyme *(Thymus pulegioides syn. T. serpyllum)* and creeping thyme *(Thymus praecox subs. arcticus)* are handsome ground covers for small spaces, useful between steps and ideal for rock gardens.
Use as seasoning in various dishes or dried as potpourri.

Chapter 28

FRUITS AND NUTS

*T*HE MID-ATLANTIC has a rich legacy of fruit cultivation dating back to George Washington's Mount Vernon and Thomas Jefferson's Monticello, to Colonial gardens and groves in Williamsburg and the Shenandoah Valley, Annapolis and Philadelphia. For nuts, the legacy extends further back to the Native Americans who harvested them before West Europeans arrived on these shores. You can carry these traditions into another century in small ways and large, with strawberry pots on your patio, a black walnut tree in your garden or a fruit orchard on a rural property.

FRUITS

GROWING FRUITS requires a certain commitment and zeal, but if you keep in mind the following general guidelines, you can raise varieties not available at the supermarket and do so with fewer pesticides:

- **SOIL AND SUN.** As a rule, fruit plants need an ordinary loam soil that's neither too heavy nor too sandy, and they must have good drainage and at least six hours of full sun.

- **FROST.** In Zone 6, especially at higher elevations, late spring frosts threaten fruit blossoms in March and April. Therefore, plant toward the tops of hillsides, not in hollows, where frost pockets form. Similarly, plant on slopes facing north or in beds facing east to delay blossoming, and select varieties designated "high chill."

- **CHEMICALS.** Most fruit cannot be grown reliably without insecticides and fungicides. However, you can select disease-resistant varieties and reduce spraying requirements.

- **DEGREES OF DIFFICULTY.** Apples, pears, figs, blackberries, raspberries, blueberries and strawberries are less difficult to grow and need less spraying than peaches, apricots, nectarines, plums, grapes and cherries. Lemons and limes can be grown as greenhouse novelties, but citrus is not hardy in the garden. Gooseberries and currants are northern plants, threaten Eastern white pine with diseases, and aren't well suited to our climate. Cranberries, too, cannot be grown here.

- **PRUNING.** There are some basic pruning requirements, but the correct training and pruning of fruit shrubs and trees is complicated and best learned through experience. Insufficient pruning will diminish fruiting, while excessive pruning will produce a tangle of unproductive stems. County extension agencies have pruning bulletins for fruit trees (see Appendix listing of extension agencies), and they also organize pruning demonstrations in late winter (look for notices in *The Washington Post*).

- **DISEASES.** To minimize diseases and pests, you need to keep the base of trees clean — free of fallen fruit, debris and leaves — and avoid mechanical injury to trunks and branches.

- **MORNING PICKING.** Soft fruit will keep longer if picked in the morning, before being warmed by the summer sun.

1. APPLES

APPLES TREES, which are handsome landscape plants in their own right, are perhaps the easiest fruit trees to grow in the home garden. Thousands of varieties are available, so it seems pointless to grow the same kinds of apples that you can buy at the supermarket.

Apple trees come in three basic sizes: Standards (which grow to 25 feet), semi-dwarfs (typically 15 to 20 feet high) and dwarfs for city gardens or smaller spaces (six to 12 feet high). Semi-dwarfs are the best choice for suburban gardens. They are far more productive and longer-lived than dwarf types — and their fruit is beyond the reach of deer.

Spur types have been bred to produce more fruiting spurs. They yield more abundant harvests and are more compact trees, but if you choose them you will have to spend more time hand-thinning young fruits in May than you would with regular trees. You may wish to grow a choice dessert apple or an heirloom variety, but first pick one that is resistant to diseases and suited to our region's climate. You will need two different varieties to assure good cross-pollination and fruit set and three if one of the pair has sterile pollen.

A young apple tree takes several seasons to train into its eventual fruit-bearing form. The object is to get a pyramidal-shaped tree with a central leader or trunk and about half a dozen permanent limbs that support the fruiting wood. These limbs, called scaffold branches, should be arranged to allow maximum air and light to the tree, and they should be wide-angled to avoid branch splitting. Pruning is done in late winter. If you have an old overgrown tree, you should prune it to achieve the same form, but training in youth is easier on the gardener and the plant.

In addition to the annual pruning regime, you will need to thin young fruit clusters in late spring to ensure that large, healthy apples develop and to keep the tree producing evenly from year to year. In May, when the infant apples are the size of grapes, reduce each cluster to just one apple, taking care not to nick the stem of the remaining fruit.

Recommended Varieties. The University of Maryland Extension Service commends these varieties for our region: Redfree, Liberty, Freedom, Jonafree, MacFree, Enterprise and Goldrush. Choice heirloom varieties include Esopus Spitzenberg, Newtown Pippin, Grimes Golden and Northern Spy. Prima, Priscilla and Pristine are disease-resistant varieties bred for home gardens.

Pests and Diseases. Just as apple fruit trees require the same cultivation as crab apples, so are they afflicted by the same ailments (see Chapter 11 on both subjects). It should be noted, though, that apple scab doesn't affect the fruit's flavor. The main additional pests specific to apple fruit trees are the larvae of the codling moth and of a beetle named plum curculio. They are controlled by spraying Imidan shortly after petals drop in April.

2. PEARS

THERE ARE TWO basic types of pear: European and Asian. European varieties have the classic sweet pear taste and shape. Asian pears are larger, rounder and typically crisper and spicier. Standards and dwarfs are available for both types.

Pear trees are easy to grow and relatively trouble-free, with the notable exception of fireblight.[†] You will save yourself years of lament by selecting a fireblight-resistant variety, even if that means passing up such favorites as Bartlett, Anjou, Comice and Bosc. Look for plants with Old Home rootstock over quince, and grow at least two varieties for cross-pollination.

Pear trees are pruned the same way as apples, except that some gardeners train multiple leaders instead of a central trunk, in case one is killed back by fireblight. Thin the young fruit in May.

Asian pears are allowed to ripen on the tree. However, if you wait for European pears to feel ripe on the outside, they will likely be mushy and gritty inside. As the fruit approaches ripeness, look for a slight darkening of the skin. Twist off the pear and store it in the refrigerator for up to two weeks, until it is evenly ripe.

Recommended Varieties. The University of Maryland Extension Service recommends these fireblight-resistant varieties: For European pears, Harrow Delight, Moonglow, Harvest Queen, Honeysweet, Seckel and Magness; for Asian pears, Tsu-Li and Ya-Li.

Main Pest: The pear psylla.[†]

3. PEACHES

PEACH TREES PROVIDE bushels of sweet, juicy fruit in summer, but at a chemical cost. You can minimize pesticide use, but you cannot eliminate it. Freestone peaches are considered best for eating fresh, clingstone for cooking. Nectarines are closely related but are more susceptible to a fruit-destroying disease named brown rot.

Peaches bloom before apples and are more prone to bud freezes. Again, find north-facing slopes and east-facing beds. By choosing early, main-season and late-season varieties, you can have fresh peaches from mid-July to September.

Peach trees, which will begin bearing fruit in their fourth season, are pruned in an open-center form. When training, remove branches with tight crotches, which are likely to crack in summer storms when the tree is laden with fruit. Once peaches reach mature form, you should prune in late winter to stimulate new growth that will bear fruit the following year. Again, local extension services will provide details and demonstrations (see Appendix for their numbers). Fruit thinning is essential for a good peach crop and for minimizing brown rot.

Recommended Varieties. Dwarf types are available; they are good for small gardens and for managing pests and diseases. The following peach varieties grow well in our region, barring abnormal seasons: Redhaven (early), Hale Haven (early), Early Elberta (mid-season), Loring (mid-season), Cresthaven (mid-season) and Redskin (late). Early Elberta and Cresthaven are more freeze-hardy than most.

Main Pests: Scale, borers, Japanese beetles and mites.[†] **Main Diseases:** Brown rot and peach leaf curl. To prevent both, spray trees with a Bordeaux mixture in February and again on a bimonthly basis from late April to just before harvest.

4. CHERRIES

FRUITING CHERRY TREES can be a little difficult, but for the patient and sanguine gardener who can shrug off the occasional disastrous season, they offer unforgettable rewards. There are two basic types of fruiting cherry trees: the tart, or sour, cherry, and the sweet cherry. Both prefer soil that is not too acidic, so you may have to add lime.

The sweet cherry tree grows much higher than the sour type, making it hard (literally) to stay on top of diseases and pests. When it rains heavily in late spring, sweet cherries at the point of ripening also are prone to splitting. Beginners are better off with the sour cherry, whose fruit, despite its name, is refreshingly sweet when picked fresh off the tree. Surplus sour cherries can be used for canning or cooking, and their later spring blooming period makes them better bets against frost damage.

Sour cherries grow to 20 feet and sweet cherries to twice that height. Natural (ungrafted) dwarf varieties of sour cherries are available. They grow to eight feet, making them easier to net against birds and squirrels. Cherries need to be cross-pollinated; since sweet cherries flower (and fruit) earlier than sour ones, you must pick two of the same type. These trees are trained in the same way as peaches, in an open-center framework.

Recommended Varieties. Select those resistant to disease and, among sweet types, to cracking as well. Among sour types, Montmorency is the most common and reliable, but it rises to 20 feet. North Star is a dwarf, growing to eight feet. Meteor is the other sour dwarf commonly planted. Among sweet varieties, Lapins or Stark Gold are used to pollinate other varieties and are good in themselves. Other favored sweet varieties are Kristin, Sam and Van, a good substitute for Bing, which struggles in our climate.

Main Pests: Fruiting cherries share the same pests as ornamental cherries (see Chapter 11), with some additions. The main fruit pests are plum curculio, cherry fruit fly and birds. Imidan is an effective spray against both insects. Birds prefer red-fruited cherries to yellow ones. If birds are a problem, cover with a fruit net as cherries ripen, preferably using a frame to hold the net. Be sure that the bottom is secure so that no birds get trapped inside the net.

5. FIGS

FIGS ARE EASY to grow and are highly ornamental plants as well, but they require protection in our cold winters. For this reason, some gardeners create a cylinder of wire around the shrub, filling it with oak leaves and wrapping the cage in two layers of burlap.

In warmer regions, figs become large shrubs, growing to 12 feet or more, and often are trained as small trees. However, because top growth isn't reliably hardy, it's better to raise them as shrubs in Greater Washington and the Mid-Atlantic.

Figs need full sun and moderately enriched but well-drained soil. They have extremely shallow root systems, so don't plant anything beneath them. Be sure to keep them watered in dry spells and in late summer, when fruit develops in the leafstalk joints.

A second plant is not needed to pollinate a fig. The important thing is to pick a variety that will be cold-hardy and mature before the first frosts. (Figs make good patio plants in large pots or barrels, but, again, be prepared to protect the container against cold weather.) If top growth dies in winter, remove the dead wood and give the plant a side-dressing of balanced fertilizer the following spring. It will take two to three seasons for the plant to start bearing fruit again.

Recommended Varieties: Brown Turkey, Marseilles, Celeste and Hardy Chicago.

Pests and Diseases: None serious, though you may need netting to keep away birds and squirrels.

6. RASPBERRIES AND BLACKBERRIES

THOUGH DIFFERENT in taste, raspberries and blackberries are grown the same way and make good companions in larger gardens. By choosing different varieties, you can harvest fresh raspberries in July and August, blackberries in August and September and fall-bearing raspberries in September and October. You should be aware that it is hard to keep these plants tidy. If you neglect them they will become thick and brambly, and fruiting will diminish.

Raspberries come in a range of colors, from the familiar red to the unfamiliar gold, purple and black. Eaten fresh, all are a blessed experience. The plants fall into two basic types, one fruiting in summer, the other in fall. Fall types, called "everbearing," are the easier to raise. Both prefer a medium loam enriched with humus. The site must be sunny, though raspberries will take (and actually prefer) light shade on hot summer afternoons. Water them well as fruit develops, but keep the water off leaves.

Pruning is central to raspberry care. Conventional summer types bloom and fruit on canes that are sent up the previous summer. If you hack the bush back in October, you will lose the next season's fruit. Once they do fruit in summer, these canes will die; that's when you should remove them. New canes, or suckers, will sprout from the ground. Canes produce more fruit if they are trained horizontally, so it makes sense to grow raspberries on a trellis. This also keeps them tidier. A modified version of the bean trellis (see Chapter 26) works well, with strands of wire strung horizontally at two, four and six feet.

Everbearing raspberries flower and fruit off new canes. Simply remove all top growth in March. A trellis is in order with these as well.

Black and purple raspberries, which grow as one plant — with a crown, not a wandering bramble — require a different pruning regime, similar to the one for blackberries. For each plant, select half a dozen sturdy canes in early summer, taking out the surplus. The remaining canes then are "tipped" (i.e., removing the top 3-4 inches). This is key to keeping the plant in bounds and fruiting the next year. Lateral branches will develop over the rest of the first season. The next February or March, cut back these laterals to about eight inches: They will grow spurs that yield the summer fruit. Once these canes have fruited, remove them entirely and tip the current year's canes to start the process again.

Recommended Varieties. For summer-bearing types, look for Algonquin (red), Killarney (red), Newburgh (red), Haut (black), Jewell (black), Cumberland (black), Brandywine (purple), Estate (purple) and Royalty (purple). Notable everbearing varieties include Fallgold (yellow), Heritage (red) and Amity (red).

As for blackberries, they essentially are grown and trained as black and purple raspberries. Thornless varieties are hardy to Zone 6 and much easier to work with than thorny types, especially at harvest time. Hull and Chester are two that do well in our region.

Pests and Diseases. The main pests other than birds are aphids, mites and Japanese beetles. For birds, use netting or streamers. **Main Diseases:** Fungal blights and viral ailments.[†]

7. STRAWBERRIES

STRAWBERRIES ARE delightful additions to herb and vegetable gardens, whether raised in pots (special clay strawberry jars with side pockets for trailing plants) or in their own patches.

Strawberries are perennials. They are grown for about three years before they are yanked and new ones are planted, preferably in another spot to avoid a buildup of soil-borne diseases. Gardeners grow two basic kinds: the traditional June-bearing type, which produces its harvest in late spring to early summer, and newer day-neutral varieties, which continue to bear fruit through the fall.

The plant is particular about its soil, and since it will grow in the same place for a few seasons, it's worth preparing the soil right. Work in sand and humus to create a well-draining light loam, with a pH between 6.0 and 6.5. You must ensure that the crown (the point where the top growth begins) is not set too deeply lest it rot. Plants are set 18 inches apart in rows separated by three feet. Watering is essential, especially as the fruit ripens in early summer and in periods of drought. A light mulch of weed-free straw will retain moisture and keep developing fruit off the soil, where it might rot. Strawberries grown in pots dry out quickly and so need daily watering in summer. Big jars are preferable to small ones.

Recommended Varieties: For June-bearing plants, Annapolis, Delmarvel, Earliglow, Allstar, Lateglow and Latestar; for day-neutrals, Tristar and Tribute.

Main Pests: Slugs, flea beetles and beetle grubs. **Main Diseases:** Verticillium wilt, leaf spot and red stele, a root-rot disease causing leaves to wilt. Pull infected plants and buy resistant varieties.[†]

8. BLUEBERRIES

OF THE THREE blueberry types, the highbush blueberry is the one to select. Growing to about eight feet, the bush is a superb ornamental in its own right, especially if it is artfully pruned. The leaves turn scarlet in the fall, and the young twigs take on a burnished coppery glow in the winter. The fruit isn't bad, either — if you can beat the birds to it.

Blueberries, too, are fussy about soil. It must be highly acidic (pH 4.5 to 5.0) heavily organic and evenly moist but not wet. Ordinary clay soil is of no use with this plant; you must thoroughly mix sand, peat moss and compost with the native soil, two feet deep and three feet in each direction from the planting hole. Plant the root ball higher if necessary for better drainage, but don't expose roots. Mulch the plant with Virginia fines or leaf mold to keep the roots damp and cool during the summer. An annual spring dressing of cottonseed meal will work wonders. Two plants in proximity will allow cross-pollination and better fruit sets.

In late winter, prune out some of the oldest canes in the center of the plant to keep an open and airy shape. Remove branches that are rubbing too much or are damaged. You will lose some of the season's flowers and fruits, but the pruning will keep the bush attractive and healthy.

Recommended Varieties: Northland (mid-season), Bluecrop (mid-season) and Blueray (late).

Main Pests: Birds. Use netting if you want to keep your crop. There are no serious diseases.

NUTS

NUT TREES FORM some of the most beautiful native hardwoods in the garden. They are fun to harvest, but you have to be patient enough to wait several years for trees to mature and produce sizable yields. Walnuts and hickories (including pecan trees) have taproots, meaning that they must be set out young, preferably from a container-grown plant.

Unfortunately, some nuts are beyond reach in our area. Pine nuts, the delicacy of the Italian stone pine or the Mexican pinyon pine, are unsuited to our climate. The pistachio tree is not hardy here. The American chestnut is no more, destroyed by a blight, though hybrid Asian and American varieties have been developed. And if you want macadamia nuts, you should book a flight to Hawaii. Nonetheless, several nut plants do well in our area:

BLACK WALNUT *(Juglans nigra).* The nuts from this large, imposing shade tree are collected as they drop and stored until the husks dry. You then break them and crack the thick shells.

ENGLISH WALNUT *(J. regia).* This is the smaller, more spreading tree found in Europe, with sweeter nuts in thinner shells. It will grow in our region, but it is rarely planted. Carpathian is an especially hardy variety.

PECAN *(Carya illinoensis).* The pecan is a large, native and beautiful shade tree and a good choice for large landscapes. Indigenous to the Southwest, it does well here, bearing nuts after eight to 10 years. It must be grown from young plants because of a taproot, and it needs to be protected against deer foraging and rutting. In colder parts of Zone 6, you will need to select a cold-hardy variety for a reliable harvest.

HAZELNUT. The hazelnut, or filbert, comes from the European hazel *(Corylus avellana).* It is not a handsome shrub, but it is a shrub, meaning that the first nut yields come sooner than with pecans or walnuts and that the plant is smaller and can be netted against squirrels, which are a problem. The native filbert *(Corylus americana)* also produces nuts, but they are not as large or as choice. Several hybrids are available for the home garden. Plant hazelnuts as naturalistic screens.

---

†See Appendix for common pest and disease ailments and remedies.

Appendix

PLANT HARDINESS ZONES

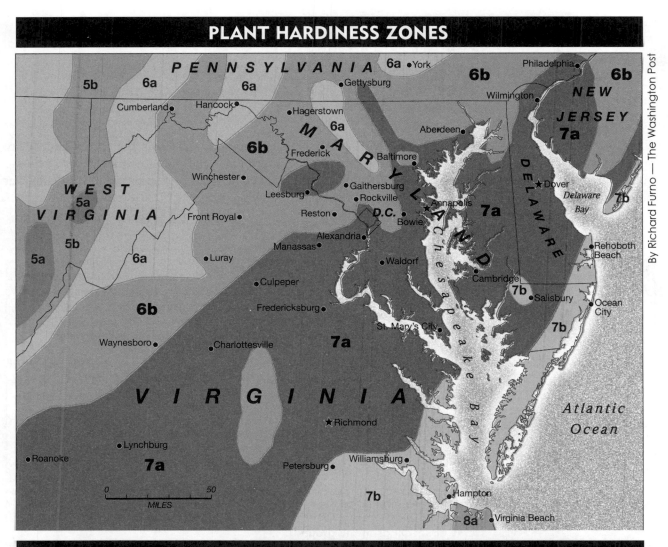

By Richard Furno — The Washington Post

AVERAGE FREEZE DATES

LOCALE	SPRING (Last Freeze)	FALL (First Freeze)
District of Columbia (National Arboretum)	May 1	October 15
Reagan National Airport	March 30	November 8
Washington Dulles Airport	April 27	October 13
College Park	April 29	October 15
Germantown	April 28	October 17
Clarksville	May 5	October 12
Frederick	April 24	October 17
La Plata	April 19	October 22
Annapolis	April 4	November 15
Woodstock (Balt. Co.)	May 1	October 10
Baltimore (Cylburn Arboretum)	May 10	October 15
Falls Church	April 21	October 22
Manassas	April 19	October 19
Warrenton	April 14	October 30
Quantico	April 13	October 30
Fredericksburg	April 22	October 17
Winchester	April 18	October 17
Richmond	April 9	November 1
Charlottesville	April 14	October 25
Wilmington (Winterthur)	May 15	October 15

Sources: Virginia Polytechnic Institute and State University; University of Maryland Cooperative Extension Service.

COMMON PESTS
AND DISEASES

There used to be a notion that we could conquer all garden pests and diseases at the squirt of a spray gun. Today it is widely recognized that toxic pesticides not only threaten our health and the environment but often are counterproductive. Pests frequently develop immunities to them, and pesticides wipe out beneficial bugs that otherwise would contain pest populations. Treatments for the following pests and diseases, therefore, favor the most benign approaches.

PESTS

NAME	DAMAGE	REMEDY
APHIDS	Flying insects, mostly green, some black. In spring, when they suck sap of new plant growth, they can appear in alarming numbers. They weaken plants and carry viruses.	Spray with hose or use insecticidal soaps or pyrethrin. Alternatively, encourage (or buy) lacewings and ladybugs, which eat aphids. Excess nitrogen fertilizer fosters aphids.
BAGWORMS	On conifers, grubs encase themselves in cone-like cocoons called "bags" and eat needles.	Handpick and destroy cocoons.
BLACK WEEVIL	A small black weevil that feeds on foliage of shrubs; grubs do greater damage to root system in the ground.	Spray with broad-spectrum insecticide as new adults emerge in mid-June and again three and six weeks later.
CUTWORMS	Subsurface caterpillar in the vegetable garden. It snips off the stems of seedlings in the ground.	Wrap vulnerable plants in a cardboard collar buried at least an inch.
GREENWORM	Superbly camouflaged green caterpillar that grows fat on rose leaves in late summer.	Handpick or spray with Bt when young.
JAPANESE BEETLES	Iridescent, purple-and-green flying beetles that are very destructive. As grubs they live beneath lawns, eating grass roots and attracting moles.	Beetle traps increase plant damage in vicinity, so don't use close to choice plants. Pick off adults and drop into a jar of diluted bleach. Grub pesticides are effective, but organic ones being developed show great promise.
LACEBUGS	Tiny sap-sucking insects that favor broadleaf evergreens in full sun.	Spray underside of leaves with horticultural oil (most effective in May) or use a systemic insecticide such as Orthene.
LEAFHOPPERS	Green, wedge-shaped flying insects, they suck sap and spread disease.	Spray with pyrethrin or horticultural oil.
LEAF MINERS	Fly or beetle grubs that exist most of the year in the safety of leaf tissue, where they form visible tunnels. Look for adult midges flying around infected plants in April.	Zap adults with a broad-spectrum insecticide. Kill larvae in early-to-mid June with a systemic insecticide such as Merit.

NAME	DAMAGE	REMEDY
MEALY BUGS	Tiny, white, waxy and oval-bodied sap-suckers, producing yellow and stunted plants.	Spray with pyrethrin or horticultural oil.
MITES	Different species of small, sap-sucking, spider-like bugs, usually red, sometimes yellow. Look for webs.	Spray with hose, or use pyrethrin, insecticidal soap or horticultural oil. Alternatively, purchase predatory mites to kill harmful ones.
PSYLLIDS	Sap-sucking psyllids (or psylla) cause new leaves to curl, particularly on boxwood. Another psylla damages pears.	Spray horticultural oil or insecticidal soap in May as new growth emerges. Repeat three weeks later. For pear psylla, spray adults on a warm day before buds break in March.
SCALE	Various species of sap-sucking insects that cover themselves in a protective shell, often resembling tiny oysters and sometimes cotton swabs.	Spray with dormant oil in winter and horticultural oil in growing season. Remove seriously infected branches and destroy.
SLUGS	Snails that have had their shells repossessed.	Handpick at night (with rubber gloves and flashlight), or use beer traps or diatomaceous earth. As a last resort, employ slug pellets.
STEM BORERS	Caterpillars that enter stalks of perennials or shrubs, causing stem dieback. Look closely for holes where the worms enter the plant.	Cut stems below dieback, put in sealed plastic bag and discard. On large shrubs and trees, use beneficial nematodes, worms that devour borers. On bearded iris, use a systemic pesticide at two-week intervals from early April to late May.
TENT CATERPILLARS	Caterpillar colonies that hatch out in early spring and form webbed nests in the crotches of trees, especially cherries and apples. In some years, they are abundant and do great damage. They feed on young leaves during the day and return to the nest at night and when it rains.	If you spy young caterpillars and small nests in late March, spray with Bt. Later you will have to use a broad-spectrum insecticide. Some people take a long pole with a nail on the end and twist filled nests like cotton candy onto the stick. Dip the nests in a bucket of bleach.
THRIPS	Brown, soft-bodied insects with wings that look like frayed string. They feed on leaves and flowers and spread disease.	Use a broad-spectrum insecticide such as malathion.
WHITEFLIES	White specks that fly like cotton when disturbed. Larvae, resembling scale, found on the underside of leaves. Sucks sap.	Spray larvae with horticultural oil, adults with pyrethrin or insecticidal soap.
WOOLLY ADELGID	Pest of hemlocks, the adelgid is seen as white specks on needles, seemingly made of cotton or wax.	Three annual oil sprayings: horticultural oil in May and October, dormant oil in late winter. On mature hemlocks, use a systemic insecticide approved for woolly adelgids.

DISEASES

NAME	DAMAGE	REMEDY
ANTHRACNOSE	Fungus damages leaves of both trees and garden vegetables. Vegetables can be pulled, but unchecked on trees, the disease can kill the plant. Look for blackening of leaves in spring.	Spray with a fungicide approved for anthracnose. (See box on anthracnose in Chapter 9 on dogwoods.)
BLIGHTS	Fungal and bacterial blights are common and frequently fatal. **Botrytis** turns petals brown and the leaves and stems gray. **Tulip fire**, for example, is a botrytis blight that afflicts tulips planted in the same bed year after year. **Verticillium** and **fusarium** cause leaves to yellow and wilt before stems and plants die. **Fireblight** causes blackened leaves and stems. **Petal blight**, prevalent on azaleas and rhododendrons, turns petals limp, brown and slimy soon after blooms open.	Select disease-resistant varieties. Otherwise, cut out and destroy infected stems, sterilizing pruners between cuts. Use a benomyl spray. Often, though, plants simply must be pulled. For tulip fire, if you can't rotate the plant bed, mix Terra Chlor into the soil at planting time. With petal blight, remove and discard faded flowers. The next year, spray the fungicide Bayleton on buds as they show color in early April. Repeat in 10 days.
CANKER	A fungal or bacterial disease such as **bytryosphaeria** that causes depressions in the bark of woody plants. It often results in dieback or death of affected stems.	Remove diseased stems. Some species can be cut to the ground and will regenerate, but check first.
CHLOROSIS	Iron deficiency causes leaves to turn pale yellow, especially on acid-loving shrubs like azaleas.	Spray or top-dress with an iron chelate supplement. Check and correct pH.
POWDERY MILDEW	White fungal coating of leaves, prevalent in late summer. Lilacs, zinnias, roses, phlox, squash, crape myrtles and honeysuckle are particularly prone to getting this disease.	Sulfur sprays or other fungicides should be used preventively. They won't reverse outbreak but will stop it from getting worse. Damage is not serious — except on vegetables.
ROOT ROT	Caused by the **phytophthora** fungus, it results in wilted foliage and dead stems. It's prevalent on rhododendrons and boxwood.	Pull up and discard affected plant. Replace it with different species.
RUST	Yellow-orange spotting of leaves. Severe infestations are fatal.	Plant disease-resistant varieties. Otherwise, minimize overhead watering, cut infected branches, spray with approved fungicides and keep dead leaves away from affected plants.
SCAB	Prevalent on fruits, both edible and ornamental. Causes raised black areas.	Buy resistant varieties. Otherwise, you'll have to use a toxic fungicide like benomyl.

DEALING WITH DEER

IN MANY RESPECTS, insects are easier to deal with than four-legged pests. Few people think twice about dispatching a Japanese beetle grub, but little rabbits are another matter.

City gardeners are most troubled by squirrels, raccoons and moles, suburbanites by deer, rabbits and voles. Farther out, add woodchucks, herons, snakes, black bears and others. There are no easy ways to handle the lot. A cat will catch moles and shrews, but it also might kill beloved songbirds or foul the garden. A dog might scare off deer — until they learn to live with each other.

Of all warm-blooded pests, none has changed gardening dynamics in recent years more than the white-tailed deer, whose habitats keep getting taken over by suburban development. With no natural predators, the deer multiply, concentrated in pockets of forest, and go on foraging binges in newly planted gardens.

This has spawned a whole new industry, with deer repellents (often with unspeakable ingredients) topping the list. These are effective temporarily but wear off with rain, or the deer come to learn that coyote urine doesn't necessarily mean that there's a real coyote out there. Some gardeners play radios day and night. Have we at last found a constructive use for Howard Stern and Rush Limbaugh? Others lay blood meal or Milorganite at crucial times, when daylilies or roses are in swollen bud, but these fleeting organic remedies obviously won't work for azaleas or other shrubs whose buds form over months.

Have we at last found a constructive use for Howard Stern and Rush Limbaugh?

One sensible approach is to select plants that are less desirable to deer, using viburnums instead of azaleas, ferns instead of hostas, perovskias instead of roses. County extension agencies have lists for you. The best way to keep deer away is with fencing. A barrier fence must be tall — seven feet is not too high — and is usually made of wiremesh simply because a wooden one would be prohibitively expensive. (The wire one is not cheap on large properties.) Gates cannot be left open.

ELECTRIFIED FENCING is the most efficient, is cheaper and is less obtrusive. People understandably have qualms about using it in populated suburban areas, though the technology is safe. The energizer converts household electricity to a pulsating charge of high voltage but extremely low amperage. The wires give a shock, but the jolt is not harmful. A common design is a portable, five-foot fence with polypropylene posts, with spikes on the bottom. Between the posts you string strands of wire or white plastic tape containing steel filaments to conduct the power. This is useful, for example, in fencing off part of a larger property to allow you to grow vegetables and have an ornamental garden around the house.

For a perimeter fence on larger, rural properties, wildlife biologist Jay McAninch has developed a slant fence that ruin's a deer depth perception, discouraging a leap. The fence is both angled and electrified. You set wooden vertical posts in the ground every 40 feet or so. To the side of each one, you bolt an eight-foot timber that is slanted out, so that the end of the timber is just 55 inches above the ground. Then you string eight strands of 12.5-gauge, high-tensile wire between the slanted timbers to form the fence.

Both types of electric fence are supplied by Gallagher Power Fence of San Antonio, Texas. Beyond the question of electrification, the slant fence is unattractive and, at a minimum, takes up a six-foot-deep strip of land along the entire fence line that must be kept free of weeds and other vegetation.

In smaller suburban gardens where space and aesthetics are at a premium, some have had success with a cheap, nylon-netted fence that is seven feet tall, comes in rolls, and is stapled to trees or fence posts. It is difficult to see, though, so you will need to tie ribbons on it to let the deer know that it is there. One gardener has built a long (40-foot) fenced garden that is so narrow (four feet) that deer simply won't enter it. As for young trees with smooth bark that are at risk in rutting season (from fall into winter), you can surround them in a cylinder of wire hardware cloth, anchored and reaching up five to six feet.

SPECIALTY PLANT SOURCES

Most plants in this book can be purchased through our area's many fine nurseries and garden centers, major garden catalogs, farmers' markets, plant society sales and hardware stores. Check your local Yellow Pages for the region's numerous plant and seed outlets.

This list is for those seeking rarer plants, mainly by mail. Some mail-order nurseries, it should be noted, charge for their catalogs, though they usually cancel that cost when an order is placed.

A nursery's inclusion on this list should not to be taken as an endorsement by the author or *The Washington Post*. Nor should the absence of a nursery be construed as a sign of disapproval. While some nurseries are cited several times, their addresses and telephone numbers are provided just once. The list follows the organization of chapters, with nurseries in alphabetical order (except when they are repeated for different plants).

AZALEAS AND RHODODENDRONS

AZALEA TRACE, 5510 Stephen Reid Rd., Huntingtown, Md. 20639, *(301) 855-2305.*
GIRARD NURSERIES, P.O. Box 428, 6839 N. Ridge East, Route 20, Geneva, Ohio 44041, *(216) 466-2881.*
GREER GARDENS, 1280 Goodpasture Island Rd., Eugene, Ore. 97401, *(541) 686-8266.*
ROSLYN NURSERY, 211 Burrs Lane, Dix Hills, N.Y. 11746, *(516) 643-9347.*
WOODLANDERS, 1128 Colleton Ave., Aiken, S.C. 29801, *(803) 648-7522.*

BOXWOOD

APPALACHIAN GARDENS, P.O. Box 82, 410 Westview Ave., Waynesboro, Pa. 17268, *(717) 762-4312.*
CARROLL GARDENS, 444 E. Main St., Westminster, Md. 21157, *(800) 638-6334 .*
HERONSWOOD NURSERY, 7530 NE 288th St., Kingston, Wash. 98346, *(360) 297-4172.*

NATIVE DOGWOODS AND DISEASE-RESISTANT HYBRIDS

FAIRWEATHER GARDENS, P.O. Box 330, Greenwich, N.J. 08323, *(609) 451-626.*
APPALACHIAN GARDENS • CARROLL GARDENS • ROSLYN NURSERY • WOODLANDERS

JAPANESE MAPLES

EASTWOOD NURSERIES, 634 Long Mountain Rd., Washington, Va. 22747 *(540) 675-1234.*
MOUNTAIN MAPLES, Box 1329, Laytonville, Calif. 95454 *(707) 984-6522.*

MAGNOLIAS

EASTERN PLANT SPECIALTIES, Box 226, Georgetown, Maine 04548, *(207) 371-2888.*
GOSSLER FARMS NURSERY, 1200 Weaver Rd., Springfield, Ore. 97478, *(541) 746-3922.*
SWEETBAY FARM, 4260 Enon Rd, Coolidge, Ga. 31738, *(912) 225-1688.*
WAYSIDE GARDENS, P.O. Box 1, Hodges, S.C. 29695, *(800) 845-1124.*
APPALACHIAN GARDENS • GREER GARDENS

ORNAMENTAL CHERRIES

FORESTFARM, 990 Tetherow Rd., Williams, Ore. 97544, *(541) 846-7269.*
CARROLL GARDENS • WOODLANDERS • GOSSLER FARMS NURSERY

CRAB APPLES

EDRICH FARMS NURSERY, 9700 Old Court Rd., Baltimore, Md. 21244, *(410) 922-5700.*
F.W. SCHUMACHER CO., 36 Spring Hill Rd., Sandwich, Mass. 02563, *(508) 888-0659.* (Seed only).
FORESTFARM • GIRARD NURSERIES

HOLLIES

MCLEAN NURSERIES, 9000 Satyr Hill Rd., Baltimore, Md. 21234 *(410) 882-6714.*

CONIFERS

CoenoSium Gardens, 4412 354th St. East, Eatonville, Wash. 98328, *(360) 832-8655.*
Colvos Creek Nursery, P.O. Box 1512, Vashon Island, Wash. 98070, *(206) 463-3917.*
Appalachian Gardens • Carroll Gardens • Girard Nurseries • Roslyn Nurseries

BEARDED AND BEARDLESS IRISES

Draycott Gardens, 16815 Falls Rd., Upperco, Md. 21155, *(410) 374-4788.*
Ensata Gardens, 9823 E. Michigan Ave., Galesburg, Mich. 49053, *(616) 665-7500.*
Nicholls Gardens, 4724 Angus Drive, Gainesville, Va. 22065. *(703) 754-9623.*
Rainbow Iris Garden, Route 1, 133358 Sagle Rd., Purcellville, Va. 22132.
Schreiner's Gardens, 3625 Quinaby Rd., N.E., Salem, Ore. 97303, *(800) 525-2367.*
Woodland Iris Gardens, 2405 Woodland Ave., Modesto, Calif. 95358, *(209) 578-4184.*

DAYLILIES

Crownsville Nursery, P.O. Box 797, Crownsville, Md. 21032, *(410) 849-3143.*
Daylily Discounters, One Daylily Plaza, Alachua, Fla. 32615, *(904) 462-1539.*
Daylily World, P.O. Box 1612, Sanford, Fla. 32772. *(407) 322-4034.*
Lady Bug Daylilies, 1852 E.S.R. 46, Geneva, Fla. 32732, *(407) 349-0271.*
Nicholls Gardens

PERENNIALS

Andre Viette Farm & Nursery, P.O. Box 1109, Fishersville, Va. 22939, *(800) 575-5538.*
Heronswood Nursery, 7530 NE 288th St., Kingston, Wash. 98346-9502, *(360) 297-4172.*
Kurt Bluemel, Inc. 2740 Greene Lane, Baldwin, Md. 21013-9523, *(410) 557-7229.*
Niche Gardens, 1111 Dawson Rd., Chapel Hill, N.C. 27516, *(919) 967-0078.*
Plant Delights Nursery, 9241 Sauls Rd., Raleigh, N.C. 27603, *(919) 772-4794.*
Carroll Gardens • Forestfarm

ANNUALS

Thompson & Morgan, Inc., P.O. Box 1308, Jackson, N.J. 08527-0308, *(800) 274-7333.*
Seeds of Change, P.O. Box 15700, Santa Fe, N.M. 87506, *(888) 762-7333.*
Seeds Blum, HC 33, Box 2057, Boise, Idaho, 83706, *(800) 742-1423.*
Harris Seeds, P.O. Box 22960, 60 Saginaw Drive, Rochester, N.Y. 14692-2960, *(800) 514-4441.*

ORNAMENTAL GRASSES

Klehm Nursery, 4210 N. Duncan Rd., Champaign, Ill. 61821, *(800) 553-3715.*
Landscape Alternatives, 1705 St. Albans St., Roseville, Minn, 55113. *(612) 488-3142.*
Plants of the Southwest, Route 6, Box 11A, Agua Fria, Santa Fe, N.M. 87501, *(505) 471-2212.*
Andre Viette Farm & Nursery • Kurt Bluemel, Inc. • Niche Gardens

GROUND COVERS

Bluestone Perennials, 7211 Middle Ridge Rd., Madison, Ohio 44057, *(800) 852-5243.*
Prentiss Court Ground Covers, P.O. Box 8662, Greenville, S.C. 29604, *(864) 277-4037.*
Eastern Plant Specialties • Forestfarm • Woodlanders

ROSES

Modern Roses
Jackson & Perkins, P.O. Box 1028, Medford, Ore. 97501, *(800) 292-4769.*
Pickering Nurseries, 670 Kingston Rd., Pickering, Ont. Canada L1V 1A6, *(905) 839-2111.*
Carroll Gardens • Wayside Gardens.
Heirloom Roses
Antique Rose Emporium, 9300 Leuckemeyer Rd., Brenham, Texas 77833, *(409) 836-9051.*
Heritage Rosarium, 211 Haviland Mill Rd., Brookeville, Md. 20833, *(301) 774-6890.*
Lowe's Roses, 6 Sheffield Rd., Nashua, N.H. 03062, *(603) 888-2214.*
The Roseraie at Bayfields, P.O. Box R, 670 Bremen Rd., Waldoboro, Maine 04572, *(207) 832-6330.*
Forestfarm • Pickering Nurseries

DAHLIAS

CONNELL'S DAHLIAS, 10616 Waller Rd. East, Takoma, Wash. 98446, *(800) 673-5139.*

MUMS

HUFF'S GARDEN MUMS, 710 Juniatta St., Burlington, Kan. 66839, *(800) 279-4675.*
KING'S MUMS, P.O. Box 368, Clements, Calif. 95227, *(209) 759-3571.*
MUMS BY PASCHKE, 12286 East Main Rd., North East, Pa. 16428, *(814) 725-9860.*

HOSTAS

BRIDGEWOOD GARDENS, P.O. Box 800, Crownsville, Md. *(410) 849-3916.*
CROWNSVILLE NURSERY • NICHOLLS GARDENS • PLANT DELIGHTS NURSERY • ROSLYN NURSERY

ROCK GARDENS

ARROWHEAD ALPINES, P.O. Box 857, 1310 N. Gregory Rd., Fowlerville, Mich. 48836, *(517) 223-3581.*
MT. TAHOMA NURSERY, 28111 112th Ave. East, Graham, Wash. 98338, *(253) 847-9827.*
WE-DU NURSERIES, Route 5, Box 724, Marion, N.C. 28752, *(704) 738-8300.*

WATER GARDENS

LILYPONS WATER GARDENS, P.O. Box 10, Buckeystown, Md. 21717, *(800) 999-5459.*
WATERFORD GARDENS, 74 East Allendale Rd., Saddle River, N.J. 07458, *(201) 327-0721.*

VEGETABLES

THE COOK'S GARDEN, P.O. Box 535, Londonderry, Vt. 05148, *(800) 457-9703* or *(802) 824-3400.*
HEIRLOOM SEEDS, P.O. Box 245, West Elizabeth, Pa. 15088, *(412) 384-0852.*
JERSEY ASPARAGUS FARMS, 105 Porchtown Rd., Pittsgrove, N.J. 08318, *(609) 358-2548.*
JOHNNY'S SELECTED SEEDS, Foss Hill Rd., Albion, Maine, 04910, *(207) 437-9294.*
PEPPER GAL, P.O. Box 23006, Fort Lauderdale, Fla. 33307, *(954) 537-5540.*
SEEDS OF CHANGE, P.O. Box 15700, Santa Fe, N.M. 87506, *(505) 438-8080.*
SEED SAVERS EXCHANGE, 3076 N. Winn Rd., Decorah, Iowa 52101, *(319) 382-5990.*
SHEPHERD'S GARDEN SEEDS, 30 Irene St., Torrington, Conn. 06790, *(860) 482-3638.*
STOKES SEEDS, P.O. Box 548, Buffalo, N.Y. 14240, *(716) 695-6980.*
TERRITORIAL SEED CO., P.O. Box 157, Cottage Grove, Ore. 97424, *(541) 942-9547.*
TOMATO GROWERS SUPPLY CO., P.O. Box 2237, Fort Myers, Fla. 33902, *(941) 768-1119.*
VERMONT BEAN SEED CO., 87 Garden Lane, Fair Haven, Vt., 05743, *(802) 273-3400.*

HERBS

Greater Washington (non-mail-order)
BITTERSWEET HILL, 1274 Governors Bridge Rd., Davidsonville, Md. 21035, *(410) 798-0231.*
DEBAGGIO HERBS, 923 N. Ivy St., Arlington, Va. 22201, *(703) 243-2498*, and 43494 Mountain View Drive,
  Chantilly, Va. 20152, *(703) 327-6846.*
WASHINGTON CATHEDRAL GREENHOUSE, Massachusetts & Wisconsin Aves., NW, *(202) 537-6263.*
SMILE HERB SHOP, 4908 Berwyn Rd., College Park, Md., *(301) 474-8791.*
Elsewhere
WELL-SWEEP HERB FARM, 205 Mt. Bethel Rd., Port Murray, N.J. 07865, *(908) 852-5390.*
WE-DU NURSERIES

FRUITS AND NUTS

ALLEN PLANT CO., P.O. Box 310, Fruitland, Md. 21826 (particularly good for strawberries), *(410) 742-7122.*
BRITTINGHAM PLANT FARMS, P.O. Box 2538, Salisbury, Md. 21802 (especially for strawberries), *(410) 749-5153.*
EDIBLE LANDSCAPING, P.O. Box 77, 361 Spirit Ridge Lane, Afton, Va. 22920, *(800) 524-4156.*
HENRY LEUTHARDT NURSERIES, P.O. Box 666WP, Montauk Hwy, E. Moriches, N.Y. 11940, *(516) 878-1387.*
JOHNSON NURSERY, Rt. 5, Box 29-J, Highway 52E, Ellijay, Ga. 30540, *(888) 276-3187.*
ST. LAWRENCE NURSERIES, 325 State Highway 345, Potsdam, N.Y. 13676, *(315) 265-6739.*
SONOMA ANTIQUE APPLE NURSERY, 4395 Westside Rd., Healdsburg, Calif. 95448, *(707) 433-6420.*
STARK BROS., P.O. Box 10, Louisiana, Mo. 63353, *(800) 325-4180.*

FOR INFORMATION AND INSPIRATION

Extension Agencies

Most communities have county or city cooperative extension agencies that dispense expert advice on common garden problems as well as providing soil tests. They generally offer pamphlets, workshops and lectures. Master Gardener volunteers also assist professional staff in plant clinics, in which homeowners bring in sick plants and bugs to be identified. Often, these clinics are in public libraries and other neighborhood sites. Call your local extension agent for details.

DISTRICT OF COLUMBIA

UDC, Cooperative Extension Service
4200 Connecticut Avenue, N.W. Bldg. 48, 20008
(202) 274-6900

MARYLAND

**Home & Garden
Information Center**
12005 Homewood Rd.
Ellicott City, 21042
(800) 342-2507 (in-state)
(410) 531-1757
Internet: www.agnr.umd.edu/hgic

Allegany County
701 Kelly Rd., Ste 101
Cumberland, 21502
(301) 724-3320

Anne Arundel County
7320 Ritchie Highway
Glen Burnie, 21061
(410) 222-6757

Baltimore City
17 S. Gay St.
Baltimore, 21202
(410) 396-1753

Baltimore County
9811 Van Buren Lane
Cockeysville, 21030
(410) 666-1022

Calvert County
P.O. Box 486
Prince Frederick, 20678
(301) 855-1150

Caroline County
207 South Third St.
Denton, 21629
(410) 479-4030

Carroll County
700 Agricultural Center
Westminster, 21157
(410) 848-4611

Cecil County
P.O. Box 326
Elkton, 21922
(410) 996-5280

Charles County
9375 Chesapeake St., Ste 119
La Plata, 20646
(301) 934-5403

Dorchester County
County Office Building
P.O. Box 299
Cambridge, 21613
(410) 228-8800

Frederick County
330 Montevue Lane
Frederick, 21702
(301) 694-1596

Garrett County
1916 Maryland Highway, Ste A
Mountain Lake Park, 21550
(301) 334-6960

Harford County
P.O. Box 663
Forest Hill, 21050
(410) 638-3255

Howard County
3525-L Ellicott Mills Drive,
Ellicott City, 21043
(410) 313-2707

Kent County
709 Morgneck Rd., Ste 202
Chestertown, 21620
(410) 778-1661

Montgomery County
18410 Muncaster Rd.
Derwood, 20855
(301) 590-9638

Prince George's County
6707 Groveton Drive
Clinton, 20735
(301) 868-9366

Queen Anne's County
505 Railroad Ave., Ste 4
Centreville, 21617
(410) 758-0166

St. Mary's County
21580 Peabody St.
Leonardtown, 20650
(301) 475-4482

Somerset County
30730 Park Drive
Princess Anne, 21853
(410) 651-1350

Talbot County
125 Bay St., P.O. Box 519
Easton, 21601
(410) 822-1244

Washington County
1260 Maryland Ave.
Hagerstown, 21740
(301) 791-1404

Wicomico County
P.O. Box 1836
Salisbury, 21802
(410) 749-6141

Worcester County
P.O. Box 219
Snow Hill, 21863
(410) 632-1972

VIRGINIA

Alexandria
1108 Jefferson St.
Alexandria, 22314
(703) 519-3325

Arlington County
3308 S. Stafford St.
Arlington, 22206
(703) 228-6400

Fauquier County
24 Pelham St., Ste 20
Warrenton, 20186
(540) 341-7950

Fairfax County
Extension agent: (703) 324-8556
Plant clinic: (703) 324-5393

Loudoun County
30B Catoctin Circle SE
Leesburg, 20175
(703) 777-0373

Prince William County
8033 Ashton Ave., Ste 105
Manassas, 20109
(703) 792-6289

Richmond
701 North 25th St, R. 104
Richmond, 23223
(804) 786-4150

Spotsylvania County
9106-A Courthouse Rd.
P.O. Box 95
Spotsylvania, 22553
(540) 582-7096

Stafford County
359 Butler Rd.
Falmouth, 22405
(540) 899-4020

For other local Virginia offices, see the Virginia Cooperative Extension Service Internet sites at www.ext.vt.edu/vce/specialty/enviro-hort/mastergard/directory.html and http://www.ext.vt.edu/

Public Gardens

The best way to see how plants grow and mature in our climate is to visit public gardens. Bring a notepad and pencil, even a camera, and don't overlook the non-flower ornament. Spring isn't the only time to view these gardens. Make a point of returning through the year to see how favored plants or landscape scenes have changed. Admission is free at most public gardens, and many hold plant society shows and plant sales as well as workshops, special tours and lectures. Call first to make sure that hours haven't changed (and leave pruners at home — it's bad form to try to take cuttings).

In addition, spring is awash with tours of private (and public) gardens. When touring, look beyond the fresh mulch and tulips and container plants to discover plant specimens, ponds and other garden features that uplift and inspire. See *The Washington Post* for information on spring garden tours, including Virginia Garden Week, the Georgetown Garden Tour and the Maryland House and Garden Pilgrimage.

DISTRICT OF COLUMBIA

U.S. National Arboretum 3501 New York Ave., N.E. (202) 245-2726 *Open daily, 8 a.m. to 5 p.m.,* *except Christmas Day.*	You'll find an extraordinary range of plant collections here in a bucolic setting. Fern Valley has native plants and Asian Valley choice exotics. Other highlights include the lily pond around the administration building, the perennials and grasses gardens at the visitor's center, the herb garden, with its collection of antique roses, the pavilions of bonsai and penjing, and the Capitol Columns garden and meadow. Conifer fans have the Gotelli Dwarf Conifer Collection.
Smithsonian Institution Gardens On the Mall	The **Enid A. Haupt Garden**, between the Smithsonian Castle and Independence Ave., is an interesting synthesis of the Victorian public garden and post-modern landscape architecture. The **Mary Livingston Ripley Garden**, between Independence Ave. and Jefferson Drive, is an inspiring blend of woody plants, ground covers, perennials, grasses and annuals. At the **Ninth Street Butterfly Border**, between Constitution Ave. and the Mall, you'll find a model mixed border designed to attract butterflies. It hits its stride in late summer and is ornamental into the fall.
U.S. Botanic Garden First St. and Maryland Ave., SW	The conservatory at First St. and Maryland Ave. was under renovation at this writing, but visit Bartholdi Park, across Independence Ave., a showcase for native, rock garden and other unusual plants suited to home cultivation.
Capitol Grounds At the U.S. Capitol	Designed by America's most famous landscape architect, Frederick Law Olmsted, the Capitol Grounds feature native and exotic shade trees of great age and size. At the height of summer, when flower gardens gasp, the Capitol's trees invite study and respect.

Kenilworth Aquatic Gardens Anacostia Ave., NE (202) 426-6905 *Open daily 7 a.m. to 4 p.m. except* *Christmas Day and New Year's.*	This government-run garden deserves more public attention. It is alive in high summer with animal and plant life, including breathtaking specimens of water lilies.
Dumbarton Oaks R and 31st streets, NW. (202) 339-6401 *Tuesdays to Sundays, 2 to 5 p.m.* *Closed for national holidays and* *inclement weather.*	An FDR-era creation of landscape architect Beatrix Farrand and owner Mildred Woods Bliss, this is a treasure. It is a triumphant blend of the designer's eye and the gardener's art, and beautiful in all seasons.
Tudor Place 1644 31st St. NW (202) 965-0400 *Monday-Saturday, 10 a.m. to 4 p.m.*	The north side of this house is marked by splendid garden rooms, including a handsome boxwood parterre. The south side reveals a landscaped ground that bows to the splendor of the house.
Old Stone House Garden 3051 M. St. NW (202) 426-6851 *Wednesday-Sunday, 9 a.m. to 5 p.m.*	Developed by former gardener George Hunsaker, this garden on the grounds of Washington's oldest standing property is ablaze in spring with old-garden roses, perennials and bulbs, and it maintains interest through the season.
Francis Scott Key Park M St. NW and Key Bridge	Built on the site of Francis Scott Key's house, the park is a good example of the perennial-and-grass-style gardens of its designer, Oehme, van Sweden and Associates.
Bishop's Garden South side of Washington National Cathedral Wisconsin & Massachusetts Aves., NW *Open daily*	This delightful terraced garden has an impressive array of boxwood, roses, yews and perennial borders, as well as a facsimile of a monastery herb garden from the Middle Ages. There are also choice specimens of cedars.

VIRGINIA

Mt. Vernon Southern End of George Washington Memorial Parkway (703) 780-2000 *Open daily, 8 a.m to 5 p.m. April to Aug.;* *9 a.m. to 5 p.m. Sept., Oct. and March;* *9 a.m. to 4 p.m. Nov. to Feb.*	Mt. Vernon's gardens and grounds have benefited from a concerted effort in recent years to focus on the horticultural and agricultural exploits of the first President. Attractions include a pleasure garden, a vegetable and fruit garden, an orchard and farm.
River Farm East Boulevard Drive, Alexandria (703) 768-5700 *Weekdays, 8:30 a.m. to 5 p.m; several* *weekends a year for seasonal events.*	Originally a satellite farm of Mount Vernon, this historic property is the headquarters of the American Horticultural Society. It features a number of display gardens.
Oatlands U.S. Route 15, 6 miles south of Leesburg. (703) 777-3174 *Monday-Saturday, 10 a.m.-4:30 p.m.;* *Sunday 1-4:30*	Oatlands is an elegant and classical house complemented by extensive garden terraces, with boxwood parterres, fine roses and lovely flower borders.
Kenmore 1201 Washington St., Fredericksburg (540) 373-3381 *Monday-Saturday 10 a.m.-5 p.m.* *Sunday noon-5 p.m.*	This is another wonderful and historic house museum, with a restored Colonial Revival garden.

Monticello Route 53 near Charlottesville (804) 984-9822 *Open daily; hours change by season.*	Thomas Jefferson's pleasure gardens and arboretum are educational and pretty. On one side of his mountain you'll find the amazing 1,000-foot-long vegetable garden and, below, the fruit orchards and vineyard. The plant shop sells interesting native and heirloom plants.
Green Spring Gardens Park 4603 Green Spring Rd., Alexandria (703) 642-5173 *Monday-Saturday 9 a.m.-4:30 p.m.;* *Sunday 12-4:30 p.m.*	This park, the horticultural jewel of the Fairfax County Park Authority, has many informative demonstration gardens, including models for foundation plantings, rock gardening, xeriscaping, shrub borders, townhouse gardens, native plant collections, vegetable gardens and a fruit orchard.
Winkler Botanical Preserve Roanoke Ave., Alexandria (703) 578-7888 *Open daily, dawn to dusk*	Winkler is a privately established, public wilderness garden showcasing the beautiful woodland plants native to the region. It is particularly attractive and instructive in spring.
The State Arboretum of Virginia **at Blandy Farm** U.S. Route 50, Boyce (near Winchester) (540) 837-1758 *Open daily, dawn to dusk*	The state arboretum has interesting collections of shrubs and trees as well as ornamental gardens, all in a picturesque setting.
Meadowlark Gardens Regional Park 1624 Beulah Rd., Vienna (703) 255-3631 *Nov-March, 10 a.m.-5 p.m.;* *April-May, 10-7:30; June-Aug, 10-8;* *and Sept-Oct, 10-7*	This park is young but brimming with horticultural energy. Its lakeside trails take you by various garden vignettes.
Bon Air Memorial Rose Garden Wilson Boulevard and N. Lexington St., Arlington	One of the finest showcases of hybrid tea roses in the region, this garden is filled with superior varieties grown by local rosarians. Most specimens are winners of the All American Rose Selection. The first great flush of bloom occurs in late May/early June and lasts for several weeks.
Richmond	Richmond is full of charming and inspiring gardens. The following properties have particularly commendable ones: **Agecroft Hall** (804) 353-4241), the adjoining estate of **Virginia House** (804) 353-4251, and **Maymont** (804-358-7166). In addition, the **Lewis Ginter Botanical Garden** (804) 262-9887, on the city's north side, has undergone extensive development as a regional showcase.

MARYLAND

Brookside Gardens 1500 Glenallan Ave., Wheaton (301) 949-8230 *Open daily except Christmas,* *9 a.m. to sunset*	This is an excellent botanical garden. Attractions include perennial gardens, woodland shade gardens, a summer butterfly garden and collections of viburnum, witch hazel, ivies and other plants. It also has large conservatories with permanent and seasonal displays and a lakeside trail.
McCrillis Gardens 6910 Greentree Rd., Bethesda (301) 949-8230 *Open daily, 10 a.m. to sunset*	Once private property, this attractive garden run by Brookside Gardens is noted for its shade gardens of rhododendrons, azaleas and other spring-flowering trees and shrubs.
London Town Foundation 839 Londontown Rd., Edgewater (410) 222-1919 *Monday-Saturday, 10 a.m.-4 p.m.;* *Sunday, noon-4*	This is a delightful, informal, riverside garden with choice, mature specimens of rhododendrons, azaleas, mountain laurels, tree peonies and other spring beauties, as well as of woodland perennials.

William Paca House and Garden 186 Prince George St., Annapolis (410) 263-5553 *Hours change by season*	On a lovely, two-acre historic site, this house has formal gardens, a pond and vegetable and wilderness gardens.
Cylburn Arboretum 4915 Greenspring Ave., Baltimore (410) 396-0180 *March-Dec, 6 a.m.-9 p.m.*	This is a 176-acre public park and arboretum with nature trails that hit their wildflower peak in mid-spring, plus various display gardens and two natural history museums. Also check out the related Druid Hill Park at Gwynns Falls Parkway and McCullough St., a city-run tropical plant conservatory and outdoor gardens. Same phone number as Cylburn Aboretum.
Ladew Topiary Garden 3535 Jarretsville Pike, Monkton (410) 557-9466 *Open April-Oct., Mon-Fri, 10-4; Sat-Sun, 10:30-5; Memorial Day-Labor Day, also open till 8 Thursdays*	The extensive gardens and grounds here were established on the historic property of Harvey Ladew and reflect much of Ladew's playfulness and sophistication as a gardener.

DELAWARE VALLEY

The Delaware Valley contains some of the finest gardens in America. As in the Richmond-Washington-Baltimore corridor, various private landscapes are open to the public during the spring tour season. In addition, once-private du Pont estates have been developed into public gardens of astonishing range and interest, notably **Longwood Gardens** in Kennett Square, Pa. (800-737-5500) and, in the Wilmington area, **Winterthur** (800-448-3883), **Nemours** (302-651-6912) and **Hagley Museum** (302 658-2400).

Other worthy gardens are at **Chanticleer** in Wayne, Pa. (610-687-4163) and, for plant history buffs, **John and William Bartram's estate** on the Schuylkill River in West Philadelphia. (215-729-5281). **The Mt. Cuba Center** is an extraordinary 20-acre woodland garden of native plants near Wilmington, peaking in spring, but it is open by appointment only (302-239-4244).

In addition, there are several outstanding arboreta whose collections run not just to trees but to shrubs and herbaceous plants as well: **Arboretum of the Barnes Foundation**, Merion, Pa. (610-667-0290), the **Morris Arboretum of the University of Pennsylvania**, Philadelphia (215-247-5777), and the **Scott Arboretum of Swarthmore College**, Swarthmore, Pa. (610-328-8025).

Plant Societies

The Mid-Atlantic region is rich in local plant societies whose members are keen to help fellow gardeners. Typically, they hold monthly meetings, organize lectures, conduct plant sales and stage annual shows at which visitors can see popular flowering plants at their best.

The following list — adapted from one provided by the American Horticultural Society — is of national societies you can write or telephone for information about the local society in your area. Most national societies publish magazines or newsletters for members.

American Boxwood Society
Box 85
Boyce, Va. 22620

American Camellia Society
100 Massee Lane
Fort Valley, Ga. 31030
(912) 967-2358

American Conifer Society
P.O. Box 314
Keswick, Va. 22947
(804) 984-3660

American Daffodil Society
4126 Winfield Rd.
Columbus, Ohio 43220
(614) 451-4747

American Hemerocallis (daylily) Society
420 Spring Haven Rd.
Dexter, Ga. 31019
(912) 875-4110

American Herb Society
P.O. Box 1673
Nevada City, Calif. 95959

Herb Society of America
9019 Kirtland Chardon Rd.
Kirtland, Ohio 44094
(216) 256-0514

American Hosta Society
7802 NE 63rd St.
Vancouver, Wash. 98662

American Iris Society
8426 Vine Valley Drive
Sun Valley, Calif. 91352
(818) 767-5512

American Peony Society
250 Interlachen Rd.
Hopkins, Minn. 55343
(612) 938-4706

American Rhododendron Society
11 Pinecrest Drive
Fortuna, Calif. 95540

Rhododendron Species Foundation
P.O. Box 3798
Federal Way, Wash. 98063
(253) 838-4646

Azalea Society of America
P.O. Box 34536
West Bethesda, Md. 20827
(301) 855-5269

American Rock Garden Society
P.O. Box 67
Millwood, N.Y. 10546
(914) 762-2948

American Rose Society
P.O. Box 30000
Shreveport, La. 71130
(318) 938-5402

Holly Society of America
11318 West Murdoch
Wichita, Kan. 67212
(316) 721-5668

International Lilac Society
David Gressley,
c/o Holden Arboretum
9500 Sperry Rd.
Kirtland, Ohio 44094
(216) 946-4400

International Water Lily Society
Santa Barbara Botanic Gardens
Santa Barbara, Calif. 93105

Magnolia Society
6616 81st St.
Cabin John, Md. 20818
(301) 320-4296

National Chrysanthemum Society
10107 Homar Pond Dr.
Fairfax Station, Va. 22039
(703) 978-7981

North American Lily Society
P.O. Box 272
Owatonna, Minn. 55060
(507) 451-2170

Society for Japanese Irises/ Society for Siberian Irises
16815 Falls Rd.
Upperco, Md. 21155
(410) 374-4788

Index

A

Aaron's Beard, 153
Aker, Scott, 79
Alliums, 147, 148
Alumroot (*Heuchera*), 124
American Boxwood Society, 246
American Camellia Society, 246
American Conifer Society, 246
American Daffodil Society, 246
American Hemerocallis Society, 246
American Herb Society, 246
American Horticultural Society,
American Hosta Society, 178, 246
American Iris Society, 246
American Peony Society, 246
American Rhododendron Society,
   60, 246
American Rock Garden Society, 246
American Rose Society, 160, 246
Anemone,
   Japanese, 125
   Bulbous, 146
Apples,
   Recommended varieties, 226
   Tree sizes, 226
   Spur types, 226
   Pruning, 226
   Fruit thinning, 226
   Pests and diseases, 226
Arbors,
   Plants for, 16
   In garden design, 16, 176
Arborvitae, 18, 19,
Austin, David, 159, 164
Azalea Society of America, 246
Azaleas,
   Washington's relationship with, 57
   Buying and selecting varieties, 57
   Cultivation, 59
   Uses, 59
   Native species, 58, 59
   In pots, 60
   Pests and diseases, 59
   Choice and rare varieties, 58, 111
   Alternative to, 109

B

Balcony gardens (see container
   plants)
Bamboo,
   Eradicating, 35
   Planting, 111
Barberry, 110
Barrenworts (Epimedium), 124

Bed (see also border),
   Definition, 17
   Filling gaps in, 20
Beebalm, 124, 196, 217, 219
Beech, 103-104
Benches, as design elements, 9, 14,
   16, 176
Birches,
   Heritage, 16, 98, 113, 195
   Paper, 113
   European white, 113
Birds (see also hummingbirds),
   Protecting grass seed from, 42
   Protecting fruit from, 230
   Attracting, 129, 197
   Habitat gardens, 197
Bishop's Garden, 243
   Blue atlas cedars at, 99
Blackberries, 228-229
Blackspot,
   Resistance to, 160
   Defeating, 163
Blowers, 24
Blueberries,
   Highbush, 229
   Soil and pH needs, 229-230
   Pruning, 230
   Ornamental qualities, 229
   Recommended varieties, 230
Blue jays, 205
Border (see also bed),
   Definition, 17
   Composing, 19
   English-style, 17
Bow saw, 22
Boxwood,
   Notable varieties and mature
     sizes, 63
   Uses, 64
   Cultivation, 64
   Snow and ice damage to, 65
   Pests and diseases, 65
   Ambivalence toward, 63
   Pruning and shearing, 65
Bugleweed (*Ajuga*), 157
Bulbs (see also listing by type),
   In containers, 135
   In grass, 146
   Forcing, 136
   Fall-flowering, 148
   Topsize designation, 137
Burlap, uses for, 83, 183
Butterflies,
   And natural habitat gardens, 197
   And wildflower meadows, 193

   Special gardens for, 198
   Plants for luring, 123, 129, 198

C

Camassia, 147
Caryopteris, 124
Catmint, 124
Cedars, 19, 99, 100, 195
Ceratostigma, 154
Cherries, fruiting,
   Sweet, 227
   Sour, 227
   Recommended varieties, 227
   Sizes, 227
   Pests and diseases, 228
Cherries, ornamental, 19, 89
   Lifespan, 89
   Varieties, 89, 90, 106
   Grafted specimens, 89
   Cultivation, 90
   Pests and diseases, 90
   Uses, 90
Chickweed, 37
Chippers/shredders, 24
Chrysanthemums,
   Potted mums, 170
   Garden hardy mums, 169
   Cushion mums, 169
   Buying rooted cuttings, 170
   Pests and diseases, 171
   Other chrysanthemum types, 171
City gardens (see container plants),
   Narrow yards, 17
Colchicums, 148
Colonial Williamsburg,
   Boxwood gardens at, 64
Compost, 29
   Bins, 30, 31
   Sources of ingredients, 29, 30, 31
Coneflowers, 125
Conifers,
   Common mistakes with, 97
   Recommended varieties, 98-99
   Varieties to avoid, 97
   Pruning, 32, 97-98
   For shade, 99
   Native varieties, 99, 195
   Pests and diseases, 97
Construction materials, 50-51
Container plants,
   Annuals for, 130
   Herbs, 217
   Bulbs, 135
   Japanese maples, 84-85
   Azaleas, 60
   Bamboo, 111

Tomatoes, 213
  Soil for, 213, 218
Contractors,
  How to hire, 51, 52
  Saving money, 52
Cosmos, 130
Cotoneasters, 74
Cottonseed meal, 230
Crab apples, 90
  Pests and diseases, 91
  Varieties to pick, 91, 106
  Varieties to avoid, 91
Crabgrass, 37
Cranesbill, 156
Crape myrtles, 71
  Recommended varieties, 72, 106
  Cultivation, 73
  Pests and diseases, 73
Crocuses,
  Spring-flowering, 145
  Fall-flowering, 149
Crows, 205
Cypress,
  Leyland, 19, 100, 112
  False, 99
  Bald, 16, 100

D

Daffodils, 133-138
Dahlias, 10, 167-169
Daisies, 171
Daylilies,
  Recommended varieties, 121
  Blooming habit, 121
  Selecting superior cultivars, 122
  Cultivation, 122
Decks,
  Design, 16-17
  As gardens themselves, 17
  For hillside gardens, 183
Deer, 9
  And apple trees, 226
  And azaleas, 60
  And dahlias, 169
  And natural habitat gardens, 197
  And pumpkins, 212
  And roses, 163, 165
  And tulips, 138
  And vegetable gardens, 204
  Fencing and repellents, 204, 237
  Resistant plants, 237
Disease resistance,
  Importance of, 10, 67, 103, 108
  And allium, 147
  And American elm (Valley Forge),
    104

And apple trees, 226
And asparagus, 206
And cabbage, 208
And conifers, 97
And crab apples, 90-91
And daylilies, 120
And dogwood, 77
And ferns, 181
And fruiting cherry trees, 227
And fruits, 225
And ground covers, 153
And ornamental grasses, 152
And pyracantha Navaho, 75
And roses, 153, 161, 165
And squash, 213
And string or snap beans, 207
And tomatoes, 214
And viburnums, 69
Dogwood,
  Flowering, 77, 112
  Kousa, 77
  Redtwig and yellowtwig, 19
  Other types, 77-78
  Cultivation, 78
  Uses, 17, 78, 79
  Pests and diseases, 78
  Dogwood anthracnose, 79
Drainage, 32
  Surface (swales), 33
  Subsurface, 34
Dumbarton Oaks, 243
  American beech and *chionodoxa*
    at, 103
  European beech at, 104

E

Edgers, 23
Egolf, Donald, 69, 72, 75
Elm,
  American, Valley Forge, 104
  Siberian, 112
  Chinese, 112
EPDM, 188

F

Fences,
  As design elements, 17
  Against pests, 204, 237
  Types, 17
  Local ordinances for, 17
Ferns, 179-181
  As ground cover, 156
  Native species, 196
Fertilizer (see also organic and
  cultivation of individual plants),
  And spreaders, 23
  And soil tests, 29, 42, 44

Accelerating plant growth with, 20
Excessive use of, 20, 39, 44, 45,
  48
Applying to newly rescued trees,
  29
Timing of application, 39
Nutrients in, 44
Fast release type, 44
Slow release type, 44
Calculating application amounts,
  44
Figs, 228
Fish for ponds, 188-190, 197
  Hideaways for, 188, 197
Floating row cover, 170
Fork, garden, 21
Fothergilla, 9, 109
Freeze dates, by locale, 233
Fringe tree, 109
Fritillaria, 147
Frogs and ponds, 188
Fruit plants,
  Requirements, 225
  Minimizing disease, 225
  Minimizing frost damage, 225
  Pruning, 225, 226, 227, 228, 230
  Suitability, 225
  Morning picking, 225

G

Gable, Joseph B., 58
Garden design,
  As outdoor rooms, 9
  Getting help with, 49, 50
Geranium (*Pelargonium*), 130
Ginkgo, 20, 105, 175
Glade, creating, 176
Glory-of-the-snow (*chionodoxa*),
  103, 146
Goldenraintree, 104
Grass seeds (see lawn)
Grasses, ornamental,
  Uses, 152
  Cultivation, 152
  For shade, 152
  Notable varieties, 151-152
Grasses, sedges and rushes,
  Native species, 196
Green Spring Gardens Park, 186,
  194, 243
  Magnolia collection at, 89
Ground Covers,
  For sun, 153-156
  For shade, 156-157
  Planting techniques, 155
Gypsum, 44

H

Hawthorn, Washington, 17
Hazelnuts (filberts), 230
Heath, Brent, 134
Heavenly bamboo, 110
Hedges,
    Clipping, 18,
    Topiary, 18,
    Natural screens, 20
    Plant spacing, 18
    Plants for,
        Arborvitae, 18
        Barberry, 18
        Boxwood, 18
        Hemlocks, 18
        Holly, 18
        Hornbeam, 18
        Juniper, 18
        Lavender, 18
        Leyland cypress, 18
        Osmanthus, 18
        Photinia, 18
        Pyracantha, 18
        Russian olive, 18
        Southern magnolia, 18
        Yews, 18
Hellebores, 125
Hemlock, Canadian, 99
Herb Society of America, 246
Herbs,
    In containers, 218
    With other garden plants, 219
    Creating an herb garden, 219-220
    Harvesting, 220
    Popular herbs,
        Basil, 221
        Chamomile, 221
        Chives, 221
        Cilantro (coriander), 221
        Dill, 221
        Fennel, 221
        Lavender, 221
        Mint, 222
        Nasturtium, 222
        Oregano, 222
        Parsley, 222
        Rosemary, 222
        Rue, 222
        Sage, 222
        Tarragon, 223
        Thyme, 223
Herons, 197
Hillsides,
    Landscaping (see also rock
        gardens), 183-184

Erosion control, 183
Planting techniques, 184-185
Plants for, 154, 185
    spreading and tiered, 185
    looking down on, 185
    looking up to, 185
Laying sod, 42, 43
Mulch, 185
Maximum slope for mowing, 43
Hoe, 21
Hollies,
    Trees and large shrubs, 93-94
    Small shrubs, 94
    For screens, 17, 93, 95
    Evergreen, 19, 93-94
    Deciduous, 94, 111
    For wet areas, 94, 111
    Cultivation, 95
    Pests and diseases, 95
Holly Society of America, 246
Hollyhocks, 130
Hornbeam, 107
Horticultural oils, 10
Hoses, 25
Hostas, 177-178
    Recommended varieties, 178
House of Meilland, 164
Hummingbirds,
    Feeding, 197, 198
    Plants that attract, 197
        Beebalm, 124, 219
        Cardinal climber, 130
        Gooseneck loosestrife, 123
        Runner beans, 207
        Tender salvias, 129
        Zinnias, 129
Humphrey, Donald, 185
Humus, 28
Hyacinths, 146-147
Hyatt, Don,
Hydrangeas,
    Lacecap, 70
    PeeGee, 71
    Oakleaf, 70, 110
    Smooth, 70
    Climbing, 70-71
    Mophead, 70
    H. serrata, 70
    Aspera, 71
    Pests and diseases, 71
    Pruning, 71
    Uses, 71

I

Impulse buying, 57, 130, 160
Insecticidal soaps, 10

International Lilac Society, 246
International Water Lily Society, 246
Irises,
    Bearded, 117-118
    Siberian, 118-119
    Japanese, 118, 119
    Bulbous, 145
    Water and bog, 119
    Display gardens, 117
Ivy,
    English, 27
    Poison, 27
    Ground, 37

J

Junipers, 97, 98, 195

K

Katsura, 104
Kordes family, 164

L

Landscape architects, 50
Landscape contractor associations,
    43
Lawn,
    Maintaining, 44
    Establishing, 42
    Endophytes, 40
    Renewing, 47
    Recommended grass varieties, 39,
        40, 41
    Overseeding, 46
    Core aeration, 46
    Mowing, 44
    Fertilizing, 44-45
    Watering, 45
    Dethatching, 45
    Pests and diseases, 43
    Replacing, 39
    On slopes, 42
        Mowing, 23 43
    Seeding, 42
    Laying sod, 42, 43
    Lawn services, 48
    In partial shade, 46
Leaf mold (leaf mulch), 30
Lilacs,
    Cultivation, 68
    Types, 67-68
    Uses, 68
    Pests and diseases, 68
Lilies, 10, 142-145
Linden tree, 105-106
Liriope, 156
Loam,
    Definition, 28

Longwood Gardens, 245
  European beech specimens at, 104
Loosestrife (*Lythrum*),
  Problems of, 111

M

Magnolia Society, 246
Magnolias, 107
  Kobus, 88
  Saucer, 87
  Southern, 19, 88
  Star, 87
  Sweetbay, 88
  Minimizing frost damage, 87, 88
  Native varieties, 19, 88, 195
Maples, 19,
  Japanese, 81, 107
    Forms, 81
    Notable varieties, 81, 82
    Other Asian varieties, 82
    Cultivation, 82,
    In containers, 84, 85
    Uses, 19, 82
    Transplanting mature
      specimens, 83
    Pests and diseases, 84
  Silver, 113
  Norway, 113
Marigolds, 130
Martin, Clair G., 164
Master plan,
  Developing, 15-20
Mattock, 22
Meadowlark Gardens,
  Daylily display at, 122
Meserve,
  Holly, 94
  Kathleen, 94
Mimosa, 113
Mitchell, Henry, 139
Morrison, Benjamin, 58
Mount Vernon, 243
  Boxwood at, 64
Mountain laurel, 73-74
Mowers, 22-23
Mulch (see also individual plant
  cultivation), 19
  Dressing beds and borders with,
    19
  Best time for applying, 19
  Checking topsoil for, 29, 30
  Building soils with, 29
  Municipal supplies of, 30, 37
  Use in weeding process, 37
Mulberries, avoiding, 111

N

National Arboretum, 64, 69, 71, 79,
  94, 104, 242
  Daylily display garden at, 122
  Lacebark pine specimen at, 99
  Magnolia collection at, 89
National Capital Daylily Club, 121,
  122
National Chrysanthemum Society,
  246
National Turfgrass Evaluation
  Program, 40
Native plants, 195-196
Natural habitat gardens, 197
Nectarines, 227
North American Lily Society, 246
Northern Virginia Daylily Society,
  122

O

Oak,
  Black, 105, 195
  Chestnut, 105
  Pin, 195
  Red, 105, 195
  Scarlet, 195
  White, 19, 105
  Willow, 105
Organic (see also disease resistance),
  Fertilizers, 48
  Disease and pest control, 234-236
  Lawn services, 48

P

Pansies, 130
Parasites, beneficial, 10
Paths,
  As design element, 16
  In shade gardens, 176
  In hillside gardens, 183, 184
  In wildflower meadows, 193
  In vegetable garden, 203-204
  Materials for, 176
Patio,
  Importance of, 16
  Trees,
    Making space for, 106
    10 best, 106-108
Peach trees,
  Minimizing bud frost damage, 227
  Recommended varieties, 227
  Fruit thinning, 227
  Pruning, 227
  Pests and diseases, 227
Pear trees,
  Asian, 226

Bradford, 19
European, 226
Recommended varieties, 226, 227
Fireblight, 226
Multiple leaders, 226
Ripening, 226
Pear psylla, 227
Pecan trees, 230
Peony,
  Double and single, 119-120
  Tree, 120
  Japanese, 120
  Cultivation, 120
Perennials (see plants by name), 117
  20 best bets for Washington, 124
  For dry soil, 122
  For damp soil, 123
  For shade, 178
  Dividing, 126
  Staking, 127
  Native species, 196
Pieris, Japanese, 73
Pines,
  Eastern white, 19, 112
  Lacebark, 99,
  Japanese black, 99
Plant clinics, 241
Plant hardiness zones, 10, 233
Plant spacing,
  Correct distances, 19
  Checking contractor's plan, 50
  Using shovel as guide, 155
Plant supports,
  Stakes, 205
    For various plants, 127, 130,
      136, 145, 168, 169, 213
  Tepees, 205
  Trellises, 205, 206, 208, 210, 213
  Wire cages, 205
Plants to avoid,
  10 plants to avoid (and
    alternatives) 111-113
  Others:
    Alberta spruce, dwarf, 97
    Anjou pear, 226
    Azaleas (unnamed varieties), 57
    Bamboos, most (except in
      containers), 35, 111
    Bartlett pear, 226
    Bing cherry, 227
    Bosc pear, 226
    Comice pear, 226
    Crab apple varieties, 91
    Firs, 97
    Irises, bearded (unnamed
      varieties), 118

Italian cypress, 97
Larches, 97
Loblolly pine, 28
Loosestrife (*Lythrum*), 111
Monterey cypress, 97
Mimosa tree, 28
Mulberry trees, 111
Ponderosa pine, 97
Red and white spruce, 97
Rocky Mountain juniper, 97
Roses graded No. 1½ or 2, 161
Sequoia tree, 97
Tiger Lily (*Lilium lancifolium*), 143
Tree-of-heaven (*Ailanthus*), 111
Planters (see also containers), 17
Plumbago (see *ceratostigma*)
Poplar,
    Lombardy black, 112
Pruners, hand, 22
Pruning, 32, 36 (see also cultivation for individual plants)
Pyracantha, 75

R

Rabbits,
    And vegetable gardens, 204
Raccoons,
    And pond fish, 188, 190
    And natural habitat gardens, 197
    And pumpkins, 212
Rakes, 21
Rarer plant sources, 238
Raspberries,
    Pruning, 228
        Summer fruiting, 228
        Everbearing, 228
        Black and purple, 229
    Recommended varieties, 229
Redwood, Dawn, 100
Rhododendron,
    Recommended varieties, 60
    Cultivation, 61
    Pests and diseases, 61
    Native species, 60
    Uses, 61
    Alternative to, 109
Rhododendron Species Foundation, 246
River Farm, 122, 243
Rock gardens (see also hillside gardens),
    Building, 185
    In sun, 186
    In shade, 186
    Plants for, 186

Demonstration garden, 186
American Rock Garden Society, 186, 246
Roses,
    All America Rose Selection, 160
    Modern (hybrid tea, floribundas, grandifloras), 10, 159
        And chemical sprays, 10, 159
        Recommended varieties, 161
    Old-Garden,
        Recommended varieties, 165
    Shrub, 163
    Rugosa, 164
    English, 164
    Climbing, 165
    As ground cover, 153
    Planting and care, 160-162
    Blackspot, 163
    Pruning, 162
Rototillers, 24
Rye,
    Annual, 37
    Winter, 37
    Perennial, 37

S

Sage,
    Perennial (*Salvia x superba*), 125
    Garden (*Salvia officinalis*), 125
    Mealy Cup (*Salvia farinacea*), 125-126
    Russian (*Perovskia*), 125
    Salvia Argentea, 126
    Salvia Gauranitica, 126
Schenk, Peter J., Jr., 141
Screens, 20 (see also trees)
Shade gardens,
    Types of Shade, 16, 175
    Turning woodlot into ornamental shade garden, 175-177
    Plants for, 177-181
Shade trees,
    10 best, 103-106
    Native species, 195
Shears, 24
Shovel, round-point, 21
Shrubs,
    Regenerating, 35,
    10 Best, 109
    Native species, 195
Siberian bugloss (*Brunnera*), 126
Silverbell, 108
Site analysis, 15
Skarphol, Brenda, 194
Snowbell,
    Japanese, 107
    American, 107

Snowdrops, 145
Soil,
    Types, 28
    Amending, 29, 30
    Buying, 30
    Dealing with clay, 29
    pH, 29
    Testing, 29
Sourwood tree, 108
Sparling, Richard, 117
Speedwell (*Veronica*), 126
Sphagnum peat moss, 218
Spider lily, 130
Spirea, 154
Sprayer, pump, 22
Spreaders, 23
Springer, Judy, 175, 176, 177
Spruces,
    Siberian, 17
    Serbian, 98
    Oriental, 98
    Colorado blue, 112
Squill (*Scilla*), 146
Squirrels, 149,
    And tulips, 142, 145
    And crocuses, 145
Stepping-stones, 19
Sternbergia, 149
Stewartia, 108
Strawberries,
    June-bearing, 229
    Day-neutral, 229
    Recommended varieties, 229
String trimmers, 24
Sunflowers, 129
Sweet Woodruff (*Galium*), 156
Swimming pools, 20

T

Tickseed (*coreopsis*), 126
Tomatoes,
    Supports for, 205
    Cultivation 213
    Recommended varieties, 214
    Pests and diseases, 214
Topiaries,
    Techniques, 18
    Ladew Topiary Garden, 245
Trees, (see also named plants)
    As weeds, 28
    Pruning, 32, 35
    Removing, 15, 27-28, 175-176
    For screening, 20
    With ornamental bark,
        Crape myrtle, 71-72, 106
        Heritage birch, 16, 98, 113, 195

Hornbeam, 107
Kousa dogwood, 77
Lacebark pine, 99
Paperbark maple, 82
Stewartia, Japanese, 108
Tudor Place,
Edging box hedges at, 64
Tulips, 138-142
Perennial, 139
Tupelo, black, 104
Turtles, 188, 197

U

University of Maryland, 40
Cooperative Extension Service,
40, 226
Home and Garden Information
Center, 45, 241

V

Vegetable gardens,
Model garden, 203, 204
Soil preparation, 204
Plant supports, 205
Cultivation, 206
Plants for,
Asparagus, 206
Beans, 206
Beets, 207
Broccoli, 207
Cabbage, 208
Carrots, 208
Cucumbers, 208
Eggplant, 209
Garlic, 209
Leeks, 209
Lettuce, other greens, 209
Onions, 210
Peas, 210
Peppers, 211
Potatoes, 211
Pumpkins, 212

Radishes, 212
Squash, 212
Tomatoes, 213-214 (see also
separate listing)
Viburnum,
Shasta, 69, 109
Shoshoni, 69
On slopes, 17
With ornamental fruit, 69
Cultivation, 70
Vines, 16, 130, 205

W

Walls, retaining, 49
Walnuts,
Black, 230
Plants to grow under, 28
English, 230
Water gardens,
Safety, 187
Siting and construction, 187
Fish, 188, 190
Fountains and waterfalls, 188
Water quality,
Algae, eliminating, 190
Filtration, 190
Municipal water, 190
pH, 190
Water plants,
Lilies, 190
Lotus, 191
Water hyacinth, 191
Thalia, 191
Horsetail, 191
Arrowhead, 191
Pickerel weed, 191
Yellow flag iris, 191
Blue water iris, 191
Submerged aquatic, 191
Bog plants, 191
Native species, 196

Pests,
Raccoons, 188, 190, 191
Mosquitoes, 188, 190
Weeds,
Broadleaf, 37
Treating, 37
Preventing, 37
Eradicating for ground covers, 155
Eradicating for wildflower
meadows, 193, 194
Preparing soil for weeding, 37
Mulching over, 37
Vines, 27
Wet ground,
Plants for, 59, 79, 88, 94, 100,
119, 123, 178, 179
Drainage, 32, 33-34
Wheelbarrow, 22
Wildlife, attracting, 197-198
Wildflower meadows, 193
Pitfalls, 193
Using perennials, 194
Wild onion, 37
Willow, weeping, 113
Winter aconite, 145
Winterhazel,
Buttercup, 109
Witch hazel,
On slopes, 17
Choice hybrids, 111
Woodpeckers, 27, 28

Y

Yellowwood, American, 105
Yews, 95-96, 100
Yinger, Barry, 120

Z

Zelkova, Japanese, 104
Zinnias, 129, 130